The Very Quick Job Search

Get a Better Job in Half the Time

Second Edition

J. Michael Farr

The Very Quick Job Search, Second Edition

© 1996, JIST Works, Inc., Indianapolis, IN

JIST Works, Inc.
8902 Otis Avenue
Indianapolis, IN 46216
Phone: 1-800-648-JIST E-mail: JISTWorks@aol.com

Other books by this author
(see the bibliography for additional details):

The Quick Resume & Cover Letter Book
The Quick Interview & Salary Negotiation Book
Getting the Job You Really Want
The Right Job for You
America's Fastest Growing Jobs
The Work Book
America's Top Jobs™ for College Graduates

*America's Top Jobs™ for People Without
  College Degrees*
America's Top White-Collar Jobs
*America's Top Medical, Education, & Human
  Services Jobs*
*A Young Person's Guide to Getting and Keeping
  a Good Job*

Instructors: This book has been widely used to support a workshop or a complete course on career planning and job seeking. Instructional materials include a complete curriculum titled *The Very Quick Job Search Instructor's Curriculum*, overhead transparencies *(The JIST Career Planning and Job Search Course Transparencies)*, *The Very Quick Job Search Activity Book*, and a 10-video series titled *The Video Guide to JIST's Self-Directed Job Search*. Please contact the publisher for additional details.

Multiple Copy Sales
Volume discounts of this book are available from the publisher, including special discounts for multiple copy orders. Contact our customer relations staff weekdays at 1-800-648-JIST.

Library of Congress Cataloging-in-Publication Data

Farr, J. Michael
    The very quick job search / J. Michael Farr. - - 2nd ed.
        p.   cm.
    Includes bibliographical references.
    ISBN 1-56370-181-2
    1. Job hunting - - United States.   I. Title.
    HF5382.75.U6F37   1996
    650. 14- -dc20   95-50811
                                            CIP

We have been careful to provide accurate information throughout this book, but it is possible that errors and omissions have been introduced. Please consider this in making any career plans or other important decisions. Trust your own judgment above all else and in all things.

ISBN 1-56370-181-2

You Don't Need to Read This Whole Book!

Just a Few Chapters Will Tell You Enough to Make a Big Difference in Your Job Search

While this is a big book, I don't intend for you to actually read it all. So, instead of staying home and reading a big book, my advice is to go out and get interviews without delay. Interviews are, after all, where the job search action is.

To get you off to a quick start, I've included, in Section 1, the information I think is most important for you to know. If you want to get a better job in less time, reading this section will make the most difference. You could read it in the morning and be out there getting interviews in the afternoon.

But there is much more to this book than the content of Section 1. For example, Section 2 provides chapters on labor market trends, career planning, exploring job alternatives, and other topics that could be very important to you. If you want to know more about resumes, you will find good information on that topic in Section 3. And Section 4 provides additional chapters on job seeking, interviewing, and related topics.

Some chapters will be more important to you than others, so review the table of contents to identify sections and chapters of particular interest.

Yes, this is a big book, but I hope you don't find it as intimidating as it seems at first. The best way to get started is to get started...

Two Quotes, One Long and One Short...

The first and longer quote is from a nineteenth century poet and philosopher. I hope it gives you something to consider as you begin this book. The second and shorter quote has to do with job seeking.

"How do you measure success?
To laugh often and much,
To win the respect of intelligent people and the affection of children,
To earn the appreciation of honest critics and endure the betrayal of false
  friends,
To appreciate beauty,
To find the best in others,
To leave the world a little better, whether by a healthy child, a redeemed
  social condition, or a job well done,
To know even one other life has breathed because you lived,
This is to have succeeded."

— *Ralph Waldo Emerson, 1803-1882*

"The best applicant doesn't typically get the job, the best job seeker does."

— *Mike Farr, 1996*

(Actually, I've been saying this for years and decided to put it in here as a quote since it seemed a good way to get you to think about it...)

Preface

This is a thorough book whose focus is quite simple: to help you get a better job and to reduce the time it takes to get it.

While the book includes a lot of information, I have organized it so that you can read its essential chapters today and be looking for a job tomorrow. Most of the information throughout this book is organized around seven major themes. These seven things are VERY important if you want to get a better job and to do it in less time. Here they are:

The Seven Steps to Getting the Job You Want

1. **Know your skills.** If you don't know what you are good at, how can you expect anyone else to figure it out? One survey of employers found about 80% of those they interview did not do a good job in presenting the skills they had to do the job.

2. **Have a clear job objective.** If you don't know where you want to go, it will be most difficult to get there. Take the time to clarify what you want to do and your job search will be far more effective.

3. **Know where and how to look for job openings.** Since three out of four job openings are never advertised, you should learn and use nontraditional job search techniques to find them. Some job search methods work better than others and, since few people have had any formal training on looking for a job, you probably know less about this than you realize.

4. **Spend at least 25 hours a week looking.** Most job seekers spend too little time actually looking and, as a result, are unemployed longer than they need to be. Organizing your job search like it is a full-time job can make a tremendous difference in your job search.

5. **Get two interviews a day.** It sounds impossible but this can be done once you redefine what "counts" as an interview.

6. **Do well in interviews.** You won't get a job offer unless you do well in interviews. I've reviewed the research on what it takes to do well in an interview and found, happily, that you can improve your performance relatively easily.

7. **Follow up on all contacts.** Following up after an interview and sending out lots of thank-you notes are just two of the little things that make a big difference.

This book provides lots of content for each of the seven steps as well as additional information that you may find helpful. I hope that you enjoy the book and that it helps bring you happiness or prosperity. Or both.

Mike Farr

Table of Contents

Section 1: Job Search Basics in Just Seven Chapters – *You Can Cut Your Job Search Time in Half with These Techniques*

This section covers those topics that I think are most important to getting a good job and in less time. It is a book within a book that you can read in a few hours and give you techniques that can have an immediate impact on your job search.

Chapter 1: What It Takes to Get a Good Job in Less Time – *And Why Traditional Methods Don't Work* . . *11*

Chapter 2: The Two Best Job Search Methods – *Why They Work and How to Use Them* *29*

Chapter 3: Identify Your Key Skills – *An Essential Step for a Successful Job Search* *61*

Section 2: Preparing for the Job Search – *Career Planning and Job Search Homework*

While "doing your homework" is not fun, this section provides important information for understanding the job market, clarifying your job objective, and preparing for interviews.

Section 3: Quick Resumes, Cover Letters, and Thank-You Notes

This section provides all that you will probably need to know on resumes, cover letters, and other job search correspondence.

Provides worksheets, tips, and sample resumes that can be completed in just a few hours as well as more advanced resume examples and tips.

Includes good examples of cover letters and how they can best be used as well as details on the often overlooked but effective thank-you note and other job search correspondence.

Section 4: Even More Good Job Search Techniques

Covers a variety of topics, some of more interest to you than others. I strongly suggest you review the chapter on using the telephone as well as other chapters that interest you.

The phone is an important tool to use in your job search and this chapter covers techniques that have been proven to work in getting interviews.

I'll explain how applications are often used to screen people out and that there are often better ways to get interviews – as well as how to complete an application without damaging your chances for employment.

This chapter reviews some interviewing methods covered in Section 1 and includes dozens of answers to specialized questions.

If you are computer literate, there are many resources available to you that you may not be aware of and this chapter reviews some of those options.

Chapter 18: Tips for Coping with Job Loss – *And Other Things You Might Want to Know* 453

Managing your money, emotions, time, and interpersonal relationships are some of the topics covered in this chapter.

Annotated Bibliography – *Sources of Additional Information* 477

Research materials organized into categories that can further assist you with your job search and career planning.

Introduction: Why This Book Could Be Worth Thousands of Dollars to You –

The Economics of Career Planning and Job Search

H ere is a quote from a study titled "Workplace Basics" completed jointly by the U.S. Department of Labor and the American Society of Training and Development:

Research shows that roughly half of the differences in earnings [between people] can be attributed to learning in school or on the job. Accidents of geography, career choices, and the selection of an employer account for the other half.

Another way to summarize their conclusion is to say that good career planning and job seeking skills can make a huge difference in how much you earn. Education and training remain very important, of course, but even a good education or advanced technical skills are not enough if you don't know where or how to find the right jobs. And then, of course, there is the issue of finding a job you really like.

Why a New Approach Is Needed

Back in the good old days, larger employers ruled the land and the job search was simple. To get a job, you sent out resumes to Personnel Departments or went there to fill out applications. You responded to want ads and you went down to the employment service office for free referrals. And you went after government jobs since there were lots of those available. Sure, there were also private employment agencies but the larger companies usually paid their fees. No problem.

Things were simpler then. College grads were in demand (there were fewer of them then) and factory jobs were plentiful. You got a job with a big employer and you kept it.

Of course, that rosy picture was not quite perfect for everyone during those times in the sixties and early seventies – there were problems. But traditional job search methods did work better back then.

Since then, the labor market has changed. An enormous number of new workers have come into the labor market: over 20 million just during the 1980s and millions more in the 1990s. Almost all of the new jobs which absorbed them have been in the service (nonmanufactuing) economy. Now, about 70% of all nongovernment jobs are with small employers (under 250 employees) and most of the new job growth has been with very small employers – those with 50 or fewer employees. People change jobs and careers far more often than in the past and few expect to stay with their current employer until retirement. And many of the new jobs require higher levels of education and training.

For these and other reasons, the old ways of looking for a job have become much less effective. Small employers, for example, usually don't have personnel offices. They are far more likely to depend on referrals from current employees than on traditional sources such as want ads or referrals from state employment agencies. They are less likely to pay private employment agency fees. And, because small employers are better able to make decisions, they are more likely to create a new job for someone they want to hire – even though there is no formal opening.

So there are a variety of reasons to believe that getting a job today requires more knowledge of how the labor market works than in the past. While the traditional job search methods still do work for some, they have become increasingly less effective for most. Which is one of the reasons that I say that career planning and job search skills are more important than ever. You will not only need to know more but, with more frequent job and career changes, you will need to use your job search skills more often.

I have concluded that career planning and job seeking skills are essential survival skills in our new economy. How well you plan your career and conduct your job search can make a tremendous difference in how much you earn, how rapidly you advance in your career, and how much you enjoy your work – and your life.

What This Book Is Designed to Accomplish

This book is about getting a job. Lots of books claim to do this but this one is different. Besides showing you how to write a good resume and find job openings, it will help you:

1. Define what you want in a job: I've included information to help you define and find "THE" job rather than just "a" job. This is an important issue since what you do for your work can be an important issue in how you feel about your life.

2. Find this job in less time: Some job search methods work better than others and I have spent many years looking for techniques that reduce the time it takes to get a job. The techniques presented in this book have been used by many thousands of people and programs and have been proven to cut job search time in half.

3. Negotiate for higher salary: There are things you can do when negotiating salary that can result in a significantly higher starting salary. It's easy enough to do and I will show you how.

4. Develop a skills language: Many people tell me that learning to identify their skills – and deciding how best to use them – is an important life experience for them. And, of course, it will help you in the interview and throughout the job search.

All of this is a tall order. In writing this book, I have tried to keep things interesting, to emphasize the most important information, and keep the book to a manageable size. I hope you like it. More importantly, I hope that it helps you find a satisfying job and more meaningful life, in less time than you could have otherwise done. And that is why this book has been titled *The Very Quick Job Search*.

The High Cost of Looking for Work

Being out of work can be an expensive proposition. Besides the obvious costs of lost income, there are less obvious psychological costs. For example, unemployed people have a higher incidence of stress-related illnesses; are more likely to have marital and other interpersonal problems; experience more alcohol and drug abuse; and even experience higher death rates – the ultimate stress-related illness.

Using more effective job search skills can mean real money to you. For example, the average length of unemployment varies between 12 and 15 weeks and has gone as high as 20 weeks during times of high unemployment. For each $10,000 in annual salary you earn, that's $2,300 (for 12 weeks) to $2,850 (for 15 weeks) of lost income. That is not a small amount of money and anything that can reduce the time you need to find a job is like money in your pocket.

Salary negotiation is another area of the job search where knowing what to do at the right time can be worth thousands of dollars to you in increased income. The cost of underemployment by people capable of more responsibility can become staggering over the years. For example, I recently interviewed a person for a job who had been working 50 hours a week for many years and making about half of what I thought her position should pay. She was comfortable in her old job and hadn't gone out looking for another job for a long time. But she had lost enough income over the past five years to buy several new cars and a trip to Europe. And a down payment on a house.

But money is not everything. There is also the matter of finding the "right" job for you. It isn't easy to determine just what to look for but if you end up in a job you don't enjoy, you probably won't do well in it either. You probably won't get promotions and raises like you might have otherwise. And you will likely look for another job because you will come to hate what you do.

So the stakes in your job search are quite high in both money and human terms. Yet most people spend more time shopping during the course of a month than planning their careers or learning how to look for a job. And for that reason, you should consider spending some time learning more about the career planning and job search process.

How Well Do the Job Search Methods Presented in This Book Work?

There is no magic to getting a job. It requires hard work and a bit of luck. Too many people muddle through their job search without learning much about how to do it. And, as soon as they find a job, they certainly don't want to think about their unemployment experience. The result is that, too often, they don't learn much that they can apply to their next job search. What they need is someone to help them who knows lots more about this job search thing than they do. Or maybe they need a book.

There are lots of job search books but hardly anyone can offer any proof that their methods work better than others. And yet it seems to me that results are what count in your job search. At various points in this book I will ask you to come up with proof to support a key interview point, support a resume statement or, in some other way, support that what you say you can do is true. So here is some proof of my credentials to write this book:

During the recession in the early 1980s, unemployment rates in many areas went well over 10 percent. That is as high as it has gotten in over 30 years, but in some areas it was much higher.

I had been operating successful job search programs since the early 1970s and won a contract to run a demonstration job search program. The U.S. Department of Labor tracks the unemployment rates for the 200 largest cities in the U.S. and our location, with lots of auto plant closings, went over 24%. That was the highest unemployment rate of any city in the entire United States at that time.

I was told by the government agency who hired us that there were no job openings there. We were to work with people who were unemployed but who were to receive no other services other than attending our job search program. We did no screening other than a two hour orientation session where we explained the program and asked them to attend only if they could commit themselves to a full-time job search and attend our program for six hours daily for four weeks or until they found a job. They were not compensated for attending. Following are some data and results from this program.

Average Length of Unemployment: 4.5 Months	
% minorities:	50%
% women:	48%
Average age:	31.6

Results: 66 percent found jobs within 2.3 weeks of program initiation. Of those who attended the first two weeks without absence, 96 percent found jobs within 2.03 weeks.

These results are incredible but true. There was no magic to it, the jobs were there all along. Our job seekers got them because they went to potential employers before the jobs were advertised and convinced the employer that they could do the job. The people waiting for a job to get advertised in the help wanted section of the newspaper stayed unemployed.

Good staff were essential in making these results happen but programs across the U.S. and Canada have obtained similar results in difficult settings using the techniques presented in this book.

The techniques in this book work and thousands of those who have used them will agree. As I was writing this, I spoke with Robert Diaz of KRBB in Wichita, following a radio interview. He had interviewed me a year earlier about this very book and told me that his wife had obtained a job as a result. She loved gardening but had no formal training in it, so he simply called a large gardening center and spoke with the owner about her. There was no job opening but she followed up, got an interview, and began working there soon after. While the job search is not always this easy, the basic techniques I present do work well for many people.

And now you have access to the same techniques. They are described in detail in this book and, taken together, represent a body of experience and common sense that has been developed and tested over many years. They can work if you make them work. Nothing more and nothing less. Making them work will, of course, be up to you.

I hope that you enjoy this book. When you are done with it, after you have found your own job, pass it along to someone else or buy another one for them. That and your offering them a little bit of caring and support will let you become part of a grass roots movement to help each other find satisfaction in our careers and our lives. And, of course, reduce our lengths of unemployment to a minimum.

Section 1:
Job Search Basics in
Just Seven Chapters –

You Can Cut Your Job Search Time

in Half with These Techniques

Section 1 Introduction

Consider this section a book within a book. Its seven chapters include what I consider to be the most important information you need to find a job in less time. You could read this section in a few hours and know a lot more about looking for a job than most people you will run into.

While this section does cover the basics to get you started in your job search, I do suggest that you review other sections of the book. Those who prepare the most seem to do the best...

Chapters in This Section

Chapter 1: What It Takes To Get a Good Job In Less Time – And Why Traditional Methods Don't Work

Provides an introduction to the job search and a review of the basic methods most people use.

Chapter 2: The Two Best Job Search Methods – Why They Work and How to Use Them

The research and my experience indicates that two job search methods work better for most people than others. These are the techniques you need to know the most about – and use the most.

Chapter 3: Identify Your Key Skills – An Essential Step for a Successful Job

Helps develop a skills language that is important for interviews, resumes, and selecting the right job for you.

Chapter 4: How to Interview for Results

You can quickly learn techniques that can substantially improve your interviewing skills.

Chapter 5: Answers to 10 Key Interview Questions

Knowing how to respond to these questions will prepare you to answer most others.

Chapter 6: JIST Cards – a Powerful New Job Search Tool

How to create and use a clever and effective mini-resume.

Chapter 7: Make Your Job Search Into a Job – Organize Your Time to Get Results

Provides specific advice on structuring your job search to get more interviews and faster results.

CHAPTER ONE

Job Search Basics

What It Takes to Get a Good Job in Less Time –

And Why Traditional Methods Don't Work

≡Quick Overview

In this chapter, I review the following:

✔ Traditional job search techniques

✔ Why nontraditional methods are more effective

✔ Two things that can cut your job search time in half

✔ Why some people take longer to find jobs

✔ The hidden job market – where most of the jobs are

✔ How people really find jobs

✔ Why many employers don't like to advertise

✔ Why resumes don't get jobs, interviews do

✔ How to search for civil service jobs

✔ How to make better use of personnel offices, application forms, help wanted ads, and resumes

✔ How to take advantage of government employment services, private employment agencies, etc.

"You can cut your job search time and get a better job!"

It's true. I have spent many years now discovering which job search methods work better than others. It is clear that some techniques can reduce the time it takes to find a job. This fact has been demonstrated many times in programs that I have run, as well as in research that I (and others) have conducted.

You can cut your job search time in half or more – and this book will teach you the basic principles of how to do it.

If you are currently looking for a job, the job search "how to" aspects of this book will probably appeal to you most. But another element of this book may be far more important to you over time: I have included a variety of things to help you understand yourself and what you want.

This self-knowledge is an essential element in helping you define just what sort of job you want.

If you know what your ideal job would be, you are more likely to find one that comes close to it. And doing so may be far more important than just finding any job quickly.

Why Some People Take Longer to Find Jobs

Looking for a job is hard work. If you are lucky, you may find one quickly. But finding even entry-level jobs can take a long time if you don't know how.

According to the U.S. Department of Labor, the average adult spends three to five months finding a new job. When unemployment rates are high, you can be out of work even longer.[1]

But some people find jobs faster than others, even in times of high unemployment. What do they do differently? While the answers can be complex, there are only two primary reasons why some people get jobs faster than others.

Doing Just Two Things Can Cut Your Job Search Time in Half

The average job seeker spends fewer than 15 hours a week looking for a job and gets fewer than two interviews.

What It Takes to Get a Good Job in Less Time

1. Job seekers who spend more time actually looking for work find jobs faster than those spending less time.

2. Job seekers who get more interviews find jobs faster because the more interviews you get, the more likely you are to get a job offer.

The bottom line is that people who spend more time on their job search and who get more interviews will usually get jobs faster.

Realizing Two Problems with Traditional Approaches Can Help

Part of the problem is that the traditional approach to the job search leads to many dead ends and rapid discouragement.

Traditional techniques encourage you to be passive in your job search, and, because they don't work well for most people, result in your being out of work longer than is necessary.

A big problem with the traditional job search is that job seekers define an interview too narrowly. By doing this, they overlook many opportunities and make obtaining an interview harder than it needs to be.

> ### Two Problems with Traditional Approaches
>
> 1. Traditional techniques encourage you to be passive in your job search.
> 2. Traditional techniques encourage you to define an interview too narrowly.

This chapter and the one that follows deal with both of these problems. Of the variety of job search methods, some clearly work better than others. The most effective ones help you remain active in your job search and do not encourage you to wait until someone calls you. These techniques can dramatically increase the number of interviews you can get. They only work, of course, if you use them.

The Hidden Job Market – Where Most of the Jobs Are

Most jobs are not advertised – and people who use traditional job search methods never find out about these jobs. In a book titled *Work in the New Economy,* Bob Wegmann concludes that as many as 70 to 75 percent of all job openings are not "visible" to job seekers using traditional job search methods.

Only about 15 percent of all people get their jobs through the want ads.

Jobs available through private and government employment agencies are also considered public knowledge. Anyone can find out about them. But these advertised openings add up to only about 25 percent of all job openings. The other 75 percent or so are hidden from you if you use traditional job search methods. So your job search should be a search for these hidden jobs, in addition to the jobs that are advertised.

How Do People Really Find Jobs?

You will hear varied opinions about how to look for a job. Yet, most job search advisors (and, sadly, many people who write job search books) seem unaware of some important facts – like just how people really do find jobs.

Good research on this is hard to find because government funds for such things have been cut back in recent years. But there is some hard evidence to indicate that some techniques work better than others.

By far the largest (and therefore the most valid) survey asking people how they found their jobs was taken by the U.S. Department of Labor back in the 1970s. They surveyed 10.4 million people and published the results in Bulletin 1886, "Job-Seeking Methods Used by American Workers." People were asked which job search method they used to find their present job, or – if they were not employed – their most recent job.

Table 1-1 summarizes the Bulletin 1886 findings along with those of another study by Camil Associates (also from the 1970s), under contract with the Department of Labor. The Camil report was based on a study of employers and did not include civil service job-holders. The studies are not precisely the same, but they do provide important information on how people find jobs.

Table 1-1	How People Find Jobs	
	Dept. of Labor %	Camil study %
Heard about opening from people I know:	28.4	34.0
Contacted employer directly:	34.9	29.8
Answered want ad:	13.9	16.6
Referred by private employment agency:	5.6	5.6
Referred by state employment service:	5.1	5.6
Referred by school placement office:	3.0	3.0
Took civil service tests:	2.1	N/A
Union hiring:	1.5	1.4
Other methods: (**Examples:** Placed ads in journals; went to places where employers come to hire people; and so on.)	5.5	4.0

How People Find Jobs

Since those large studies were conducted, a variety of smaller studies have supported their general findings. I have taken the liberty of developing a composite picture of how people actually find jobs. Chart 1-1 averages the data obtained in the studies mentioned above and incorporates some more recent information. It provides a composite of what we know about how people find jobs and simplifies it to make a point.

The pie chart clearly shows that informal and nontraditional job search methods are a far more important source of job leads than traditional sources.

Chart 1-1   How People Find Jobs

Traditional vs. Informal Job Search Methods

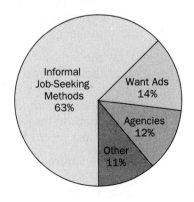

The chart shows that only two job-seeking methods – direct contact with employers and getting leads from people you know – are used to find about three out of every four jobs. Consequently, most of this chapter (and this book) emphasizes nontraditional or informal job-seeking methods. These are the methods that open doors to the hidden job market.

Should "Luck" Be How You Find a Job?

For most people, "luck" is the most important element in their job search – but should it be?

In spite of all the books telling us how to read want ads and send out resumes, and in spite of the national "system" of private and public employment agencies, most people get their jobs by informal methods, such as word of mouth or going directly to an employer. Even though these are clearly the most effective methods, few people are organized in their use of these methods. The result is lost time – and time is money. Since very few people have any formal job search training, they waste much of their time using ineffective methods that needlessly lengthen their unemployment and drain their confidence.

Traditional Ways of Finding Job Leads

Very few people have any real training on how to find jobs. Few have even read a book on job seeking, and very few have attended a seminar, workshop, or class on job seeking. As a result, they go about using well-known job search methods that may or may not work well.

In this chapter, I review job search techniques that are traditionally used by most people. "Traditional" means it's the way people have always done things. That doesn't mean it's the best way, it's just the way that everyone knows. Traditional job search methods are not always the most effective ones, but some people do find jobs using them. One or more of these methods can result in your getting a good lead.

Six Frequently Used Traditional Job Search Methods

1. Reading the help wanted ads in the newspaper
2. Going to personnel offices and filling out applications
3. Sending out resumes
4. Going to the local employment service office
5. Signing up with a private employment agency
6. Applying for civil service jobs

As you will soon discover, the traditional job search methods all have their limitations. It is important for you to understand these limitations so that you do not rely on these methods too heavily.

Because so many people know and use traditional job search methods, let's take a closer look at each of them. For each one, I present their disadvantages as well as some nontraditional tips on increasing the effectiveness.

Traditional Job Search Method 1: Help Wanted Ads

Since almost everyone who is looking for a job reads the newspaper's want ads, they must be a good place to look for jobs, right? Not entirely. One of the very reasons they are *not* great sources for good job leads is that so many people do read them. The odds, simply, are not in your favor (see sidebar).

As if that is not bad enough, another problem is that most jobs are never advertised. (To understand why, see the Quick Case Study later in this chapter "Why many employers don't like to advertise.")

Various studies have found that about only 15 percent of all jobs are advertised, which leaves 85 percent that are not.

These unadvertised jobs often include the best jobs.

Advertised jobs, on the other hand, often include the following:

➤ Jobs that are fairly difficult to fill

➤ Jobs that are relatively low paying

➤ Jobs that have other limitations

With Want Ads, the Odds Are Not in Your Favor

Let's do a little arithmetic to illustrate my point.

The research indicates that about 10 percent of the workforce reads the want ads at any given time.

It's pretty easy to accept that 10 percent or more read the want ads each week. The unemployment rate is often half or more of that percentage. Then add to that the people who are looking for better jobs; wanting full-time instead of part-time; soon to graduate students; and those entering or re-entering the labor market.

So, for example, in a city of 200,000 people, 130,000 people (about 65 percent) would be in (or want to be in) the workforce. This means that about 13,000 will be reading the want ads at any given time. If the local paper presented 500 want ads for real jobs, that would be an average of 260 people per advertised job!

But it can get even worse for the most desirable jobs. For a want ad that said something like "good pay and benefits, no previous experience required," there would be even more interested people. Let's say that twice as many people as usual are interested in this ad. That would be 520 people interested in that particular advertised job. If you were one of them, you would be about one-fifth of 1 percent of those interested – a slim chance indeed of getting that job.

This is one reason that those who depend too much on the want ads get so discouraged – it always seems that someone else is more qualified. Figure out the odds for your own newspaper's distribution area. The competition is fierce!

Some people <u>do</u> get jobs from the want ads

While the want ad odds are not in your favor, some good jobs *are* advertised and this makes want ads worth looking at on a regular basis. Here are some tips to make the search worthwhile.

Quick
Tip

Making Good Use of Want Ads

➤ Sunday and Wednesday newspapers typically have the most ads, and you should look at all the ads on those days.

➤ The ones that interest you may not be listed in an obvious way. An accounting job, for example, could be listed under "Accounting," or "Bookkeeper," or "Controller," or several other key words. So make it a policy to read each and every ad in the newspaper. Mark any job that appears interesting and respond to each one, even if you don't have all the qualifications listed. Employers sometimes list things they do not require to limit the response.

➤ Look at want ads that were placed in newspapers that are a month or so old. You can be certain that those organizations will need people with those same skills at some time in the future. Or perhaps the person they hired is not working out. Or maybe there is a similar job that might open up soon.

➤ If an ad does not include an address or phone number, you can often look them up in a "criss-cross" directory. Such a directory is available at many larger libraries, and it will allow you to look up by address, phone number, person, or organization name. Ask your friendly librarian.

Why Many Employers Don't Like to Advertise

Quick Case Study

A business associate of mine recently advertised for a receptionist and said 80 applicants responded. The large number of inquiries disrupted the phones and office routine and required considerable time to handle. All but five were screened out based on their applications and resumes. They interviewed five and got down to the final two, one of whom came in after hearing about the opening from the receptionist who was leaving. After all that work, they hired the job seeker who had never read the ad because they knew more about her from the recommendation they got from their trusted employee.

While many ads encourage you to send in your resume or to fill out an application, you don't have to follow those rules. It is often to your advantage to call the organization and attempt to speak directly with the person who will supervise that position. Ask for an interview, even if they resist. Set up a specific time to meet with the hiring authority.

Employers don't advertise job openings for a variety of reasons. Let's consider a couple of the most important ones. Doing so will help you understand why employers often prefer to hire people using other methods.

Employers find that advertising can cause a lot of extra work

When employers put an ad in the paper, they often receive many responses, and they have to interview all sorts of strangers. Most employers are not trained interviewers and don't enjoy it. They have to interview job seekers who do their best to create a good impression. And they have to eliminate most of them by finding their weaknesses. It's not fun for either side.

Phone calls have to be handled, applications and resumes collected and reviewed, interviews scheduled, and follow-up activities conducted. It takes lots of time. And employers know that screening strangers is a risky business because few are willing to present their weaknesses.

Some organizations get hundreds or even thousands of applicants for each job opening. To the employer, they are all strangers that may or may not be telling the complete truth. And employers would really rather not have to interview strangers unless they have to.

Often, employers don't need to advertise

Most jobs are filled before advertising is needed. The employer may already know someone who seems to be right for the job. Or someone hears about the job and gets an interview before it is advertised. Often, employers hire someone who's been recommended to them by a friend, employee, or associate. Employers are much more comfortable hiring a person they know is good rather than someone they don't know at all. It's that simple.

There is also some evidence that employees who are hired as a result of a personal referral make better employees than those hired through want ads. I think this is the result of a current employee only being willing to refer someone that they think is a good match – and not recommending those who are not.

Traditional Job Search Method 2: Personnel Offices and Application Forms

Quick Alert

The personnel office is not a job seeker's best friend, and neither is an application form.

When you think about it, just why does a personnel office exist, anyway? A person who works there might tell you that their job is to help their organization find qualified people to fill jobs by screening applicants. The question is, from the job seeker's point of view, who is getting screened? It's the job seeker – and it usually means getting screened out.

If you don't believe this, ask someone who has worked in a personnel office. They will tell you that for each person who is hired, 20 or more are not. Sometimes hundreds are screened out for each one hired. What makes this even worse is that personnel people don't actually *hire* anyone unless they will be working in personnel. They screen most job seekers out and then, if the position is still open, and *if* you weren't screened out, you get to meet the person who could eventually hire you.

If you make it to the interview stage – and the chances are slim that you will – you are just one of several others being interviewed. This further reduces your chances of getting a job offer to maybe 5 percent or less.

While those odds seem terrible, they are even worse when you consider that many employers end up hiring someone who wasn't even referred by personnel. Jobs are often filled before personnel even knows they are open. (I have hired many people while working within larger organizations, and I know this to be a fact.)

I often would recruit informally for weeks before the position I was trying to fill worked its way through the formal channels and became posted in the personnel office. By then, I often had one or more good candidates who had the inside track on that job. The last thing I wanted was to get a lot of people referred to me from personnel. They would all be strangers, they would all try to manipulate me into thinking they were great, and they would take up a lot of my time.

Finding the personnel office

If you are still skeptical, have you ever noticed how job seekers are treated in a personnel office? The furniture is usually inexpensive, sturdy, and uncomfortable. The walls are decorated with signs saying everything but "sit down and be quiet." But if the signs don't say that, the clerk might. When I was job seeking, I had applications pushed at me with an announcement like, "Take one of those pencils and complete this application, and then wait until someone can give you an interview." It makes you feel unimportant, doesn't it?

And one more thing – only larger organizations have personnel offices. Smaller organizations don't have them at all, nor do many branch offices of larger organizations. A job seeker who assumes that getting a job requires finding personnel offices will miss most of the jobs that are out there.

Filling out applications

There is some evidence that filling out applications is a more effective method for youth than for adults. This is because many of the jobs they seek are entry level jobs that do not pay well, require night and weekend hours, require little training, and have high turnover rates. Many employers have more difficulty filling these positions and are more willing to hire someone based on an application and a brief interview.

Much of what I said about personnel offices applies to applications as well. Application forms are specifically designed to collect information that can be used to screen you out. And many smaller organizations don't even have them. It is always better to ask to see the person in charge than to ask to complete an application. Fill out an application if you are asked to, but don't expect it to get you an interview.

I'll give you more details on completing applications in a later chapter.

Traditional Job Search Method 3: Sending Out Resumes

The resume has been around for ages. So have the "experts" who will advise you to send yours out by the hundreds. This approach does have its appeal because it seems easy, and almost every job search and resume book recommends it. The problem is that it doesn't work very well.

Like an application, a resume is the near-perfect tool for an employer to use to screen you out. As a result, you should expect a very low response rate, in the neighborhood of 2 to 5 percent, if you mail out unsolicited resumes.

The effectiveness of sending out unsolicited resumes varies by industry and job. It might be that you have skills in short supply, such as those of a computer network engineer; so sending out unsolicited resumes might work to get you interviews. But overall, it is clear that this is not an effective technique for most people.

In an older study of resume effectiveness conducted by Deutsch, Shea and Evans, Inc., and titled "Technical Manpower Recruitment Practices," it took an average of 1,470 resumes for each job offer actually accepted using this method. That is not what I would consider good odds. Of course, you could be the exception, but for most people, sending out unsolicited resumes only helps support the post office.

Farr's Rule: Resumes don't get jobs, interviews do

Many resume books will tell you that the way to get an interview is to create a superior resume that will somehow jump out of a pile of resumes and get the employer's attention. If you only follow their advice, they say, they will show you how to create a better, best, or perfect resume.

While this advice seems to make sense, it assumes that the job search consists of sending in your resume to someone who will compare it to many others. In spite of this assumption, it is almost always better to contact an employer directly (an active approach) rather than to send them a resume and hope for the best (a passive approach). Once you have set up an interview, then send or bring your resume to the interviewer before the interview.

I do think that resumes have their place in the job search and that most people can write a superior resume in a matter of hours – once they have done their homework on what they want to do and have to offer in support of that objective.

Quick Reference

I cover resumes in more detail in a later chapter and also in *The Quick Resume & Cover Letter Book,* published by JIST.

Traditional Job Search Method 4: The Federal/State Employment Service

Quick Fact

Only about 5 percent of all workers get their jobs from public employment services. And most offices know of only about 5 percent of the existing job openings in their area.

Required by federal law, each state has local offices that provide assistance to job seekers in locating job openings. Going by different names in different states, these offices also administer the unemployment compensation program and are often referred to as the "unemployment office" as a result. You should also note that these agencies are publicly funded and *never* charge a fee.

For many years, the results obtained by the Employment Service have been criticized since only one in six who went there actually got a job as a result. Even worse, about half of those jobs lasted fewer than 30 days and paid much lower wages than average.

That all sounds very negative, and I will show you better sources of job leads. But some offices, in some areas, are *much* more active than in others, listing as many as 30 percent of the available openings in that area. Some states now provide job search workshops and other helpful services, too.

Using the Employment Service

➤ Even with its limitations, I suggest you visit the local employment service office on a weekly basis. Some jobs are listed there, and the staff will refer you to openings if you meet the employer's criteria.

➤ Many offices have staff and services for specific groups of people such as veterans, professionals, temporary workers, and others. Ask what services are available and then use those that make sense to you.

➤ Try to see the same staff person each week, so that they get to know you over time. It is important that you create a good impression with them, so dress like you will be going to an interview and treat the staff with respect. If you impress them, they might remember you when they see a good job opening being listed and refer you to it.

Traditional Job Search Method 5: Private Employment Agencies

Quick Fact

Only about 5 percent of all people get their jobs through private employment agencies. And only one in 20 who use them actually get their jobs through them.

To put it mildly, a 95 percent failure rate is not a good record.

Unless the employer pays the fee, using a private employment agency is not a good idea for most people. The exceptions might be if you have skills that are very much in demand or are working full-time and have a limited amount of time to look. Remember that most of the jobs they find are uncovered by calling up businesses listed in the *Yellow Pages* or by reading the want ads. You can do this yourself and keep the money. I show you how in this very book.

While I paint a rather negative picture of the services provided by private employment agencies, they do work for some people. Their effectiveness has also increased over the years, particularly for jobs that tend to be in high demand such as accounting.

Private agencies are slightly more effective for women than for men and more people have had success in using them than in the past. While this appears to support the use of private agencies, I still suggest that you use them with caution.

Quick Alert

Why You Should Use Private Employment Agencies with Caution

➤ Employment agencies charge fees – often substantial ones – to either you or the employer. Fees range from 10 to 15 percent of your annual salary. For each $10,000 you earn a year, your fee will be between $1,000 and

$1,500. Figure it out for your annual salary. That is a lot of money – entirely too much, I think, for most people to consider.

➤ You should also watch out for want ads placed by these agencies. There are lots of them in most papers. The advertised job may not exist, and they may try to refer you to another one paying less money. And NEVER sign an agreement without taking it home and studying it. Never. If you are pressured to sign, walk away.

➤ The people who work in private employment agencies are typically sales people who are paid a commission on the fees they earn. They are not career counselors, so you won't get much help if you have a problem (been fired, changing careers, etc.). What they will want is a quick fee, payable before you start your next job or soon after. And to get that, they may encourage you to accept a position that is less than you are qualified for.

➤ Don't expect much meaningful counseling from them either, especially if the employer pays the fees. It's obvious the agencies are working for *them*, not you.

Traditional Job Search Method 6: Civil Service Jobs

Quick Fact

About 80 percent of all people who work support the 20 percent who earn their living in government-paid jobs.

Almost any job you can imagine can be found somewhere within the public sector: teachers, police, laborers, engineers, secretaries, managers, short-order cooks, librarians, etc. These jobs can be obtained from federal, state, province, county, city, township, and local government sources.

Most civil service jobs require you to fill out lots of forms, take tests, or meet other criteria in order to be considered. These procedures are intended to make the hiring process fair to all who apply. But you should know that applying and actually being considered are two different things.

Quick Alert

The procedures for being considered for government jobs often take a long time before a decision can be made; so if you are in a hurry to find a job, this source is probably not for you. It takes months to be considered for some positions, and then more time to get an interview – and there is often intense competition for the more desirable jobs. In spite of all this, it could be worthwhile to find out what jobs you may qualify for and how to apply for them.

In many areas, the white pages section of the phone book includes a special listing of government agencies. This section is usually on blue paper, making it, I suppose, the blue pages. Many potential places to apply are listed there, but it may require some digging.

You can use the white pages to look up listings under your city, county, state, province, parish, or town name. Most will have a general information number you can call to inquire about the agencies or departments which interest you. Larger governmental systems also typically have a centralized office that screens applicants and lists what openings they know about.

Looking for government jobs can be quite specialized, and there are a variety of good books that have been written on this. Check the bibliography in the back of this book for suggestions of books on this topic.

Who knows, it may be worth the wait.

Traditional Methods Encourage You to Be Passive

The problem with traditional job search methods is that they encourage you to be passive. Traditional methods all require you to depend on *someone else* to do something to let you know about an opening.

They assume that you can't do anything until *someone else* places an ad in the paper, reads your resume, decides to create a position, or in some other way allows you to talk to them about a job opening.

You send in a resume and hope someone else will call you back. You depend on an employer to place a help wanted ad – and hope you don't get screened out. You fill out an application – and hope you get an interview.

I believe that traditional methods are designed to help the employer screen people out. They all create barriers to a job seeker getting in and talking to the person who is most likely to supervise a person with his or her skills. And they all assume that a prospective employer and a job seeker can't see each other unless there is a job opening.

But now you know otherwise.

I believe that many of these traditional methods made more sense in a labor market dominated by a relatively few large employers. While they make much less sense now, most people still assume that these techniques are the way things work. This old-fashioned way of doing things can result in frustration and a longer job search than is necessary. This is not how things have to be.

The techniques that I encourage you to use throughout this book are active ones. I teach you to look at the job search in a new and different way from the traditional approach. I encourage you to be self-reliant, self-directed, and active rather than passive.

Traditional Methods Lead to Hopelessness

By narrowly defining who can talk to whom, traditional job search methods have the effect of encouraging people to believe that there are few jobs out there for which they are qualified.

Private or governmental employment agencies know about only a small percentage of openings; so those who go there will never know of the 95 percent of jobs never listed there. Newspapers only list 15 percent (or fewer) of all openings, and other sources are even worse.

After people use the traditional methods and nothing happens, they tend to believe that there is nothing more they can do. Eventually, they tend to sit at home becoming increasingly discouraged.

The longer a person is unemployed, the fewer hours they tend to spend looking for a job. So even those who have good work habits, years of reliable work experience, and many skills begin to believe that there are no jobs out there for them and that *they* are undesirable and unemployable.

While any one of the traditional methods can and does work for some people, they represent, in total, only about 25 percent of the methods people use to actually get jobs. Therefore, each technique should be used only as one of several methods. With virtually every traditional job search method, the odds are stacked against you.

I suggest that you can do much better.

In the rest of this book, you will learn about more effective and – nontraditional – job search methods. Other techniques explained in this book will be far more effective for most people.

⟩⟩⟩ *Quick Summary*

✓ You can cut your job search time in half (or more) and get a better job.

✓ Some job search methods work better than others.

✓ If you are currently looking for a job, the job search "how to" aspects of this book will probably appeal to you most.

✓ Self-knowledge (regarding your skills and interests) is an essential element in helping you define just what sort of job you want. If you know what your ideal job would be, you are more likely to find one that comes close to it.

✓ Job seekers who spend more time actually looking for work find jobs faster than those who spend less time.

✓ Job seekers who get more interviews find jobs faster because the more interviews you get, the more likely you are to get a job offer.

✓ One of the things that traditional job search methods have in common is that they encourage you to be passive. The result is discouragement and being out of work longer than is necessary.

✓ Traditional job search approaches have job seekers define an interview too narrowly and make obtaining an interview harder than it needs to be.

✓ The most effective job search methods help you remain active in your job search and can dramatically increase the number of interviews you can get.

✓ Most jobs are not advertised. Only about 15 percent of all people get their jobs through the want ads.

✓ Studies show that only two job-seeking methods – direct contact with employers and getting leads from people you know – are used to find about three out of every four jobs.

✓ In this chapter, I review job search techniques that are traditionally used by most people. For each one, I present their disadvantages as well as some non-traditional tips on increasing the effectiveness.

✓ Traditional job search methods include reading the help wanted ads in the newspaper, going to personnel offices and filling out applications, sending out resumes, going to the local employment service office, signing up with a private employment agency, and applying for civil service jobs

✓ The techniques that I encourage you to use throughout this book are active ones. I teach you to look at the job search in a new and different way from the traditional approach. I encourage you to be self-reliant, self-directed, and active rather than passive.

CHAPTER TWO

Job Search Basics

The Two Best
Job Search Methods –

Why They Work and How to Use Them

Quick Overview

In this chapter, I review the following:

✓ Why nontraditonal methods work best

✓ What frictional unemployment is

✓ The four stages of a job opening

✓ How to make warm contacts

✓ Networking basics

✓ How to make cold contacts

✓ A new definition of a job interview

✓ How to use the *Yellow Pages* for job leads

✓ A preview of some other job search methods discussed in greater detail in later chapters

✓ Some "little things" that you can do to make a big difference in your job search

I mentioned in the previous chapter that some job search methods work better than others. It turns out that two methods – getting leads from people you know and direct contacts with employers – work better than the traditional techniques.

In this chapter, I review these methods and give you a good idea of how to use them during your job search. I also present a few key ideas about where to look and why the nontraditional techniques I suggest work.

I've already shown you the data on how people find jobs and, as you know, the most effective technique is getting leads from people you know. And I've also pointed out that most jobs are with small organizations.

Well, you might say, all this is very enlightening, but just going around talking to people doesn't seem like a substantial job search method. It's true, there is more to it than that, and I will provide the details later in this chapter. But to understand just how to be most effective in your job search, I want you to understand a bit about the *why*.

Some Reasons Why Nontraditional Methods Work Best

Many of the traditional job search methods made more sense 20 or more years ago. Back then, a larger percentage of our workforce was employed in large organizations. But, while many people continue to use outmoded job search methods, the labor market has changed.

Small Organizations – Where Most of the Jobs Are

Whatever job search methods you use, it is essential that you begin with a sense of where those jobs are, and most jobs are now with smaller organizations.

My most recent review of the data indicates that about 70 percent of all non-governmental workers now work for small employers. These are employers with 250 or fewer workers. Look at the following chart to see the importance of small organizations in your job search.

Most of the new jobs in our economy now come from small organizations, and this has been true for many years now. Some studies indicate that virtually all of the net job growth in recent years has come from very small employers – those with 20 or fewer employees.

Smaller employers tend not to have personnel offices, so asking to fill out an application or to send in a resume to the personnel department just doesn't make much sense with them. And,

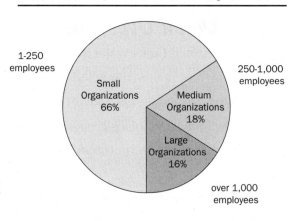

Chart 2-1   Where People Work

1-250 employees

Small Organizations 66%

250-1,000 employees

Medium Organizations 18%

Large Organizations 16%

over 1,000 employees

because there are many more small employers than large ones, they are often harder to find or even to know about. Even larger corporations have begun to decentralize, passing along hiring decisions to smaller local branches that are too small to have a personnel office. This results in larger organizations acting more like small ones in the way they hire people – and the traditional job search approaches are even less effective.

Quick Tip

It is clear that more people are working for small employers than large ones and this trend is likely to continue. You should also note that the opportunities for learning and advancement are often better in smaller organizations than in larger ones.

Many of the nontraditional methods presented in this chapter and throughout this book are very effective with smaller organizations, and the same methods also work well with larger, more formal organizations. The traditional job search methods reviewed in the previous chapter were designed for a very different time and economy, when large employers dominated the labor market. They just don't make as much sense today.

Frictional Unemployment – Where the Job Search Action Is

Friction, according to the dictionary, is "a resistance to motion when two surfaces touch." According to the U.S. Department of Labor, a similar phenomenon occurs in the job market. Called "frictional unemployment," it is a situation where job openings exist and qualified job seekers are looking for them but the employer and job seeker don't connect with each other right away.

An example of frictional unemployment is when a job opening occurs because of someone leaving, but the position remains unfilled for a time before a qualified candidate is selected and actually begins working. The U.S. Department of Labor estimates that over 40 percent of all unemployment is due to this friction. The other sources of unemployment indicated in the chart include "cyclical" unemployment, which is the product of a sluggish economy, and "structural" unemployment, which stems from the restructuring of our economy in fundamental ways such as new technologies.

Some researchers believe that 40 percent of unemployment attributed to friction is a conservative estimate. They argue that frictional unemployment *is* unemployment since the longer it takes to fill or find a job, the higher the unemployment rate.

Chart 2-2   The Sources of Unemployment

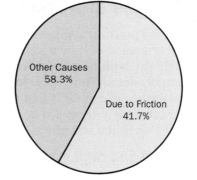

If you could reduce the average length of time it takes to find a job by just one day, it would reduce the number of unemployed by more than 300,000 people. If you could reduce it by just 10 percent, it would have the same economic impact as creating 2.5 million jobs.

This may all seem somewhat theoretical until you realize that the major cause of frictional unemployment is that most job seekers do not know how to find the jobs that exist at any given time. On an individual basis, that means that a job you would accept is open right now but the employer has not yet found anyone to fill it.

This reduction in job search time is something that I have demonstrated in programs many times – people can cut their job search time if they use the right techniques. In a book titled *The Job Market*, author Richard Lathrop concludes that the lack of a national policy to provide job search training is nothing short of a

Chapter 2 *(side tab)*

national scandal. I agree. It is relatively easy to increase your job-getting skills and a shame that it is not taught in more schools and programs.

More recent studies by the Department of Labor also acknowledge the increasing importance of unemployment due to friction. A 1990 article published in the *Monthly Labor Review* indicated that 41 percent of the increase in the unemployment rate was attributable to the increased *frequency* of unemployment. That is to say that, as more people have experienced at least some unemployment each year, the overall unemployment rate has also gone up. With more job and career changing and relatively higher unemployment rates, the implication for national policy is enormous but largely ignored.

The good news for you is that, once you learn the proper job search techniques, you can dramatically reduce the time it takes to find a job. In job-search programs that I have managed, we have routinely decreased the time it takes to get a job to a matter of several weeks. Though these results are from a highly structured job search program, many people who use the methods I suggest in this book have cut their job search time in half – or more.

Once you understand that jobs are out there for you that are not advertised – and that you qualify for these jobs – the next step is learning how to find them.

The Four Stages of a Job Opening

There is a practical application to the idea of frictional unemployment. It comes in an examination of how a job opening comes to be. Jobs, you see, don't just open up one day with no notice. Someone typically knows a job might open up before it actually does. Often, these jobs get filled by someone before the employer needs to advertise. The result is that the job is never advertised at all, because it is filled before there is a need. But how do you find these openings if they're not advertised? Here is the answer:

Quick Advice

Learn to find employers before they advertise the job you want.

To do this, you need to understand how most jobs become available.

I have found it useful to think of a job opening as a process that occurs over time. Before a job is filled, a series of events occur. Thinking in these terms, I have identified four major stages that most job openings go through before they are filled. Each of the four stages represents a distinct phase in the history of a job opening. To help you understand this, let's go through each stage of a job opening in more detail. Each stage is defined and illustrated in the graphic that follows.

The Four Stages of a Job Opening

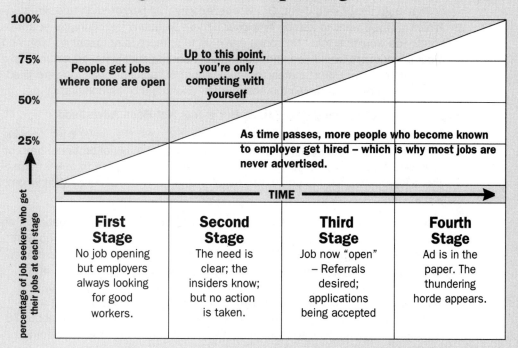

People get jobs where none are open	**Up to this point, you're only competing with yourself**		

As time passes, more people who become known to employer get hired – which is why most jobs are never advertised.

percentage of job seekers who get their jobs at each stage

TIME →

First Stage	**Second Stage**	**Third Stage**	**Fourth Stage**
No job opening but employers always looking for good workers.	The need is clear; the insiders know; but no action is taken.	Job now "open" – Referrals desired; applications being accepted	Ad is in the paper. The thundering horde appears.

Stage 1: There Is No Job Open Now

At some point in time, before a job is actually created or available, it does not exist. If you asked an employer if they had a job opening at this stage, they would say "No." Perhaps no openings are planned or all positions are occupied.

In the conventional job search, there would be no basis for you to have an interview with this employer. And most job seekers will completely ignore the opportunities that exist in this situation. Yet, should an opening become available at any time in the future, those who are already known to the employer will be considered before all others. About 25 percent of all jobs are filled by people the employer knows before the job is even open.

Stage 2: No Formal Opening Exists, But One or More Insiders Know of a Possibility

As time goes on, someone in an organization can usually anticipate a possible future job opening before one actually opens up. It could be the result of a new marketing campaign or product, an increase in business, an observation that someone is not doing well on the job, or a variety of other things. It's not always the boss who knows either.

In previous jobs, I have often known that a coworker was looking for another job even though the boss did not. Or I wondered why that person didn't get fired. Typically, if you were to ask an employer if there were any job openings at this stage, you would be told "No" once again. In fact, there is no opening – yet. And most job seekers would keep on looking, not realizing that a job opportunity is right before them. Unfortunately for them, about 50 percent of all jobs are filled by people who are known to the employer by this stage of an opening.

Stage 3: A Formal Opening Now Exists, But It Has Not Been Advertised

At some point in time, the boss will finally say that, yes, they have a job opening and that they are looking for someone to fill it. But, with few exceptions, days or even weeks go by before that job will be advertised. If you were to ask if there was a job opening at this stage, you might still get a "No," depending on whom you ask.

In larger organizations, even the personnel office doesn't get formal notice of an opening for days or even weeks after the opening is known to people who work in the affected department. In large organizations, people who work there often don't know of openings in other departments. In smaller organizations, of course, most staff would know of any formal openings. In either case, once a job opening finally reaches this stage, it is the first time a person using a conventional approach to the job search might get a "Yes" response. And about 75 percent of all jobs are filled by someone who finds out about the job before it leaves this stage.

Stage 4: The Job Opening Is Finally Advertised

As more time goes by and a job opening does not get filled, it might be advertised in the newspaper, a sign hung in the window, the Employment Service notified, or some other action taken to make the opening known to the general public. This is the stage where virtually every job seeker can know about the opening and, if the job is reasonably desirable, a thundering horde of job seekers will now come after it.

What the Four Stages Mean to You

The "four stages of a job opening" concept shows that you can be considered for a job opening long before a formal opening exists – and long before it is advertised. In fact, that is why most jobs are never advertised. Someone like you gets there before it needs to be. Employers don't like to hire strangers. They prefer to hire people they already know or who are referred to them by someone they know. Many are willing to talk to a job seeker even before they have a job opening – if you approach them in the right way. Once you know each other, of course, you are no longer strangers.

About 25 percent of the people who get hired become known to the employer before a job opening exists. Another 25 percent or so of those who get hired find out about the opening during the second stage of a job opening. Jobs that are filled during the first and second stages of a job opening are simply not available to someone using traditional job search methods. Half of all jobs are gone by then.

Only about half of all jobs make it to the third stage of a job opening. During this stage the job is at least available to a job seeker using traditional methods. If that job seeker just happens to ask the right person at the right time and if there is a job opening they will, for the first time get a "Yes" response. During this third stage another 25 percent get their jobs. With 75 percent of the jobs getting filled during the first three stages, that leaves the remaining 25 percent that get advertised and, in other ways, made available to the public.

The most important job search rule of all

The four stages of a job opening make it clear that most jobs are filled before they are advertised. This pattern illustrates the most important job search rule of all:

Don't wait until the job is open!

The best time to search for a job is before anyone else knows about it. Most jobs are filled by someone the employer meets before a job is formally "open." So the trick is to meet people who can hire you before a job is available.

Instead of saying "Do you have any jobs open?" say "I realize you may not have any openings now, but I would still like to talk to you about the possibility of future openings." With this simple approach many employers will say "Yes" instead of "No." Not all, but many.

More bad news for traditional job search methods

Besides missing out on half of the available job openings, there are other disadvantages to those using traditional job search methods. The first is that the jobs that remain unfilled by the third and fourth stages of a job opening tend to be less desirable or harder to fill. The best jobs are often gone by then. This is even more true for the jobs that are left unfilled long enough to get advertised. There are exceptions, of course, but the better jobs tend to get taken long before they are advertised.

Jobs that make it to the third and fourth stage of a job opening face another distinct disadvantage – they have more competition. This is particularly true for advertised jobs since there are often many applicants for these jobs.

During the third and fourth stages an employer has the task of screening out all but one of those who are interested. Virtually all of the applicants are now strangers who will manipulate the employer by "marketing" or "selling" themselves, which means emphasizing the positive and hiding the negative. Employers know this, so they try to find out something "wrong" with each applicant in order to eliminate them from consideration. It is the nature of the game and it is not nice.

So the job search takes on a decidedly competitive and distasteful flavor for those seeking jobs in the third and, more so, in the fourth stage of a job opening. I am not saying you should not consider jobs that are advertised – you should – it's just that you need to find ways of finding potential openings before others do. Or, if you prefer, you can remain unemployed longer than you really need to.

A new concept for interviewing

You can "interview" even before a job opening formally exists.

You may not have noticed that what I have done in the previous narrative is to redefine what an "interview" is. In the conventional job search, an interview is something you can obtain only when an employer has a clearly defined job opening that you qualify for. But that definition eliminates opportunities available during the first two stages of a job opening. Here is my new definition of an interview:

A New Definition of an Interview

An interview is any face-to-face contact with a person who hires or supervises people with your skills – even if there is no job opening now.

This definition is a very important one to remember because it allows you to "interview" all sorts of people you would otherwise overlook in a job search. For example, it allows you to talk to a potential employer during the first or second stages of a job opening – before a job is formally open at all.

Instead of waiting for a job to be advertised in the newspaper, this definition allows you to go out and talk to potential employers who may not have job openings at all but who might in the future. Understanding and using this new definition will give you a distinct advantage in finding job possibilities while others use traditional job search methods – and remain unemployed longer than they need to.

The rest of this book assumes this new definition of an interview. This mind-set opens a world of possibility. And it can help you get a job in much less time than would be possible otherwise.

The Two Most Effective Job Search Methods – Warm and Cold Contacts

I find concepts easier to understand if I keep things simple. One simple idea that I have applied to the job search is that of warm and cold contacts. Let me explain:

Sales people who call on potential customers via phone or by dropping in without an appointment call this technique making "cold contacts." While I do not think that the sales analogy is completely appropriate when applied to the job search, I like the "cold contacts" term. It quickly communicates a style of contact that can be adapted for the search for potential job openings.

Quick Definition

So, in the job search context, cold contacts are job leads obtained from contacting people you don't know – employers in particular. Using this term also allows me to create the term "warm contacts" to describe leads for job openings that come from people you already know. These warm contacts include friends, relatives, and acquaintances.

Warm Contacts: The Most Effective Job Search Method

If you remember the data on how people find jobs presented in the previous chapter, you may recollect that warm contacts – from friends and relatives – account for about one-third of all job leads. It is probably higher than that. More recent studies which asked job seekers for lead sources other than friends or relatives, found that other groups such as "business associates" and "acquaintances" provided leads as well.

Quick Fact

All personal referrals together probably account for about 40 percent of how people find jobs. That makes using personal contacts the most important job search technique of all.

Leads developed from direct contacts with employers are also very important. About 30 percent of all job seekers find their jobs using this method. Together, these two techniques account for about 75 percent of all job leads. With a little practice, getting leads from your warm contacts may be the only job search techniques you need.

Just Three Steps to Identify Hundreds of Warm Contacts

Quick Tip

The people who know you are the same ones who are most likely to help you – if only they knew what to do. Yet few job seekers seem willing to ask for meaningful help from the people they know in developing job leads. If they are asked to help a job seeker at all it is of the vague, "Tell me if you hear anything," variety. While this crude approach does work often enough, people you know – your warm contacts – can and will be much more helpful if you learn to ask them to help you in more specific ways.

Knowing that leads provided by warm contacts is the most effective source of jobs for most people, it makes sense to systematically develop these contacts. Yet few job seekers go about developing their warm contacts in an organized way. With just a few simple techniques that I will soon review, you might be amazed at how many people you know – or can come to know.

Step 1: List contact groups of people you know

To give you an idea of how this works, let's start by defining just who you know – your "warm" contacts. You know far more people than you may at first realize. To prove this, I suggest you begin by listing the *types* or *categories* of people you know.

Look over the list of contact groups that follows. It includes categories that often come up in workshops that I teach, and it will give you some ideas for your own list. Notice that some of the listings are of groups of people with whom you might share something in common, even though you would not know all those within the group.

A Sample List of Warm Contact Groups

Friends	Present or former teachers
Relatives	Neighbors
Former employers	People in my athletic club
Former coworkers	People I play sports with
School friends	Members of a professional organization I belong to (or could join)
Alumni lists	
Members of my political party – in and out of elected positions	People who sell me things or provide me with professional services (insurance, hair salon, mechanic, shop clerks, etc.)
Members of my church	
Members of social, fraternal, or other clubs	People I play cards with

Warm Contact Groups Worksheet

Directions: Now create your own list of groups of people you know. Use any of the groups from the previous sample as well as your own groups and list them in the spaces below. I have already included the friends and relatives groups since almost everyone has some – and because they are an important source of job leads. Be as specific as possible in the categories you add.

Groups	#	Groups	#
Friends			
Relatives			

Step 2: Create warm contact lists

While most people agree that "you have to know someone to get a job" most job seekers often tell me they "don't know anyone." One of those assumptions *is* true, namely, that people very often *do* get jobs through someone they know. But job seekers are mistaken if they think they don't know people. To show you what I mean, let's take a few of the groups you listed in the preceding exercise and see how many people they represent.

You know far more people than you might realize

Right now, if I asked you to take the first group on your list (which is "friends," since I put it there) and write a list that included everyone you are friendly with or who is even somewhat friendly to you, how many people would you guess that is? Ten? Twenty-five? Two-hundred?

Don't feel insecure here: some very good people just can't call a lot of people "friends." The truth is we all would be very fortunate to have just a *few* good friends during our lives. Instead, I'm suggesting that you think of people who are "friendly" to you, not close friends. Jot that number on your Warm Contact Groups Worksheet, next to the "friends" entry. Next, estimate how many people are in each of the other groups and note your estimate next to each entry.

When you are finished, don't be surprised if the number of people you know is larger than you anticipated. It's not at all unusual for someone to get hundreds of potential contact people this way. Some groups, such as people who belong to your religious group or who went to the same school, can be enormous. They don't all know about job openings, of course, but they are a place to start. And each contact on your list is a source of potential job leads.

Some contact groups are ideal for making out of town contacts. For example, while you may not personally know everyone who graduated from your school, an alumni list can help you locate past graduates who live all over the country. If you ask them to help you to locate contacts in their area, many will. I'll provide more details on looking for a job out of town later in this book.

Create lists of specific contacts

I know from experience that leaving you with the idea that you know lots of people is not enough. To make this an effective job search technique, you will have to contact those people. To accomplish this, it is essential that you make – you guessed it – more lists.

For each of the contact groups you listed previously, use a sheet of paper to make a separate list. Begin with friends and write as many friends' names on that list as you can think of. Then do the same thing for relatives. When you have completed these two lists, you should have a significant number of names of people who know you. You can save the other lists to do later in your job search. You may only need the first two.

Step 3: Use your warm contacts to develop an expanding network of contacts

Armed with your lists of friends and relatives, you have the beginning of a list of people who, in turn, can refer you to others. This process is what is called "networking."

Networking basics

Networking sounds sophisticated and complicated, but it's really a pretty simple idea. You use one person you know as a source to introduce you to one or preferably two other people you don't know. Like this:

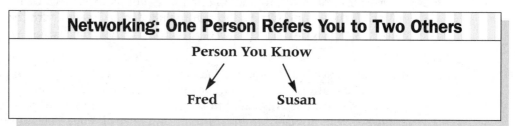

Networking: One Person Refers You to Two Others

Person You Know

Fred   Susan

The first person you contact is clearly a warm contact, since you know them directly. The people your warm contact then refers you to will also give you a warm reception, since you have a personal connection with them. In a sense, they are also warm contacts once you get to know them.

After meeting with Fred and Susan (or chatting with them on the phone), they will often be willing to give you names of others to contact. As you repeat this referral process with each person, this is what happens:

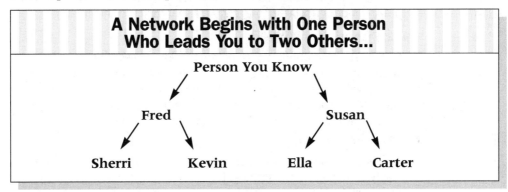

**A Network Begins with One Person
Who Leads You to Two Others...**

Person You Know

Fred   Susan

Sherri   Kevin   Ella   Carter

Networking arithmetic

The number of people you could contact through networking is amazing. In the example I just presented, if you kept getting two referrals from each person, you would have 1,024 people in your network after only the tenth level of contact. And that is starting with only one person!

The Six Rules for Developing a Successful Network of Contacts

Networking is a simple idea and it does work. It helps you meet potential employers you would not find using any other method. These employers may be a friend of a friend of a friend. And they will be willing to see you for this reason. Of course, not all of your contacts will be helpful to your job search, but there are some things you can do to increase this possibility. Here are my basic rules of networking:

Rule 1: Get Started – Set Up a Meeting

An essential criteria for a person to be in your network is that they are willing to talk to you. This should include just about everyone, so select those who seem most likely to know lots of other people. Friends, relatives, and other warm contacts are an ideal place to start, because they are usually very willing to help you if they can.

To set up a meeting, simply call your contact and say something like:

"Hi there, Uncle Albert, I'm looking for a job and wonder if you could help me out. When would be a good time for me to come over?"

Quick Reference

While some short explanatory conversation is in order in your initial phone call, your objective is to get an appointment.

In a later chapter you will learn about a job search tool called a JIST Card and use this as a basis for making phone calls. These techniques will assist you in making more effective phone contacts, but more on this later.

Rule 2: Present Yourself Well

It is most important that each contact in your network ends up thinking well of you. To increase the chances that they will, it helps to be friendly, well organized, polite, and interested in what they have to say. Even Uncle Albert doesn't *have* to see you, so be on your best behavior and behave as if you are going to an interview with a stranger, even if you know the person well.

Rule 3: Learn Something

Be open to learn from your contacts, even if they don't know very much about the type of job you are seeking. Do try, however, to keep things centered on your goal. Your goal, of course, is to get more job leads.

In situations where the contact does know about the type of job you want, there is often much that they can tell you about what is going on in the field and other details that would be helpful for you to know.

Rule 4: Get Two Referrals

Getting referrals is essential to developing a network, so don't give up until you have at least two names of other people who might help in your job search. You can get referrals from virtually anyone but only if you keep asking for them. I have developed three questions that will typically get you one or more referrals, but often only after you ask the second or third question.

The Three Essential Questions to Get Referrals

1. Do you know of anyone who might have an opening for a person with my skills? If no, then,

2. Do you know of anyone else who *might* know of someone who would? If still no, then,

3. Do you know someone who knows lots of people?

Quick Tip

It is essential that you ask all three questions.

It is unusual to get a "No" if you ask all three questions. But I know from many years of experience that you will resist asking the second and, particularly, the third questions. Most people are willing to ask the first question and stop there.

42   The Very Quick Job Search   *Section 1: Job Search Basics*

Even untrained job seekers ask the first question, though typically using less direct language than I suggest here. And they get about 40 percent of all their job leads in this way – more than from any other method. But my point here is that asking the second and third questions can dramatically increase the effectiveness of your warm contacts.

So get used to asking each of the three questions until you get what you want: either a lead for a possible job opening or the names of two people who might be of assistance to you in your search.

As you ask each of the three questions, be prepared for an occasional "yes" response to your first question. Whenever this happens, get the details of the person to contact about the job opening, including the correct spelling of their name and how to contact them. Then call them yourself and ask for a time to come in and talk to them as soon as possible.

Rule 5: Follow Up on Referrals

There will be occasions when you do get the name of a person who has a job opening. When this happens, obviously you should follow up on this right away. In most cases, you are better off to make the contact yourself, rather than to wait for your warm contact to call for you. This approach allows you to make sure that there is no delay in making the contact and assures that you maintain control of the contact process.

The networking process is far more likely to provide you with contacts that don't have a job opening for you at this time. In these situations, you can call them and say something like this:

> *Hello, my name is Jean Porter, a friend of Fred Janney. He suggested*
> *I call and ask you for help. I am looking for a position as a retail*
> *sales manager and he thought you might be willing to see me and*
> *give me a few ideas . . .*

The conversation pretty much takes care of itself from here on but do keep your phone conversation short. Remember that you want an interview in person, not over the phone.

One thing leads to another and, before you know it, you are in the hidden job market. Once you make the first few contacts with people you know, you will quickly begin to be referred to people you don't know. The nature of the process encourages each person to refer you to someone who knows even more about the sort of job you want than they do.

As you get referred along, you will begin to meet some very knowledgeable people who will tell you things you need to know. The more of them you see, the more you learn, and the better prepared you are for future contacts and for interviews. With each level of referrals, you are also more likely to meet people who have the ability to hire you or who know someone who does.

You are now in the hidden job market. Most of the people you meet through networking in this way do not have jobs open or are unlikely to hire someone like you. But they do know other people and are often willing to refer you to them – or tell someone else about you who, in turn, *does* have an opening.

This is networking and it really does work. After just a few levels of contacts, you will begin to talk to people who do supervise or need people with skills similar to yours. They may or may not have a job opening now, but you are now in a position to be considered for future openings. You have come to be known to them in the early stages of a job opening. While others are waiting for jobs to be advertised in the want ads, you are getting there before it is – and have a chance to get the job before it is ever advertised.

If you are shy and conversation does not come easily to you, here are a few questions you can ask in your referral interviews that should keep things moving:

Questions You Can Ask in a Referral Interview

➤ How did you get into this line of work?

➤ What are the things you like best (or least) about your work?

➤ Do you have any ideas how a person with my background and skills might find a job in this field?

➤ What trends do you see in this career field? How could I take advantage of them?

➤ What projects have you been working on that excite you?

➤ From your point of view, what problems are most important to overcome in this career area?

Rule 6: Send Thank-You Notes

Sending someone a thank-you note is a simple act of appreciation. While sending a thank-you note is good manners, very few people do it today. Good manners alone justify sending thank-you notes to people who help you in your job search. They may have spent an hour or so interviewing you, given you the name of someone else to contact, or helped you in some other way. I believe that the job search can and should be conducted on a person-to-person level. Thank-you notes help reinforce this one-on-one relationship.

Your sending thank-you notes also has a practical benefit since the person who receives it is far more likely to remember you. They will perceive you as being thoughtful and well-organized. I have been told by hundreds of employers that they rarely or never get a thank-you note from the people they interview. They describe the people who *do* send them as being "thoughtful," "well-organized," "thorough," and in other positive terms.

While thank-you notes will not get you a job for which you are not qualified, they will often help people remember you in a positive way. Thank-you notes can also help these referrals become effective members of your network of people willing to help you. If they do know of a job opening, or meet someone who does, you will be remembered when others will not.

Thank-you notes are an important and often overlooked tool in the job search. I cover them in more detail in a later chapter and I encourage you to use them regularly. They are a small detail that can make a big difference in your job search.

Cold Contacts: Making Direct Contacts with Prospective Employers

Many people need only use their warm contacts to develop a network that results in a job offer. As I have pointed out, warm contacts are the number one source of job leads, accounting for about 40 percent of how people find jobs. With the techniques I presented earlier in this chapter, you can use your warm contacts even more effectively than the norm.

Even though networking with your warm contacts may be the only job search method you really need, it is wise to use a *variety* of job search methods. This section will present basic techniques that you can use to develop direct contacts with prospective employers. This is an important topic because the research indicates that contacts made in this way account for about a third of how people find jobs. This makes this method one of the two most effective job search methods.

Although getting jobs by directly contacting an employer is clearly an important source of leads, there are things you can do to dramatically improve your results when doing so. While making cold contacts is intimidating for many people, doing so can make a dramatic difference if you know how.

There are two basic methods for making cold contacts. The first is using the phone to set up interviews with people who work in organizations that are likely to use or need someone with skills similar to yours. The second involves your personally dropping in to a potential employer's location and asking for an interview. Let me cover each of these methods in turn.

Remember the New Definition of an Interview

When making cold contacts with employers, it is important for you to remember just what your objective is. Your objective is to get an interview. But you also need to keep reminding yourself that you are not just looking for an interview in the traditional sense. Instead, you are looking for interview opportunities in a broader context and with a nontraditional definition.

Just to help you remember this definition of what it is you are looking for, let me again present the definition I provided earlier in this chapter:

Quick Definition

A New Definition of an Interview

An interview is any face-to-face contact with a person who hires or supervises people with your skills – even if there is no job opening now.

Keep this in mind at all times as you consider how to make cold contacts. It is a key concept and, if you fully use it, will help you find many opportunities that others will overlook.

Using the Yellow Pages as a Source of Job Leads

If you think about it, the *Yellow Pages* telephone directory is the ideal source for finding prospective employers. Virtually every business, not-for-profit, and governmental organization is listed in this one place. Big organizations as well as the smallest of organizations are listed. And the *Yellow Pages* book is free and readily available. Even if you are considering looking for a job in a distant location, the *Yellow Pages* for that location is an important source of job leads.

The Fabulous Four-Step *Yellow Pages* Cold Contact Process

Once again, it pays to be systematic in how you go about your job search. The *Yellow Pages* can be intimidating unless you approach it in an organized way. After considerable trial and error on my own I have developed an approach to using the *Yellow Pages* that I suggest you use too. If you do, *the Yellow Pages* can become one of your best friends.

Yellow Pages Step 1. Identify Index Headings

Begin by looking at the index that is usually in the front of the *Yellow Pages*. It lists the categories within which the various businesses and other organizations are listed. From "Abrasives" and "Accident & Health Insurance" through "Zoning Consultants," most *Yellow Pages* list hundreds of categories. And each category, of course, refers to a listing of organizations under that heading. The *Yellow Pages* is a gold mine of job leads once you know how to use it. Here are some tips to get the best effect.

Go through each and every heading in the index of your *Yellow Pages* and, for each, ask yourself this question:

Could this organization use a person with my skills?

The only possible answers are "Yes" or "No." There will be some strange options that come up when doing this, things you would never seriously consider, but humor me, and just answer yes or no for each listing.

Yellow Pages Step 2. Define Which Headings Are of Most Interest

If your answer is "Yes," to a particular category, then mark it with one of the following numbers:

Mark each "Yes" index entry with a 1, 2, or 3

1 = This type of organization sounds very interesting as a possible place to work.

2 = This type of organization sounds somewhat interesting.

3 = This type of organization does not appeal to me at all (or is possible but weird).

Actuaries
✓ **Acupuncture** See
    1 Chiropractors-Doctors of Chiropractic
      (D.C.)
    2 Clinics
    1 Physicians & Surgeons-Medical-M.D.
    1 Physicians & Surgeons-Osteopathic-
      D.O.
Adding & Calculating Machines &
  Supplies See
    Calculating & Adding Machines &
      Supplies
Additions-Homes See
    Building Contractors
    Carpenters
    Contractors
      Alteration
    Contractors
      General
    Home Improvements
Addressing-
    & Letter Service See
      Letter Shop Service

Addressing-(Cont'd)
    Machines & Supplies
Adhesives-
    & Glueing Equipment
    & Glues
Adjusters See
    Insurance Adjusters Company
    Insurance Adjusters Public
✓ **Adoption Services Adult-**
    Day Care See
    2 Day Care Centers Adult
    1 Human Services Organizations
    2 Senior Citizens' Organizations
    2 Senior Citizens' Services
    1 Social Service Organizations
    Education See
    3 Schools-Academic-Colleges &
      Universities
    3 Schools-Academic-Secondary &
      Elementary
    Foster Care See
    3 Homes for the Aged
    3 Homes-Adult

Adoption Services Adult-(Cont'd)
    2 Nursing Homes
    3 Retirement & Life Care
      Communities & Homes
✓ **Advertising-**
    3 Aerial
    3 Art & Layout Service See
      Artists-Commercial
      Graphic Designers
    3 Calendars See
      Calendars
    Copy Writers See
    1 Advertising Agencies & Counselors
    3 Writers
    Coupons See
    2 Advertising-Direct Mail
    2 Advertising-Directory & Guide
    1 Sales Promotion Service
    Direct Mail
    See Also
    3 Letter Shop Service
    Directory & Guide Displays See
    2 Display Designers & Producers

Yellow Pages Step 3. Identify Specific Prospects

Each and every index entry refers you to a section in the *Yellow Pages* which, in turn, lists specific organizations and businesses to contact. Each and every one of these individual listings is a potential target for you. Let's look at a way to identify which organizations you should contact.

The obvious place to begin would be the ones you rated with a "1" – those that sounded particularly interesting to you. But these entries may not be the best place to begin. If you are just beginning your job search it is often a good idea to improve your job-search and interviewing skills with organizations where you have less to lose. Consider contacting organizations you listed as a "3" first.

Even if you mess up these contacts you can't hurt yourself badly. If you are looking for a specialized job where few positions – and even fewer organizations – exist, it is also wise to start with your "3s" until your techniques improve. As you do this, though, you just may get a job offer. It happens often enough, even from the least likely of sources. And you just might want to consider such an offer, too.

By now, you should have expected me to suggest you create yet another list. And why not? In identifying specific places to contact, I have found it most effective to write down the name of each specific targeted organization on a simple list along with the phone number for each. Use a separate form for each general type of organization that you identify in the index.

Yellow Pages Contact List

Desired Position: *accountant*

Employer Name	Phone Number
John Murphy – Aetna Insurance	*555-9936*
Jim Anderson – Acme Corporation	*555-7835*

For many jobs, there are hundreds (and in larger cities, perhaps thousands) of places you can identify using just this technique. The odds are excellent that one of them will hire you. And you only need one.

Yellow Pages Step 4. Make the Phone Call

In most cases, you can just pick up the phone and call. If you are calling a smaller organization, ask for the manager or person in charge. In a larger organization, ask for the person in charge of the functional area you are interested in, like accounting, or computer operations, or whatever.

In making cold phone contacts, remember that you are not looking for a job opening – you want to meet with the person who has the authority to hire or supervise someone with your skills, even if there is no job opening now. This is a very important point, because doing otherwise will result in many more negative outcomes than would otherwise be the case.

Never ask for the personnel department when making these kinds of calls!

Keep in mind that you want to get to the person who directly hires or supervises someone with your skills. Unless you want to work in a personnel department, you should not be asking for that department.

Most people who make cold calls based on the *Yellow Pages* techniques I have outlined here get one or more interviews with each hour of using the telephone. There are few other techniques that can get you this kind of result.

Making Cold Telephone Calls Is Not Easy, But It Does Work

While making a telephone call to an unknown prospective employer is not easy for most people, ask yourself what is the worst thing that can happen to you. At worst, the employer might be annoyed that you called. They might even get angry and hang up on you. But my experience – and that of many job seekers who have used this technique – is that most employers don't mind your calling at all. You see, employers are interested in talking to good people, even if they don't have an opening when you call. Employers are people, too – and they know from experience that they just might need someone soon.

The chapter, "Dialing for Dollars," later in this book provides considerable detail on how to create and use a telephone script that you can adapt for use in making contacts with people you know or in making cold contacts. While there is a bit more to learn to make cold phone contacts work well, the basic techniques are quite easy and they do work.

Another Effective Cold Contact Technique: Dropping in Without an Appointment

If you keep your eyes open, there are sources of job leads everywhere you go. For example, if you are interested in photography, drop in at a camera store. If you are looking for a position in accounting, drop in any business or other organization and ask for the person in charge of that function. On your way to a job interview at 2 p.m., look for places along the way that might need someone with your skills. On your way home, when you don't have anything important to do anyway, stop in at these places.

Managers in many small organizations will see you if you just drop in and ask to see them. Even managers in large organizations will often see you if you ask to see the person in charge. While doing this may frighten you, it does work and you might be surprised at how many people are willing to talk to you if you approach the situation correctly.

It is important that you are dressed appropriately for an interview if you are making cold contacts in person. First impressions do count. Because an opportunity can present itself in unexpected ways, you should pay more than normal attention to your dress and grooming throughout your job search. Doing so will allow you to create positive impressions with even casual contacts and to pursue cold contact and interview opportunities on short notice.

Be willing to call or come back

You will often enough find that the person you want to see is busy or not available. You do need to be sensitive to this and don't push for an interview if you sense that this is a bad time for the person.

If the person you want to see is busy, offer to get back with him or her at a better time. Make sure that you have the correct name and title, then set a specific time that would work out best for him or her by getting a specific day (next Tuesday, for example) and time (between 9 and 10 a.m.) for you to call or come back. In most cases, you will be better off to call at that time and set up an appointment for a later time, since this will save you transportation time. An exception to this would be if you sense that this would be an above average opportunity for you based on what you observed in your initial contact.

Follow up!

Next Tuesday, at 9:00 a.m., the odds are very good that this particular employer is not even thinking about or expecting you to call. Of course, since you WILL call then, as you had promised, you are bound to make a positive impression. In your phone call, go after setting up a specific time to come in. If no job is open now, ask to come in and "discuss the possibility of future openings."

Persistence pays off, so get over your fear of rejection in making cold contacts in person or by phone. Keep asking for an interview, even if there is no job opening just yet. Doing so will help you identify opportunities long before they would be known to job seekers using traditional methods.

Little Things Make a Difference

I often observe that if you take care of the little things the big things will take care of themselves. In closing off this chapter, I want to review a variety of little things that matter in the job search. In some cases, other sections of the book will cover these things in more detail but, should you not take the time to read all that, I wanted you to know about them.

Know What You Want to Do

Too many people look for a job without having a clear sense of what they really want to do. This lack of a job objective puts an employer in the position of having to figure this out for you and this is not the way you want this done. Worse yet, not having a clear objective greatly increases your chances of getting a job that you hate.

A few chapters in Part II of this book can help you define what you want to do and put it into the form of a job objective. It is essential that you spend the time to do this because it is so very important.

Emphasize Your Skills and Accomplishments

Few people can quickly tell me why someone should hire them over someone else. Yet the key question you will have to answer in an interview (though it is rarely asked this clearly) is "Why should I hire you?" Answering this question requires you to have a thorough understanding of the skills you have that can be used in the job you want. And this requires most of us to do some homework.

Some of the chapters later in this book give you lots of information to use in the interview process, and I strongly suggest that you review those chapters carefully.

Send Thank-You Notes

Thank-you notes make a difference and are covered later in this book. You should routinely send them right after each significant contact you make in your job search: after an interview, after setting up an interview, after getting the name of someone to contact from a friend, and in many other situations.

To help you understand why I emphasize thank-you notes, consider their effect. For example, if you had made a cold contact but had only arranged to make a call back again on next Tuesday at 9:00 a.m., it is highly likely that employer will quickly forget about this discussion. But, on the same day you spoke with them, you send them a thank-you note telling them you appreciate their willingness to talk to you and that you look forward to calling them next Tuesday morning. My experience is that most employers are impressed with this attention to detail, and that impression will help you just a little bit.

As a few days past, that potential employer is likely to put you out of his or her mind again, but not as much. When you call next Tuesday as you promised, he or she is likely to be just a bit more receptive to setting up a time to see you. You send *another* thank-you note, thanking that person for seeing you and enclosing a JIST Card (more on this later) or resume. If you do this, you will have again created a positive impression and increased your chances of getting a good reception.

Little things count, in the job search as well as in life. I've always appreciated people who send thank-you notes – and so will most potential employers.

Spend More Time Looking

Plan on looking full time for your next job. The next chapter will help you organize your job search as if it were a job in itself. This approach, along with some nontraditional techniques I present in this book, can reduce your job search time substantially.

Set a Goal of Two Interviews per Day

If you use traditional job search methods, getting two interviews a day just isn't possible for most people. That's why I suggest a nontraditional definition of an interview because this new definition allows you to get more interviews. Lots of people using the techniques I present in this book do get two interviews a day. And they get better jobs in less time as a result.

Stay in Touch

Stay in touch with the meaningful contacts you make during your networking. Ask them if it is OK to call them up every few weeks during your job search, then do so if it is OK (and it almost always is). If you sent them a thank-you note after your first contact, they will probably remember you fondly. When you call, let them know what happened from your following up with any referrals they gave you.

People in your network will hear of job openings that they did not know of when you last had contact. In a very real sense, they will know of jobs in the first, second, or third stages of the job opening – long before they are advertised. Since they already know you, staying in touch with them is often a far more effective source of good job leads than making new contacts.

Organize Your Contacts

In case you haven't noticed, using the techniques I have covered in this chapter can solve one of the major problems job seekers normally have – not having enough job leads or interviews. While that problem is solved if you use the job search methods I suggest, a new one is often created – having too many job leads to keep track of in your head. The only way to solve this new "problem" is to organize your contacts on paper. Computers can do this and there are even contact management programs designed for this use, but for most job seekers, simple noncomputer systems will work just fine. For example, you can use a follow up system based on 3-by-5-inch cards which have the advantage of being inexpensive, easy to get, and portable. In the next chapter I'll show you how to use these index cards to build an effective system for organizing and tracking contacts.

More Good Job Search Methods

There are a lot of clever job seekers out there, so almost anything you can imagine has been tried by someone and has probably worked. Let's look at some of the more important of these other techniques. Most are covered in more detail later in the book.

> **JIST Cards:**
>
> JIST Cards are covered in more detail in a chapter later in this book, but I want to show you an example here, since they are excellent tools for enclosing in a thank-you note, giving to people in your network, and for other uses. They work.

John Kijek **Home:** (219) 232-9213
Message: (219) 637-6643

Position Desired: Management position in a small- to medium-size organization.

Skills: B.A. in business plus over five years experience in increasingly responsible management positions. Have supervised as many as 12 staff and increased productivity by 27 percent over two years. Was promoted twice in the past three years and have excellent references. Started customer follow-up program that increased sales by 22 percent within 12 months. Get along well with others and am a good team worker.

Willing to travel and can work any hours

Hardworking, self-motivated, willing to accept responsibility

Quick Fact

➤ School or Other Placement Office:

About 5 percent of all people get their jobs either from school placement programs or from referrals from teachers.

That may not sound like much, but it is almost as important a source as the employment service. There are some very good (and free) job search and placement programs operated by schools, government agencies, and other places. Some people even sign up for schools because of their records for helping graduates find jobs. If you have access to any such program, use it. Often, these services can be of excellent quality.

➤ Take an Entry-Level Job:

For example, if you want to manage a restaurant but you are short on experience, get a job as a waiter or waitress. Take the jobs that are easy to get, then volunteer to help out at other, more responsible tasks. Ask to move up and keep after that goal.

➤ Ask for the Job:

Once you decide you are interested in a particular job, saying you want it is a way to communicate your enthusiasm for it. Be prepared to say exactly why you want that job and why you think you can handle it well. An employer is likely to be impressed with your enthusiasm for this particular job and assume you will be more energetic and committed to it. Say you want the job and you are more likely to get it. It's amazing how many people don't do this. Just say "I'm really interested in this position. When can I start?!" It makes a difference when it is true.

➤ **Define a Problem You Can Solve:**

If you look for them, opportunities for you to solve an employer's problem will often become obvious in your job search. Let's say you know something about marketing. During an interview, you conclude that you could substantially increase the sales of that organization.

Go home and develop a simple written plan, including projected income and expenses, and set up a later interview to present your ideas. You could do this at any place you really wanted to work.

➤ **The Armed Services:**

Don't overlook them as a source of training and employment. They are a major employer of young people and have a lot to offer, including funds for college.

➤ **Volunteer to Work for Free:**

In some situations, consider offering an employer a day or more of your time to demonstrate that you can do the job. If you really do want the job, this is a technique that can get an employer to take you seriously over other candidates who might appear to have better credentials.

➤ **Self-Employment:**

Often overlooked as a source of jobs, you could create your own. It's not easy, but some jobs – such as painting or consulting – cost very little to start. People with substantial management or professional experience often offer consulting services while continuing their job search. Some people successfully turn their unemployment into opportunities to start a business they have always dreamed of.

If you are considering this yourself, do be cautious. While some people succeed in starting up a profitable business, many more do not. The best way to approach this may be to define what sort of activity you want to be self-employed in and begin doing that part-time while employed elsewhere. Many hobbies help you develop the necessary skills to later avoid business failure.

If you are now unemployed – or soon will be – consider self-employment as a way to earn temporary income. Paint houses, do tax returns, or whatever else you know how to do to earn cash. The extra income will help get you through to your next "real" job.

If you know you want to be self-employed or start a particular type of business, it may also be wise to seek a job in your area of interest. Depending on the job, you can then gain the skills and contacts you need to succeed in it on your own.

Self-Employment Resources

I've included several books on self-employment in the bibliography including two published by JIST Works. *MInd Your Own Business* by LaVerne Ludden and Bonnie Maitlen is a good book to start with if you are considering self-employment, as it covers a variety of things you should know before "jumping in." *The Franchise Opportunities Handbook* lists more than 1,500 franchise opportunities. It provides good advice if you are considering franchising and could prove to be extremely helpful.

➤ **Employment Contractors/Temporary Help Agencies:**

Under these headings in the *Yellow Pages* you will find organizations that can hire you for short-term jobs. Assignments can last from a day or two to many months. Some specialize in office help, others in accounting or other specialized areas. A few of these agencies provide testing and training in such areas as word processing. These are good places to go if you need a source of income quickly.

Another distinct advantage is that the job assignments often give you good work experience in a variety of work settings. It is not unusual, if you do a good job, to get job offers from the same employers to whom you were assigned as a temporary. Some employers routinely use these services to screen for good employees instead of using conventional hiring procedures.

➤ **Head Hunters:**

True head hunters look for you and are not interested in most unemployed job seekers. They are hired by employers to look for specific kinds of highly compensated people who are in short supply. Unless you are employed now in a responsible job, making good money, and on your way up, head hunters are not likely to be interested in you.

➤ **The Public Library:**

The library is a wonderful place for a job seeker. The research librarians there can help you find answers to the most difficult questions you might have. And it is quiet, free, and open evenings and weekends – the times you should reserve for the library.

A good library will have a variety of newspapers, professional journals, business directories, career information and job search books, and other resources. Some even have typewriters and word processors to use and quiet places to research an organization's background between interviews.

A library is a job seeker's friend. Chapter 17 provides additional information on using the library in your job search and the bibliography in the back of this book mentions many resources you can find there.

Quick Summary

✓ Whatever job search methods you use, it is essential that you begin with a sense of where those jobs are, and most jobs are now with smaller organizations. About 70 percent of all nongovernmental workers now work for employers with 250 or fewer workers.

✓ *Frictional unemployment* is a situation where job openings exist and qualified job seekers are looking for them, but the employer and job seeker don't connect with each other right away. The U.S. Department of Labor estimates that over 40 percent of all unemployment is due to this friction.

✓ The Four Stages of a Job Opening:
Stage 1: There is no job open now
Stage 2: No formal opening exists, but insiders know of a possibility
Stage 3: A formal opening exists, but it has not been advertised
Stage 4: The job opening is finally advertised

✓ Learn to find employers before they advertise the job you want.

✓ Don't wait until the job is open.

✓ You can "interview" even before a job opening formally exists.

✓ A New Definition of an Interview: An interview is any face-to-face contact with a person who hires or supervises people with your skills – even if there is no job opening now.

✓ The two most effective job search methods: Warm contacts and cold contacts.

✓ All personal referrals together probably account for about 40 percent of how people find jobs. That makes using personal contacts the most important job search technique of all.

✓ Cold contacts are job leads obtained from contacting people you don't know – employers in particular. Using this term also allows me to create the term "warm contacts" to describe leads for job openings that come from people you already know. These warm contacts include friends, relatives, and acquaintances.

✓ Armed with your lists of friends and relatives, you have the beginning of a list of people who, in turn, can refer you to others. This process is what is called "networking."

✓ Three steps to identify hundreds of warm contacts:
Step 1: List contact groups of people you know
Step 2: Create warm contact lists
Step 3: Use your warm contacts to develop an expanding network of contacts

✓ The six rules for developing a successful network of contacts:
Rule 1: Get started – Set up a meeting
Rule 2: Present Yourself Well
Rule 3: Learn Something
Rule 4: Get Two Referrals
Rule 5: Follow Up on Referrals
Rule 6: Send Thank-You Notes

✓ The *Yellow Pages* is an important source of job leads.

✓ Other techniques discussed in this chapter provide important job search methods which are discussed in further detail in later chapters of the book.

CHAPTER THREE

Job Search Basics

Identify Your Key Skills –

An Essential Step for a Successful Job Search

≡Quick Overview

In this chapter, I review the following:

- ✓ What skills are
- ✓ How to develop a skills language
- ✓ The skills triad: Job-related skills, Adaptive skills/Personality traits, and Transferable skills
- ✓ The skills that employers want
- ✓ Three basic employer expectations
- ✓ How to use your skills knowledge to help you find a satisfying job

While this is a book on getting a job, I believe that this chapter is one of the most important in the book. It will help you identify the skills you have and begin to develop a "skills language" that is tremendously important to you throughout your job search and, more importantly, your life.

Knowing what you are good at is an essential part of doing well in an interview. But it is also important to you in other ways. For example, unless you use those skills that you enjoy and are good at, it is unlikely that you will be fully satisfied with your job.

Most people are not good at expressing the skills they have. I can tell you this based on many years of working with groups of job seekers. When asked, few can quickly tell me what they are good at, and fewer yet can quickly present the specific skills they have that are needed to succeed in the job they want.

Quick Fact

Many employers also note that most job seekers don't present their skills effectively. According to one survey of employers, more than 90 percent of the people they interview cannot adequately define the skills they have to support their ability to do the job. They may have the necessary skills, but they can't communicate them.

In an exhaustive study titled "Job Search: A Review of the Literature," Steve Mangum cites a variety of research studies and concludes that "No single factor carries more negative connotations in the interview than an inability to communicate." It is "Problem #1" in the job search and interview process. This chapter is designed to help you fix that problem.

Skills: They May Not Be What You Think They Are

Webster's Dictionary defines a skill as an ability to do something well, especially as the result of long, practical experience. But, like the definition of "love," there is much more to understanding skills than what a dictionary can tell you. Because knowledge of your own skills is such an important issue, it is worth more space than the chapter I have provided in this book. Since one chapter is all there is, let's get started.

A Skill Is Something You Can Do

True enough. There are many skills that any of us could show someone else. These demonstrative skills relate to performance of various kinds, such as riding a bike or baking a cake. In turn, most of these types of activities can be broken down into "smaller" skills that must be used together to do the more complex tasks. For example, baking a cake seems simple enough to do, but only if you have some of the component skills such as: using measuring cups and other devices; reading a cookbook (and following directions); shopping for ingredients; using timing devices; using a stove properly; organizing the work area; and other skills.

In turn, each of the above skills can be further broken down. For example, in order to use a stove, you would have to be able to read the numbers or words on the dial and be able to manipulate the dial with your fingers (or toes), which requires fine motor coordination. You surely get the point. If you carefully analyze even simple tasks, more skills are required than you at first realize.

A Skill Can Be Something You Own, as Part of Your Personality

This can also be true. For example, some people just seem to be "organized." Others just seem to "get along well with others" or have "leadership abilities." Still others might be "creative thinkers" or "good writers." Such skills are more abstract than riding a bike or baking a cake, and it may be difficult to say just how you acquired them. Nevertheless, they are legitimate and important skills.

How Many Skills Do You Have?

Many people don't realize that everyone has hundreds of skills, not just a few. When I ask someone in a job search workshop what skills they have, too often they say, "I can't think of any."

Quick Case Study

Some time ago, I was leading a workshop for a group of about 30 people, and we were doing a series of group exercises to help each person in the group identify their skills. Most of those in the group had been unemployed for a long time and they lived in a small town with an unemployment rate of about 15 percent. I asked one man in the group to tell me what he was good at. He couldn't think of one thing! I asked him some questions and found out that he had worked as a cabinet maker on the same job for over 15 years. He never missed a day of work and had been late once, over 10 years ago. He took pride in his work and had one of the lowest reject rates in his department of over 20 people. No skills?

Young people often underestimate their skills in the same way. So do women who have "just" been a homemaker and have "no work experience." So do some people who have had very responsible and well-paying professional positions. In my workshops over the years, countless job seekers have told me they have "no skills" when in fact, they have hundreds. And so do you.

The Three Types of Skills

Simple skills such as closing your fingers to grip a pen (which is not simple at all if you consider that miracle of complex neuromuscular interaction which computers can only approximate) are building blocks for more complex skills such as writing a sentence and even more complex skills such as writing a book.

Even though you have hundreds of skills, some will be more important to an employer than others. And some will be far more important to you in deciding what sort of job you want. So, to keep it simple, I have found it useful to think of skills in the three major categories described next.

The Skills Triad

As I have suggested, analyzing the skills required for even a simple task can become quite complicated. But a useful way to organize skills, for our purposes, is to divide them into three basic types. Each of these are explained briefly below and much of the rest of this chapter will help you identify your own key skills in each of these areas.

Adaptive Skills/Personality Traits

You probably take for granted the many skills you use every day to survive and get along. I call these skills adaptive or self-management skills because they allow you to adapt or adjust to a variety of situations. Some of them could be considered part of your basic personality. Such skills that are highly valued by employers include getting to work on time, honesty, enthusiasm, and getting along with others.

Transferable Skills

These are general skills that can be useful in a variety of jobs. For example, writing clearly, good language skills, or the ability to organize and prioritize tasks would be desirable skills in many jobs. These are called transferable skills because they can be transferred from one job – or even one career – to another.

Job-Related Skills

These are the skills people typically first think of when asked, "Do you have any skills?" They are related to a particular job or type of job. An auto mechanic, for example, needs to know how to tune engines and repair brakes. Other jobs also have job-specific skills required of that job in addition to the adaptive and transferable skills needed to succeed in that job.

This system of dividing skills into three categories is not perfect. Some things, such as being trustworthy, dependable, or well-organized are really not skills as much as they are personality traits. There is also some overlap between the three skills categories. For example, a skill such as being organized might be considered either adaptive or transferable. For our purposes, however, the Skills Triad is a very useful system for identifying skills that are important in the job search.

Identify Your Skills

Because it is so important to know your skills, I include a series of checklists and other activities in this chapter to help you identify your key skills. These skills are important to know in selecting jobs that you will do well in and to emphasize in an interview. Developing a skills language can also be very helpful to you in writing your resume and conducting your job search.

The skills you just wrote may be among the most important things that an
employer will want to know about you. Most (but not all) people write adaptive
skills when asked this question. Whatever you wrote, these skills are often very
important things to mention in the interview. In fact, presenting these skills well
will often allow a less experienced job seeker to get the job over someone with
better credentials.

Identify Your Adaptive Skills and Personality Traits

I have created a list of adaptive skills that tend to be important to employers. The
ones listed as "The Minimum" are those that most employers consider essential
for job survival and they will typically not hire someone who has problems in
these areas.

Look over the list and put a check mark next to each adaptive skill that you have.
Put a second check mark next to those skills that are particularly important for
you to use or include in your next job.

Adaptive Skills Checklist

The Minimum

__ Good attendance   __ Meet deadlines

__ Honesty   __ Get along with supervisor

__ Arrive on time   __ Get along with coworkers

__ Follow instructions   __ Hard-working, productive

Other Adaptive Skills

__ Able to coordinate	__ Intuitive	__ Solve problems
__ Friendly	__ Discreet	__ Patient
__ Ambitious	__ Learn quickly	__ Spontaneous
__ Good-natured	__ Eager	__ Persistent
__ Assertive	__ Loyal	__ Steady
__ Helpful	__ Efficient	__ Physically strong
__ Capable	__ Mature	__ Tactful
__ Humble	__ Energetic	__ Practice new skills
__ Cheerful	__ Methodical	__ Take pride in work
__ Imaginative	__ Enthusiastic	
__ Competent	__ Modest	__ Reliable
__ Independent	__ Expressive	__ Tenacious
__ Complete assignments	__ Motivated	__ Resourceful
__ Industrious	__ Flexible	__ Thrifty
__ Conscientious	__ Natural	__ Responsible
__ Informal	__ Formal	__ Trustworthy
__ Creative	__ Open-minded	__ Self-confident
__ Intelligent	__ Optimistic	__ Versatile
__ Dependable	__ Sincere	__ Sense of humor
	__ Original	__ Well-organized

Other Similar Adaptive Skills You Have

Add any adaptive skills to the list above that were not listed but that you think are important to include.

_____

_____

_____

_____

Your Top Adaptive Skills

Carefully review the checklist you just completed and select the three adaptive skills you feel are most important for you to tell an employer about or that you most want to use in your next job. These three skills are EXTREMELY important to include in your resume and to present to an employer in an interview.

1. _____

2. _____

3. _____

Identify Your Transferable Skills – Skills That Transfer to Many Jobs

Over the years, I have assembled a list of transferable skills that are important in a wide variety of jobs. In the checklist that follows, the skills listed as "Key Transferable Skills" are those that I consider to be most important to many employers. The key skills are also those that are often required in jobs with more responsibility and higher pay, so it pays to emphasize these skills if you have them.

The remaining transferable skills are grouped into categories that may be helpful to you. Go ahead and check each skill you are strong in, then double-check the skills you want to use in your next job. When you are finished, you should have checked 10 to 20 skills at least once.

Transferable Skills Checklist

Key Transferable Skills

__ Meeting deadlines

__ Planning

__ Speaking in public

__ Controlling budgets

__ Supervising others

__ Increasing sales or efficiency

__ Accepting responsibility

__ Instructing others

__ Solving problems

__ Managing money or budgets

__ Managing people

__ Meeting deadlines

__ Meeting the public

__ Negotiating

__ Organizing or managing projects

__ Written communications

Other Transferable Skills:

__ Using my hands, Dealing with things

__ Assemble or make things

__ Build, observe, inspect things

__ Construct or repair buildings

__ Operate tools and machinery

__ Drive or operate vehicles

__ Repair things

__ Good with my hands

__ Use complex equipment

Dealing with Data

__ Analyze data or facts

__ Investigate

__ Audit records

__ Keep financial records

__ Budget

__ Locate answers or information

__ Calculate, compute

__ Manage money

__ Classify data

__ Negotiate

__ Compare, inspect, or record facts

__ Count, observe, compile

__ Research

__ Detail-oriented

__ Synthesize

__ Evaluate

__ Take inventory

Working with People

__ Administer

__ Patient

__ Care for

__ Persuade

__ Confront others

__ Pleasant

__ Counsel people

__ Sensitive

__ Demonstrate

__ Sociable

__ Diplomatic

__ Supervise

__ Help others

__ Tactful

__ Insightful

Transferable Skills Checklist *continued*

__ Teach   __ Tough   __ Understand
__ Interview others   __ Listen   __ Outgoing
__ Tolerant   __ Trust
__ Kind   __ Negotiate

Using Words, Ideas

__ Articulate   __ Correspond with others   __ Design
__ Inventive   __ Speak in public
__ Communicate verbally   __ Remember information   __ Edit
__ Logical   __ Write clearly
__ Research   __ Ingenious
__ Create new ideas

Leadership

__ Arrange social functions   __ Direct others
__ Motivate people   __ Self-controlled
__ Competitive   __ Explain things to others
__ Negotiate agreements   __ Self-motivated
__ Decisive   __ Get results
__ Plan   __ Solve problems
__ Delegate   __ Mediate problems
__ Run meetings   __ Take risks

Creative, Artistic

__ Artistic   __ Perform, act   __ Expressive
__ Music appreciation   __ Drawing, art   __ Present artistic ideas
__ Dance, body movement   __ Play instruments

Other Similar Transferable Skills You Have

Add any transferable skills to the list above that were not listed but that you think are important to include.

_____   _____
_____   _____
_____   _____
_____   _____

Your Top Transferable Skills

Write in the margins any other transferable skills you have that were not listed. Then select the five top transferable skills you want to use in your next job and list them below.

1. _____

2. _____

3. _____

4. _____

5. _____

The Skills Employers Want

Since I am particularly interested in personal and career development issues, it is nice to know that employers value those who have done their homework in these areas. The reason they do is that people who have done career planning have a better idea of what they want to do long-term and understand the training and skills needed to get there. Because they are clearer in what they want to do, they are more likely to be in the right jobs for the right reasons – and they are also more likely to be motivated and prepared to do them well.

Finding Out What Employers Want – The Results of a Survey of Employers

As a way to illustrate that employers value adaptive and transferable skills very highly, I have included the results of a survey of employers here. This information comes from a study of employers conducted jointly by the U.S. Department of Labor and the American Association of Counseling and Development. The study, titled *Workplace Basics – The Skills Employers Want*, was conducted to discover what employers wanted in the people they hired. It turns out that most of the skills they want are either adaptive or transferable skills. Of course, specific job-related skills will remain important, but basic skills form an essential foundation for success on the job.

Here are the top skills employers identified in the Workplace Basics survey:

The Top Skills Employers Want

1. Learning to learn
2. Basic academic skills in reading, writing, and computation
3. Good communication skills including listening and speaking
4. Creative thinking and problem solving
5. Self-esteem, motivation, and goal setting
6. Personal and career development skills
7. Interpersonal/negotiation skills and teamwork
8. Organizational effectiveness and leadership

Note that all of these skills are either adaptive or transferable skills. What is most interesting is that most of these skills are not formally taught in school. Just try to find a course on creative problem solving or personal goal setting, for example. Yet these "soft" skills are those that employers value most. Of course, job specific skills are also important – an accountant will still need to know accounting skills – but the adaptive and transferable skills are the ones that allow you to succeed once on the job.

So, once again, this study shows the importance of knowing your skills and using them well in a career planning sense. If you have any weaknesses in one or more of the skills that were listed, consider improvements. And if you are already strong in one or more of them, look for opportunities to develop and use them in your work – or to present them clearly in your next interview.

You can never assume that you are exempt from new training because your duties involve routine tasks. Competitive pressures compel employers to shift employees between jobs and responsibilities, which places a premium on your ability to absorb, process, and apply new information quickly and effectively.

From the organization's perspective, having an employee who knows how to learn is more cost-effective because it reduces the time and resources spent on training. Your adaptability also means you'll have reason to stay longer, and every employer values the money he or she can save by hiring a long-term employee.

Meeting Employer Expectations

Meeting employer expectations in an interview can get you the job over those with better credentials.

I've been playing around with the "Employer's Expectations" concept since the early 1970s, when I was looking for a way to help people in my job search workshops improve their performance in an interview. After looking at the research on how employers make decisions, I concluded that there are a few simple concepts that could help one job seeker be seen more positively by an employer than another. While there is considerable research to support what I suggest on this topic it is also good common sense.

Back in the 1970s Sidney Fine, a labor market expert who was the principal researcher for the U.S. Department of Labor's job classification system, had estimated that one-half of all jobs could be learned by the average adult in two weeks or less. To do so, they would use their adaptive and transferable skills to compensate for their lack of specific job knowledge and job-related skills.

While many jobs have become more complex since then, it is still true that you could use your current skills and abilities to quickly learn to handle many, many jobs that you had not previously done. The point is that many employers are willing to overlook a lack of job content skills or "credentials" and hire a person who presents themselves more effectively in an interview. If an employer has two job seekers with similar credentials, the one who makes a better impression will get the job. Even if one has better credentials, the one who *presents* their ability to learn and do the job best will often get the job over the more qualified candidate.

Identifying Your Job-Related Skills

Many jobs require skills that are specific to that occupation. An airline pilot will obviously need to know how to fly an airplane, and, thankfully, having good adaptive and transferable skills would not be enough to be considered for that job.

Job-related skills may have been gained in a variety of ways including education, training, work, hobbies, or other life experiences.

Quick Reference

I've included a variety of information and activities in chapter 9 to help you identify your job-related skills. These skills can be found in education, work, and other life experiences. You should find chapter 9 particularly thorough in helping you identify key job-related skills to emphasize in your job search and interviews.

Knowing Your Skills Is the Basis for Your Job Search

Knowing what you are good at is an essential part of your job search. It will help you answer interview questions, write a resume, and complete applications. More importantly, knowing the skills you *like* to use can help you make a better decision about what sort of job you really want. Your jobs, careers, and personal situations will change, but your adaptive and transferable skills will be with you throughout your life. They are important for an employer to know, but even more important for you to know.

Three Basic Employers' Expectations

An important principle throughout this book is that the opinion of an employer *does* matter. In the interview, where an employer's opinion matters most, there are three basic employers' expectations for you to meet and each is covered below.

Employer Expectation 1. Appearance: Do You Look Like the Type of Person Who Will Do Well in the Job?

There is a variety of research that indicates that employers react to how a job seeker looks, and one survey indicates that 40 percent of all interviewees create a negative first impression based on their appearance. Once you create a negative impression it is most difficult to overcome, yet an appearance-related problem is often relatively easy to correct.

Employers react within a few seconds to people they first meet – just as all people do. If their initial reaction to you is negative, you probably will not be hired. I suggest that "appearance" in this context is more than just dress and grooming, though these things are clearly of great importance in an interview. Employers will also react to a variety of things including whether you are on time to the interview, your dress and grooming, your verbal skills, body language, ability to handle "small talk," and other adaptive skills.

In an interview, if the employer feels you will not fit in or will not get along well with coworkers, you will not be hired – even if you have the experience to handle the job. Job seekers who can effectively present their ability to adapt to a new work situation often get jobs over people with more experience and training. I have seen this happen countless times. It is the better *prepared* job seeker who gets the job, not necessarily the better qualified one.

Quick Fact

To further illustrate how important adaptive skills are to employers, note that most people who are fired or lose their jobs do so because of an inability to adapt and get along rather than an inability to do the job itself.

Robert Half & Associates conducted a survey of personnel directors from the 1,000 largest U.S. corporations. Only 4 percent listed "not doing job" as the most disturbing employee behavior. Responses related to actual job performance totaled only 32 percent. The remaining responses related to poor adaptive skills. The most frequently noted problems were: lying and dishonesty (14%), absenteeism and tardiness (12%), arrogance and overconfidence (10%), and lack of dedication (6%).

Employer Expectation 2. Dependability: Can You Be Counted on to Get the Job Done?

Even if you have superior job-related skills, you won't get an offer unless the employer feels that you are a reliable sort who does not miss work, can be relied upon to get things done, and will hang around long enough to pay off their training investment.

Many interview questions are designed to probe this very issue. An employer will not hire a person who may move out of town soon, take another job (overqualified), has a history of leaving jobs, may have an attendance problem (alcoholism, sick kids), has no family or friends living in town (will move soon), is late often, or for any other reason can't be depended upon. Some of the issues may not seem fair for an employer to wonder about – and some are probably illegal to ask about – but are a legitimate concern to an employer. And it would be your concern as well, if you were hiring someone.

An employer is clearly not concerned with job-related skills here but in your adaptive skills and motivations for wanting to work. Once an employer is satisfied that you have acceptable adaptive skills, your transferable skills are often next in importance. Your ability to learn the new job quickly, for example, together with other desirable personal traits or skills will be more important than if you simply have the necessary experience.

Most employers have learned that, despite whatever you already know, you will have to be retrained in their system. If a job seeker impresses the employer as disorganized, rigid, unmotivated, or lacking in other important transferable or adaptive skills, someone else with less experience may get the job. Your skill in organizing things could be more important to the employer in the long run than someone else's knowledge of a specific procedure.

Employer Expectation 3. Credentials: Do You Have the Job-Related Skills, Experience, and Training?

Your education, training, and prior work experiences are weighted heavily by employers in determining whether you are capable of doing a particular job. I have listed this expectation third since it becomes important only if you don't get screened out based on the first and second criteria above.

People without the minimal job-related skills required for a job typically will not get an interview. But many employers will waive their requirements for education, training, and previous experience for the right candidate. That's why I have listed job-related skills third among the three employer expectations.

This is not to say that job-related skills are unimportant, especially in certain professional or technical jobs. They are. For example, no matter how nice you are or how good you are with your hands (another transferable skill) you can't get a job as an airline pilot unless you know how to fly an airplane and have the appropriate credentials. This is a fact that I am very, very comfortable with since I'm on airplanes so much. But if you do meet the minimal criteria for a job *and* get an interview, you will be considered, unless you create a negative impression based on expectations #1 and #2.

Quick Summary

✓ Most job seekers don't present their skills effectively. According to one survey of employers, more than 90 percent of the people they interview cannot adequately define the skills they have to support their ability to do the job. They may have the necessary skills, but they can't communicate them.

✓ One researcher concludes that "No single factor carries more negative connotations in the interview than an inability to communicate." It is problem number one in the job search and interview process.

✓ Most people underestimate their skills. A skill can be something you do, or something you own as part of your personality.

✓ Three types of skills, making up The Skills Triad, are: Adaptive skills/Personality skills, Transferable skills, and Job-related skills.

✓ The top skills employers want: 1) Learning to learn, 2) Basic academic skills in reading, writing, and computation, 3) Good communication skills including listening and speaking, 4) Creative thinking and problem solving, 5) Self-esteem, motivation, and goal setting, 6) Personal and career development skills, 7) Interpersonal/negotiation skills and teamwork, 8) Organizational effectiveness and leadership.

✓ Three basic employers' expectations: 1) Appearance: Do you look like the type of person who will do well in the job?, 2) Dependability: Can you be counted on to get the job done?, 3) Credentials: Do you have the job-related skills, experience, and training?

✓ Most people who are fired or lose their jobs do so because of an inability to adapt and get along rather than an inability to do the job itself.

✓ Meeting employer expectations in an interview can get you the job over those with better credentials.

CHAPTER FOUR

Job Search Basics

How to Interview for Results

Quick Overview

In this chapter, I review the following:

✓ Tips on traditional and nontraditional interviews

✓ Five things to do to have a successful interview

✓ The three types of interviews

✓ The seven phases of an interview

✓ The three-step process for answering problem interview questions

The interview is the most important 60 minutes in the job search. There is a lot at stake, yet the research indicates that most people are not well prepared for the interview process. In an odd way, this can be good news for you, since I believe it is fairly simple to substantially improve your interviewing skills – thereby giving you an advantage over other job seekers who do not know what you will soon learn.

I have observed many employers willing to hire someone who presents themselves well in an interview over others with superior "credentials."

This chapter is based on substantial research into how employers actually decide on hiring one person over another. While the interview itself is an incredibly complex interaction, I have found that there are certain simple things you can do that make a big difference in getting a job offer. This chapter will present some of the things I have learned over the years, and I hope you find them helpful.

The 60 Minute Drill – Essential Tips on Traditional and Nontraditional Interviews

Most interviews last about 60 minutes. One hour. It is the most important 60 minutes in your job search, and you should do everything in your power to see that it goes well. Even though you are likely to have many interviews, each one is hard to get and each one could be the one that gets you the job offer.

There is good research indicating that interviews are not a valid way to select good employees. Most employers would agree. But while it is not always the best method, the fact is that how you do in an interview is very important in whether or not you will be considered for a job. Doing well in an interview is, more or less, a requirement for getting a job.

Five Things You Must Do to Have a Successful Interview

While we know that the interview is important to both you and the employer, few job seekers have a clear sense of what they need to accomplish during those critical minutes. So, before I teach you interview techniques, I ask you to consider just what it is you want to accomplish in an interview. Here are the things I believe are most important:

Five Things to Do to Have a Successful Interview

1. Make a positive impression.
2. Communicate your skills.
3. Answer problem questions.
4. Help the employer know why they should hire you.
5. Follow up after the interview.

These are interview essentials, and if you do them well, you can dramatically increase your chances of getting a job offer. This chapter will show you, step-by-step, how to do well in a job interview. By dividing the interview into sections and mastering one section at a time, those crucial 60 minutes won't seem so intimidating.

Don't Be Intimidated by the Interview Process

An interview is intimidating and stressful to most people. We aren't often evaluated as intensely as we are in an interview and the stakes are high. I believe one of the reasons so many people withdraw from an active job search is because of their fear of rejection, which is unavoidable in most traditional interviews. If you don't get a job offer, does it mean that you are a bad person? Of course not. Even so, it is hard not to avoid the stress of hoping to be selected and the disappointment of not getting the job. But there are some things you can do to reduce the stress of interviews.

Reject rejection

The word "interview" has two parts: "inter," which means "between" and "view," which surely means "look at." I do not claim to be an expert on root words, but it does seem that "interview" means, roughly, "two people looking at each other." In a job interview, that is precisely what should be going on. More often, however, there is the one-sided feeling that the all-powerful employer is giving the job seeker a thorough looking over.

The job seeker conducting a conventional job search is likely to get rejected, which does not feel good. You need to get over these feelings and understand that rejection is a necessary part of eventual success in the job search. The more rejections you get (and the faster you get them), the closer you are to being accepted.

You Have to Get Rejected Before You Can Get Accepted

One way to look at the interview is as a series of rejections, like this: No No No No No No No No No No No No No No No No No No No No No No No No No No No No No No No No No No No No No No No No No No No No No No No No No No No No No No No No No No No No No No No No No No No No No No No No No No No No No No No No No No No Yes

Finally, you meet someone who makes you a job offer. If you accept, that's a "yes." Along the way, however, the rejection doesn't have to be one-sided. An interview should be, after all, a two-way communication. Employers are not the only ones who can say no.

Understand "intuition" and use it to your advantage

Many employers claim they get a "feel" for a person during an interview. I have often heard interviewers say they did or did not hire someone based on a "gut reaction." This can be a very unnerving thought until you understand that what they feel can often be predicted. And if you know what might cause a negative reaction, you can try to change your behavior accordingly.

Quick Fact

Most gut reactions are really responses to nonverbal cues.

Many of your most powerful signals can be nonverbal. As evidence of this, think about how a lie detector works. Your body gives off electrochemical signals that can be measured. Even if you try, you can't keep this from happening – and the machine can read your "real" reaction. Your voice, facial expressions, posture, and other subtle signals give you away, too.

Obviously, the only way to avoid this problem in a job interview is to be honest. If you overstate your abilities, you often unconsciously communicate that you are hiding something, which many interviewers will notice.

Often, you may be completely unaware of how your nonverbal signals are creating a negative impression. Perhaps your grooming is inappropriate or out-of-date;

maybe you play with your hair or slouch in your chair; or you may have a hard time expressing yourself without moving your hands too much. Employers notice these things.

Some time ago, I worked with a college graduate who had been chronically unemployed or underemployed for over 10 years. His credentials were great – a prestigious school, good grades, a desirable degree in business. Yet I immediately knew why he had such a hard time getting a decent job – his handshake was limp, he slouched terribly, his hair looked oily, and he looked like he slept under a bridge. While many of his problems were personality-related, his job search was bound to be unsuccessful simply based on his appearance. Any employer would react negatively to him.

The good news is that you can change many of your undesirable mannerisms. Ask an objective person or friend to role-play interviews with you and provide constructive feedback on your nonverbal image. By becoming aware of negative signals, and by practicing to eliminate or change them, you can make an employer's "intuition" work for you.

Interviewers are people, too

If you tend to think of an interviewer as the enemy, you should reconsider. It is helpful to remind yourself that most bosses started out as job seekers and will very likely take on that role again. You should also realize that most interviewers have reasons of their own to be nervous. For example:

Reasons for Interviewers to Be Nervous

➤ **Most employers have no training in interviewing.** Just as most job seekers don't know how to find jobs, interviewers often don't know how to interview. How would they have learned? It is not at all unusual for a well-trained job seeker to be a better interviewer than the interviewer. (Really!) I often hear job seekers say, "They didn't even ask me any hard questions! I had to tell them what I was good at because they never asked."

➤ **If they hire you, and you don't work out, they lose.** If they make a mistake, their boss will know. Since it costs lots of money to train new staff, their decision is literally worth thousands of dollars. In small organizations or departments, if one person does not work out, everyone else feels the extra workload. The person who hired you could lose credibility (and maybe even his or her job).

➤ **Everyone likes to be liked.** I've known employers who hate to interview because they don't like to turn people down. They are not comfortable in screening people out. You don't have to feel sorry for them, but it is something to think about.

So, you see, interviewers are not to be feared at all. Employers are just like us because they *are* us. Their roles are just a little different at the moment.

The Three Types of Interviews – A Very Important Concept

Too many people think of a job interview too narrowly. One of the big tasks in a successful job search is to get more interviews. But if you define an interview in a narrow and traditional way, you will miss out on meeting many perspective employers who in many cases are willing to talk to you even before a job opening exists.

For this reason, how you define an interview is a critical part of a successful job search. To open yourself up to a more creative and effective job search, consider that there are many types of interviews. I've defined just three major types of interviews. Understanding the distinctions among them can help to find jobs that others may overlook.

The Three Types of Interviews
1. The traditional job search interview
2. The information interview
3. The JIST job search interview

Much of this book works on the assumption that an interview can include something more than the "traditional" interview. All three types of interviews share some characteristics, but there are significant differences too. If you know how to conduct yourself in each type of interview, you will have a distinct advantage over most job seekers. Let's take a closer look at each type.

The First Interview Type: The Traditional Job Interview

The following is what job seekers usually think of when the word "interview" is used.

Quick Definition

A Traditional Interview is. . .

a meeting with a person who has a job opening for which you might qualify, who is actively looking for someone to fill it, and who has the authority to hire you.

While this is certainly an interview, it does have a few problems. For one thing, most jobs get filled before a traditional interview is needed. Employers often hire people they came to know before the job became available. An important lesson to learn is that if you wait until the opening, the job is likely to be filled.

This is not to say that traditional job interviews are not important. They are. But it would be irresponsible not to tell you that more than half of all jobs are filled in a different way. If you believe in your heart that an interview can happen only if you get a "Yes" to your question, "Do you have any job openings for me?", you will miss some of the very best opportunities.

Manipulation and Counter-Manipulation Are the Basis for the Traditional Interview

In the traditional interview, your task is to present yourself well. The task of the interviewer is to find out what's wrong with you so you can be eliminated from consideration. This is not the friendliest of social situations. If the interviewer has any training on how to interview, you will face techniques intentionally designed to reveal your flaws.

In a book considered by many to be required reading for interviewers, *The Evaluation Interview*, Richard Fear wrote,

"Since most applicants approach the interview with the objective of putting their best foot forward, the interviewer must be motivated from the very beginning to search for unfavorable information."

In a traditional interview, any good interviewer will encourage you to be yourself and let your guard down. In an article by John and Merna Galassien titled "Preparing Individuals for Job Interviews: Suggestions from More Than 60 Years of Research" they conclude that the primary role of interviewers is to weed out the "undesirables." Their goal is to manipulate you to reveal negative information, if at all possible.

A job seeker's reaction to all this manipulation is natural enough: you try to hide your faults and emphasize your strengths. Your objective, in these traditional interviews, is to get a second interview. If you leave the interview and that decision has not been made, go after a second interview in your follow-up efforts. I'll tell you more about following up later in the chapter.

The Major Types of Traditional Interviews

In addition to much manipulation, you are likely to encounter different interviewing styles. So that you will not be taken by surprise, let's review some of the more common methods used in traditional interviews.

The Preliminary Screening Interview

This is by far the most common preliminary interview, where you meet with a person whose role is to screen applicants and arrange follow-up interviews with the person who has the authority to hire. Other times, you may meet directly with the hiring authority whose primary focus is to eliminate as many applicants as possible, leaving only one or two. These one-on-one interviews are the focus of the techniques presented later in this chapter.

The Group or Panel Interview

While still not as common as the one-on-one interview, group interviews are gaining popularity. It's possible you could be asked to interview with two or more people involved in the selection process. I've even known of situations where a group of interviewers met with a group of applicants – all at the same time. Many of the techniques used in this book will work well in these settings too.

The Non-Directive Interview

Some interviewers will ask few direct questions and, instead, encourage you to tell them whatever you want. For example, instead of asking "How did you do in your math classes?", they might ask, "What did you like best about school?" If you are not prepared for such open-ended questions, you could quickly put your foot in your mouth.

The Stress Interview

Some interviewers intentionally try to get you upset. They want to see how you handle stress, whether you can accept criticism, or how you react to a tense situation. They hope to see how you are likely to act in a high-pressure job.

For example, they might try to get you angry by not accepting something you say as true. "I find it difficult to believe," they might say, "that you were responsible for as large a program as you claim here on your resume. Why don't you just tell me what you really did?"

Another approach is to quickly fire questions at you but not give you time to completely answer, or to interrupt you midsentence with other questions. Not nice.

But now you've been warned. I hope you don't run into this sort of interviewer, but if so, be yourself and have a few laughs. The odds are the interview could turn out fine if you don't take the bait and throw things around the room. If you do get a job offer following such an interview, you might want to ask yourself whether you would want to work for such a person or organization. (It might be fun not to accept the job and then tell them what you think of their interviewing technique.)

The Structured Interview

In light of current legislation overseeing hiring practices, a structured interview is becoming more common, particularly in larger organizations. The interviewer may have a list of things to ask all applicants and a form to fill out. Your experience and skills may be compared to specific job tasks or criteria. Even if highly structured, there is usually the opportunity for you to present what you feel is essential information.

The Reality Interview

Many Fortune 1000 companies, including Radisson Hotels International, Hershey's, and S.C. Johnson & Co., have switched to an interviewing method known most often as "reality interviewing." These companies believe that the more traditional way of rating candidates' answers to questions only encourages the interviewers to pick new employees who are just like themselves.

According to Arthur H. Bell, author of *Extraviewing,* there are three simple steps to the reality interview.

Three Simple Steps to the Reality Interview

1. **Ask applicants to describe their realities – what they did do or are doing – rather than their impressions, attitudes, or ideals.**

   The idea here is to sidestep canned answers. So instead of being asked "What do you believe is the best way to handle conflict?" the question will be phrased, "Tell me about a time you experienced conflict with another worker. How did you handle it?"

2. **Probe the applicant's past and present realities in direct relation to his or her future responsibilities with the company.**

   Simply stated, the past is dead and buried as far as the interviewer is concerned. In the reality interview, the person on the other side of the desk wants to know which parts of your past will be useful for the specific job you now want with his or her company. In this situation, do not expect any questions that require you to judge or give value to anything – that is the interviewer's task. As Bell reports one interviewer's explanation, "I want an applicant to tell me about what he ate, not how he liked it. I want the meal, not the burp." Questions here will be posed as, "What were the events that led to the incident?" "Who was involved?" "What exactly did you do and say?" "What was the outcome?"

3. **Pose situational questions in addition to past experience questions.**

   Again, the situational questions are specific, which prevents you from answering vaguely. For example: "As a seafood buyer, you are responsible for the availability of halibut to 30 supermarkets in our chain. You manage to lock in a large purchase of halibut at an attractive price from suppliers. Based on this purchase, management decides to feature halibut prominently at rock-bottom prices in its double-page newspaper ads. The ads work too well: Within hours of ad publication, customers have cleaned out the supermarkets of their halibut stock. Managers from most of the stores are calling you for more halibut. What would you do?"

Notice this does not invite an "I-think-buying-should-always-be-done-within-budget" answer! Nor is it a good idea to blurt out, "I'd just buy more halibut as fast as I could and get it out to the stores," Bell said. Your answer must keep the company's situation firmly in mind, as well as save your own rear end.

Although the reality interview demands more than the surface research we all wish we could get by on, it definitely can stack the cards in your favor. The *Wall Street Journal* reported that S.C. Johnson & Co. interviewed a woman for a sales position using this situational method. Her background was in theater – not exactly an area that excited interviewers. Furthermore, she was up against several experienced salesmen and the interviewers had never hired a woman for such a position. However, the reality interview gave her a chance to score higher than the other applicants and get the job offer. She eventually broke sales records in the company.

Similarly, L'Oréal has used this interview method since 1988. From 1988 to 1990, the number of employees hired through this method was lower (33 versus 41), but of those 33, only five were separated from the company compared to 17 people who were let go after passing the more traditional interview. Furthermore, two reality interview graduates were promoted to management, whereas none from the other interview styles were so honored.

The Disorganized Interview

Let's face it, you will come across many interviewers who will not know how to interview you. They may talk about themselves too much or neglect to ask you any meaningful questions. Many people are competent managers but poor interviewers. The best way to help such lost souls learn about the true you is by providing some answers to questions they may not have asked.

The Second Interview Type: The Information Interview

This type of interview has become widely used (and often abused) since the mid-1970s, when Richard Bolles popularized it in his book *What Color Is Your Parachute?* Other forms of information interviews had been popularized by Bernard Haldane and others in prior years. It is supposed to be used by job seekers who have not yet decided what they want to do – or where.

Quick Definition

An Information Interview is. . .

used by someone who isn't yet sure of what they want to do, to obtain career information or advice from a knowledgeable person who shares a common interest or who works in a career area of possible interest to the interviewee. It is not supposed to be used by someone who is actively seeking a job.

To correctly use the technique, you must first define your ideal job in terms of skills required, size and type of organization, salary level, interests, what sort of coworkers, and other preferences. The next step is to gather information on just where a job of this sort might exist and what it might be called.

If you are interested in defining your ideal job, if you do your homework before using this method, and if you are truly honest and sincere about seeking information but not a job, then the information interview technique is both effective and fun.

Unfortunately, this technique has often been misused. People who really want to get a job have used the technique as a trick to get in to see someone. ("I'm not looking for a job but I am conducting a survey ...") Well, that is dishonest and most employers resent the misrepresentation. Many employers are now wary about anyone, even the sincere ones, asking to see them for any reason. Many who support the use of information interviews lament this and point out that some career counselors and others who should know better have encouraged this dishonesty. Proponents do point out, however, that the technique is still useful, particularly outside larger cities and with smaller organizations.

"Profit" interviews

Years before "information interviewing," Bernard Haldane developed a similar technique for those seeking managerial and professional positions. He explained his approach in a book that I consider to be a classic, titled *How to Make a Habit of Success*, originally published in 1960. In it, you identify an employer that is of particular interest. That organization meets most of the criteria set by the job seeker *and* the job seeker clearly sees how that organization could benefit from employing him or her.

Once that happens, the job seeker carefully puts together a written business proposal to be presented to the person (or persons) within that organization who makes decisions. The plan would address what you propose to do; how it would be done; how much money (or other benefits) the project or activity will generate; how much it will cost (including your salary and benefits); and why you are the one person uniquely qualified to successfully fill the position.

The key word in all this is "profit," since if you propose other benefits, but not more profit, your case is surely weakened. If all goes well, you have a job created for you where none existed before. It *does* happen! In fact, Haldane and Associates, the career counseling firm founded by Bernard Haldane, provides data indicating that almost two-thirds of the people they work with have jobs created just for them by using this technique.

The Third Interview Type: The JIST Job Search Interview – An Essential Concept for Getting More Interviews

Over the years, I have come to define an interview in a way that is quite different from how most people define an interview. Instead of the narrow definition of a traditional interview (where your job search consists of looking for job openings),

I suggest that an interview can also be one where no job exists at all. Here is my simple definition of an interview:

Quick Definition

A JIST Job Search Interview Is:

any face-to-face contact with someone who hires or supervises people with your skills – whether or not they have a job opening now.

The implications of this new definition of an interview are enormous; it allows you to talk to people who might hire you in the future but may not have an opening now. For example, if you seek an interview for a job that is now open (a traditional job opening) you would ask, "Do you have any job openings?". And very often, the answer would be "No." If, on the other hand, you had said "I would like to speak with the person in charge of (this or that)," you would probably get to talk to them. That would be an interview in the way I define it, even if there is no job opening yet.

Almost everyone thinks of the job search in the traditional way: of getting in to talk to employers about jobs that are now open. But I believe that this traditional approach results in those people being out of work longer than they need to be.

While I encourage you to look for traditional interviews during your job search, I believe that these interviews represent only a small percentage of the opportunities for jobs. Opening up your job search to include an emphasis on interviews with potential employers that don't have a job opening now allows you to access the 75 percent or so of all jobs that are never advertised. Understanding and using this new definition of an interview fundamentally changes how you approach your search for a new job and it has profound implications on your ability to get more "interviews," both traditional and nontraditional.

The Criteria for a Successful JIST Job Search Interview

Since there are far more employers who don't have a formal job opening at any one time, it should be obvious that this new definition of an interview will allow you to talk to more employers than restricting your search to specific openings. But not every conversation with an employer is an interview. To get the most from this type of interview, here is what you need to know or do.

The JIST Job Search Interview provides a tremendous advantage to you. Now you can interview with employers before they have a job opening and often completely avoid the competition from other job seekers. And, because the employer won't be trying to eliminate you from the pool of applicants (as is done in the traditional interview), the interview can be much more relaxed.

Keep the new definition of an interview in mind as you continue reading this book. It is an important definition that can make a very big difference in how effective you are in finding job openings.

The Seven Phases of an Interview

In a traditional interview, the objective is to get a job offer. It is that simple. But in situations where there may not be a job opening just yet, the objective may be to make a good impression and get referrals to other people.

A certain amount of judgment is required for you to know how to act in various sorts of interviews. If there is a job opening and you want it, you would behave differently than in an interview where no opening existed. But just what *do* you do during the interview?

Fortunately, there has been much research on the interview process. That research indicates that some things are clearly very important to an employer in deciding on one person over another. For example, it should be obvious that your dress and grooming can create a positive or negative first impression. But just how *should* you dress and groom for an interview? What else do employers find important – and what can you do about it? The answers to these and other questions fill this book, but I think you will find the following review of the interview process will give you enough information for most situations (see sidebar).

Overview of the Seven Phases of an Interview

A job interview is a complex interaction, but dividing one into distinct sections makes it easier to understand. After extensive consideration, I've divided a typical interview into seven distinct sections (actually, it could have been some other number, but seven seemed just right). Here they are:

Farr's Seven Phases of an Interview

Phase 1: Before You Go In.

Before you even meet the interviewer, you will create an impression. If it's bad, nothing good can come of it.

Phase 2: Opening Moves.

An interview isn't a game, exactly, but how you begin it will often affect whether you win or lose.

Phase 3: The Interview Itself.

This is the longest and most complex part of an interview. It's here that you are asked problem questions and have the opportunity to present your skills. The impression you make here is highly dependent on your self-understanding of what you have to offer and your ability to communicate it.

Phase 4: Closing the Interview.

There is more to ending an interview than simply saying good-bye. This phase can allow you to wrap up the interview in a positive way and can be used to arrange for the next phase.

Phase 5: Following Up.

In my opinion, an interview is not over until you send a thank-you note and schedule additional follow up. People who follow up get jobs over those who do not. It's that simple.

Phase 6: Negotiating for Salary and Other Benefits.

Discussing money in an initial interview can quickly get you screened out. Knowing what to do, and how, can be worth many, many dollars.

Phase 7: Making a Final Decision.

Once you get a job offer, you have to decide to accept it, reject it, or negotiate for something "better." The stakes are high here and you may have to live with a bad decision for some time. I'll provide you with a simple decision-making process and other tips to help you evaluate such an important life decision on its own merits.

A Thorough Review of the Seven Phases – Including Tips on Handling Each One

Once the interview process has been cut into more manageable chunks, each one becomes easier to master. The section that follows provides information on each phase along with tips on improving your performance. Pay attention: even small improvements in your interviewing skills can make the difference between getting an offer or getting screened out.

Phase 1: Before You Go In – You Make a Positive Impression Before You Even Get There, so Make Sure It Is a Good One.

While often overlooked, what happens before the interview is very, very important. Before you actually meet prospective employers, you often have indirect contact with those who know them. You might even contact the interviewer directly, through correspondence or a phone call. This contact creates an impression. Let's take a look at the issues here and see what you can do to prepare yourself.

Create a positive impression in preliminary contacts

There are three ways an interviewer may form an impression of you before meeting you face-to-face:

1. The interviewer already knows you

There are many situations where an interviewer may know you from previous contacts or from someone else's description of you. When this is so, your best approach is to acknowledge that relationship, but to treat the interview in all other respects as a business meeting. Even if you are the best of friends, remember that a decision to hire you involves hard cash. It will not be done lightly.

2. Through previous phone contacts

The phone is an important job search tool. How you handle yourself on the phone will create an impression, even though the contacts are brief. If you set up an interview with the employer, you have already created an impression.

Secretaries (and other staff you have contact with) may also mention their observations to the interviewer, so be professional and friendly in all encounters with staff.

You should consider calling the day before the interview to verify the time. Say something like: "Hi, I want to make sure our interview for two o'clock tomorrow is still on." Get any directions you need. This is just another way of demonstrating your attention to detail and helps communicate the sense of importance you are giving this interview.

3. Through previous paperwork

Prior to most interviews, you will provide the employer with some sort of paperwork that will create an impression. Sending a note or letter beforehand often creates the impression that you are well organized. Copies of applications, resumes, and JIST Cards sent in advance help the interviewer know more about you. If they are well done (as they must be), they will help create a positive impression. For these reasons, all paperwork you present to an employer must be as professional as possible.

Quick Tip

The JIST Card presented on this page is a type of mini-resume that presents key information about yourself on a 3″ by 5″ card. It is covered in more detail in chapter 6, but here is an example of one, just so that you know what it is:

Jonathan Michael
Home: (614) 788-2434
Messages: (614) 355-0068

Objective: Management

Skills: Over 7 years of management experience plus a B.S. degree in Business. Managed budgets as large as $10 million. Experienced in cost control and reduction, cutting over 20% of overhead while business increased over 30%. Good organizer and problem solver. Excellent communication skills.

Prefer responsible position in a medium to large business

Cope well with deadline pressure, seek challenge, flexible

Research the organization, interviewer, and job

Knowing something about the organization and the interviewer will pay off. This is not practical in situations where you call or drop in unexpectedly, as when making a cold contact, but it does make sense in other situations.

For example, let's say you have targeted a particular organization as one of the few that seem able to provide you with the kind of job you want. Because of that interview's importance to you, it would be wise to be well prepared for it. Briefly, there are three ways of researching for an interview.

The library is a good place to start. Ask the librarian for sources of information on the organization that interests you. There are often national, state, and local directories listing businesses and other organizations that provide some information. Newspapers might contain articles and news releases regarding the organization, and back issues are often available at the library. Major newspapers are indexed and articles are cross-referenced to help you find what you are looking for. Libraries also often have access to computerized databases of information or on-line services that can provide detailed information.

The organization itself is a good source of information. Call the receptionist or even the interviewer and ask them to suggest materials you might read. Annual reports or catalogs are sometimes available but anything you get will help. It won't hurt for your interviewer to know how thorough you are either.

Ask others who might know about the organization or the interviewer. This is one of the best sources of information. An hour on the telephone can give you information you could not obtain otherwise. Use the networking technique by contacting someone who seems likely to know what you want or knows someone who would. Find out what you can, then ask for the name of someone else who would know more.

Here are some things you might want to find out about before you go to a job interview:

The Organization: Size, number of employees; major products or services; competitors and the competitive environment; major changes in policies or status; reputation, values, and major weaknesses or opportunities.

The Interviewer: Level and area of responsibility; special work-related projects, interests, or accomplishments; personal information (family, hobbies, etc.); and management style.

The Position: If an opening exists or if similar jobs now exist; what happened to others in similar positions; salary range and benefits; duties and responsibilities; and what the last person did wrong (to avoid it) or right (to emphasize it).

The more you can find out before you begin, the better you are likely to do in the interview. Employers appreciate someone who does their homework. You will be better prepared for any questions that may come up, and you will be able to more readily direct the interview to concentrate on presenting your skills well.

Quick Reference

I provide much more advice on researching for employer information in chapter 11, and there are lots of reference sources noted in the bibliography, too.

Getting to and waiting for the interview

There are several details to consider before the interview itself and each one makes a difference.

Get there on time. Try to schedule several interviews within the same area of town and time frame to avoid wasted time in excessive travel. If you are driving, get directions from the receptionist and be sure you know how to get there and how long it takes. Allow plenty of time for parking and plan on arriving for the interview 5 to 10 minutes early. If you are using public transportation, make sure you know what to do to get there on time.

Check your grooming. Arrive early enough to slip into a restroom and correct any grooming problems your travel may have caused (wind-blown hair, etc.).

Be nice to the receptionist. Many organizations have a receptionist and this person is important to you. Assume that everything you say or do will get back to the interviewer. (It typically will.) A friendly chat with the receptionist can also be a productive way to find out more about the organization. For example, if it seems appropriate, ask the person what it is like to work there, what he or she does in the job, or even what sort of a person the boss is. They are often happy to share these things with you in a helpful way. A thank-you note to him or her following your interview will surely create a positive impression. Treat all support personnel with respect and they will help you by saying nice things about you to the boss; mistreat them and you will probably not get a job there.

I once worked in a busy office that had a public waiting room that was often crowded. When I was interviewing people, the receptionists often interacted with applicants as they waited for me. If the person being interviewed acted strangely or did not treat all staff with respect, they would give me a thumbs down sign in a way that the applicant could not see. Those interviews were very short. I figured that if that applicant did not treat one of my staff well before the interview, they would only show the same lack of interpersonal skills on the job. The moral: Receptionists are real people and their opinions of you do count.

Use appropriate waiting room behavior. It is important to relax and to look relaxed as you wait for the interview to begin. Occupy yourself with something businesslike. For example, this could be a good time to review your notes on questions you might like to ask in the interview, key skills you want to present, or other interview details. Bring a work-related magazine to read or pick one up in the reception area. They may also have publications from the organization itself that you may not have seen yet. During the entire interviewing process, I advise you not to smoke since a nonsmoker is often seen as a more desirable worker. You may have other mannerisms that create negative impressions, too. Don't slouch in your seat. Don't create a mess by spreading out your coat and papers across the next seat.

Be prepared if the interviewer is late. Hope that it happens. If you arrive promptly but had to wait past the appointed time, that puts the interviewer in a "Gee, I'm sorry, I owe you one" frame of mind. If the interviewer is 15 minutes late, approach the receptionist and say something like: "I have an appointment to keep yet today. Do you think it will be much longer before (insert interviewer's name) will be free?"

Be nice, but don't act like you can sit around all day either. If you have to wait more than 25 minutes beyond the scheduled time, ask to reschedule at a better time. Say it is no problem for you and you understand things do come up. Besides, you say, you want to be sure Mr. or Ms. So-and-So doesn't feel rushed when they see you. Set up the new time, accept any apology with a smile, and be on your way. When you do come back for your interview, the odds are that the interviewer will apologize – and treat you very well indeed.

Phase 2: Opening Moves – First Impressions Do Count!

You've gotten to the right office, on time, and the interviewer now walks into the room. What is the first thing that will happen? While this may seem obvious, the first thing that will happen is that he or she will see and react to you.

Appearance counts

In a monumental and thorough work entitled *Job Search, A Review of the Literature*, Steven Magnum found that "Appearance, communication skills, and attitudes dominate the research. Attire and physical attractiveness visibly influence the hiring process."

I cannot stress enough the importance of your appearance in the job search. It is a major factor in the interview process and in getting a job offer – or getting eliminated from consideration.

The importance of appearance is highlighted by the results of a study which evaluated the effect of nonverbal communication style on employers. Two actors, one male and one female, were videotaped while role-playing an interview. Two tapes were made of each, using precisely the same responses to the same questions. In one tape, the actors made good eye contact while speaking, spoke clearly, and presented good posture. In the other, they did not. They dressed the same for each series of tapes and, I emphasize, used the same words in responding to the same questions.

These tapes were then randomly shown to 52 professional interviewers who were asked to score the interviews in various categories. No interviewer saw the same actor in both roles. What do you suppose happened? Naturally, the "good" interview was chosen over the "bad" one.

What was astonishing was that, of all the interviewers, not one would have invited back the person who had poor nonverbal skills. The same people using the same responses but who had good nonverbal communication skills would have been invited back by 88 percent of the interviewers. The results of this study show that your appearance and various personality traits (adaptive skills) are observed by interviewers.

Let's look at some of the other appearance-related issues employers use to define your personality and make hiring decisions.

Be particular about your dress and grooming

How you dress and groom can create a big negative or positive impression even during the first few seconds of an interview. With so many options in styles, colors, and other factors, the "correct" approach can get quite complex. Entire books have been written on the subject and there are many differences of opinion on just what is right for various occasions. To avoid the complexity, I present this simple rule for you to follow:

Mike Farr's Interview Dress and Grooming Rule

Dress and groom like the interviewer is likely to be dressed – but cleaner.

My rule means that a bank teller would dress, when going to an interview, like his or her boss would dress. An auto mechanic, on the other hand, would look inappropriate going to an interview dressed like the manager of a bank. If there is any doubt about just how to dress or groom, guess conservatively. Pay attention to details. Do your shoes look presentable? Are your clothes clean and pressed? Is your hair neat? Are you absolutely clean? Have you looked closely at yourself in the mirror?

It is best to get someone else's opinion on the impression you make. A better clothing store can help you select a coordinated job-search outfit. Plan to invest some money in at least one set of good quality interviewing clothes. Notice, when you are all spruced up, how good you feel. That can affect your whole performance in the interview.

A firm handshake and good eye contact

Shaking hands is a common custom and, while it seems a small detail, do learn to execute this formality properly. If the employer offers his or her hand, give a firm-but-not-too-firm handshake as you smile.

As ridiculous as it sounds, a little practice helps. Avoid staring but do look at the interviewer when either of you is speaking. It will help you concentrate on what is being said as well as indicate to the employer that you are listening closely and have good social skills.

Other nonverbal behaviors make an impression

The very best way to see yourself as others see you is to role-play an interview while it is videotaped. Looking at and listening to the video playback is sometimes shocking to people. If video equipment is not available to you, all is not lost. Pay close attention to your own posture, mannerisms, and other body language. Ask yourself how employers might evaluate you if they saw that behavior. Look at other people and copy the posture and behavior of ones you think would look good in an interview situation. Here are some additional tips on improving your interview behavior.

Act interested. When you are sitting, lean slightly forward in your chair and keep your head up, looking directly at the interviewer. This helps you look interested and alert.

Eliminate annoying behaviors. Try to eliminate any distracting movements or mannerisms. A woman in one of my workshops saw herself in a videotape constantly playing with her hair. It was only then that she realized she did it at all, and how distracting it was. Listen to yourself and you may notice that you say "aaahhh" every 10 seconds, or say "you know what I mean?" over and over, or use other repetitive words or phrases. You may hardly be aware of doing this, but do watch for it. Seek out and eliminate similar behavior from the interview.

Pay attention to your voice. If you are naturally soft-spoken, work on increasing your volume slightly. Listen to news announcers and other professional speakers who are good models for volume, speed, and voice tone. I, for example, have a fairly deep voice. I have learned to raise it up and down while doing presentations, so everyone doesn't go to sleep. Your voice and delivery will improve as you gain experience and conduct more interviews.

Tips to help you quickly establish a positive relationship

Open the interview with an approach intended to establish a relaxed, social tone. Here are some ideas of what to say in the first few minutes.

Use the interviewer's name as often as possible. Do this particularly in the early part of the interview and again when you are ending it. Be formal, using "Mr. Jones" or "Ms. Smith," unless they suggest otherwise.

Play the chit-chat game for awhile. The interviewer will often comment on the weather, ask if you had trouble getting there, or some other common opening. Be friendly and make a few appropriate comments. Do not push your way into the business of your visit too early because these informal openings are standard measures of your socialization skills. Smile. It's nonverbal and people will respond more favorably to you if you smile at them.

Comment on something personal in the interviewer's office. "I love your office! Did you decorate it yourself?" or "I noticed the sailboat. Do you sail?" or "Is that a Phantom II computer I noticed downstairs? How do you like it?" or "Your receptionist is great! How long has he been here?" The idea here is to express interest in something that interests the employer and encourage her or him to speak about it. It is a compliment if your enthusiasm shows. This tactic can also provide you the opportunity to share something you have in common, so try to pick a topic you know something about.

Ask some opening questions

As soon as you have both completed the necessary pleasant chit-chat, be prepared to ask a few light questions to get the interview off in a useful direction. This can happen within a minute of your first greeting, but is more likely to take up to five minutes. Some of the transitional questions that follow could be used in a traditional interview setting, while others assume that you are interviewing before a job is actually open.

Some Questions to Ask Early in an Interview

"How did you get started in this type of career?" (or business or whatever)

"I'd like to know more about what your organization does. Would you mind telling me?"

"I have a background in _____ and am interested in how I might be considered to work in an organization such as yours."

"I have three years experience plus two years of training in the field of _____. I am actively looking for a job and know that you probably do not have openings now but would be interested in future openings. Perhaps if I told you a few things about myself, you could give me some ideas of whether you would be interested in me."

Phase 3: The Interview Itself – A Few Simple Techniques Can Dramatically Improve Your Performance

If you have created a reasonably positive image of yourself so far, an interviewer will now be interested in the specifics of why they should consider hiring you. This back-and-forth conversation usually lasts from 15 to 45 minutes and many consider it to be the most important – and most difficult – task in the entire job search.

Fortunately, by reading this book, you will have several advantages over the average job seeker:

1. You know what sort of job you want.

2. You know what skills are required to do well in that job.

3. You have those very skills.

The only thing that remains to be done is to communicate these three things. This is best done by directly and completely answering the questions an employer will ask you.

Quick Fact

Be prepared for problem interview questions

According to employers in the Northwestern University's Endicott Survey, about 80 percent of all job seekers cannot provide a good answer to one or more problem interview questions.

All employers will try to uncover problems or limitations you might bring to their job. Everyone has a problem of some sort and the employer will try to find yours. Expect it. Let's say, for example, that you have been out of work for three months. That could be seen as a problem, unless you can provide a good reason for it.

Meet an employer's expectations or you are unlikely to get the job

Your task in the interview is to understand what an employer is looking for. After reviewing the research on what employers react to in an interview, I've selected three things that are of particular importance (as discussed in Chapter 3). If any of these "employer's expectations" are not met, it is unlikely that you will get a job offer. They are:

Quick Reminder

The Three Major Employer Expectations

1. Appearance – Do you look like the type of person who will succeed on the job?

2. Dependability – Can you be depended on to be reliable and to do a good job for a reasonable length of time?

3. Credentials – Do you have the necessary training, experience, skills, and credentials to indicate that you are able to do the job well?

Most problem questions have to do with either the second or third expectations.

View every interview question as an opportunity to support your ability to do the job. Your interview will be short, so you must make the most of it. Each question provides a chance to present the skills you have that are needed by the employer. Remember that the interviewer is a person just like you. You must be honest and be able to support, with proof, anything you say about yourself. If you have carefully selected your job objective and know your skills, you will find it easy to present reasons why the employer should hire you.

You should also be prepared to ask some questions early on. Some interviewers are happy to discuss details of the position you seek. If possible, find out as much as you can about the position early in the interview. Ask about the type of person they are looking for to fill this position, what sort of people have done well in those jobs before, or what sorts of responsibilities the job requires. Once you know more about what the interviewer is looking for, you can "fit" your later responses to what you now know the company wants.

Let's say you've found out that the position requires someone who is good at meeting people and who is organized. Assuming you have those skills, you could later emphasize how good you are at meeting people. The examples you use to support this skill could also provide evidence of how organized you are.

The Three-Step Process for answering interview questions

There are thousands of questions that could be asked of you in an interview and there is no way you can memorize a "correct" response for each one. Interviews just aren't like that. They are often conversational and informal. The unexpected often happens. For these reasons, it is far more important to develop an *approach* to answering an interview question rather than memorizing a "correct" response for each.

I have developed a technique that you can use to fashion an effective answer to most interview questions. To make it easy, I have given the technique a name – The Three-Step Process for Answering Interview Questions and here it is:

The Three-Step Process for Answering Interview Questions

Step #1: Understand What Is Really Being Asked.

Most questions relate to Employer Expectation #2 – regarding your adaptive skills and personality. This includes such questions as: can we depend on you?; are you easy to get along with?; are you a good worker? The question may also relate to Employer Expectation #3, namely, do you have the experience and training to do the job if we hire you?

Step #2: Answer the Question Briefly, In a Non-Damaging Way.

A good response to a question should acknowledge the facts, and present them as an advantage, not a disadvantage.

Step #3: Answer the Real Question by Presenting Your Related Skills.

Once you understand the employer's real concern, you can answer the often hidden question by presenting the skills you have related to the job.

An Example of an Answer Using the Three-Step Process

To show you how the Three-Step Process can be used, let's use it to answer a specific question:

> *Problem Question: "We were looking for someone with more experience in this field than you seem to have. Why should we consider you over others with better credentials?"*

Here's how one person might construct an answer to this question, using the Three-Step Process.

Step 1: Understand What Is Really Being Asked

The question above is often asked in a less direct way, but it is a frequent concern of employers. To answer it, you must remember that employers often hire people who present themselves well in an interview over those with better credentials. Your best shot is to emphasize whatever personal strengths you have that could offer an advantage to an employer. The person wants to know whether you have anything going for you that can help you overcome a more experienced worker.

Well, do you? Are you a hard worker? Do you learn fast? Have you had intensive training or hands-on experience? Do you have skills from other activities that can transfer to this job? Knowing in advance what skills you have to offer is essential to answering this question.

Step 2: Answer the Question Briefly, in a Non-Damaging Way

Here is an example of how one person might answer the question without damage:

> *"I'm sure there are people who have more years of experience or better credentials. I do, however, have four years of combined training and hands-on experience using the latest methods and techniques. Because my training is recent, I am open to new ideas and have gotten used to working hard and learning quickly."*

Step 3: Answer the Real Question by Presenting Your Related Skills

While the above response answers the question in an appropriate – and brief – way, it might continue with additional details that emphasize key skills needed for the job:

> *"As you know, I held down a full-time job and family responsibilities while going to school. During those two years, I had an excellent attendance record both at work and school, missing only one day in two years. I also received two merit increases in salary and my grades were in the top 25 percent of my class. In order to do all this, I had to learn to organize my time and set priorities. I worked hard to prepare myself in this new career area and am willing to keep working to establish myself. The position you have available is what I am prepared to do. I am willing to work harder than the next person because I have the desire to keep learning and to do a good job. With my education complete, I can now turn my full attention to this job."*

This response presents the skills necessary to do well in any job. This job seeker sounds dependable, which meets Employer Expectation #2 (Dependability). And he gave examples of situations where he had used the required skills in other settings, thus meeting Employer Expectation #3 (Credentials). It was a good response.

Quick Reference

Chapter 5 provides thorough answers to ten interview questions that, in one form or another, are asked in most interviews. If you can answer those questions well, you should be prepared to answer most others. I strongly suggest you carefully review these answers in chapter 16 since they will show you how to use the Three-Step Process in more detail. That chapter also includes a list of 94 additional questions that are frequently asked in an interview. And, since you are probably curious, here is my list of 10 most frequently asked problem questions.

The Top 10 Problem Interview Questions

1. Why don't you tell me about yourself?

2. Why should I hire you?

3. What are your major strengths?

4. What are your major weaknesses?

5. What sort of pay do you expect to receive?

6. How does your previous experience relate to the jobs we have here?

7. What are your plans for the future?

8. What will your former employers (or teachers, if you are a recent student) say about you?

9. Why are you looking for this sort of position and why here?

10. Why don't you tell me about your personal situation?

Questions you might ask the interviewer

Even if you don't ask any questions during an interview, many employers will ask you if you have any. How you respond will affect their evaluation of you. So be prepared to ask insightful questions about the organization.

Good topics to touch on include:

➤ The competitive environment in which the organization operates

➤ Executive management styles

➤ What obstacles the organization anticipates in meeting its goals

➤ How the organization's goals have changed over the past three to five years

Generally, it is most unwise to ask about pay or benefits or other similar areas. The reason is that it tends to make you seem more interested in what the organization can do for you. It is also not a good idea to simply have no questions at all. Doing so makes you appear passive rather than curious and interested.

Phase 4: Closing the Interview – The Last Few Minutes Are Important

There are a few things to remember as the interview is coming to an end. Let's review them briefly.

Don't let the interview last too long. Most interviews last 30 to 60 minutes. Unless the employer asks otherwise, plan on staying no longer than an hour.

Watch for hints from the interviewer, such as looking at a watch or rustling papers, that indicate he or she is ready to end the interview. Exceptions to the one-hour rule should be made only at the interviewer's request.

Summarize the key points of the interview. Use your judgment here and keep it short! Review the major issues that came up in the interview. This is an optional step and can be skipped if time is short.

If a problem came up, repeat your resolution of it. Whatever you think that particular interviewer may see as a reason not to hire you, bring it up again and present your reasons why you don't see it as a problem. If you are not sure, be direct and ask, "Is there anything about me that concerns you or might keep you from hiring me?" Whatever comes up, do as well as you can in responding to it.

Review your strengths for this job. This is another chance for you to present the skills you possess that relate to this particular job. Emphasize your key strengths only, and keep it brief.

Use the "Call-Back Close." This is an approach that is quite strong. You may not be comfortable with it at first but role-play and practice in your early interviews will help you get more comfortable. The Call-Back Close does work, and it works as follows:

The Call-Back Close

1. Thank the interviewer by name. While shaking his or her hand, say: "Thank you (Mr. or Mrs. or Ms. _____) for your time today."

2. Express interest. Depending on the situation, express your interest in the job, organization, service, or product:

> *"I'm very interested in the ideas we went over today." or,*
>
> *"I'm very interested in your organization. It seems to be an exciting place to work." or, if a job opening exists and you want it, definitely say,*
>
> *"I am definitely interested in this position."*

3. Mention your busy schedule. Say "I'm busy for the next week, but..."

4. Arrange a reason and a time to call back. Your objective is to leave a reason for you to get back in touch and to arrange for a specific day and time to do so. For example, say "I'm sure I'll have questions. When would be the best time for me to get back with you?"

Notice that I said "When" rather than "Is it OK to...." The first way does not easily allow a "no" response. Get a specific day ("Monday") and a best time to call ("between 9 and 10 a.m.").

5. Say "thank you" and "good-bye."

Phase 5: Following Up – Effective Follow Up Actions Can Make a Big Difference in Getting a Job Offer Over More Qualified Applicants

The interview has ended, you made it home, and now it's all over, right? Not right. You need to follow up. As I've said throughout this book, following up can make the difference between being unemployed and getting a good job fast. Here is what you should do when you get home.

Make notes on the interview. While it is fresh in your mind, jot down key points. A week later, you may not remember something essential.

Schedule your follow up. If you agreed to call back next Monday between 9:00 and 10:00 A.M., you are likely to forget unless you put it on your schedule.

Send your thank-you note. Send the note the very same day if possible.

Call when you said you would! If you call when you said you would, you will create the impression of being organized and wanting the job. If you do have a specific question, ask it. If a job opening exists and you do want it, say that you want it and why. If no job opening exists, just say you enjoyed the visit and would like to stay in touch during your job search. This would also be a good time to ask, if you had not done it before, for the names of anyone else with whom you might speak about a position for a person with your skills and experience.

Schedule more follow up. The last thing to do is to schedule the next time you want to follow up with this person.

Phase 6: Negotiating for Salary and Other Benefits – If You Handle This Well, You Can Earn Thousands of Dollars a Minute

Once a job offer is made, negotiations can be as simple as saying "When can I start?" However, there is far more you should know about negotiating a job offer and I will provide additional details on this in chapter 18. But, in the interim, here are a few essential tips to remember:

1. The time to negotiate is after you've been offered the job.

Do not discuss your preferred salary or an other negotiable subject in an interview until after a job offer has clearly been made. Many, many job seekers have been eliminated from consideration over this very issue.

2. Don't say "no" too quickly.

NEVER, EVER turn down a job offer in an interview! Even if you are certain that you won't accept the job because, say, it pays too little, always ask to consider it overnight. You can always say no tomorrow. If your decision to refuse the job as offered remains firm, you can always suggest (tomorrow) that you appreciate the offer but ask that they consider you for other opportunities, give you higher wages, or whatever. This is no time to be playing games, but many people have turned down one job only to be offered a better one later simply because the employer had time to think about things.

3. Don't say "yes" too quickly either.

As with saying "no" too quickly, take time to think about accepting a job too. If you do want it, do not jeopardize obtaining it with unreasonable demands. Ask for 24 hours to consider your decision and, when calling back, consider negotiating for something reasonable. A bit more money, perhaps – or the promise of a salary review after 90 days. But make it clear that you do want the job in any case and don't be difficult. If you want the job, say so – and don't quibble over things that are not important to you.

Money Isn't Everything: Some Other Things You Might Negotiate

Let's assume that you get a job offer that is close to, but not quite in the pay range you wanted. Before you turn it down, think about what other things you might ask for that would make the job acceptable. Then ask for them.

Title: Some job titles look better on a resume and sound better in an interview. Just by changing the wording, you can position yourself for more responsibility ("office manager" vs. "secretary," for example).

Hours: I once accepted a job that paid a bit less than I wanted, but it let me take one afternoon off per week. I still worked over 40 hours but those afternoons sailing sure felt good.

Salary Review: Ask to have your salary reviewed for an increase after three to six months. Negotiate a specific increase to be given then, if your performance is good.

Advancement: Discuss the next level of responsibility toward which you might work. Find out how you might get there and how long it might take.

Education and Training: Some organizations pay for course work, seminars, or other training. This can be a tremendous benefit, if you can get it.

Vacations: Smaller organizations are more flexible on this. Ask for more and you just might get it.

Fringe Benefits: "Fringes" are often standard for everyone in the same organization, but sometimes there is flexibility. For example, negotiation for special insurance benefits (by showing that you are more valuable than some other employees), could be worth real money to you.

> **Working Conditions:** Perhaps you like to do some work from home, come in at 8:15 a.m. instead of 8:00, prefer to have your own office (with a window), or some other special request. The time to negotiate these things is before you start working there.

Phase 7: Making a Final Decision

It is rare to find the perfect job. There are usually compromises to be made. But, too often, a job is accepted without thorough knowledge of just what it would be like to actually work there. At the time, it seems to be a good idea. Unfortunately, what seemed good at first doesn't always turn out that way later. The major problem is that many people never make a careful decision at all. They don't take the time to weigh the pros and the cons of their decision. One job leads to another and careers develop by accident. There is an alternative.

In a book entitled *Decision Making*, Irving Janis and Leon Mann present research and theory on the process – and consequences – of making important decisions. They found that various groups who used this process were more likely to stick to their decision and have fewer regrets afterwards then those who did not. To make any important decision they suggest that you consider the alternatives in a systematic way.

You can easily adapt their decision-making process for use in making career decisions. Let's say that you are considering a job offer, but it requires you to move – something you would rather not do. They suggest that you create a simple form with four boxes, like the sample one that I have provided. Simply writing in the pros and cons for yourself and for others (if this is an issue for you) will help you make a good decision. It's that simple.

The Career Choice Balance Sheet	
Positives	**Negatives**
For me:	
For others:	

Quick Summary

✓ **Five things you must do to have a successful interview:**

1. Make a positive impression.

2. Communicate your skills.

3. Answer problem questions.

4. Help the employer know why he or she should hire you.

5. Follow up after the interview.

✓ The three types of interviews: 1)Traditional, 2) Information, and 3) JIST Job Search.

   ✓ Several types of traditional interviews include: The Preliminary Screening Interview, The Group or Panel Interview, The Non-Directive Interview, The Stress Interview, The Structured Interview, The Reality Interview, The Disorganized Interview.

   ✓ One type of information inteview is called the Profit interview.

✓ **The Seven Phases of an Interview:**

Phase 1: Before You Go In – You Make a Positive Impression Before You Even Get There, so Make Sure It Is a Good One.

Phase 2: Opening Moves– First Impressions Do Count!

Phase 3: The Interview Itself – A Few Simple Techniques Can Dramatically Improve Your Performance

Phase 4: Closing the Interview – The Last Few Minutes Are Important

Phase 5: Following Up – Effective Follow-Up Actions Can Make a Big Difference in Getting a Job Offer Over More Qualified Applicants

Phase 6: Negotiating for Salary and Other Benefits – If You Handle This Well, You Can Earn Thousands of Dollars a Minute

Phase 7: Making a Final Decision

✓ **The Three-Step Process to Answering Interview Questions**

Step 1: Understand What Is Really Being Asked

Step 2: Answer the Question Briefly, in a Non-Damaging Way

Step 3: Answer the Real Question by Presenting Your Related Skills

Chapter 4

CHAPTER FIVE

Job Search Basics

Answers to 10 Key Interview Questions

Quick Overview

In this chapter, I review the following:

✓ The 10 Most Frequently Asked Interview Questions

✓ Comments and analysis of each question

✓ Sample answers to each question

✓ The Prove It Technique

✓ How to handle obvious and not-so-obvious problems

I considered putting this chapter later in the book but decided it was just too important. Doing well in the interview is often essential to your getting a job and being prepared to answer the questions covered in this chapter can make an enormous difference to you in getting a job over other qualified applicants.

Let me also suggest to you that reading this chapter can be worth thousands of dollars to you, because one of the questions is "What sort of pay do you expect to receive?" Knowing how to answer this one question will quickly pay for this book – and, over the years, leave enough left over to buy a new car. . .

The 10 Most Frequently Asked Interview Questions

Knowing and practicing answers to a relatively small but important cluster of difficult questions will prepare you to answer many others. Some questions are asked more than others. Others are seldom asked directly but are the basis for other questions. For example, a conversational question about your family relationships may really be an attempt to discover whether or not you will be a reliable worker.

From the thousands of questions that could be asked, I have constructed 10 questions that represent the types of issues that concern most employers. The following list of questions is partly based on questions employers actually ask, and partly on my sense of which questions provide the best patterns for teaching you the principles of constructing good overall responses.

The Top 10 Problem Interview Questions

1. Why don't you tell me about yourself?
2. Why should I hire you?
3. What are your major strengths?
4. What are your major weaknesses?
5. What sort of pay do you expect to receive?
6. How does your previous experience relate to the jobs we have here?
7. What are your plans for the future?
8. What will your former employers (or teachers, if you are a recent student) say about you?
9. Why are you looking for this sort of position and why here?
10. Why don't you tell me about your personal situation?

Quick Reminder

Recall that in the last chapter, I discussed the Three-Step Process for answering interview questions. Because each of you is different – and each interview is different – there can be no one correct way to answer an interview question. For this reason, it is important for you to learn a strategy for answering any interview question. One important strategy presented in the previous chapter is the Three-Step Process reviewed on the following page.

> ## The Three-Step Process to Answering Interview Questions
>
> **Step 1: Understand What Is Really Being Asked.** It usually relates to Employer's Expectation 2, regarding your adaptive skills and personality: Can we depend on you? Are you easy to get along with? and Are you a good worker?
>
> **Step 2: Answer the Question Briefly, in a Non-Damaging Way.** Acknowledge the facts, but present them as an advantage, not a disadvantage.
>
> **Step 3: Answer the Real Question by Presenting Your Related Skills.** Once you understand the employer's real concern, you can get around to answering the often hidden question by presenting your skills and experiences related to the job.
>
> The Three-Step Process is important for understanding that the interview question being asked often is looking for underlying information. The technique that follows will help you provide that information in an effective way.

The "Prove It" Technique

1. Present a Concrete Example: People relate to and remember stories. Saying you have a skill is not nearly as powerful as describing a situation where you used that skill. The story should include enough details to make sense of the who, what, where, when, and why.

2. Quantify: Whenever possible, numbers should be used to provide a basis for what was done. For example, give the number of customers served or the amount of cash handled.

3. Emphasize Results: It is important to provide some data regarding the positive results you obtained. For example, sales increased by 3 percent over the previous year or profits went up 50 percent. Use numbers to quantify your results.

4. Link It Up: While the connection between your story and doing the job well may seem obvious to you, make sure it is clear to the employer. A simple statement is often enough to accomplish this.

If you do a thorough job in completing the activities in Part II of this book, it should be fairly easy to provide proof to support the skills you discuss in an interview. This technique is the basic interview strategy to use. I will refer to it in sections that follow and it is most important that you remember the basic steps.

Answers to the Top 10 Problem Interview Questions

In this section, I use the Three-Step Process and "Prove It" techniques to create sample answers to the 10 problem questions listed earlier in this chapter. For each question, I provide an analysis of what the question is really asking, followed by a strategy for answering it. I also provide one or more sample responses. In each case I use the Three-Step Process, including the "Prove It" approach for constructing a response.

While your answers will differ from the sample answers provided, you will learn how to use the basic techniques and apply them to your own situation.

Problem Interview Question #1: "Why don't you tell me about yourself?"

Analysis of the question:

This is an open-ended question. You could start anywhere, but telling your life's history in two hours or less is not what is really being asked. Instead, such a question is a test of your ability to select what is important and communicate it clearly and quickly. Obviously, the questioner expects you to relate your background to the position being considered.

A strategy to use in answering the question:

There are several basic approaches that could be used. One would be to go ahead and provide a brief response to the question as it is asked and the other is to request a clarification of the question before answering it. In both cases, you would quickly turn your response to focus on your skills, experience, and training that prepared you for the sort of job you now want.

Sample answer #1:

If you answered the question as it was asked you might say something like this:

> "I grew up in the Southwest and have one brother and one sister. My parents both worked and I had a happy childhood. I always did well in school and by the time I graduated from high school I had taken a year's worth of business courses. I knew then that I wanted to work in a business setting and had several part-time office jobs while still in high school. After high school I worked in a variety of business settings and learned a great deal about how various businesses run. For example, I was given complete responsibility for the daily operations of a wholesale distribution company that grossed over two million dollars a year. That was only three years after I graduated from high school. There I learned to supervise other people and solve problems under pressure. I also got more interested in the financial end of running a business and decided, after three years and three promotions, to go after a position where I could have more involvement in key strategies and long-term management decisions."

Comments on this answer:

Notice how this job seeker provided a few bits of personal history, then quickly turned the interviewer's attention to skills and experiences directly related to the job now sought.

You could ask the interviewer to help you narrow down things he or she really wants to know with a response such as this:

Sample answer #2:

> *"There's so much to tell! Would you like me to emphasize my personal history, the special training and education I have that prepared me for this sort of position, or the skills and job-related experiences I have to support my objective?"*

Comments on this answer:

If you do this well, most employers will tell you what sorts of things they are most interested in and you can then concentrate on giving them what they want.

Quick Tip

Honesty is always the best policy, but that old adage doesn't rule out marketing yourself in the best light during an interview. As James Huntington-Meath, owner of Career Directions, a private guidance agency in Chapel Hill, N.C., puts it, "I am always going to counsel individuals to be positive about themselves. I don't think it's unethical to coach people in that direction, either." So stay away from taking credit for something you don't deserve, claiming to have experience you don't have, or bragging about a poor performance. But feel free to talk up your achievements, awards, and promotions with no fear of misrepresenting yourself.

Problem Interview Question #2: "Why should I hire you?"

Analysis of the question:

This is a direct and fair question. Though it is rarely asked this clearly, it is the question behind any other question that will be asked. It has no hidden meaning.

A strategy to use in answering the question:

A direct question deserves a direct response. Why should they hire you? The best response provides advantages to them, not to you. This often involves providing proof that you can help them make more money by improving efficiency, reducing costs, increasing sales, or solving problems (by coming to work on time, improving customer services, organizing one or more operations, or a variety of other things).

Sample answer:

Here is an example of a response from a person with considerable prior experience:

> *"You should hire me because I don't need to be trained and have a proven track record. I have over 15 years of education and experience related to this position. Over 6 of those years have been in management positions similar to the one available here. In my last position, I was promoted three times in the 6 years I was there. I most recently had responsibility for supervising a staff of 15 and a warehousing operation that processed over 30 million dollars worth of materials a year. In the last 2 years, I managed*

a 40 percent increase in volume processed with only a 6 percent increase in expenses. I am hard-working and have earned a reputation as a dependable and creative problem solver. The opportunities here excite me. My substantial experience will help me know how to approach the similar situations here. I am also willing to ask questions and accept advice from others. This will be an important factor in taking advantage of what has already been accomplished here."

Comments on this answer:

This job seeker's response emphasized the "Prove It" technique. While she presented her skills and experience in a direct and confident way, she avoided a know-it-all attitude by being open to others' suggestions.

Quick Tip

Completing this brief activity might be quite a challenge unless you have first completed the activities in Part II of this book. If you do find it difficult to clearly identify why someone should hire you, you'll need to consult Part II.

The Reasons Why Someone Should Hire You

• •

In the spaces below, list the major advantages you offer an employer in hiring you over someone else. Emphasize your strengths. These could be personality traits, transferable skills, special training, prior experience, or anything else you think is important. These are the things to emphasize in your interview.

1. _____

_____

_____

2. _____

_____

_____

3. _____

_____

_____

Problem Interview Question #3: "What are your major strengths?"

Analysis of the question:

Like the previous question, this one is quite direct and has little hidden meaning.

A strategy to use in answering the question:

Your response should first emphasize your adaptive or self-management skills. The decision to hire you is very much based on these skills and you can deal with the details of your specific job-related skills later. Remember that here, as elsewhere, your response must be brief.

Quick Reference

Chapter 6 provides details on the JIST Card. Once you have done a JIST Card of your own, it lists the key skills to emphasize in your response to this question.

Sample answer:

Here is a response from a person who has little prior work experience related to the job he now seeks:

> "One of my major strengths is my ability to work hard towards a goal. Once I decide to do something, it will probably get done. For example, I graduated from high school four years ago. Many of my friends started working and others went on to school. At the time I didn't know what I wanted to do, so furthering my education at that point did not make sense. The jobs I could get at the time didn't excite me either, so I looked into joining the Navy. I took the test and discovered a few things about myself that surprised me. For one thing, I was much better at understanding complex problems than my grades in high school would suggest. I signed up for a three-year hitch that included intensive training in electronics. I worked hard and graduated in the top 20 percent of my class. I was then assigned to monitor, diagnose, and repair an advanced electronics system that was worth about 20 million dollars. I was promoted several times to the position of Petty Officer and received an honorable discharge after my tour of duty. I now know what I want to do and am prepared to spend extra time learning whatever is needed to do well here."

Comments on this answer:

Once you begin speaking about one of your strengths, the rest of your response often falls into place naturally. Remember to provide some proof of your skills, as this response did. It makes a difference.

Problem Interview Question #4: "What are your major weaknesses?"

Analysis of the question:

This is a trick question. If you answer the question as it is asked, you could easily damage your chances of getting the job. By trying to throw you off guard, the employer can see how you might react in similar tough situations on the job. I have often asked this question to groups of job seekers and usually get one of two types of responses. The first goes like this:

"I really don't have any major weaknesses."

That response is obviously untrue and evasive. The other type of response I usually get is an honest one like this:

"Well, I am really disorganized. I suppose I should do better at that, but my life has just been too hectic, what with the bankruptcy and embezzlement charges and all."

While this type of response might get an "A" for honesty, it gets an "F" for interview technique.

A strategy to use in answering the question:

What's needed here is an honest, undamaging response followed by a brief, positive presentation to counter the negative.

Sample answer #1:

"Well, I have been accused by coworkers of being too involved in my work. I usually come in a little early to organize my day and stay late to get a project done on time."

Sample answer #2:

"I need to learn to be more patient. I often do things myself just because I know I can do them faster and better than someone else. This trait has not let me be as good at delegating tasks as I want to be. But I am working on it. I'm now spending more time showing others how to do the things I want done and that has helped. They often do better than I expected if I am clear enough about explaining what I want done – and how."

Comments on these answers:

These responses could both be expanded with some "Prove It" content but they successfully use the three basic steps in answering a problem question as outlined earlier in this chapter.

Problem Interview Question #5: "What Sort of Pay Do You Expect to Receive?"

Analysis of the question and tips for a good answer:

If you are unprepared for this question, it is highly probable that any response will damage your ability to get a job offer. The employer wants you to name a number which can then be compared to a figure the company has in mind. For example, suppose that the employer is looking to pay someone $25,000 a year. If you say you were hoping for $30,000, you will probably be eliminated from consideration. They will be afraid that, if you took the job, you may not stay. If you say you would take $20,000 one of two things could happen:

1. You could get hired at $20,000 a year, making that response the most expensive two seconds in your entire life or,

2. The employer may keep looking for someone else, since you must only be worth $20,000 and they were looking for someone, well, worth more.

This question is designed to help the employer either eliminate you from consideration or save money at your expense. You could get lucky and name the salary the company had in mind but the stakes are too high to recommend that approach. Which brings me to the most important salary negotiation rule.

Quick
Advice

Farr's Salary Negotiation Rule 1

Never talk money until after they decide they want you.

Your objective in an initial interview is to create a positive impression. It is unlikely you will get a firm job offer in a first interview. If salary comes up, avoid getting nailed down. Here are some things you could say:

"Are you making me a job offer?" (A bit corny, yes, but you just might be surprised at the result) or,

"What salary range do you pay for positions with similar requirements?" or,

"I'm very interested in the position and my salary would be negotiable" or,

"Tell me what you have in mind for the salary range."

Quick
Tip

"Employers are anxious to know how your joining the organization will impact their bottom line, and they'll try to get to the subject as soon as possible," says Doug Matthews, managing director of Right Associates' Cincinnati office – an executive outplacement firm. Salary issues are the main reasons candidates are knocked out of the running during screening interviews and informational meetings, according to outplacement industry surveys. In fact, responding appropriately to salary questions can get you past screening interviewers, who rarely have authority to negotiate salaries, and in front of decision-makers with whom the real negotiations take place.

So, always be coy and defer the question as many times as you have to until you are sure it's the real thing and not just part of a screening process. Then, when the timing is right, maneuver the interviewer into naming the starting point. Remember the most important rule: He who speaks first loses.

In most situations, these responses will either get the employer to name a salary range, or put the subject to rest until the proper time. But let's suppose you run into a clever, demanding interviewer who insists you disclose your salary expectations before telling you what he or she is willing to pay. Here is what I suggest:

Farr's Salary Negotiation Rule 2

Know, in advance, the probable salary range for similar jobs in similar organizations.

To find out comparable salary ranges, phone around and ask questions. Those in the business will know what similar jobs in your area are paying. The trick here is to think in terms of a wide range in salary.

I have developed a list of about 250 jobs and the salary ranges you can expect for each. Look for it in chapter 16 of this book. These jobs cover about 85 percent of the workforce and the list will give you a good place to start in finding out what pay to expect for various jobs.

Let's say that in the previous example you figure the employer's range to be somewhere between $22,000 and $27,000. That is a wide range, but you could then say: "I was looking for a salary in the mid to upper twenties."

That covers a lot of territory! It would include from $22,000 to $29,000 a year or so. You can use the same strategy for any salary bracket you may be considering. For example, if you wanted $28,000 a year and their range might be $25,000 to $33,000, you could say "A salary in the mid-twenties to low-thirties." This technique is called "bracketing" and is the third salary negotiation rule:

Farr's Salary Negotiation Rule 3

Always bracket your stated salary range to begin within their probable salary range and end a bit above what you expect to settle for.

If you are offered the job, you are likely to get offered more than they (or you) may have originally been willing to consider. Which brings me to the last rule:

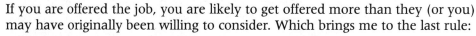

Farr's Salary Negotiation Rule 4

Never say no to a job (or salary) offer either before it is made or within 24 hours afterwards.

Perhaps you think it impossible to say no before an offer is made but I have seen it done many times. In a first interview, let's say that salary does come up. If you were hoping to get a minimum salary of $25,000 a year and the interviewer mentions that he is hoping to pay $23,000, you just might show some disappointment. You might even say something like, "Oh no, I couldn't consider that!" and if you did, that would be the end. Before you were even offered the job, you turned it down.

But suppose that particular job turned out to be (if you had only hung around to find out more) the perfect job for you in all respects except the salary. You may have been delighted to take it. Suppose also that the employer (if only it had gotten to know the delightful person you are) found you to be the kind of person to hire even if it took a few extra dollars – say $2,000 – to get you. In either case, you would strike a bargain.

Quick Alert

For this reason, NEVER give a hint that the salary mentioned is not acceptable to you.

You might say, instead,

Quick Reminder

> *"That is somewhat lower than I had hoped but this position does sound very interesting. If I were to consider this, what sorts of things could I do to quickly become more valuable to this organization?"*

Remember that a discussion of salary is not necessarily a job offer.

Do not let an employer eliminate you from consideration unless and until you get a firm job offer. If you are not sure ask "Is this a job offer?" If it is, and if the pay they offer is low, say something like,

> *"Thank you for the offer. The position is very much what I wanted in many ways and I am delighted at your interest. This is an important decision for me and I would like some time to consider your offer."*

Even if their offer is an insult, do not break their office furniture and stamp out. Be nice (any job offer is good for your ego when you get to turn it down). At worst, you can call them tomorrow and say:

> *"I am flattered by your job offer but feel that it would not be fair of me to accept. The salary is lower than I would like and that is the one reason I cannot accept it. Perhaps you could reconsider your offer or keep me in mind for future openings that might allow me to be worth more to you?"*

Even as you say no, leave the door open for negotiation. If the employer wants you, it may be willing to meet your terms. It happens more than you might imagine.

Comments on these answers:

Do not use this example as a technique to get a higher wage. Understand that once you say no to their offer, the deal is off. You must be willing to lose that job forever.

Problem Question #6: "How Does Your Previous Experience Relate to the Jobs We Have Here?"

Analysis of the question:

This is another direct question that requires a direct response. It relates to Employer Expectation #3 (credentials) and your response will be very important if you have created a good impression up to this point. This question does require you to overcome any weaknesses your background might present when you are compared to other job seekers.

Here are some common typical stumbling blocks: You are just out of school and have limited experience in this career; this is your first job or you have not worked for a period of time; your prior work experience was not the same as the tasks required in this job; your previous level of responsibility was lower or higher than this job; you have had lots of jobs but no clear career direction; you do not have the educational or other credentials many other applicants might have.

A strategy to use in answering the question:

Lead with your strengths. If it is obvious that other job seekers might have more education, more years of experience, or whatever, acknowledge that, then present your strengths. Use the standard Three-Step Approach to answering a problem question. And, again, your JIST Card often will provide a starting point.

Sample answer #1:

"As you know, I have just completed an intensive program in the area of computer programming (or whatever). In addition, I have over three years' work experience in a variety of business settings. That work experience included managing a small business during the absence of the owner. I learned to handle money there and a variety of basic bookkeeping tasks. I also inventoried and organized products worth over three hundred thousand dollars. These experiences helped me understand the consequences of computer programming in a business setting. While I am new to the career of programming, I am familiar with computer language. My educational experience was very thorough and I have over 300 hours of interactive computer time as part of my course work. Because I am new, I plan to work harder and will spend extra time as needed to meet any deadlines."

Comments on this answer:

This response emphasizes transferable skills (knowledge of accounting procedures) and adaptive skills (meeting deadlines and working hard). This is necessary to counter a lack of previous work experience as a programmer. In this situation, what was learned in school is also very important and should be emphasized as the equivalent of "real" work.

Sample answer #2:

"In my previous position I used many of the same skills needed to do this job well. Even though it was in a different industry, managing a business requires the types of organizational and supervisory skills that I possess. Over the past seven years I guided my region to become one of the most profitable in our company. Sales expanded an average of 30 percent per year during the years I worked there, and profits rose at a similar rate. Since this was a mature company, such performance was highly unusual. I received two promotions during those seven years and rose to the executive level at a

pace, I was later told, no one had previously achieved. I am now seeking a challenge in a smaller, growth-oriented company such as yours. I feel my experience and contacts have prepared me for this step in my career."

Comments on this answer:

This response acknowledges that the previous career field differed from the one now being considered, but emphasizes achievements and prior success. To accomplish this, all sorts of executive skills would have had to be used. The response also includes the motivation to move on to the challenge of a smaller organization.

Problem Interview Question #7: "What Are Your Plans for the Future?"

Analysis of the question:

This question really explores your motives for working. It is asking whether you can be depended on to stay on at this job and work hard at it.

A strategy to use in answering the question:

As always, your best approach is an honest one. I'm not encouraging you to reveal negative information, but you should be prepared to answer the employer's concern in a direct and positive way. Which issues are of concern to an employer will depend on the details of your background.

For example:

➤ Will you be happy with the salary? (If not, might you leave?)

➤ Will you want to have a family? (If so, will you quit to raise children?)

➤ Do you have a history of leaving jobs after a short period of time? (If so, why won't you leave this one too?)

➤ Have you just moved to the area and appear to be a temporary or transient resident? (If so, you probably won't stay here long either, right?)

➤ Are you overqualified? (If so, what will keep you from going to a better job as soon as you find one?)

➤ Do you have the energy and commitment to advance in this job? (If not, who needs someone without energy and drive?)

➤ Might you appear to have some other reason to eventually become dissatisfied? (If so, the employer will certainly try to figure out what it is.)

Any of these reasons, and others, can be of concern to an employer. If your situation presents an obvious problem, use the standard Three-Step Approach to answering problem interview questions. If you feel you do not have any problem to defend, use steps #2 and #3 of the Three-Step Approach to assure the employer that, in effect, this is the precise organization you want to stay with and do well for – for at least the rest of your adult life.

Sample answer #1:

For a younger person or one just entering a new career:

"I realize I need to establish myself in this field and am very willing to get started. I've thought about what I want to do and am very sure my skills are the right ones to do well in this career. For example, I am good at dealing with people. In one position, I provided services to over 1,000 different people a week. During the 18 months I was there, I served well over 72,000 customers and not once did I get a formal complaint. In fact, I was often complimented on the attention I gave them. There I learned that I enjoy public contact and am delighted at the idea of this position for that reason. I want to learn more about the business and grow with it. As my contributions and value to the organization increase, I hope to be considered for more responsible positions."

Comments on this answer:

The employer wants to know that you will stay on the job and work hard for your pay. This response helps the employer feel more comfortable with that concern. (Note that this response could be based on work experiences gained in a fast-food job!)

Sample answer #2:

For a person with work history gaps or various short-term jobs:

"I've had a number of jobs (or one, or have been unemployed) and I have learned to value a good, stable position. The variety of my experiences are an asset since I have learned so many things I can now apply to this position. I am looking for a position where I can settle in, work hard, and stay put."

Comments on this answer:

This would be an acceptable response, except it is too short and no proof was offered. The ideal place to introduce a story would have been right before the last sentence. Some positions, such as sales-oriented ones, require you to be ambitious and perhaps aggressive. Other jobs have requirements particular to the career field or specific organization. You can't always predict what an employer might want, but you should have a good idea based on the work you will do in Section 2 of this book. If you do it correctly, you have what the position requires. You will simply need to say so.

Problem Interview Question #8: "What will your former employers (or teachers, references, warden, or keeper...) say about you?

Analysis of the question:

This question again refers to Employer Expectation #2. The employer wants to know about your adaptive skills – are you easy to get along with, are you a good worker, etc.? Your former employers may tell of any problems you had – or they may not. As you know, many employers will check your references before they hire you, so if anything you say here does not match what a former employer says, it could be bad news for you.

A strategy to use in answering the question:

Be certain to discuss your job-search plans with former employers. Do the same with anyone else who may be contacted for a reference. Clearly tell them the type of job you now seek and why you are prepared to do well in it. If a previous employer may say something negative, discuss this openly with your former supervisor and find out what he or she will say in advance.

If you were fired or resigned under pressure, you can often negotiate what would be said to a prospective employer. Lots of successful people have had personality conflicts with previous employers. If these conflicts are presented openly and in the best light possible, many interviewers are likely to understand. It may also be wise to get a written letter of reference, particularly from a not-too-enthusiastic employer. They will rarely be brave enough to write you a totally negative letter. And the letter may be enough to satisfy a potential employer. Larger organizations often don't allow phone references to be given, and this may be a great relief to you. Check it out by calling them and finding out.

If possible, use references that will say nice things about you. If your ex-boss won't, find someone who will. Often, an interviewer appreciates an honest response. If you failed in a job, telling the truth is sometimes the best policy. Tell it like it was but DO NOT be too critical of your old boss. Doing that will make you sound like a person who blames others and does not accept responsibility. Besides, you were partly at fault. Admit it, but quickly take the opportunity to say what you learned from the experience.

Sample answer:

> *"My three former employers will all say I work hard, am very reliable, and loyal. The reason I left my previous job, however, is the result of what I can only call a personality conflict. I was deeply upset by this, but decided that it was time I parted with my former employer. You can call and get a positive reference, but I thought it only fair to tell you. I still respect (that old hog). While there, I received several promotions and as my authority increased, there were more conflicts. Our styles were just not the same. I had no idea the problem was so serious because I was so involved in my work. That was my error and I have since learned to pay more attention to interpersonal matters."*

Comments on this answer:

This response could be strengthened by some introduction of positive skills along with a story to support them.

Problem Interview Question #9: "Why are you looking at this sort of position and why here?"

Analysis of the question:

The employer wants to know if you are the sort of person who is looking for any job, anywhere. If you are, she or he will not be impressed. Employers look for people who want to do what needs to be done. They rightly assume that such a person will work harder and be more productive than one who simply sees it as "just a job." People who have a good reason to seek a particular sort of position will be seen as more committed and more likely to stay on the job longer. The same is true for people who want to work in a particular organization.

A strategy to use in answering the question:

It is most important that you know in advance which jobs are a good match for your skills and interests. Section 2 of this book will help you clarify and explain your assets. In responding to the question, mention your motivations for selecting this career objective, the special skills you have that the position requires, and any special training or credentials you have which relate to the position.

The question actually has two parts. The first is why this position, and the second is why here? If you have a reason for selecting the type of organization you are considering or have even selected this particular organization as highly desirable, be prepared to explain why. If at all possible, learn as much as you can about the organizations you interview with in advance. Call other people to get details, use the library, ask for an annual report, or whatever else it takes to become informed.

Sample answer:

"I've spent a lot of time considering various careers and I think that this is the best area for me. The reason is that this career requires many of my strongest skills. For example, my abilities in analyzing and solving problems are two of the skills I enjoy most. In a previous position, I would often become aware of a problem no one had noticed and develop a solution. In one situation, I suggested a plan that resulted in reducing customer returns of leased equipment by 15 percent. That may not sound like much, but the result was an increase in retained leases of over $250,000 a year. The plan cost about $100 to implement. This particular organization seems to be the type that would let me develop my problem-solving skills. It is well run, growing rapidly, and open to new ideas. Your sales went up 30 percent last year and you are getting ready to introduce several major new products. If I work hard and prove my value here, I feel I would have the opportunity to stay with the business as it grows – and grow with it."

Comments on this answer:

This response uses "Prove It" nicely. It could have been said by an experienced manager or a good secretary.

Problem Question #10: "Why Don't You Tell Me About Your Personal Situation?"

Analysis of the question:

A good interviewer will rarely ask this question so directly. Casual, friendly conversation will often provide the information sought. In most cases, the interviewer is digging for information that would indicate you are unstable or undependable. For instance:

What they ask vs. what they really want to know. . .

The Issue	The Reason
Do you have marital or family troubles?	Missed work, poor performance, poor interpersonal skills
Do you handle money and personal responsibilities poorly?	Theft of property, irresponsible job-related decisions
Do you live in a good, stable home?	Socio-economic bias, renters less stable than owners
How do you use leisure time?	Drinking, socially unacceptable behavior
Do you have young children?	Days off and child care problems
Marital status?	If single, will you stay? If married, will you devote the necessary time?

A strategy to use in answering the question:

There are other issues that may be of concern to an employer. Often, these are based on assumptions the person has about people with certain characteristics. These beliefs are often irrelevant, but if the employer wonders whether you can be depended upon, it is in your own best interest to deal with these doubts. Be aware that even your casual conversation should always avoid reference to a potential problem area. In responding to a question about your personal situation, be friendly but positive.

Examples of appropriate answers:

Young children at home:

> *"I have two children, both in school. Child care is no problem since they stay with a good friend."*

Single head of household:

"I'm not married and have two children at home. It is very important to me to have a steady income and so child care is no problem."

Young and single:

"I'm not married and if I should marry, that would not change my plans for a full-time career. For now, I can devote my full attention to my career."

Just moved here:

"I've decided to settle here in Depression Gulch permanently. I've rented an apartment and the six moving vans are unloading there now."

Relatives, upbringing:

"I had a good childhood. Both of my parents still live within an hour's flight from here and I see them several times a year."

Leisure time:

"My time is family-centered when I'm not working. I'm also active in several community organizations and spend at least some time each week in church activities."

Comments on these answers:

While all of these responses could be expanded, they should give you an idea of the sorts of approaches you can take with your own answers. The message you want to give is that your personal situation will not hurt your ability to work and, indeed, could help it. If your personal life does disrupt your work, expect most employers to lose patience quickly. It is not their problem, nor should it be.

Handling Obvious and Not-So-Obvious "Problems"

Most job seekers have at least one problem which they fear will cause an employer to respond negatively. Some of these are obvious, that is, they can be seen by an employer during an interview; others are not so obvious but are the sort of thing an employer might not be enthusiastic about. How you handle these or similar problems differs depending on the situation. Many employers will not react in the way you expect and will give you a fair chance. They will be interested in your ability to do the job you seek. Your task is to convince them that your problem will not be an issue. Here are some considerations:

Does the problem affect your ability to do the work you seek? If it is a serious limitation or safety hazard, you should consider this in your selection of a position and consider changing your objectives. This does not necessarily mean you need to change careers, but it does mean that you should look for a position where the limitation is not serious. For example, a person with a prison record should not seek a job as a bank teller. A person with seizures should not paint tall houses. A person with back problems should not dig ditches.

Avoid Being Screened Out Early

Assuming your job objective is reasonable, but you still are concerned that you won't be seriously considered because of your problem, use job-search techniques that don't require you to reveal it too early.

If the problem is obvious or comes up in the interview, deal with it. Use the standard Three-Step Approach to Answering an Interview Question. If the problem is not obvious and won't seriously affect your ability to do the job, don't bring it up. Do not discuss your problem unless you fear you will eventually lose your job if it is found out. Wait until you have received or are negotiating a job offer. Too many job seekers reveal a problem on an application when they could have simply left the space blank. Too many bring up a problem that is not a problem at all in a preliminary interview ("I want you to know, madam, that a great aunt, once removed, had some odd habits.") Save your secret until after they like you and want to hire you.

Quick Case Study

Some time ago, I was helping a man who used a wheelchair to find a job. He wanted to work as a dispatcher. This position used his voice and his mind but not his legs and was a good job objective for him. Yet employers were often unwilling to hire him. The wheelchair probably was an issue. I helped him learn to get interviews by using the phone rather than filling out applications. Employers had no idea he was in a wheelchair until he came for the interview. He was direct about the problem and said he got there and would do the same every day. He then presented his skills and abilities to do the job. His approach forced the employer to focus on his ability to do the job rather than the fact that he was in a wheelchair. He got the job and was still there three years later.

Some Topics That Should Not Be an Issue – But Sometimes Are

Employers are people. They often want to know things about your personal situations that, perhaps, you think they have no right to know. Or perhaps you wonder whether an employer will treat you differently because of your status or some other factor that does not seem to affect your ability to do the job. For example, the following topics are sometimes an issue, even though they shouldn't be.

➤ Age

➤ Arrest record

➤ Disabilities or limitations

➤ Being unemployed

➤ Being fired

➤ Being overweight

➤ Gender

➤ Race or ethnicity

Chapter 5

➤ Religion

➤ Your plans to have children

I review these and other issues in chapter 16, always trying to give you a productive way to deal with them. There are laws that are designed to protect you from being treated unfairly in the hiring process. You can learn more about these in chapter 16. But the more important issue is how you can overcome whatever obstacle may be put before you so that you can get the best job you can handle. That is what this book is really about.

Some Final Interview Tips

You can't prepare for everything that might happen in an interview. But you will find that interviewing for jobs before they are advertised will be much easier and more comfortable than the traditional interview setting. But whatever interview you find yourself in, remember to be yourself and tell the employer why she or he should hire you.

You are now much better prepared to do well in the interview than most job seekers. And, if you read the rest of this book, you will be even better prepared.

Quick Summary

✔ **The Top 10 Problem Interview Questions:**

1. Why don't you tell me about yourself?

2. Why should I hire you?

3. What are your major strengths?

4. What are your major weaknesses?

5. What sort of pay do you expect to receive?

6. How does your previous experience relate to the jobs we have here?

7. What are your plans for the future?

8. What will your former employers (or teachers, if you are a recent student) say about you?

9. Why are you looking for this sort of position and why here?

10. Why don't you tell me about your personal situation?

CHAPTER SIX

Job Search Basics

JIST Cards –
A Powerful New Job Search Tool

Quick Overview

In this chapter, I review the following:

- ✓ JIST Cards – A powerful job search tool
- ✓ Six things a JIST Cards does
- ✓ How to use JIST Cards
- ✓ Why JIST Cards work so well
- ✓ Tips for creating JIST Cards

In this chapter, I introduce you to a powerful job search tool that I first developed back in the early 1970s. Many find it helpful to think of a JIST Card as a mini resume or as a special business card. While both analogies are helpful, I believe that a JIST Card is something very special in that it is a far more useful and effective job search tool than a resume and provides more information and impact than a business card.

I have included JIST Cards in the first part of the book because they are so different and because they work so well.

Let's Begin with Your Reaction to One

The best way to understand the impact of a JIST Card is to look at and react to one. I've provided a sample JIST Card on this page but, before you look at it, try to imagine that you are an employer who hires or supervises people with similar skills. While you may or may not have a job opening right now, try to react to the information you will be presented as you likely would if you were an employer in this situation. Simply react naturally, as yourself, when you read what follows.

```
Jonathan Michael                          Home: (614) 788-2434
                                       Message: (614) 355-0068

Objective: Management

Skills: Over seven years of management experience plus a B.S. degree in
Business. Managed budgets as large as $10 million. Experienced in cost
control and reduction, cutting over 20 percent of overhead while business
increased over 30 percent. Good organizer ad problem solver. Excellent
communication skills.

Prefer responsible position in a medium to large business

Cope well with deadline pressure, seek challenge, flexible
```

What Was Your Reaction?

Don't get too analytical about this, just note how you reacted as the JIST Card information was presented to you in your imagined role as an employer. With that mind-set, answer the questions that follow:

1. **Do you feel good about this person and how he presented himself?** (yes or no) _____

2. **Would you be willing to see him if you had a job opening?** (yes, no, or maybe) _____

3. **If he asked, would you be willing to see him even if you did not have a job opening?** (yes, no, or maybe)_____

It's Amazing, But Most People Are Willing to Set Up an Interview with Just 30 Seconds of Information

The odds are good that you reacted positively to the JIST Card you read. Most people can read a typical JIST Card in fewer than 30 seconds. Yet, in that short period of time, most people react in a positive way to what they read. I know because I constantly survey those who attend seminars I give and over 95 percent react positively to reading their first JIST Card. In fact, most people who read it say they would interview such a person – based on just this much information.

A few people do react negatively to the sample JIST Card you just read, saying that it does not present enough information or that the person sounds *too* good. It is true that a JIST Card does not present much information. It certainly does not give enough information to hire someone – but neither does a resume, application, or any other job search tool I know of.

Six Things a JIST Card Does

My observation is that a JIST Card's brevity is one of its major advantages.

It is the only job search tool I know of that can does all of the following:

1. **Creates a positive first impression**

2. **Provides specific details related to what a job seeker can do**

3. **Presents performance-related information in a memorable way**

4. **Provides both an effective tool for generating job leads and for presenting information**

5. **Predisposes most readers to consider giving the job seeker an interview**

6. **Provides information that can be presented or read in under 30 seconds**

Quick Comment

You might ask why this clever tool is called a JIST Card. Well, JIST is the name I came up with in the early 1970s that identified the job search program I had developed. I developed the idea of using 3-by-5 inch cards to overcome the limitations of resumes, cover letters, and applications and I continued to develop the concept into what you see here. I felt then that the cards deserved a unique name, hence JIST Cards.

Some Ways You Can Use a JIST Card

JIST Cards can help you get results in a way no other job search tool can. I have seen them posted on a grocery store bulletin board in Texas and on a table at a hairdresser's salon in southern California. I've even had friends tell me they found them under their windshield wiper after going to a movie. But here are some of the best uses.

✓ **Give to friends and relatives.** The odds are good that the people who know you best could not describe what you can do as clearly as a JIST Card can. Give some cards to the people you know best and ask them to circulate them to others who might know of openings for someone with your skills. Friends and relatives are a major source of job leads and you can quickly get hundreds of your cards into circulation this way. This can expand your network and increase the results dramatically.

✓ **As a business card.** Like a business card, you can give your JIST Card to almost anyone you meet during the time you are looking for a job. One example was a job seeker who gave a handful of JIST Cards to her insurance agent who put them in the waiting room where customers could see them. This resulted in several phone calls from employers and one job offer. This is an excellent way to equip your network contacts with a tool that they can use to help you.

✓ **Send to an employer before an interview.** Think about it. Send an informal note thanking someone for setting up an interview with you and enclose a JIST Card. It's just enough to arouse their interest.

✓ **Enclosed with a thank-you note after an interview or phone contact.** Sending an informal thank-you note is simply good manners. Enclosing a JIST Card is good sense. It's just one more way to tell the prospective employer about yourself and give them a tool for contacting you. I also know that this approach has often resulted in the person sending the thank-you note getting the job over those with better credentials.

✓ **Attached to an application.** When you have to complete an application (knowing as you do that it is not a good way to get an interview), attaching a JIST Card will allow the viewer to quickly get a positive overall impression. It can't hurt.

✓ **Attached to a resume.** Unlike a resume, you can read a JIST Card in 30 seconds. It provides a clear and direct presentation of what you want and what you can do. It can also help give the reader a positive perception of you as they get into the details of your resume.

✓ **As the basis for a telephone presentation.** With just a few changes, the JIST Card can be easily adapted to use as a telephone script for obtaining interviews. I'll show you how this is done in another chapter in this book.

✓ **As a source for answering interview questions.** Small as it is, a well-prepared JIST Card includes a variety of things you can use as the basis for answering interview questions. For example, in response to the question "Why don't you tell me about yourself?" you might say "You might want to know that I am a hard worker..." Or you can select almost any key skill, experience, or accomplishment statement from your JIST Card and use it as the basis for answering many interview questions.

In fact, even though the JIST Card is an effective job search tool, I believe that its greatest value is the way it forces us to get to the essence of what we have to offer an employer. It can foster a sense of identity and self-definition that comes through in an interview. I have seen it happen and know that it is true.

✓ **Creative uses.** People have found very creative ways to use their JIST Cards and I encourage you to do so as well. I will mention them from time to time elsewhere in this book as a tool to use in combination with another job search technique and you will think of other uses that I may not specifically mention.

For example, in chapter 2, I suggest that you develop a list of groups of people you know, then use them as a potential source of job leads. One group would be "people I went to school with." With that thought in mind, consider what might happen if you got the alumni list from your high school or college and sent ten JIST Cards to each person on that list along with a letter asking them to help you out. Think about it.

Why JIST Cards Work So Well

JIST Cards are clearly a different and nontraditional type of tool in the job search. Before I review why I think they work so well, let me tell you how I originally discovered their power.

How They Were First Developed

I developed JIST Cards in response to a need I saw. Back in 1972, there wasn't as much information on job seeking as there is now. In those days resumes, applications, personnel offices, and state and private employment agencies were the tools of the job search (and, unfortunately, remain the tools for many uninformed job seekers today). I was running a job search program and noticed that the traditional tools did not work well for me or most others.

Sending out lots of resumes, for example, netted few responses. Filling out applications at personnel offices seemed a process that took time but got few interviews. And the jobs available from the employment agencies were depressingly low skilled and entry level. I figured there had to be a better way.

I had been sending job seekers in my job search program out to knock on potential employer's doors without appointments, and a number of job seekers were getting jobs in this way. Most employers they visited were in small businesses that had no personnel department and no applications and the jobs sought (such as auto mechanic, factory worker, and food service worker) did not typically require resumes. So I suggested to the job seekers I had doing this to leave a 3-by-5 inch card with their name, job objective, and credentials. I also had them include my office phone number, which was professionally answered 24 hours a day. The first ones were handwritten.

Well, the reaction was interesting. Within days, I began to get calls asking for one of my people who had dropped in to an employer a few days earlier. It seemed that, while the employer did not have an opening at that time, they did now. And they wondered if so and so (who had dropped in and left their card) would give them a call. People got jobs as a result, lots of them. I paid attention.

As the weeks went by, I began getting calls from employers for job seekers who had dropped in weeks or even months earlier. They now had a job opening and wanted to know if the job seeker who had left the card was still available. Often they had already found a job but I could usually send out someone else. I learned from these employers that they had been impressed by the cards and the people who had left them behind. The employers liked the fact that these job seekers

Chapter 6

seemed more assertive, were clear about why they wanted this particular type of job, and communicated the skills they had to do it. They also told me that the cards were interesting and, since they didn't know what to do with them (since they did not file easily, like a resume or application) they had put them on their bulletin board or just left them on their desks.

Hmmm. I began to make the cards a bit better, by adding more details related to skills, experience, and credentials. Since they worked so well, I also produced several hundred of the cards for each person in the program so that they would pass them out freely. Phone calls from employers looking for those who had dropped off those early cards came rolling in. I got lots of good leads in this way from contacts others had made and lots of job seekers got jobs from these leads for jobs that were never advertised. I continued to develop the cards and came to call them JIST Cards since JIST was the name I had given to the job search program I ran way back in the early 1970s.

Seven Reasons JIST Cards Work So Well

Over the years, I have been continually surprised at how well JIST Cards work and I have some thoughts on why this is so.

✓ **1. They are short:** Since it takes less than 30 seconds to read, a JIST Card typically holds the reader's complete attention without interruption. Resumes, letters, applications, and conversations are unable to do this without distraction or the mind wandering. And, because they are short, they are "polite" and to the point in such a way that few will react negatively to the presentation.

✓ **2. They are clear:** A JIST Card quickly communicates what it is about. It gets to the point quickly and efficiently.

✓ **3. They create a positive impression:** While a well-done resume or application can also create a positive impression, they take longer to do so and often provide details that can be interpreted negatively (such as not having a degree or enough experience). A well-done JIST Card includes nothing that could be interpreted negatively and most readers are left with a positive (though admittedly general) first impression.

✓ **4. They are easy to pass along:** Because of their size and brevity, JIST Cards are far more likely to be passed along to another person than a resume or application. For this reason, they become a tool used by others in our network in ways that more traditional approaches never could. JIST Cards generate job leads in the hidden job market more effectively than any other job search tool I know of. Put a hundred of them in the right hands and they do get around in unexpected ways.

✓ **5. They are hard to file:** Resumes and applications get put away, thrown away, or lost in a pile. JIST Cards are less likely to be handled that way because of their format. Their small size also makes them more likely to be put on a bulletin board or in some location where they are seen.

✓ **6. They are memorable:** While I have been teaching people about JIST Cards since 1972, this is a very big country and they are new to most employers. The novelty of the format is memorable in itself but the content of a well-crafted JIST Card is also easily remembered by an employer, particularly when included in a thank-you note. It tends to help an employer remember (and be positively impressed by) one person over another.

✓ **7. They present the essence of what an employer wants to know:** In a very compact format, a typical JIST Card accomplishes the following:

> ➤ Introduces you by name

> ➤ Provides a way to contact you by phone

> ➤ Clearly states your job objective

> ➤ Summarizes your key credentials including relevant training and experience

> ➤ Presents the most important skills you have to do the job, often including specific accomplishments to support them

> ➤ Provides any extra flexibility such as willingness to relocate or work weekends (an optional section)

> ➤ Closes with a summary of important adaptive skills, personality traits, or other characteristics that make you a good choice for the job you seek without any negatives

A JIST Card can't replace a resume, it's simply different and I think that its power to help you generate leads in the hidden job market is justification enough for their use.

Tips on Creating Your Own JIST Cards

There is no doubt that the JIST Card is an effective new tool in the job search. Employers respond positively to JIST Cards and they can be used in ways a traditional resume cannot. But you may also find that they are more difficult to create than they at first appear. The reason is that they are sophisticated in their simplicity.

Quick Tip

If you have not done your homework, JIST Cards can be quite difficult to write. For example, you do need to have a clear idea of your job objective and the skills that best support it. A number of chapters in Part II of this book will give you lots of self-assessment activities and information that will help you sort out your job objective, skills, and other matters. If you need to get on with your job search right away, consider doing a basic JIST Card now and a better one later...

In order to create a good JIST Card you must know yourself very well, know what sort of job you are looking for, and be able to sort through all your personal information to find the few words that best describe your ability to do that job. It is also essential that every statement on your JIST Card be both accurate and true. Copying someone else's just won't do.

Writing an effective JIST Card may require some time on your part. The tips that follow should help you create each section of the card. As you assemble your own, consider asking others for feedback before you create your final version.

The Anatomy of a JIST Card

Identification ———

Job Objective ———

Skills Summary ———

Contact Information ———

John Kijek   **Home:** (219) 232-9213
                        Message: (219) 637-6643

Position Desired: Management position in a small- to medium-size organization.

Skills: B.A. in business plus over five years experience in increasingly responsible management positions. Have supervised as many as 12 staff and increased productivity by 27 percent over two years. Was promoted twice in the past three years and have excellent references. Started customer follow-up program that increased sales by 22 percent within 12 months. Get along well with others and am a good team worker.

Willing to travel and can work any hours

Hardworking, self-motivated, willing to accept responsibility

A JIST Card doesn't contain many details, but consider what John Kijek's card (the sample card at the beginning of this chapter) does include:

Identification: A simple courtesy, John's name is given.

A Way to Be Contacted: Few employers will write, so two phone numbers are provided. The first number is his home phone and the second is that of an answering service that is professionally answered 24 hours a day. This approach makes sure that John will get every call.

Related Education and Training: His JIST Card includes his education related to the job he wants.

Length of Experience: John lists his total length of work experience as well as the fact that he was promoted.

Skills and Accomplishments: This section tells what John can do and how well he can do it. These are job-related skills. John also mentions several important transferable skills such as his ability to supervise others and get results.

Preferred Working Conditions: John lists two preferences for the type of work he wants. Both of these are positives.

Good Worker Traits: John lists his adaptive skills that would be important to most employers.

And he does all this on a 3-by-5 inch card! If you didn't see it you may not have believed it possible to do all this in such a small format, but there it is.

Quick Tip

Suggestions for Completing Each Section

Following are suggestions for completing each section of your own JIST Card. Plan on writing several drafts before you write your final version.

Your name

Don't use nicknames or initials if possible. Keep it simple and don't include your middle name unless you go by that name.

Phone numbers

If you have an answering machine at home, you can use just one phone number. Remember that an employer will probably not call you twice, so make sure that you have a phone number that will be reliably answered 24 hours a day. If using a home number, make certain that family members are trained on how to answer calls professionally and be certain that they know how to take good notes, including repeating the name and phone number of the caller so that they get it right.

My preference is to include a second number if possible. Some people do not like leaving a message on an answering machine and a second number for "messages" makes it clear that an employer will leave a message there rather than speak with you directly. You can get a telephone answering service to give you a number that is answered by a real person 24 hours a day for about $30 a month. Commercial voice mail services are available for as low as $15 a month and this gets you a phone number as well as 24 hour service. And then there are pagers, cellular phones, call forwarding, and other phone options that might make sense for you.

Some JIST Cards also now include an Internet address or other way to leave computer E-mail, though this is appropriate only for jobs such as computer engineer and others where the employers are likely to be using those on-line services.

Notice that some of the sample JIST Cards give some information such as "message" or "answering service" before a phone number to inform the caller of what to expect. I also suggest that you always include your area code, since you never know how widely your JIST Cards might get distributed.

Job objective

Don't be too narrow in your job objective. Avoid job titles by saying "general office" rather than "receptionist," "accounting" rather than "controller," or "data processing" rather than "programmer" if you would consider a variety of jobs. If you are more specific in your job objective, try to avoid a job title but give other details. For example, say "management position in an insurance-related business" or "working with children in a medical or educational setting."

Chapter 16 provides lots of information on exploring career and job possibilities. If you aren't sure of what to include in your JIST Card's job objective, consider completing that chapter as soon as possible.

Don't limit yourself to entry-level jobs if you have the potential or interest in doing more. If you say "office manager," instead of secretary, or "business manager" instead of "supervisor," you just might get the better job. If you are not too sure of your ability to get a higher paying job, it is still best to keep your options open. Say "office manager" or "responsible secretarial position," for example.

Length of experience

You want to take advantage of all the experience you have that supports your job objective. If you are changing careers, have been out of the work world for awhile, or do not have much work experience related to the job you want, you may want to include other experiences to convince the employer you can do the job. Depending on your situation, here are some examples of things you might include:

Paid Work. You can list any work you were paid to do. Experience related to the job you are seeking is best, of course, and should be emphasized if you have it. But the work does not have to be similar to the job you are looking for now. Working in a fast food place while you went to school can count and so can a job in an unrelated career.

Volunteer Work. You can include volunteer work as part of your experience total. Consider doing so if you don't have very much paid work experience. The fact that you were not paid is not all that relevant and does not need to be mentioned until later.

Informal Work. If your paid work history is scanty, you can also include work you did at home or as an unpaid hobby. It is best if this work relates to the job, but it doesn't have to be. For example, if you worked on cars at home and want to be an auto mechanic, there is an obvious connection. You may have experience working in the family business or taking care of kids. Use this experience if your job-related paid work experience is weak.

Related Education and Training. Any training or education that might help you should be mentioned. Job-related classes in high school, in the military, in college, or any other setting can be used.

To figure out your total experience, complete the following table. Write either years or months (if you don't have much experience) in the spaces beside each question.

Your Total Experience Includes:	
1. Total paid work experience:	_____
2. Total volunteer work experience:	_____
3. Total informal work experience:	_____
4. Total related education or training:	_____
Total Experience:	_____

Other tips for writing your experience statement

Because everyone has a different background, no single rule for writing a good experience statement can be given for everyone. Here are some tips for writing your own experience statement.

If you have lots of work experience: If part of your work experience is not related to the job you want now, you can leave it out. For example, if you have 20 years of experience, say "Over 15 years of work experience" or include just the experience that directly relates to this job. This keeps the employer from knowing how old you are, should you be concerned about this.

If you don't have much paid work experience: You need to include everything possible. If you have no paid work experience in the field you want to work in, emphasize training and other work. For example, "Nearly two years of experience including one year of advanced training in office procedures."

Remember to include the total of all paid and unpaid work as part of your total experience. Include all those part-time jobs by saying "Over 18 months total work experience..."

If your experience is in another field: Just mention that you have "Four years work experience" without saying in what.

If you had raises and promotions: If you earned promotions, raises, or have other special strengths, this might be the time to say so. For example, "Over seven years of increasingly responsible work experience including three years as a supervisor. Promoted twice."

Education and training statement

Depending on your situation, you can combine your education and training with your experience (as in one of the examples just discussed) or list it separately. Don't mention it at all if it doesn't help you. If you have a license, certification, or degree that supports your job objective, you may want to mention it here, too. For example: "Four years of experience plus two years of training leading to certification as an Emergency Medical Technician."

Skills and accomplishments section

Think about the skills you have that are most important to do well in the job you want. This is the section where both transferable and job-related skills are mentioned. Use the language of the job to describe the more important things you can do. It is best to use some numbers to strengthen what you say and emphasize results. Instead of saying "Skills include typing, dictation," (and so on) say "Type 60 wpm accurately and take dictation at 120 wpm." You might mention any job-related tools or equipment you can use if that is appropriate.

Several chapters in Part 1 of this book can help you identify skills to emphasize in your JIST Card. Chapter 3 does a thorough job in identifying the adaptive and transferable skills you have while chapter 9 will help you identify job-related skills and accomplishments.

Emphasize results: It is too easy to overlook the importance of what you do unless you organize it correctly. Add up the numbers of transactions you handled in a previous job, the money you were responsible for, the results you got. Some examples:

➤ "Expanded sales territory to include over seven new states and increased sales by $1,500,000."

➤ A person with fast-food experience might write "Handled over 50,000 customer contacts with total sales over $250,000, quickly and accurately." (These figures are based on a five-day week, 200 customers a day for one year, and an average sale of $5.)

➤ Someone who ran a small store could say "Responsible for managing a business with over $250,000 in sales per year. Reduced staff turnover by 50 percent by introducing employee training and retention program."

➤ Present a successful fund-raising project as: "Planned, trained, and supervised a staff of six on a special project. Exceeded income projections by 40 percent."

Also include in this section one or more of your transferable skills that are important for that job. A manager might mention "Ability to train and supervise others," a receptionist might add "Good appearance and pleasant telephone voice." I recommend you give numbers to support these skills, too. A warehouse manager might say "Well-organized and efficient. Have reduced expenses by 20 percent while orders increased by 55 percent."

Preferred working conditions, flexibility, or other positive information

This is an optional section of your JIST Card. You can add just a few words to let the employer know what you are willing to do. Do not limit your employment possibilities by saying "Will only work days" or "No travel wanted." It is better to leave this blank than give anything negative. Look at the sample JIST Cards for ideas. Then write your own statement.

Adaptive skills/"good worker" traits

List three or four of your key adaptive skills. Choose skills that are important in the job you are seeking. You identified these skills in chapter 3.

Writing and Production Tips

The best way to write a JIST Card is to begin with longer versions until your content is getting pretty clean. Then edit, edit, edit. When you are working with such a small format, every word has to count. Use short, choppy sentences. Get rid of any word that does not directly support your job objective. Add more information if your JIST Card is too short. Then read your card out loud to see how it sounds.

After you have edited it down, ask someone else to help you with the final version. It is amazing to see how many typographical errors slip onto these little cards. (Hey, did you notice that there is a typo in Jonathan's sample JIST Card earlier in this chapter?) An employer might notice such an error and it will *not* create a positive impression. Here are some other tips for creating the final version.

✓ **Formatting**: You can type individual JIST Cards – or even handwrite them – but it is much better to have them printed in large quantities. Four copies of the same card can fit on one standard sheet of 8-1/2-by-11 inch paper. Make sure your final version is error-free and typed on a good typewriter or printed on a letter quality printer if using a computer-based word processor. Never use a dot-matrix printer or poor quality typewriter.

✓ **Making Copies**: Take the final version to a local print shop and have at least a hundred sheets printed. That will get you 400 JIST Cards, once they are cut. The cost for printing and cutting the cards should be $30 or so. You can also get them photocopied for a reasonable price at many quick print shops with copy machines. If you do this, make certain that you get excellent copy quality and that the copy machine can copy onto light card stock. If they don't carry light card stock, you can get it at most office supply stores.

✓ **Computer Generated JIST Cards:** If you have access to a word processor, you can print out excellent quality JIST Cards on a laser printer. While hard to obtain, you can also get special micro-perforated card stock that allows you to print out on 3" by 5" card stock and then tear off separate cards.

Quick Reference

JIST publishes a book titled *Using WordPerfect in Your Job Search* that provides details on creating JIST Cards, resumes, and other job search documents with WordPerfect, the most-used of all word processors. Written by David Noble, this is a very good book that provides lots of details on creating superior documents for use in the job search as well as tips for making your search more effective. It is the only book of its kind that I know of.

- ✓ **Desktop Publishing/Typesetting**: If you don't have your own computer and laser printer, you still have options. Many print shops can "typeset" your JIST Cards for a modest fee and it is usually worth it to get a professional appearance. Also note that this approach allows you to put more content on your card if you feel you need to.

- ✓ **Paper**: I recommend you use a light card stock in a buff, off-white, or pastel color such as light gray. Most print and copy shops will have a selection of card stock to show you and many office supply companies also carry it.

- ✓ **Design**: Some of the sample JIST Cards have been created using desktop publishing and employing different typefaces and simple design elements such as lines. Keep your design simple and uncluttered as well.

I have seen a variety of creative formats over the years, including business-sized cards, cards printed on both sides, folded cards with name and phone number on the front and other information inside, different ink colors, fancy printed papers, gold embossed printing, and other features. I liked some of these things but did not like others, so be as creative as you wish in your design, but do use good taste. Remember that the JIST Card's message is simple and the design should complement the message and not compete with it.

You might also want to consider coordinating the look of your JIST Card so that it matches your resume and stationery. You can use the same paper colors and textures, same ink color, and similar design elements.

You Have to Use JIST Cards for Them to Work

JIST Cards work best if you have hundreds of them in circulation, so once you have them, use them! Give them away freely because they will not help you get a job if they sit on your desk. To avoid delay, you may want to start with a few handwritten or typed JIST Cards reproduced on a photocopy machine. The better ones can come as you have time to improve them. But before you get a chance to, they may just help you get a job. . .

More Sample JIST Cards

Here are some more sample JIST Cards. To save space, they are less than full-size and vary from those for entry-level jobs (for persons just out of school) to those for professionals and other occupations. Study them and use any ideas that help you with your own card.

Sandy Zaremba   **Home:** (512) 232-7608
                                     Message: (512) 234-7465

Position Desired: General Office/Clerical

Skills: Over two years work experience plus one year of training in office practices. Type 55 wpm, trained in word processing operations, post general ledger, handle payables, receivables, and most accounting tasks. Good interpersonal skills and get along with most people. Can meet deadlines and handle pressure well.

Willing to work any hours

Organized, honest, reliable, and hardworking

Joyce Hua   **Home:** (214) 173-1659
                                     Message: (214) 274-1436

Position Desired: Programming/Systems Analyst

Skills: Over 10 years combined education and experience in data processing and related fields. Competent in programming in COBOL, FORTRAN, RPG II, BASIC PLUS, and database management on DEC and Prime computers. Extensive PC and network applications experience. Have supervised a staff as large as seven on special projects and have a record of meeting deadlines. Operations background in management, sales, and accounting.

Desire career-oriented position, will relocate

Dedicated, self-starter, creative problem solver

Paul Thomas
Home: (214) 173-1659
Message: (214) 274-1436

Position Desired: Research Chemist, Research Management in a small- to medium-size company

Skills: Ph.D. in Biochemistry plus over 15 years of work experience. Developed and patented various processes having current commercial applications worth many millions of dollars. Experienced with all phases of lab work with an emphasis on chromatography, isolation and purification of organic and biochemical compounds. Specialized in practical pharmaceutical and agricultural applications of chemical research. Have teaching, supervision, and project management experience.

Personal: Married over 15 years, stable work history, results and task oriented, ambitious, and willing to relocate

---

Richard Straightarrow
Home: (602) 253-9678
Answering Service: (602) 257-6643

Objective: Electronics installation, maintenance & sales

Skills: Four years work experience plus two year A.A. degree in Electronics Engineering Technology. Managed a $300,000/yr. business while going to school full-time, with grades in the top 25 percent. Familiar with all major electronics diagnostic and repair equipment. Hands-on experience with medical, consumer, communications, and industrial electronics equipment and applications. Good problem-solving and communication skills. Customer service oriented.

Willing to do what it takes to get the job done

Self-motivated, dependable, learn quickly

Juanita Rodriquez
Home: (639) 247-1643
Message: (639) 361-1754

Position Desired: Warehouse Management

Skills: Six years experience plus 2 years of formal business coursework. Have supervised a staff as large as 16 people and warehousing operations covering over two acres and valued at over $14,000,000. Automated inventory operations resulting in a 30 percent increase in turnover and estimated annual savings over $250,000. Working knowledge of accounting, computer systems, time & motion studies, and advanced inventory management systems.

Will work any hours

Responsible, hardworking, and can solve problems

Deborah Levy   **Home:** (213) 432-8064
                                    Message: (213) 888-7365

Position Desired: Hotel Management

Skills: Four years experience in sales, catering, and accounting in a 300-room hotel. Associate's degree in Hotel Management plus one year with the Boileau Culinary Institute. Doubled revenues from meetings and conferences. Increased dining room and bar revenues by 44 percent. Have been commended for improving staff productivity and courtesy. I approach my work with industry, imagination, and creative problem-solving skills.

Enthusiastic, well-organized, detail-oriented

Jonathan Michael   **Home:** (614) 788-2434
                                    Message: (614) 355-0068

Objective: Management

Skills: Over seven years of management experience plus a B.S. degree in Business. Managed budgets as large as $10 million. Experienced in cost control and reduction, cutting over 20 percent of overhead while business increased over 30 percent. Good organizer and problem solver. Excellent communication skills.

Prefer responsible position in a medium to large business

Cope well with deadline pressure, seek challenge, flexible

Quick Summary

✓ Six Things a JIST Card Does: A JIST Card's brevity is one of its major advantages. It is the only job search tool I know of that does all of the following:

1. **Creates a positive first impression**

2. **Provides specific details related to what a job seeker can do**

3. **Presents performance-related information in a memorable way**

4. **Provides both an effective tool for generating job leads and for presenting information**

5. Predisposes most readers to consider giving the job seeker an interview

6. Provides information that can be presented or read in under 30 seconds

✓ **Some Ways You Can Use a JIST Card:**

Give to friends and relatives.

As a business card.

Send to an employer before an interview.

Enclosed with a thank-you note after an interview or phone contact.

Attached to an application.

Attached to a resume.

As the basis for a telephone presentation.

As a source for answering interview questions.

✓ **Seven Reasons JIST Cards Work So Well:**

1. They are short.

2. They are clear

3. They create a positive impression.

4. They are easy to pass along.

5. They are hard to file.

6. They are memorable.

7. They present the essence of what an employer wants to know.

CHAPTER SEVEN

Job Search Basics

Make Your
Job Search into a Job
– *Organize Your Time to Get Results*

<table>
<tr><td>

Quick Overview

In this chapter, I review the following:

✓ How to set up your job search office

✓ How to organize your contacts

✓ How to set up a job search schedule

✓ More planning and scheduling tips

</td><td>

It's amazing, but if you have read the previous chapters in this book, you already know more about finding a job than most people in North America. But knowing and doing are two separate things. This chapter will help you develop a job search schedule and other techniques designed to turn getting a job into a job itself. It will give you a variety of techniques to conduct your job search campaign in an organized and efficient manner.

</td></tr>
</table>

Doing so can cut your job search time in half and that is the reason I have included this information in the first section of the book.

Your Objective: Get Two Interviews a Day

After many years of analyzing what works in the job search process, I have come to one very simple conclusion:

The more interviews you get, the sooner you will get a job offer.

This is a very simple thought, but accomplishing it seems to be a big block for most job seekers. I observe that a big part of the problem is that few job seekers have an organized plan. They muddle through their day without much discipline, work on their job search less than full time, and often don't get much done. The longer they remain unemployed, the less time is spent on looking for a job. Clearly, this is not a good thing to do.

Quick Fact

The average job seeker gets about two interviews per week and spends fewer than 15 hours a week on the job search. At that rate, it takes an average of three to four months to find a job. For most people, that is much longer than it needs to be.

Quick Advice

As an alternative to the normal and ineffective job search, I suggest two things:

1. That you set out to spend more time on actually looking for work

2. You get at least two interviews each day throughout your job search.

Quick Reminder

With the new definition of an interview I am using in this book, getting those two interviews a day can suddenly become quite possible. Remember, an interview can now be any face-to-face contact with a person who hires or supervises people with your skills – whether or not they have a job opening now.

Armed with my new and broader definition of what counts as an interview, getting them becomes much easier. While getting two interviews a day is not possible for someone conducting a traditional job search, nontraditional methods make it quite possible for you to get two interviews a day. If you do, there is a fairly simple arithmetic that begins to work to your advantage and I present it below.

The Arithmetic of Getting Two Interviews a Day

2 interviews a day x 5 days a week = 10 interviews a week

10 interviews a week x 4 weeks = 40 interviews a month

Contrast this with the fact that the average job seeker gets fewer than two interviews a week and takes three to four months to get a job. At that pace, it takes 24 interviews or so to get a job. With 40 interviews in just one month it's easy to understand how people using my approach cut their job search time in half. So part of the secret of job search success is to devote as much time and energy to *getting* a job as you will to keeping it once you have found it. In a very real sense, getting a job *is* a job. If you approach it in this way you are much more likely to get a job in less time. It's simple arithmetic.

Set Up Your Job Search Office

To organize your job search as if it were a job, you need a place where you can work. Usually, this will be a place in your home that can be set aside as your job search office. Following are some essentials you'll need to help you set up this office.

Even if you don't have the luxury of a home office, it is important that you set up a place where you can conduct your job search work without interruption. It is important that you can concentrate on your work, so if you have children or other at-home responsibilities, arrange for someone else to care for them during your "office hours." Ask for cooperation from all family members to avoid interference during your job search time.

It is best to select a place where you can safely leave your materials and equipment so that you won't have to set up your work space every day. At the very least, you will need a table or desk to write on, a chair, and enough space to store your materials and accommodate your office equipment.

Basic materials and equipment

As you work on your job search, you will find a variety of reference materials, office supplies, and other things that will help you get your job search work done. Here are the basics you will need:

➤ **A telephone.** It is essential that you have access to a telephone throughout your job search. If you don't have one, set up your office in the home of a friend or relative who does.

➤ **Erasable ball-point pens.** I prefer black or blue ink pens and erasable ones are helpful in correcting errors on, say, an application form.

➤ **Lined paper or note pads.** Use these for notes and contact lists.

➤ **3-by-5 inch cards.** These can be used in a variety of ways and I suggest that you have several hundred of them on hand.

➤ **A 3-by-5 inch card file box with dividers.**

➤ **Thank-you notes and envelopes.**

➤ **Multiple copies of your resumes and JIST Cards.**

➤ **Business-sized envelopes.** Get ones that match your resume paper if possible, as they create a better impression

➤ **Postage stamps.** You will need lots of these and the post office has a plastic holder for dispensing a roll of stamps one at a time – a cheap and time saving approach.

➤ **A current copy of the *Yellow Pages* phone book.** You might want copies of the *Yellow Pages* for surrounding areas as well. These books are no longer free in most areas but you can buy copies for anywhere in the country. Contact your local phone company to find out how.

➤ **Calendars and planning or schedule book.**

➤ **Access to a good print quality typewriter or computer word-processor.**

➤ **A copy of this book, of course.**

If you have a computer

More and more people have computers at home now, and they provide an obvious advantage when doing correspondence, revising a resume, and for other tasks. I'll mention their use from time to time throughout this book, providing a few tips on using them in the job search.

If you don't have a computer

If you know how to use a computer for word-processing but don't have one at home, try to get access to someone else's. Some libraries have them available for use there, or borrow one from a friend.

If you are not computer literate, don't get distracted from your job search by trying to learn now. You can get resumes done professionally at many print shops, secretarial services, and other sources. I'll provide more details on doing so in the chapter on resumes and cover letters.

Organize Your Contacts and Follow Ups

By using the job search methods you have learned so far, you can quickly develop hundreds of contacts. Keeping track of them all is more than your memory can handle, and they will quickly become disorganized unless you develop some sort of a system to keep them.

My earliest attempts at doing this involved putting one page per contact in a three-ring binder. This was better than the loose pieces of odd sized notes I had been putting on a bulletin board to remind me to follow up on things. Over the years, I developed some simple systems that work very well and that I highly recommend you use in your own job search.

Contact-management software

There are a variety of commercially available contact-management software packages that are designed to assist salespeople and others to follow up on personal contacts. Most allow you to enter information on a contact (including name, address, and phone numbers) and then make notes related to each. They typically allow you to set up a follow up date for the computer to remind you to call them back or to take some other action as that date approaches. Many allow you to create form letters that can be modified and sent as needed, sort contacts by your criteria, and do other helpful tasks.

You will find these types of programs at virtually any larger software store, and they can be quite useful if you have access to a computer and are reasonably computer literate.

Quick Alert

There are also some software packages that take many hours to set up and learn and that don't work particularly well. So before you run out and buy such a program consider whether it is worth doing at all.

My own opinion is that you can get by just fine with the low-tech alternative I will present in the next section. I have used contact-management software and like the better ones, but I prefer the simpler and noncomputerized system for use in the job search. Read on and you can decide for yourself.

Manual systems work just fine

There is something to be said for simplicity, and the manual system I will describe has evolved after many years of experience and it works just fine.

Job lead cards

Look at the following 3-by-5 inch card. It shows the kinds of information you can keep about each person who helps you in your job search.

Organization: *Mutual Health Insurance*
Contact Person: *Anna Koch*   **Phone:** *701-355-0216*
Source of Lead: *Uncle Bob*
Notes: *4/10 called. Anna on vacation. Call back 4/15.*
4/15 interview set 4/20 at 1:30. 4/20 Anna showed
me around. (Friendly people) Sent thank-you note and
JIST card. Call back 5/1. 5/1 second interview 5/8 at 9 a.m.!

Quick Tip

Although the card used in this example is specially printed, you can keep the same kind of information on blank 3-by-5 inch cards available at most department and stationery stores. You should create one card for each person you contact during your job search. Include anyone who gives you a referral, interviews you, or who is a potential employer or contact. Keep brief notes on the cards each time you talk with them to help you remember important details for your next contact.

Develop a job lead card box

Most department and stationery stores have small boxes made to hold 3-by-5 inch cards. They also have tabbed dividers for these boxes, with room to write on. Buy an inexpensive card file box and enough dividers to set up a box as described here.

Set up a file box divider for each day of the month, numbering them 1 through 31. Once this has been done, file each completed Job Lead Card under the date you want to follow up. Here are some examples of how this system can be used.

Example 1: You get the name of a referral to call, but you can't get to it right away. You create a Job Lead Card and file it under tomorrow's date.

Example 2: You call someone from a *Yellow Pages* listing, but the person is busy this week and tells you to call back in two weeks. You file the Job Lead Card under the date exactly two weeks in the future.

Example 3: You get an interview with a person who doesn't have any jobs now, but he gives you a name of someone else who might. After you send a thank-you note, you file this Job Lead Card under a date a few weeks in the future.

As you contact more and more people in your job search, the number of people you file away for future follow-up will keep increasing. You will develop more and more "new" leads as you follow up with people you've already contacted one or more times in the past.

Quick Reminder

Following up makes a difference. Once you have contacted someone, it often pays to send them a thank-you note and then stay in touch with them repeatedly throughout your job search. While following up is a simple concept, it does work. Remember that most people get their jobs from people they know and following up allows you to maintain these contacts in a more effective way. This is one of the most effective ways of getting a job.

At the beginning of each week, you simply review all the Job Lead Cards you filed for the week. On your weekly schedule, list any interviews or follow-up calls you promised for a particular time and date. At the beginning of each day, pull the Job Lead Cards filed under that date and list them on your Daily Contact Sheet (described in the following section) for that day.

Use a daily contact sheet

To help you organize your daily activities, I have found that it helps to create a simple listing of people you plan on contacting that day. You can create this simple form on regular lined sheets of paper. The sheet has four columns as in the following example:

Daily Contact Sheet

Daily Contact Sheet
Date: _____

Contact Name/ Organization	Referral Source	Job Lead Card	Phone Number

Quick Advice

Complete one of these forms each day. I suggest that you list at least 20 people or organizations to contact before you begin any phone calls that day. Use any source to get these leads – referrals, Job Lead Cards from your card file box, potential contacts from the *Yellow Pages*, jobs listed in the want ads, warm contacts you have not yet called, and any other legitimate lead or contact. Check the Job Lead Card column on the form if you have made a card for that contact.

Establish and Stick to a Job Search Schedule

At work, I have a variety of ways that I schedule my time so that I set priorities and get high priority tasks done. But when you are out of work, you don't have a lot of the structure that you take for granted at work. You have to create this structure beginning with the basics, such as how many hours a week you plan to work on your job search.

Quick Tip

I know that this may seem silly to you but trust me on this: doing what I suggest in this section is important. Having a detailed schedule made out in advance makes it far more likely that, come next Tuesday, you will be productively involved in getting interviews rather than goofing off.

Begin with a Weekly Job Search Schedule

Here are five simple steps that will help you get started in setting up your job search as a job.

Step 1: Decide how many hours per week to look

How many hours per week do you plan to spend looking for a job?

In most cases, I recommend at least 25 hours per week for a person who is looking for full-time work. An active job search is difficult work, and 40 hours per week is too much for many people. Since the average job seeker spends fewer than fifteen hours per week actively looking for work, 25 hours per week is a big improvement.

Whatever you decide is fine but you should realize that the less time you spend, the longer you are likely to be unemployed.

> Write here the number of hours per week you plan to spend looking for a job: _____.

Step 2: Decide which days to look

Decide which days each week you will use to look for work. Since most businesses are open Monday through Friday, these days are often the best days to look. In the first column of the following form check the days you plan to use for your job search. Don't mark in the other columns yet.

Weekly Planning Worksheet

Day	Number of Hours	Time
_____ Monday	_____	_____
_____ Tuesday	_____	_____
_____ Wednesday	_____	_____
_____ Thursday	_____	_____
_____ Friday	_____	_____
_____ Saturday	_____	_____
_____ Sunday	_____	_____
Total No. Hours/Week	_____	_____

Step 3: **Decide how many hours per day to look**

Decide how many hours you will spend looking for work on each of the days you selected on the Weekly Planning Worksheet. For example, if you selected Mondays, you may decide to spend five hours each Monday looking for work. You would then write "5" in the "Number of Hours" column on the form. Do this with all the days you checked until the total equals or exceeds the number of hours per week you listed in Step 1.

Step 4: **Decide what times each day to look**

Using the same Weekly Planning Worksheet, use the remaining time column to list the times you will use each day to look for work. For example, if you decided to spend six hours each Monday looking for work, you might decide to begin at 8 a.m. and work till noon (4 hours), take an hour off for lunch, then work from 1 to 3 p.m. (2 hours).

Go ahead and complete this section of the worksheet now, though I know you are resisting doing this.

Step 5: **Transfer your job search schedule to a calendar**

Use a monthly calendar to mark off the days and times you've scheduled each day of each week to look for a job. A regular calendar sheet will do for this, allowing you to see your basic schedule for an entire month at a glance. I've provided a generic calendar page for you to use, although you would be better off using a larger and current calendar sheet with the correct preprinted dates on it.

SUN	MON	TUE	WED	THU	FRI	SAT

Develop a Daily Job Search Schedule that Gets Results

You have now decided what days and what hours to spend each week on your job search. But what will you do each day? You still need a more specific daily plan to get the most out of each hour of your job seeking schedule.

After much experimentation, I have developed a simple daily schedule that I recommend you consider. It emphasizes your setting up interviews in the morning and going to interviews in the afternoon. This is the same basic daily activity schedule that I have used in structured job search programs where participants achieved dramatic reductions in time spent getting jobs. Look it over carefully and adapt it to fit your needs.

A Recommended Daily Job Search Schedule	
7:00 a.m.	Get up, shower, dress, and eat breakfast.
8:00 to 8:15 a.m.	Organize your job search office, review schedule for interviews or promised follow-ups, update daily schedule as needed.
8:15 to 9:00 a.m.	Review Job Lead Cards and old leads for follow-up, develop new leads (from want ads, *Yellow Pages*, warm contact lists, etc.), complete Daily Contact Sheet.
9:00 to 10:00 a.m.	Make new and follow-up phone calls to get interviews and referrals.
10:00 to 10:15 a.m.	Take a break.
10:15 to 11:00 a.m.	Make more phone calls.
11:00 to Noon	Make follow-up calls, send follow-up notes and resumes as needed.
Noon to 1:00 p.m.	Lunch break.
1:00-3:00 p.m.	Go on interviews, cold contacts in the field, research for interviews at library.

Quick Tip

Of course, you can adapt the schedule that I recommend to meet your own needs. It is, after all, your schedule. But do pay attention to the principles involved as they have been used successfully by many thousands of people. For example, my recommended schedule encourages you to use the telephone as a primary tool for developing job leads because it is quite effective in doing so. It creates blocks of time that allow you daily changes in activities that include getting you out of your job search office into the real world. And it helps you resist the natural inclination to sit home and feel sorry for yourself.

Additional Planning and Scheduling Tips

Quick Reminder

Remember that we have redefined an interview. An interview now includes seeing people who hire people like you but don't necessarily have a job opening.

With this in mind, consider the following additional tips.

✓ Set a Daily Objective for Interviews

Your goal should be to get at least two interviews per day, every day. Remember that since we redefined what an interview is, they are now easy to get. Many people get more than two interviews per day if they use the techniques I suggest.

✓ Expect to Get Rejected

While I haven't met many normal people who handle rejection well, the job search process requires that you seek rejection. I say this because. . .

> ### The more you get rejected, the closer you are to getting accepted. Somewhere.

One example of how seeking rejection pays off is in making cold contact phone calls. After many years of experience in running job search programs, I know that you will need to make 10 to 15 of these calls to get one interview. While that sounds like a lot of rejection (and it is), most people can make that many calls in an hour; so two hours of calls can result in two interviews. The calls that don't get you an interview are often friendly and rarely unfriendly, so the rejection you experience is really no big deal.

✓ Make Phone Calls, Be Active

You won't get a job by reading job search books or working on your resume. Save those activities for weekends, evenings, and other times. During the day, concentrate on active job search methods that result in your setting up interviews.

✓ Stick to Your Schedule

Arrange interviews at times other than those you planned to spend in your job search office. In my suggested daily schedule, I leave each afternoon open for interviewing and for cold contacts in the field. Job search office hours are in the mornings and focus on setting up interviews. Blocking your time use in simple ways such as this will help you do what you need to get done without loss of focus. Plan to take care of your personal business after your office hours, too.

✓ Don't Get Discouraged

Looking for a job is hard work, so take time for breaks and take time to take care of yourself. It's easy to get discouraged, but find a way to keep a positive attitude and keep going out to get interviews.

Unemployment is a good time to reflect on what is really important in life, and most people learn that it is other people that matter most to them. Don't lose contact or reject support from others because they often want to help you in your job search. The best antidote to unemployment is work, so find a way to get out there and find someone to hire you.

✓ Use Commercially Available Schedule Books

I use a pocket-sized schedule book sold by Day-Timers, Inc. (phone 215-266-9000) and can't imagine being without something like this. There are a number of similar organizing books and systems available in good department and stationery stores. Consider getting one for keeping track of daily appointments and tasks.

✓ Try Computerized Scheduling

Though some people use scheduling software on their computers, I prefer a system that is portable and more readily updated when a computer is not accessible, such as a schedule book.

Now You Know How to Find a Job, But. . .

You now know far more than the average job seeker about finding job leads and getting interviews. With what you know now, you can probably go out and find a job in less time. But there are other things for you to learn that will be of great value to you in your job search. For example:

➤ Do you know precisely the kind of job you want? Most people have only a general idea.

➤ Will you be able to handle the tough interview questions you will be asked? Perhaps not as well as you might.

➤ Do you have a specific plan on how to spend your time each day during your job search? Very few people do.

The rest of this book prepares you for the job search in three ways:

1. The first is by helping you to better understand yourself. Knowing who you are, what you have done, and what you are good at are important things to know.

2. Once you explore yourself, you then need to consider what it is you want in a job. Not just any job should do, you see.

3. When you have figured out the type of job you want, then – and only then – are you ready to learn more about job seeking techniques such as interviewing, making phone contacts, writing resumes, organizing your time, and others. That is what the rest of this book is about – job search methods that work.

You now know enough about finding job leads to go out and find one in less time. I hope you go out and find a great job before you finish this book. It happens. . .

In Conclusion

Quick Advice

The final lessons I can offer as I end this section are these:

Trust yourself. No one can know you better than you.

Decide to do something worthwhile. Whether it is raising a family or saving the whales, believe in something you do as special, as lasting, as valuable.

Work well. All work is worth doing, so put your energy into it and do it as well as you are able.

Enjoy life. There is always something to marvel at if you look for it.

Send thank-you notes. Many people will help you throughout your life, in large and small ways. Let them know you appreciate them. The more you give, the more you seem to get in return.

Quick Summary

✓ The more interviews you get, the sooner you will get a job offer.

✓ The average job seeker gets about two interviews per week and spends fewer than 15 hours a week on the job search. At that rate, it takes an average of three to four months to find a job. For most people, that is much longer than it needs to be.

✓ As an alternative to the normal and ineffective job search, I suggest two things:

1. That you set out to spend more time on actually looking for work.

2. You get at least two interviews each day throughout your job search.

✓ To organize your job search as if it were a job, you need a place where you can work. Usually, this will be a place in your home that can be set aside as your job search office.

✓ Basic materials and equipment include: A telephone, erasable ball-point pens, lined paper or note pads, 3-by-5 inch cards, a 3-by-5 inch card file box with dividers, thank-you notes and envelopes, multiple copies of your resumes and JIST Cards, business-sized envelopes, postage stamps, the *Yellow Pages* phone book, copies of the *Yellow Pages* for surrounding areas, calendars and planning or schedule book, access to a good print quality typewriter or computer word-processor, and a copy of this book, of course.

✓ Contact-management software packages are designed to assist salespeople and others to follow up on personal contacts. Most allow you to enter information on a contact including name, address, and phone numbers and then makes notes related to each. You can keep the same kind of information on blank 3-by-5 inch cards and set up a job lead card box.

✓ To help you organize your daily activities, create a daily contact sheet, listing the people you plan to contact for the day. Complete one of these forms each day. List at least 20 people or organizations to contact before you begin any phone calls that day. Use any source to get these leads.

✓ Establish and stick to a job search schedule. Five simple steps that will help you get started in setting up your job search as a job:

Step 1: Decide how many hours per week to look (I recommend at least 25 hours per week)

Step 2: Decide which days to look

Step 3: Decide how many hours per day to look

Step 4: Decide what times each day to look

Step 5: Transfer your job search schedule to a calendar

✓ Develop a daily job search schedule. My recommended schedule encourages you to use the telephone as a primary tool for developing job leads because it is quite effective in doing so. It creates blocks of time that allow you daily changes in activities that include getting you out of your job search office into the real world. And it helps you resist the natural inclination to sit home and feel sorry for yourself

Section 2:
Preparing for
the Job Search –

Career Planning and

Job Search Homework

Section 2 Introduction

The title of this section is not exciting and you will probably not want to review it. But before you pass it over completely, let me argue that this section is well worth your time.

I say this because much of the information it provides will help you make more informed career plans or be more effective in your job search. For example, Chapter 8 presents an important overview of the labor market and emphasizes trends that you should consider in making career plans. Chapters 9 and 10 are designed to help you clearly identify just what kind of job you want and the experiences that best support your ability to handle it. And the last chapter in this section reviews a variety of sources of information on jobs and employers.

While this is not all "fun" reading, taking the time to complete the chapters will give you a competitive advantage over those who have not. Its just like doing homework: not fun but necessary if you want to do well...

Chapters in This Section

Chapter 8: Labor Market Trends – Looking for Work in the New Economy

Provides important information for you to consider in planning your career or educational options, including lots of interesting data.

Chapter 9: Document Your Experience and Accomplishments

Reviews your work, education, leisure, and other life experiences to identify strengths and to document specific situations that can support your key skills.

Chapter 10: Define Your Ideal Job – Then Identify Specific Job Targets

It seems obvious that you should be as clear as possible about what you want in a job before you go looking for it. This chapter will help even those with a clear job objective by helping you identify just what it is you really want.

Chapter 11: Research Before the Interview – Print and Computer Resources

Reviews the many excellent sources of information available on jobs and employers.

CHAPTER EIGHT

Preparing for the Job Search

Labor Market Trends –
Looking for Work in the New Economy

≡Quick Overview

In this chapter, I review the following

✓ Some hard facts about the new economy – 12 employment trends to be aware of and understand.

✓ How often people change jobs (or careers), and the real cost of unemployment.

✓ The good news: Jobs are out there, and you can find them. Where the jobs are – 9 positive trends to put to your advantage.

✓ How career planning and job seeking skills can give you the competitive edge.

If you like facts, this chapter should be one of your favorites. It provides a thorough review of labor market trends and how this relates to your career planning and job seeking. This is an important chapter because it forms a basis for understanding much of what I suggest in the rest of this book.

This is one of the more difficult chapters to write because it requires so much research and thought on my part. There has been so much change in the labor market that affects how we look for work and plan our careers, yet few people are aware of how old-fashioned their concepts are. I hope this chapter helps you to understand why you need to act differently in today's labor market.

Some Hard Facts About the New Economy

Things are not like they used to be. Our economy has changed so rapidly that, for most of us, our concepts about how to plan our careers – and how to find a job – are completely out of date. This can be a dangerous and expensive situation. The average person will change jobs far more frequently than their parents. They will also change their careers more often than in the past. While there are a variety of reasons for this, the fact is that there are now huge negative economic consequences for those who are unprepared for our changed economy.

Think about it. At its simplest level, a job search now costs more money than it used to. The average length of unemployment is longer, varying between 15 and 20 weeks, depending on the rate of unemployment. Lost earnings and benefits during this time can be substantial. Even at modest salary levels, it adds up to thousands of dollars. Making things even worse is the fact that people change jobs more frequently now. Over your work life, the average cost of looking for work can be enough to buy a very nice car. Or a big yacht.

Our economy has changed dramatically since the end of World War II. Even in the more recent years from the mid-1970s, change has been more rapid than most people realize. Newspaper articles and other media sources constantly present stories on the many economic and demographic changes now occurring. For example, most of us know that there are more women in the paid workforce than ever before and that the baby boomers are aging. But what does all of this mean? And how do these changes affect each of us?

The fact is that literally every person who works now or in the future will be affected by the changed labor market. Following are some of the major trends.

How Much Does Unemployment Cost?

With the average length of unemployment hovering at about 19 weeks, figure it out:

For each $10,000 of annual income, your cost is $3653.85. And that's just for one bout of unemployment!

Even worse than the financial cost of a protracted job search is the long-term consequences of poor career planning: unhappiness, loss of self-esteem, missed promotions, and other problems. The need for improved job search and career planning may not be obvious if you have not thought about it much. If that is the case for you, consider the details that follow in this chapter.

A Closer Look at the Unemployed

At the time I wrote this book, there were 126 million people in the workforce and 5.9 percent of them were counted among the unemployed. Only about half of these people, 46.7 percent of the unemployed or 2.7 percent of the workforce, lost their jobs involuntarily. Of the remaining 3.2 percent who were unemployed, 1.8 percent are reentering the workforce, and another .7 percent are first time job seekers.

Only about half of the unemployed are "unemployed" in the traditional sense. But about one in six people experience at least some unemployment each year.

Table 8-1	The Reasons People Are Unemployed*		
	1992	1993	1994
Job Losers	56.4	54.6	46.7
On temporary layoff	13.3	12.6	10.3
Not on temporary layoff	43.1	42.0	36.3
Job Leavers	10.4	10.8	11.7
Reentrants	23.7	24.6	33.7
New entrants	9.5	10.0	8.0

* Percentages of the unemployed, by reason.

One way to look at this data is that less than half of the unemployed are unemployed in the traditional sense. Consider the arithmetic:

Those who left their jobs voluntarily	11.7%
Looking for a job after having been out of the labor market for awhile	33.7
First-time job seekers	8.0
On temporary layoff/expect to return	10.3
Percent of the unemployed who are not normally considered as "unemployed" by most people	63.7
Percent of the unemployed who most would consider as "unemployed" in the traditional sense	36.3

With an overall unemployment rate of 5.9 percent, this means that only 2.14 percent of the workforce is "unemployed" in the way most people define it.

Those unemployment rates may not sound all that high to you until you consider that about 17 percent of men and 12.5 percent of women in the workforce experience some unemployment during each year. That is about one in six of us. And, if you are unemployed, the unemployment statistics, either good or bad, offer no consolation.

Unemployment Varies by Age, Gender, Race, and Other Factors

Being unemployed is typically a solitary experience. Statistics just don't apply to individuals. Even so, you may find it of interest that unemployment statistics do change based on various sociological factors. For example, I present information elsewhere in this chapter that shows a direct relationship between higher levels of education and lower levels of unemployment. People who make more money also tend to take longer to find a job than those whose earnings are lower. Higher-earning individuals also tend to be older, so you have to ask whether it is the age or earnings that results in a longer or shorter job search. Or both?

Women, on average, experience fewer bouts of unemployment than men, and they tend to find jobs more rapidly when they need to. Is that because they accept lower paying jobs than men do? Or is it because women have tended to be in service sector jobs (where all the job growth has been) while more men have traditionally been in the goods producing sector? Do women earn less than men with comparable levels of education because they are women, or because women of the same age and educational level as men have fewer years in the labor force?

There has been a lot of research into all of these questions, and my observation is that no one seems to know for sure.

 Some people are unemployed for long periods of time. The recent average length of unemployment was 18.1 weeks. While half of all people found jobs in 8.4 weeks, over 20 percent were unemployed longer than 15 weeks. And this does not count "discouraged workers," those who were unemployed but not actively looking.

It is clear that many people suffer severe economic hardship from unemployment. You can look at all sorts of statistics to try to understand why the job market is so bad for you, but the more important issue remains an individual one: "What can I do to get a good job in as little time as possible?" Answering that question is the focus of this book.

Trend #1: People Change Jobs More Often

My father retired from an organization where he had worked for almost 30 years. It was one of the FORTUNE 500 companies, and – believe it or not – they gave him a gold watch when he retired. That wasn't all that unusual a situation for people who retired in the 1960s and 70s. They tended to stay with an organization for many years.

It's different today. The average 35-year-old has changed jobs between six and seven times since he or she began working. Even those over 35 change jobs fairly frequently – on average, every three years or so. That represents a lot of job changes over the average person's working life.

How Often a Person Changes Jobs

How often a person changes jobs is closely related to age and income, which is, in turn, related to educational level. An article titled "Occupational Tenure, Employer Tenure, and Occupational Mobility" (published in *the Occupational Outlook Quarterly*, volume 34, number 2) provides a good review of how all this works.

The mean duration on the job for 16 to 24-year-olds is only 1.9 years, while for 25 to 34-year-olds, it jumps to 5.4 years and goes to 10 years for 35 to 44-year-olds. Averages are considerably higher since they include people who change jobs very often and the mean, as used in the figures above, may be a more meaningful way to look at this.

Trend #2: More Career Changes Expected

People change their careers more frequently now, too. A change in careers is more significant than a job change because it involves changing from one occupational group to another. A teacher who moves into real estate sales is but one example.

It is now estimated that the average worker will change *careers* from five to seven times. Five to seven times! That is a lot of career changing.

The following contribute to this trend:

➤ Changing technologies

➤ More frequent job changing

➤ More adults attending post-secondary training and educational programs

➤ Corporate downsizing

➤ Many other factors

Data on Career Changes

Years ago, a study by Ellen Sehgal titled "Occupational Mobility and Job Tenure in 1983," (*Monthly Labor Review* volume 107, number 10) indicated that over 7 percent of employed adults were changing careers that year – a rate of between 6 and 7 career changes during the average person's work life. More recent data indicates that the average occupational tenure is 6.6 years (Occupational Outlook Quarterly, volume 34, number 2). Over a work life of 45 years, that would result in 6.8 career changes.

Trend #3: The Older We Get, the More Stable We Become (Occupationally Speaking)

How does your work history stack up against others' – or what should you expect as "normal" for your future job and career changes? As you might guess, the answer varies. The U.S. Department of Labor recently released some information that might interest you. It indicates that the median time in the same occupation was 6.5 years but only 4.5 years with the same employer. But there are significant differences among types of workers.

Length of time with an employer – and in the same occupation – increase with age. Given that, men had more tenure than women, whites more than blacks or Hispanics, and college grads more than those with less education.

It makes sense that age is related to tenure. Young workers have not been in the labor market very long and tend to change jobs often. Older workers gain skills in particular occupations and often have more to lose in starting over in either a new occupation or with a new employer. The table below will help you learn what is "normal" for your age group:

Table 8-2	The Relationship of Age to Tenure	
Age	Years with Employer	In Same Occupation
16-24	1.2	2.0
25-34	3.5	5.1
35-44	6.0	9.9
45-54	10.0	13.2
55-64	12.4	17.4
65+	11.1	18.1

Women tend to have less tenure than men, particularly as they mature, because many have taken time off from jobs to handle home and family responsibilities. No great differences in tenure exist between white or black men, but there are among women, with black women tending to have more continuous employment than white women. Hispanics have shorter tenures for a variety of reasons including a lower average age, employment in high-turnover jobs, and a mix of newly arrived immigrants. Self-employed workers have higher tenure, as do those in declining or slow growth industries, since those with more seniority tend to keep the jobs and few younger workers are added.

Through all the details, what does come through is that we continue to change jobs and occupations fairly often but less so as we age – and even less so if we have more education and good jobs.

Quick Advice

The results of the studies also make clear a point that I make over and over: We all need to spend more time on career planning and learning job seeking skills. With more job and career changes probable in our futures, ignoring this will cost us dearly.

Trend #4: Most Jobs Are Still Not Advertised

It has been true for many years that most jobs are not advertised. Only about 15 percent of all people actually get their jobs through the want ads. That leaves the other 85 percent or so of jobs, including most of the more desirable ones, to be filled in some other way. Even if you consider jobs available through other publicly accessible sources, such as the state-run Employment Service and private employment agencies, most jobs are still filled informally.

Unfortunately, there is a shortage of solid and recent research on job seeking skills. Even the Department of Labor has not conducted serious research on this for some time, though there is good evidence to support what I suggest. Robert

Wegmann's book, *Work in the New Economy*, does a thorough job of looking into the available research on how people find jobs. Following an extensive review of the literature, he concludes that about 75 percent of all jobs are filled without ever being advertised or listed in any publicly available data bank or job posting.

Trend #5: Jobs Changing or Being Eliminated at a Rapid Pace

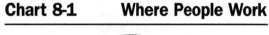

Chart 8-1   **Where People Work**

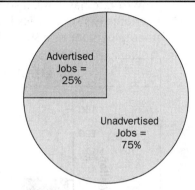

As you are surely aware, many thousands of manufacturing jobs have been eliminated in just the past decade. New technologies, foreign competition, consolidation and restructuring of large companies, and other factors have eliminated millions of manufacturing jobs since the mid-1970s. Manufacturing jobs are not the only ones being affected either, with virtually no sector of the job market escaping the effects of rapid economic and technological change.

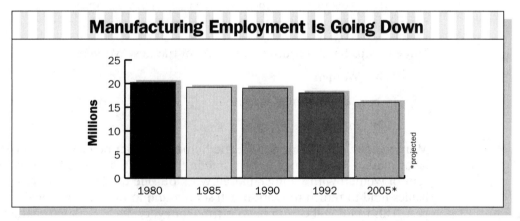

Manufacturing Employment Is Going Down

It may be that the factory is going the same way of the farm. Before the industrial revolution, over half of all people worked on farms. Now it is under 3 percent. Just as improved farm technology allowed more food to be produced with fewer workers, factories are becoming more productive as the result of improved technology. We are in the midst of a manufacturing technology revolution right now, which may eventually result in a small percentage of our workers producing all the goods we need.

Trend #6: More Workers Are Looking for More Jobs Than Ever Before

According to the U.S. Department of Labor, there were 20 million new workers added to the labor market between 1976 and 1988, a 30 percent growth rate. Many more new workers have entered the job market since then, although the growth rate has slowed some. During this time, the competition for available openings has sometimes been rather fierce. This has resulted in a higher average unemployment rate since the mid-1970s than in any period since World War II.

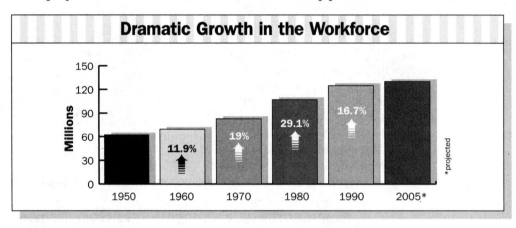

Dramatic Growth in the Workforce

Three groups have accounted for many of the new workers:

➤ Women

➤ Baby boomers

➤ Immigrants

More women now work outside the home than ever before, and they stay in the labor market longer. For the first time in the history of this country, over 50 percent of women with young children work outside the home. Those who do have babies tend to return to work much sooner and in higher numbers than in the past. This trend will continue with three of every five new labor market entrants being female.

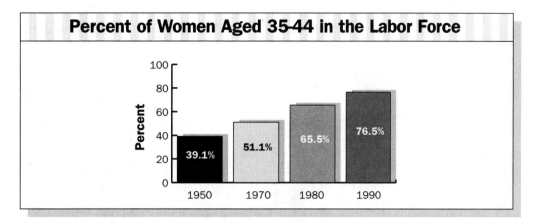

Percent of Women Aged 35-44 in the Labor Force

Percent

- 1950: 39.1%
- 1970: 51.1%
- 1980: 65.5%
- 1990: 76.5%

Most of the baby boomers now have entered the workforce, and their large numbers have swelled the number of more experienced workers to unprecedented levels. New immigrants have also helped increase the number of available workers and will continue to do so. Since 1970, over 12 million legal immigrants have been absorbed into our labor market, plus an estimated 8 to 12 million illegal immigrants.

Even though projected growth in the labor force is expected to moderate, another 33 million new workers are anticipated by the year 2005, a 19 percent increase. This slower but still substantial growth rate has been affected by the declining number of 16 to 24-year-olds entering the labor force. The typical new worker will be older and more educated, on average, than in the past.

Trend #7: Fewer Jobs in Large Organizations

Besides the millions of factory workers who lost their jobs, the ranks of middle management were also greatly reduced over the past decade. Long-term employees from all levels of the corporate hierarchy were suddenly looking for work. With frequent layoffs, few new people were hired, and far fewer opportunities for advancement were created.

While many more people have poured into the job market, larger companies have actually decreased the number of people they hire. Each year, *FORTUNE* magazine provides data on the 500 largest corporations in America – the FORTUNE 500. Look at the following chart that shows the numbers employed by the FORTUNE 500. From 1979 to 1990, the FORTUNE 500 corporations reduced the number of people they employed by over three million people. The percentage of the workforce they employed dropped from 18 percent to 11 percent during the same period.

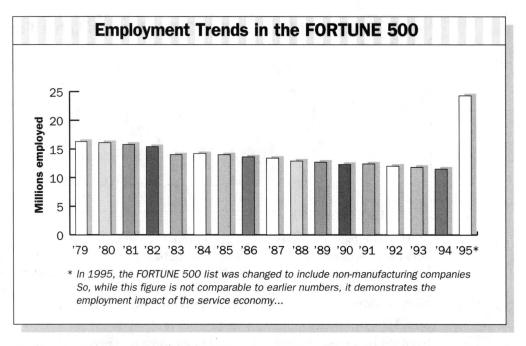

Employment Trends in the FORTUNE 500

In millions employed — years '79 through '95*

* In 1995, the FORTUNE 500 list was changed to include non-manufacturing companies So, while this figure is not comparable to earlier numbers, it demonstrates the employment impact of the service economy...

During the 1980s, the FORTUNE 500 reduced the number of people they employed by over almost four million people, a 24 percent decrease. This "down-sizing" of large corporations continues as a result of competitive pressures and new technologies. The factories and refineries are simply more efficient, putting out more goods and services with fewer workers.

Trend #8: College Graduates Experience a Tighter Market

I recently completed a book titled *America's Top Jobs for College Graduates*. In researching it, I found lots of interesting information regarding college graduates and how they are doing in the labor market. Here are some facts:

Quick Fact

➤ Overall employment is projected to grow about 20 percent by the year 2005, to 147 million workers. An astounding 39 percent of these new jobs will require a college degree.

➤ There were about 1.1 million new graduates entering the labor force during the 1980s, and projections are for about 1.32 million per year in the decade to come.

➤ An additional 1 million college graduates enter or reenter the workforce each year, mostly women and new immigrants.

➤ A college graduate earns about $16,000 a year more, on average, than a high school graduate.

As the baby boomers have moved through the educational system, unprecedented numbers have gone on to a rapidly expanded college system. More college-educated people have joined the workforce than ever before. Because the economy could not absorb them rapidly enough, many ended up competing for jobs not normally held by college graduates. That resulted in others, without degrees, being bumped out of those jobs. And they, in turn, bumped out those with even less education. As a result, the educational level required for entry to many jobs has increased. Competition for entry-level jobs held by college graduates has also gone up during the employers' market of the 1980s and 1990s, though future demand for college graduates looks quite good.

All the data I see indicates that a college degree pays off in the labor market. But having a college degree does not guarantee success. Many new graduates, for example, have found it difficult to find jobs related to their majors. Projections indicate that while many jobs will be created for college graduates, even more will enter the labor market in the years to come.

This situation will result in as many as 30 percent of new college graduates:

➤ Having to take initial jobs not typically held by college graduates

➤ Taking longer to find jobs

➤ Experiencing higher unemployment rates

And, as some experienced college graduates have found, it can be very hard to find certain jobs, particularly those that pay better or are more specialized.

Even so, the overall projections for college graduates are quite positive. Most will find jobs that they like and most will end up doing quite well, though it may not be as easy as it was back when college graduates were in short supply. College graduates will have to stay up-to-date with the changing technologies in their fields, just like everyone else. And they will probably face more frequent job changes than in the past. For these reasons, they will also have to plan their careers more carefully and learn more about job seeking – skills they will need more now than ever.

Trend #9: More Women Are in the Job Market (and Some Are Struggling)

As I've noted previously, women are now a major part of the labor market and are now much more likely to work outside the home. One study on women in their forties provides some interesting information on their working and family experiences over the years. The study, released by the U.S. Department of Labor and titled *Work and Family, Women in Their Forties*, tracks a group of women (who were then between 30 and 49 years old) since 1967. The information I present here covers only those who were in their forties during the years 1967 through 1986. While that may seem like a limited group, there are implications here for all working women.

The study found that over 85 percent of these women worked at least some during their forties, and on average, they worked 289 weeks over the 10 year period. Since working "full-time" would have required 480 to 520 weeks, this means that these women worked the equivalent of about 60 percent of full time. While only 15 percent did not work at all during their forties, almost 25 percent worked full time throughout that decade.

Nonwhite women in their forties worked slightly more weeks than white women, mostly due to the higher percentage of white women who did not work at all. Women with more education worked more. For example, those with college educations worked more weeks than those without college educations, and women with high school diplomas worked more weeks than those without high school diplomas.

There are clear indications that women with lower levels of education did not fare as well as those with more. For example, high school dropouts, when compared with their more educated counterparts, worked fewer hours, were less likely to be in the labor force, and were less likely to be married.

This study also provides striking evidence of the frequent changes in life situations experienced by so many women even during their "settled" forties. For example, about 40 percent who were in the labor market at age 40 were out of it at age 49. These and many other changes in work and marital status indicate rapid and substantial changes in these women's lives.

Although a lot has changed in the workforce since 1967, it seems clear from this and other studies that women and men with more education tend to fare better in the workforce. I believe that this trend will increase in the years to come, as more jobs require advanced technical training. Even for more mature women and men, change seems unavoidable. Given that, it is best to prepare for it now – before change is forced on you.

Table 8-3 Some General Data on Women in the Workforce

Women as a Percentage of...

The labor force	52%
The employed	45
Employed full-time workers	41
The unemployed	45
Employed executive, administrative, and managerial workers	40
Employed professional specialty workers	51
Employed administrative support workers	80

Trend #10: Good Paying, Low-Skill Jobs in Short Supply

Before 1975 or so, many high school graduates and even drop-outs could get a reasonably well-paying job at the local factory. Now, there are far fewer well-paying, low-skill-level jobs, particularly due to the following factors:

➤ The downsizing of larger corporations

➤ The loss of union dominance in many industries (the percentage of union workers has been dropping for many years)

➤ The overall huge reduction in manufacturing jobs

The relatively few such jobs that do open up are quickly filled by more experienced older workers or those with more seniority or training. Younger workers without technical training or college education are doing very poorly in today's economy. And for most of them, it's not going to get any better.

Trend #11: Education and Earnings Closely Related

It is clear that people with lower educational attainment are not doing well in our new economy. Young males are now marrying later, for example, because most cannot afford families unless they obtain more education or become established in their careers.

Quick Fact

In 1992, median earnings for college graduates were $37,000 a year, compared with $21,000 a year for high school graduates.

A college graduate earns over $16,000 a year more than a high school graduate. Over a decade, a college graduate's earnings will be about $160,000 more, enough to make a big difference in lifestyle and more than enough to pay off any cost of attending college. Over a 40-year worklife, the difference in earnings is staggering, well over a half million dollars – enough to buy a fleet of Porsches!

Table 8-4	Relationship of Education to Earnings	
Education Level	**Earnings**	**% Premium Over High School Grads**
High School Diploma	$21,242	n/a
Bachelor's Degree	34,385	62%
Master's Degree	40,666	91
Ph.D.	52,403	147
Professional	67,131	216

Not only do those with more education earn more money, they are also more likely to be in the labor market. About 85 percent of women and 95 percent of men with college degrees are in the labor market, as compared to 78 percent of male high school drop-outs and only 47 percent of female high school drop-outs. This one-two punch of significantly lower earnings and lower labor market participation has profound effects on family income. Women with little education who are single heads of households are likely to have a particularly bleak economic future.

Following is a chart showing the average earnings for various family situations. The information comes from the Department of Labor's *Employment and Earnings* report and clearly shows the earnings differential for various family situations. Note that these figures are averages and that the effect of educational level would make them far more dramatic.

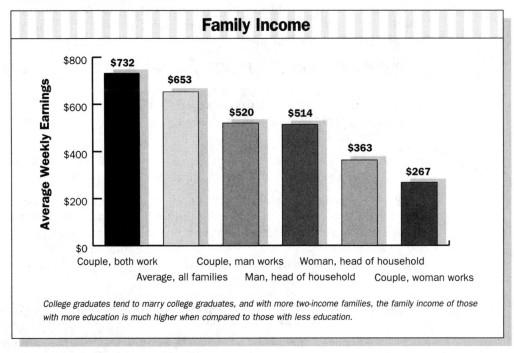

Family Income

College graduates tend to marry college graduates, and with more two-income families, the family income of those with more education is much higher when compared to those with less education.

Quick Fact

The rich get richer...

It is now true that the poor (and uneducated) get poorer and the rich (and educated) get richer. The solution is to obtain higher levels of education and academic achievement.

Trend #12: Computer Skills Are Increasingly Important

Most people now understand that knowing how to use a computer in their work has become increasingly important. But few realize how important it is and how quickly the demand for these skills has increased.

A recent study from Olsten Temporary Services found that over 90 percent of secretaries and clerical support staff are required to have computer literacy to be considered for employment. That shouldn't be any surprise to people who work in those jobs, since computers are now a routine part of the office environment in most places. But just three years earlier, only about 70 percent of those workers were required to have computer skills.

Quick Fact

For years, many professionals and managers seemed to be immune from needing to know much about computers. I've heard more than one brag that they didn't know how to do even simple word processing. Just three years ago, only 30 to 40 percent of employers required professionals and managers to be computer literate. But things have changed. Now, 75 percent of professionals and 78 percent of middle managers are required to be computer literate. Even 64 percent of senior managers are expected to have computer skills, compared to only 36 percent just three years ago.

This is the most dramatic change in the workplace in decades.

Millions of people who have lost their jobs over the past few years do not have the computer skills now required. New entrants to the labor market who do not have the necessary computer literacy are finding fewer jobs they can qualify for. Both groups are finding it more and more difficult to find jobs comparable to those they held in the past or new jobs that pay reasonably well.

Quick Advice

Other studies have indicated that computer skills pay a premium of 36 percent to over 50 percent in higher wages for those with similar education.

So here is my advice:

1. Use a computer often.

If you work now, look for ways to use a computer to make your work more productive, and use it every day – even if you have to buy one yourself.

2. Take classes.

If you are in school, take as many computer literacy courses as possible, and use a computer for your word processing and other work – even if you have to buy one yourself.

3. Upgrade you knowledge and skills.

Plan on continually upgrading your computer knowledge and skills by taking night classes, reading computer magazines, learning and using new programs, and any other activity you can – even if you have to spend your leisure time doing so. In today's labor market, it is no longer optional.

The Good News: Good Jobs Are Out There and You Can Learn to Find Them

Even though our economy has experienced a great upheaval, there is ample evidence that many people are doing quite well in it. Let's look at the trends in our economy having a positive side and examine ways to benefit from them.

Positive Trend #1: More Jobs Than Ever Before

Our economy has been able to absorb almost all of the new workers who have poured into it. As I mentioned earlier, many millions of new jobs have been created to employ the new workers who have come into the workforce during the past 20 years. Although our unemployment did go up during the 70s and 80s, it would have been much higher if it were not for the rapid expansion of our economy. Only during the recession of the early 1980s did the unemployment rate go above 9 percent. It has steadily decreased since then to rates well below 6 percent.

Positive Trend #2: Many New Jobs in Small Businesses

Over two-thirds of all workers in the private sector work in small businesses. Small businesses, as defined by the U.S. Department of Labor, are those with 250 or fewer workers. These businesses are clearly the source of most of the new jobs in our economy. Look at the chart that follows. It is based on information gathered by the U.S. Department of Labor and clearly shows the importance of smaller employers to our workforce.

An economist named David Burch has researched the job-generating ability of various sized businesses. His striking conclusion is that the smallest companies, those with 20 or fewer employees, are responsible for creating as many as 80 percent of the net new jobs. While larger employers will remain an important source of employment, small businesses seem to be far more important in our new economy than ever before.

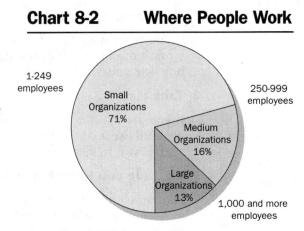

Chart 8-2   Where People Work

They cannot be ignored as a major source of employment opportunities.

Positive Trend #3: The Service Economy Is Growing Rapidly

There is great misunderstanding about our becoming a service economy and what that means. So let's begin by defining our terms.

Quick Definition

The "Service Economy" consists of all jobs that are not in the "Goods Producing" sector. The Goods Producing industries are: Construction, Agriculture, Forestry and Fishing, Manufacturing, and Mining

If you are not employed in one of the "goods-producing industries," you are in the "service economy." Much of the confusion comes from a subcategory of occupations, called "service occupations," that includes jobs such as police officers, restaurant workers, nursing aids, and janitors. While these jobs are often in "Service Industries" (such as health care), the "service industry" is far larger.

In general, the goods-producing industries have not been growing, and in some cases, have declined in the numbers of people they employ. Yet our economy continues to create many new jobs – and virtually all of them are in the service sector.

Table 8-5	Services-Producing Industries Account for Virtually All Job Growth*		
	1979	*1992*	*2005* (projected)
Service-Producing	63	84.7	109.2
Goods-Producing	26.5	23.1	23.7
Total	89.5	107.9	133
*In millions employed			

About 80 percent of our workforce is now employed in the service sector, and the percentage is expected to gradually increase to about 82 percent by the year 2005. Virtually all of the new jobs that have been created since 1960 have been in the service economy.

Jobs in the services sector include occupations such as those in the health, business, education, wholesale and retail trade, banking, real estate, transportation, and other industries. This is the fastest growing sector of our economy, and many of the jobs pay quite well. Doctors, lab technicians, optometrists, attorneys, accountants, and other specialists are some of the jobs included in this sector. These higher-paying and fast-growth jobs also tend to require high levels of skill and specialized training or education.

Positive Trend #4: The Number of Jobs in Manufacturing and Government Is Not Expected to Decrease

The graph that follows shows the number of people working in major sectors of our economy since 1950 as well as projections through 2005. Notice that government jobs have increased modestly during this time, and manufacturing jobs, while down from historic highs, are projected to increase slightly in the years to come. So, while almost all of the employment growth has been in the service industry, manufacturing and government will remain important sources of employment. Here are the facts:

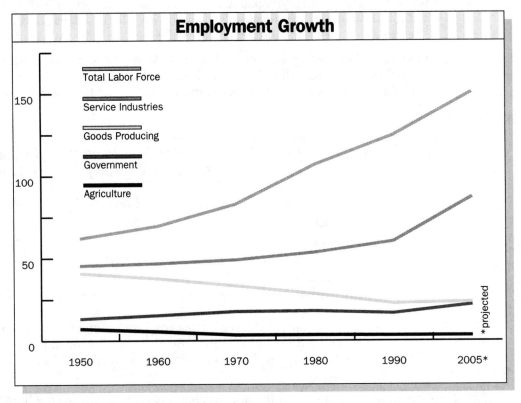

Clearly, manufacturing will remain important, even though it now employs fewer people than in the past. This result is similar to what happened during what has come to be called the "Industrial Revolution" that occurred during the last century. Before then, well over half of the American workforce was in agriculture. Over the years, technological improvements reduced the percentage of workers on farms to about 3 percent, while those working in manufacturing increased dramatically.

We may now be in the midst of a similar "Service Revolution" of equivalent magnitude. As manufacturing processes become more efficient and goods become more reliable, we will require fewer and fewer workers to produce and maintain the goods we need. Just as we have more food now than ever before with only a small percentage of our workforce producing it, we are moving towards fewer workers producing the manufactured goods we need.

The new jobs in the new economy are not in agriculture, farming, or government; they are in the service economy. This has been true for some time, and the projections indicate that this will continue to be true in the years ahead.

Positive Trend #5: Many New Jobs Pay Well – But Require More Education or Training

The average job in our economy pays over $22,000. To many, that is a higher amount than they would have guessed. Averages, however, can be misleading. If you separate the levels of compensation by education, a different picture emerges.

In the chart titled "More Education = Higher Earnings" presented earlier in this chapter, you saw that the average high school graduate earns about $21,000 per year, while the average college graduate earns about $34,000 per year. That is a considerable difference for the four years of additional education it took to obtain it.

Quick Reminder

But remember that these are average earnings. People just starting out will often make considerably less, and some will earn considerably more.

It is clear that average earnings go up with educational attainment. Some people with lower educational attainment do have higher-than-average earnings, but dramatically fewer than those with higher levels of education. Earnings of those in the top 20 percent of income (about $31,000 per year or more) are also education-related as indicated in the chart that follows. Note that very few of those with a high school education or less are among the highest earners.

Table 8-6	High Earnings by Level of Education	
Percent Earning Over...	**$600/Week**	**$1,000/Week**
Less than 4 years of high school	6.0%	0.6%
4 years of high school	11.9	1.5
1 to 3 years of college	19.4	3.6
4 years of college	34.9	10.3
5 or more years of college	47.9	18.5
All levels of education average	19.5	4.8

The types of occupations are related to education, too. About 95 percent of those with five or more years of higher education are in professional specialty, managerial, technical, and sales occupations while only 17 percent of those with less than four years of high school were.

Generally, occupations that are growing rapidly also require higher educational attainment. For example, technicians, professionals, and executives/administrators/managers are the three fastest growing major occupational groups. All of these usually require education or training beyond high school.

The occupations that are declining most rapidly include machine operators, fabricators, laborers and agriculture, forestry, and fishery workers. All of these groups have the highest proportion of workers with less than a high school education and also have the lowest earnings.

Though some high school graduates do find well-paying jobs, they are becoming the exception. Some better-paying jobs for high school graduates include truck driver, secretary, data processing equipment repairers, police and firefighters, machinists, computer operators, tool and die makers, and others. But many of these occupations also require substantial on-the-job training and considerable academic proficiency and talent.

Chapter 11 will show you how to obtain additional information on various jobs, their anticipated growth rates, earnings, and entry requirements. If you are considering changing careers or want to advance to higher levels of responsibility in your current field, that chapter will be of particular interest.

Positive Trend #6: The Outlook for College Graduates Is Improving

In spite of a tighter job market for college graduates in recent years, 92 percent of new graduates are expected to find jobs typically held by college graduates. As I have pointed out elsewhere, college graduates have higher earnings and lower unemployment rates than those with less education, and the future looks favorable.

In 1992, there were about 30 million college grads in the workforce. By 2005, the demand for grads is projected to grow by an enormous 40 percent – more than double that for the labor market as a whole.

All this good news indicates that having a college degree is a very good thing. For most college grads, this will clearly be true, but there are other things to consider to fully understand these projections.

For one thing, about 6 million (about 20 percent) of the college grads in the workforce are either unemployed (1 million or about 3 percent) or are holding jobs not typically held by grads (6 million or about 17 percent). Some of those appearing to be "underemployed" chose to be so (as they attend graduate school or for other reasons), but many were simply unable to find better jobs due to intense competition.

Another factor is that while about 1.05 million jobs requiring grads are projected to open up each year, there will be about 1.38 million new and returning grads joining the labor force each year. That means that the demand (though high) will be exceeded by the supply (which is even higher).

The bottom line here is that while a college degree can be of great value, it will not guarantee success in the job market any more than it has in the past. About one in four new grads will have to accept jobs that are not typically held by grads – though many will do better over time. This reinforces my observation that career planning is more important than ever. For college grads and those considering additional education, it is more important than ever to know in advance which degrees and occupations offer the best opportunities for employment.

Positive Trend #7: Trade and Technical Training Serve as Alternatives to a College Degree

More education clearly pays off in the job market, but it should be noted that college is not the only route to higher earnings, since many trade, technical, sales, and other fields offer similar benefits. A well-trained plumber, auto mechanic, chef, computer repair technician, police officer, tool and die maker, or medical technologist can all do quite well in our economy.

These and many other occupations require one to two years of specialized training, and some apprenticeship programs allow for on-the-job training. Outstanding people in sales, small business, management, self-employment, and other activities can still do quite well without a college degree or technical training, though more education is often required to compete for the better positions. Plenty of jobs exist in large but slower-growing occupations.

There is plenty of glamour in occupations that are growing rapidly, but many jobs will continue to become available in occupations that are growing slowly or even declining. Jobs will become available to replace those who retire or leave for other reasons, and opportunities will exist in virtually all areas for those with superior abilities, motivation and/or preparation.

Positive Trend #8: More Education Pays Off in Less Unemployment Too

It is clear that education and training pay off in higher average earnings. These people are in more demand in the job market. Look at the chart that follows to see how unemployment rates go down as educational attainment goes up. People with more education not only earn more money, they also experience lower unemployment rates. This combination results in much higher average earnings and less economic disruption.

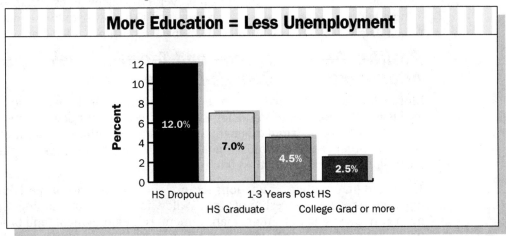

Positive Trend #9: Demand for Most Jobs Is Expected to Grow

Overall, employment is projected to grow by about 22 percent by 2005. But this growth is not even, since the occupations having the highest growth rates are those that tend to require more education or training. Following are recent projections for you to consider.

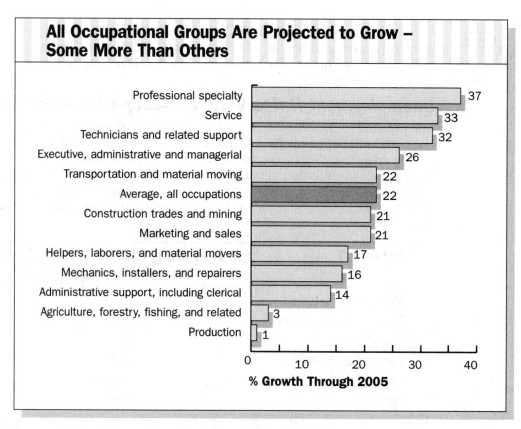

All Occupational Groups Are Projected to Grow – Some More Than Others

Occupation	% Growth Through 2005
Professional specialty	37
Service	33
Technicians and related support	32
Executive, administrative and managerial	26
Transportation and material moving	22
Average, all occupations	22
Construction trades and mining	21
Marketing and sales	21
Helpers, laborers, and material movers	17
Mechanics, installers, and repairers	16
Administrative support, including clerical	14
Agriculture, forestry, fishing, and related	3
Production	1

% Growth Through 2005

Lower-paying jobs, such as those in retail trade (food service workers, cashiers, etc.) have been typically filled by young people, those with few job-related skills, or low educational attainment. In many parts of the country, employers cannot hire these workers at minimum wage any longer. A big reason is that there are fewer young people entering the job market. The number of new entrants peaked in 1979 and has continually decreased since.

While immigrants and women without post high school education have taken many of these jobs, our rapidly expanding economy has generated more demand for people to fill these positions. In accord with the law of supply and demand, entry wages for these jobs are going up. Many of the fast-food chains are even actively recruiting older workers – a previously untapped source of employees.

Other occupations have also experienced or are anticipating shortages of qualified workers for a variety of reasons. As a result of expanded opportunities for women, fewer qualified women now seek jobs such as secretaries, nurses, teachers, and other occupations that have traditionally employed many females. Shortages in these occupations now make them good occupational choices for qualified men or women.

Quick Reference

Chapter 16 provides growth projections for various jobs, and note that most of them are expected to require additional workers. But note also that, as mentioned earlier, almost all of the fastest growing occupations require special training or advanced education.

Unemployment Rates Vary for Occupational Groups

One measure of the demand for various skill levels of workers is the unemployment rate. I have already presented the data on unemployment rates based on level of education that showed lower rates of unemployment for those with higher levels of education. If you examine various types of jobs, you will find that some types of jobs have lower unemployment rates than others. Once again, it is clear that occupations requiring higher levels of training and education are in more demand.

Table 8-7	Jobs Requiring Higher-Level Skills Have Lower Unemployment Rates
Manager/Professional:	2.1%
Technical/Sales/Clerical:	4.2%
Craft/Repair:	5.8%
Farm/Forest/Fishing:	6.2%
Service:	6.6%
Labor/Operators:	8.6%

The Bottom Line: Career Planning and Job Seeking Skills Give a Competitive Edge

The following factors all point to continued disruption in the employment of most working people:

➤ More frequent job and career changes

➤ Less long-term security with any one organization

➤ Rapid technological change

➤ An ongoing demand for new job-related skills

For those who are unprepared, this can spell economic and personal disaster. New economic survival skills are needed for our new economy and you can ignore them only at your peril.

Change presents both problems and opportunities. While the new labor market realities do create problems for many people, there are, in my opinion, many ways that you can take advantage of the current job market – if you know how. So, in closing this chapter, I offer you a few things to consider.

Six Things You Should Do to Get Ahead
1. Upgrade your job skills and keep doing it

Too many people think that once they get their "credentials" they are set for life. Not so. No matter how much education or training you already have, you will need more to move ahead in your present job or even to keep it.

It is increasingly important for people in all occupational areas to keep learning new things. Computers, for example, have revolutionized the way many people work.

If you are unfamiliar with a new technology that might affect your job, you should consider going back to school or learn to use it in some other way. Constantly look for ways to apply new techniques to your own job to increase your productivity. Finish that degree you have always wanted to get. Sign up for any relevant training related to your job. Be willing to try out new things. It is no longer enough to "put in your time" because the world will surely continue to change around you.

2. Avoid the "boxes" in your life

Most people separate their life activities into the three major categories of playing, learning, and working. One way they do this is by age, emphasizing playing as the major activity for young children, learning and being educated for youth, working for adults and, finally, retirement and a return to playing again.

Richard Bolles, in a book titled *The Three Boxes of Life* has defined these three activities – playing, learning, and working – as the three boxes that too many people use to limit themselves. Instead, he suggests we should strive to incorporate playing, learning, and working into all aspects of our lives. Working, for example, can also be playing as well as an ongoing learning experience. Ideally, that is what good career and life planning should help you achieve – a balance between leisure, learning, and working rather than a separation.

3. Incorporate life planning into your job search

Your current priority may be to find your next job. That is a worthy objective, and this book will show you a variety of techniques to accomplish that. But before you begin, take a bit more time to define more clearly what, precisely, you want and need from a job. And consider how that job might help you go where you want to go with your life. It will be time well spent.

Good career planning is extremely important, but it should be done in the context of what you want to do with your life. How can you, for example, incorporate elements of pleasure and learning into your next job?

4. Develop your life-long skills

You will likely change jobs and careers again and again during your life. And whatever job skills you have now will need to be continually upgraded. This makes it increasingly important for you to know what you are particularly good at doing and develop those skills throughout your life.

5. Consider small organizations

More and more of us now work in small organizations. Over time, an increasing number of us will spend at least part of our working lives working in (or starting up) a small business. Smaller organizations offer excellent opportunities for young people to gain experience and for more experienced workers to apply their skills. And smaller organizations are now just as secure, on the average, as larger ones. They will become increasingly important as a source of jobs in the future. If working in a small organization is a new idea to you, consider it.

6. Do things you enjoy doing

Having been unemployed myself, I know very well that earning a living can be a difficult task. And over the years I have done many things that I did not enjoy to earn a living. But having fun or finding satisfaction with what we do with our lives is what it is all about. Get both if you can.

Quick Summary

✓ **The 12 General Employments Trends to Consider:**

Trend #1: People Change Jobs More Often

Trend #2: More Career Changes Expected

Trend #3: The Older We Get, the More Stable We Become (Occupationally Speaking)

Trend #4: Most Jobs Are Still Not Advertised

Trend #5: Jobs Changing or Being Eliminated at a Rapid Pace

Trend #6: More Workers Are Looking for More Jobs Than Ever Before

Trend #7: Fewer Jobs in Large Organizations

Trend #8: College Graduates Experience a Tighter Market

Trend #9: More Women Are in the Job Market (and Some Are Struggling)

Trend #10: Good Paying, Low-Skill Jobs in Short Supply

Trend #11: Education and Earnings Closely Related

Trend #12: Computer Skills Are Increasingly Important

✓ **The 9 Positive Employment Trends to Consider**

Positive Trend #1: More Jobs Than Ever Before

Positive Trend #2: Many New Jobs in Small Businesses

Positive Trend #3: The Service Economy Is Growing Rapidly

Positive Trend #4: The Number of Jobs in Manufacturing and Government Is Not Expected to Decrease

Positive Trend #5: Many New Jobs Pay Well – But Require More Education or Training

Positive Trend #6: The Outlook for College Graduates Is Improving

Positive Trend #7: Trade and Technical Training Serve as Alternatives to a College Degree

Positive Trend #8: More Education Pays Off in Less Unemployment Too

Positive Trend #9: Demand for Most Jobs Is Expected to Grow

✓ **Six Things You Should Do to Get Ahead:**

1. Upgrade Your Job Skills and Keep Doing It

2. Avoid the "Boxes" in Your Life

3. Incorporate Life Planning into Your Job Search

4. Develop Your Life-Long Skills

5. Consider Small Organizations

6. Do Things You Enjoy Doing

Chapter 8

CHAPTER NINE

Preparing for the Job Search

Document Your Experience
and Accomplishments

≡≡Quick Overview

In this chapter, I review the following:

✓ How your accomplishments can reveal
your skills

✓ How to complete the Life Experience
Worksheets

✓ The Education and Training Worksheets

✓ The Job and Volunteer Worksheet

✓ The Other Life Experiences Worksheet

✓ Key accomplishments and skills to tell an
employer

Throughout your job search, you will need ready access to a large number of facts from your life's history. This chapter will help you organize those facts into a type of "database." You can use this information in later chapters to select or research a job objective, complete applications and resumes, answer interview questions, and perfect many other job search skills.

The language of your skills that you developed in Chapter 3 will help you examine your background in this one. Knowing which things to emphasize from your life's history will be very important to you in your job search.

Emphasize Your Accomplishments

When reviewing your history, remember the situations where you felt some joy or sense of accomplishment. Identify the skills you were using when you experienced these feelings.

Quick Tip

Understand that an "accomplishment" could be something small, that only you know about.

For example, perhaps you never won an award or do not consider yourself outstanding in any particular way. But you did figure out how to make an unauthorized announcement over your school's public address system, releasing everyone early on the last day of school in your senior year. (An action for which you did not get an award but that was quite creative.) Or you collected more canned food for the homeless than anyone else in your homeroom. Or whatever. Almost every month of your life there is something that you accomplish. These things are the basis for identifying your skills.

Here is an example of what one person selected as an accomplishment. I listed to the right of her story some of the skills needed to do what she described.

Accomplishment	Skills Needed
"Last summer, my cousin got ill and could not run his concession at the city fair. Even though I had never run a concession before, I bought the supplies and handled all the details in time to open the stand the first day with only one day's notice! There are usually two people who run the stand, but without help I ran it myself. I served over 5,000 customers that week and took in over $20,000. That is an increase of 36 percent over last year. Because I bought supplies wholesale and in quantity, the profits were 50 percent over last year, too. I worked 12-hour days but always opened on time."	Accepts responsibility Risk taker Problem solver Meets deadlines Good scheduler, prioritizer Efficient, fast Good customer contact Interpersonal skills Gets results! Budgets money & time Good negotiator Saves money Hard worker Responsible

Do you see how one accomplishment, once you analyze it, can help reveal your skills? John Crystal, a pioneer in career planning, developed this way of analyzing skills many years ago. You may find it helpful to identify five or so things that you felt you did particularly well *and* that you enjoyed doing.

When you are done, write down, in as much detail as you can, what you remember about each accomplishment. Then go back over each story and look for the skills you used. A pattern of similar skills being used again and again will usually develop in the things you do well and enjoy doing. These are probably the skills you are particularly good at and enjoy using most. And they are almost always adaptive or transferable skills.

The Life Experience Worksheets

As you complete the various worksheets that follow, keep in mind that you are looking for skills that you have demonstrated as well as your accomplishments. Pay special attention to those experiences and accomplishments that you really enjoyed – these often demonstrate skills that you should try to use in your next job. When possible, include numbers to describe your activities or their results.

For example, saying "spoke to groups as large as 200 people" has more impact than "did presentations."

In some cases, you may want to write a draft on a separate sheet of paper before completing the form in this book. Use an erasable pen or pencil on the worksheets to allow for changes. In all sections, emphasize the skills and accomplishments that best support your ability to do the job you are seeking.

Education and Training Worksheets

Most of us, in our early years of schooling, managed to acquire some basic skills that are important in most jobs: getting along with others, reading instructions, and accepting supervision. Later on, courses became more specialized and relevant to potential careers.

Use this worksheet to review your educational experiences. Some courses may seem more important to certain careers than others. But even courses that don't seem to support a particular career choice can be an important source of certain skills.

High School Worksheet

Unless you are a recent high school graduate, most employers won't be interested in too many details related to your work in high school. Still, it can be worthwhile to emphasize highlights, particularly if you are a recent graduate.

Name of school(s)/years attended:

_____

Subjects you did well in or might relate to the job you want:

_____

Extracurricular activities/hobbies/leisure activities:

_____

Accomplishments/things you did well (in or out of school):

_____

_____

_____

_____

_____

College Worksheet

If you graduated from college or took college classes, this is often of interest to an employer. If you are a new graduate, these experiences can be particularly important. Consider those things that directly support your ability to do the job. For example, working your way through school supports your being hard working. If you took courses that specifically support your job, you can include details on these as well.

Name of school(s)/years attended:

_____

Courses related to job objective:

_____

Extracurricular activities/hobbies/leisure activities:

_____

_____

Accomplishments/things you did well (in or out of school):

_____

_____

_____

_____

_____

Specific things you learned or can do that relate to the job you want:

_____

_____

_____

_____

_____

Post-High School Training Worksheet

List any training that might relate to the job you want. Include military and on-the-job training, workshops, or informal training such as from a hobby.

Training/dates/certificates:

_____

_____

_____

Specific things you can do as a result:

_____

_____

_____

_____

_____

Specific things you learned or can do that relate to the job you want:

_____

_____

_____

_____

_____

The Job and Volunteer History Worksheet

Use this worksheet to list each major job you have held and the information related to each. Begin with your most recent job first, followed by previous ones.

Include military experience and unpaid work here, too. Both are work and are particularly important if you do not have much paid civilian work experience. Create additional sheets to cover all of your significant jobs or unpaid experiences as needed. If you have been promoted, consider handling that as a separate job.

Whenever possible, provide numbers to support what you did: number of people served over one or more years; number of transactions processed; percent sales increase; total inventory value you were responsible for; payroll of the staff you supervised; total budget you were responsible for; and other data. As much as possible, mention results using numbers, too.

I have provided several of the worksheets, but, if you need more, please feel free to photocopy extras for each of the jobs you need to document.

Job and Volunteer History Worksheet #1

Name of organization: _____

Address: _____

_____

Employed from: _____ to: _____

Job title(s): _____

Supervisor's name: _____

Phone number: _____

Machinery or equipment you used:

_____

_____

Data, information, or reports you created or used:

_____

_____

People-oriented duties or responsibilities to coworkers, customers, others:

_____

_____

_____

_____

Services you provided or products you produced:

_____

_____

_____

_____

_____

Reasons for promotions or salary increases, if any:

_____

_____

Details on anything you did to help the organization, such as increase productivity, simplify or reorganize job duties, decrease costs, increase profits, improve working conditions, reduce turnover, or other improvements. Qualify results when possible—for example, "Increased order processing by 50 percent, with no increase in staff costs."

_____

_____

_____

_____

_____

Specific things you learned or can do that relate to the job you want:

_____

_____

_____

_____

_____

What would your supervisor say about you?

_____

_____

_____

_____

_____

Job and Volunteer History Worksheet #2

Name of organization: _____

Address: _____

_____

Employed from: _____ to: _____

Job title(s): _____

Supervisor's name: _____

Phone number: _____

Machinery or equipment you used:

_____

_____

_____

Data, information, or reports you created or used:

_____

_____

_____

People-oriented duties or responsibilities to coworkers, customers, others:

_____

_____

_____

_____

_____

Services you provided or products you produced:

_____

_____

_____

_____

_____

_____

Reasons for promotions or salary increases, if any:

_____

_____

Details on anything you did to help the organization, such as increase productivity, simplify or reorganize job duties, decrease costs, increase profits, improve working conditions, reduce turnover, or other improvements. Qualify results when possible—for example, "Increased order processing by 50 percent, with no increase in staff costs."

_____

_____

_____

_____

_____

Specific things you learned or can do that relate to the job you want:

_____

_____

_____

_____

_____

What would your supervisor say about you?

_____

_____

_____

_____

Job and Volunteer History Worksheet #3

Name of organization: _____

Address: _____

_____

Employed from: _____ to: _____

Job title(s): _____

Supervisor's name: _____

Phone number: _____

Machinery or equipment you used:

_____

_____

_____

Data, information, or reports you created or used:

_____

_____

_____

People-oriented duties or responsibilities to coworkers, customers, others:

_____

_____

_____

_____

_____

Services you provided or products you produced:

_____

_____

_____

_____

_____

_____

Reasons for promotions or salary increases, if any:

_____

_____

Details on anything you did to help the organization, such as increase productivity, simplify or reorganize job duties, decrease costs, increase profits, improve working conditions, reduce turnover, or other improvements. Qualify results when possible—for example, "Increased order processing by 50 percent, with no increase in staff costs."

_____

_____

_____

_____

_____

Specific things you learned or can do that relate to the job you want:

_____

_____

_____

_____

_____

What would your supervisor say about you?

_____

_____

_____

_____

Job and Volunteer History Worksheet #4

Name of organization: _____

Address: _____

_____

Employed from: _____ to: _____

Job title(s): _____

Supervisor's name: _____

Phone number: _____

Machinery or equipment you used:

_____

_____

_____

Data, information, or reports you created or used:

_____

_____

_____

People-oriented duties or responsibilities to coworkers, customers, others:

_____

_____

_____

_____

_____

Services you provided or products you produced:

_____

_____

_____

_____

_____

_____

Reasons for promotions or salary increases, if any:

_____

_____

Details on anything you did to help the organization, such as increase productivity, simplify or reorganize job duties, decrease costs, increase profits,
improve working conditions, reduce turnover, or other improvements.
Qualify results when possible—for example, "Increased order processing by
50 percent, with no increase in staff costs."

_____

_____

_____

_____

_____

Specific things you learned or can do that relate to the job you want:

_____

_____

_____

_____

What would your supervisor say about you?

_____

_____

_____

_____

The Other Life Experiences Worksheet

Think about any hobbies or interests you have had – family responsibilities, recreational activities, travel, or any other experiences in your life where you feel some sense of accomplishment. Write any that seem particularly meaningful to you below, and name the key skills you think were involved in doing them.

Other Life Experiences Worksheet

Situation 1: _____

Details and skills used:

_____

_____

_____

_____

_____

Specific things you learned or can do that relate to the job you want:

_____

_____

_____

_____

_____

Situation 2: _____

Details and skills used:

_____

_____

_____

_____

_____

Specific things you learned or can do that relate to the job you want:

_____

_____

_____

_____

_____

Situation 3: _____

Details and skills used:

_____

_____

_____

_____

Specific things you learned or can do that relate to the job you want:

_____

_____

_____

_____

_____

Key Accomplishments and Skills to Tell an Employer

In this chapter, you had the opportunity to examine the job-related skills you have from education, work, and other life experiences. As you have surely noticed, these skills exist only in the context of your using your adaptive and transferable skills.

Doing the activities I suggest in this chapter may have given you a few more adaptive or transferable skills to add to your list – or more insight into how you use them. Now it is time to consider which skills are likely to be most valuable to you and a prospective employer in a work situation. Answering the following questions may help.

Questions for Review

1. What are the most important accomplishments and skills you can present to an employer regarding your educational and training experiences?

_____

_____

_____

_____

_____

2. What are the most important accomplishments and skills you can present to an employer regarding your paid and unpaid work experiences?

_____

_____

_____

_____

_____

3. What are the most important accomplishments and skills you can present to an employer regarding your other life experiences?

_____

_____

_____

_____

_____

If you find that your opinions about the skills you have or want to use on your next job have changed since the earlier chapter on skills, that's okay. These are your lists, and you can do anything you want with them. So feel free to go back and do those activities again as you learn new things – or simply if you change your mind.

Defining your skills and figuring out what to do with them is a process that is never completely done. In the next chapter, you will use your skills knowledge in a new way to help define what sort of job you want – even if you already have a job objective.

Quick Summary

✓ When reviewing your history, remember the situations where you felt some joy or sense of accomplishment, and identify the skills you were using when you experienced these feelings. Understand that an "accomplishment" could be something small, that only you know about.

✓ One accomplishment, once you analyze it, can help reveal your skills. John Crystal, a pioneer in career planning, developed this way of analyzing skills many years ago.

✓ You may find it helpful to identify five or so things that you felt you did particularly well *and* that you enjoyed doing. When you are done, write down, in as much detail as you can, what you remember about each accomplishment. Then go back over each story and look for the skills you used.

✓ A pattern of similar skills being used again and again will usually develop in the things you do well and enjoy doing. These are probably the skills you are particularly good at and enjoy using most. And they are almost always adaptive or transferable skills.

✓ As you complete the various worksheets, keep in mind that you are looking for skills that you have demonstrated as well as your accomplishments. Pay special attention to those experiences and accomplishments that you really enjoyed. When possible, include numbers to describe your activities or their results.

✓ In this chapter, you have the opportunity to examine the job-related skills you have from education, work, and other life experiences. These skills exist only in the context of your using your adaptive and transferable skills.

CHAPTER TEN

Preparing for the Job Search

Define Your Ideal Job –

Then Identify Specific Job Targets

Quick Overview

In this chapter, I review the following:

✓ Why a job title is not a job objective

✓ What most people want from work

✓ How to define what you really want to do

✓ The eight components of an ideal job description

✓ How to determine the field and industry to work in

✓ How to take advantage of several guides to occupations (OOH, CGOE, DOT, EGOE, and other resources)

✓ How to clarify and refine your ideal job objective

✓ Questions you need to be able to answer before you begin your job search

If you are reading this, you:
1) Either have a clear job objective, or 2) You don't. In either case, this chapter will provide important things to consider. It is divided into two major sections. The first will help you explore what you really want from your work in terms of your values, interests, skills, work environment, and other preferences. Most people don't give these things much thought in their selection of a job and risk their long-term happiness and success by doing so.

The second section introduces you to the more traditional way to approach career planning by showing you ways to select specific job titles as targets. Even if you already have a job objective, it is likely that you are overlooking many opportunities in related jobs and industries, and the information in this section will help you throw a wider net in your search for openings.

Even if your objective is general, it allows you to select those details to present to an employer that best support what you want to do next. But whether you do or do not have a clear job objective, this chapter will help by showing you how to explore career and job alternatives that you may not have considered. It pays to be both well-informed and flexible.

A Job Title Is Not a Job Objective

Defining your "ideal" job is a tricky business. There are over 20,000 job titles – far too many jobs for you or anyone else to really know well. Add to that the obvious variable of different work environments. You might be delighted to work in one place (it being all that you could hope for in a great place to work) and entirely miserable working in another. Yet both could *look* very much the same to a job seeker. And both could have the very same job title.

Many people confuse their job objective with a job title, but they are not the same thing at all. For example, if you were looking for a job as an accountant, secretary, or computer programmer, those are job titles. But a job objective is more complex and specific to you and your needs.

Here is an example of a job objective: "A position requiring skills in organizing, communicating, and dealing with people. Prefer a small- to mid-size organization engaged in creative activities. Background in office management, skilled in word processing, spreadsheets, and other computer programs."

Although it doesn't mention a job title, this is just the sort of thing that a person who had worked as a "secretary" in the past might write on a resume. It mentions skills and preferences without limiting the choices. This approach leaves open a variety of options that would not be called "secretary," and it also provides more information on what the person wants and is good at doing. This sample job objective would clearly allow this person to do a wide variety of jobs that would not be called "secretary" such as: office manager, sales associate, customer services representative, business manager, and many other job titles.

Most people don't take the time to clarify what they have to offer and want to do. Their resumes often show this lack of clarity by listing a job title without providing information on what they *want* to do. They often present the same lack of clarity in their search for a job by seeking a title – rather than the type of work, employer, and work environment they prefer. As a result, they often end up being a "secretary" (or whatever) instead of doing something they really want to do. Employers don't consider them for jobs with different titles and responsibilities, so opportunities are lost. People end up being secretaries, accountants, and computer programmers because that's what they did in the past.

Quick Advice

So don't limit yourself by looking for a job title. Instead, be clear about what you want and have to offer and seek an employer who will allow you to do those things. Then let *them* figure out where you would best fit in.

What Most People Want from Work

Years ago, there were studies that indicated a high percentage of people were not happy in their jobs. Of course, back then, many people didn't expect to be happy in their work. Work was…well…work, and enjoyment was something you got outside of work. But there has been a change in attitude for many people in recent years, with more and more people looking for both meaning and even some joy from the same activities they do to earn their livings. While many people still go to work simply to earn a living, many want more. And the good news is that many are finding it.

Surprise! Money is *not* number one!

The Gallup Poll study

A study by the Gallup Poll indicated that 78 percent of those surveyed rated "interesting work" as being very important in being satisfied with their jobs. Only one measure, "good health insurance and other benefits" was rated higher. While many people do value making good money (particularly if you don't make enough to live reasonably well), only 56 percent rated "high income" as being very important to them. It's not that money isn't important – it is; it's just that most working people value other things, too. Table 10-1 shows some other things that were rated higher than money:

Table 10-1	A Few Things Rated Higher Than Money!
Factor	**Percent of People**
Interesting work	78%
Job security	78
Opportunity to learn new skills	68
Having a week or more of vacation	66
Being able to work independently	64
Recognition from coworkers	62
Regular hours, no weekends or nights	58
Being able to help others	58
Limiting job stress	58
High income	56

While some of these things are clearly self-serving (job security and benefits), they don't seem unreasonable. And most are really related to wanting recognition, opportunity, and other values that seem to me to be good things. Still, while people are clearly looking for more from their jobs, some dissatisfaction remains.

In most of the measures surveyed, the respondents rated their satisfaction with the measures at about half the level of their importance to them. Only 41 percent, for example, said that their work was satisfying enough to please them. But even here, there are indications that people are getting more satisfaction from their jobs than in the past, with another survey (this one by Research & Forecasts) saying that over half of those surveyed are enjoying their work more now than five years ago. Or, in other words, more of us are having more fun. If you are not among them, it may be time to make a change, either by looking for more challenge where you are or by looking elsewhere.

The Louis Harris & Associates survey

Table 10-2 shows the results of another survey, this one by Louis Harris and Associates, asking people to rate those things they considered to be very important in their work.

Table 10-2	What People Want from Work
Factor	**Percentage of People***
A challenging job	82%
Good benefits	80
Good pay	74
Free exchange of information	74
Chance to make significant contributions	74
The right to privacy	62

*The percentage of people who indicated that each of the factors were important.

The Survey by Media General Associated Press

In another survey conducted by Media General Associated Press, working adults were asked to name the one thing they liked most about their work. The responses are listed in Table 10-3, along with the percentage who rated each as being most important to them. Once again, notice that the money is not in first place.

Table 10-3	The One Thing That People Like Most About Their Jobs
Factor	**Percentage of People**
The work itself	32%
People at work	23
Money	12
Hours	7
Benefits	6
Boss	3
Other reasons	17

The Research & Forecasts survey

I have believed for many years that your life situation affects what is most important to you, and sure enough, there is some research to support that. In a study asking working people to select the two factors that were most important in their current jobs, there are distinctly different answers based on level of education. And, it has been clearly established, the more education you have, the higher your earnings are likely to be. Table 10-4 presents the results of the survey taken by Research & Forecasts:

Table 10-4	Work Values Differ by Level of Education and Earnings		
	High School Grad or Less	**Some College**	**College Graduate**
Pay	46%	42%	29%
Amount of independence	31	35	40
Pleasant working conditions	30	23	17
Liking the people at work	29	24	19
Gratifying work	25	32	43
Contribution to the public good	11	14	23
Important career step	10	15	19

As you can see, pay is less important for those with higher levels of education and earnings. For them, having independence and gratifying work are the highest rated values, with pay a distant third. But for those earning less, money becomes far more important. No surprise here – it makes sense. Once you are making a living, other things become more important. But even then, the research indicates that most people *did not* select pay as one of their top two choices. Over 50 percent of the high school grads or those with less education picked other things as being more important.

The research makes it clear that most people rate various measures of personal satisfaction very high in their jobs. For this reason, you would be wise to spend some time considering what *you* want out of your work before you go out and look for it.

Step I: Begin by Defining Just What It Is You Really Want to Do

The information and activities that follow will help you consider a variety of things that most people don't spend the time to think about in an organized way. Yet it is these very things that will make a huge difference to you in your long-term career satisfaction and success.

The Eight Components of an Ideal Job Description

Many experts have considered what is involved in helping a person define a job that would be particularly well suited to them. Among the more helpful approaches is one that defines eight clusters of issues to consider in defining the ideal job. While a variety of people have contributed to the process that follows, Bernard Haldane, John Crystal, and Richard Bolles have articulated it most clearly in their writings. The eight issues to consider are:

The Eight Components of an Ideal Job

1. Skills required

2. Personal values or interests

3. Preferred earnings

4. Level of responsibility

5. Location

6. Special knowledge

7. Work environment

8. Types of people you like to work with or for

All of these elements interact, so before you can define your ideal job, let's explore each of these factors in more detail.

1. What skills would you prefer to use?

Knowing what you are good at, and which of these skills you would like to use in your next job, is essential in developing a job objective. Chapters 3 and 9 should have given you a good sense of what skills you want to use on your next job. Think about those skills that you enjoy using *and* are good at. Then list the five that you would most like to use in your next job.

The Five Skills You Would Most Like to Use

1. _____

2. _____

3. _____

4. _____

5. _____

2. What values are important or have meaning to you?

What are your values? I once had a job where the sole reason for the existence of the organization was to make money. Not that this is necessarily wrong, it's just that I wanted to be involved in things that I could believe in. For example, some people work to help others, some to clean up our environment, and others to build things, make machines work, gain power or prestige, care for animals or plants – or something else. I believe that all work is worthwhile if done well, so the issue here is just what sorts of things are important to you.

The checklist that follows will help you identify one or more of the values that others have identified as being important or satisfying to them in their work. It was developed by Howard Figler, author of *The Complete Job Search Handbook* and used in a book titled *Exploring Careers*.

Work Values Checklist

This checklist presents 33 common "satisfaction factors" that people get from their jobs. Begin by reading the entire list, then rate each item, using the scale that follows.

1 = **Not Important at All**

2 = **Not Very Important**

3 = **Somewhat Important**

4 = **Very Important**

____ **Help Society:** Contribute to the betterment of the world I live in.

____ **Help Others:** Help others directly, either individually or in small groups.

____ **Public Contact:** Have lots of daily contact with people.

_____ **Work with Others:** Have close working relationship with a group. Work as a team toward common goals.

_____ **Affiliation:** Be recognized as a member of an organization whose type of work or status is important to me.

_____ **Friendship:** Develop close personal relationships with coworkers.

_____ **Competition:** Pit my abilities against others. There are clear outcomes.

_____ **Make Decisions:** Have the power to set policy and determine a course of action.

_____ **Work Under Pressure**: Work in a situation where deadlines and high quality work are required by my supervisor.

_____ **Power and Authority:** Control other people's work activities.

_____ **Influence People:** Be in a position to change people's attitudes and opinions.

_____ **Work Alone:** Do things by myself, without much contact with others.

_____ **Knowledge:** Seek knowledge, truth, and understanding.

_____ **Intellectual Status:** Be regarded by others as an expert or a person of intellectual achievement.

_____ **Artistic Creativity:** Do creative work in any of several art forms.

_____ **Creativity (general):** Create new ideas, programs, organizational structures, or anything else that has not been developed by others.

_____ **Aesthetics:** Have a job that involves sensitivity to beauty.

_____ **Supervision:** Have a job in which I guide other people in their work.

_____ **Change and Variety:** Have job duties that often change or are done in different settings.

_____ **Precision Work:** Do work that allows little tolerance for error.

_____ **Stability:** Have job duties that are largely predictable and not likely to change over a long period of time.

_____ **Security:** Be assured of keeping my job and a reasonable financial reward.

_____ **Fast Pace:** Work quickly, keep up with a fast pace.

____ **Recognition:** Be recognized for the quality of my work in some visible or public way.

____ **Excitement:** Do work that is very exciting or that often is exciting.

____ **Adventure:** Do work that requires me to take risks.

____ **Profit, Gain:** Expect to earn large amounts of money or other material possessions.

____ **Independence:** Decide for myself what kind of work I'll do and how I'll go about it, not have to do what others tell me to.

____ **Moral Fulfillment:** Feel that my work is contributing to a set of moral standards that I feel are very important.

____ **Location:** Find a place to live (town, geographic area) that matches my lifestyle and allows me to do the things I enjoy most.

____ **Community:** Live in a town or city where I can get involved in community affairs.

____ **Physical Challenge:** Have a job with physical demands that are challenging and rewarding.

____ **Time Freedom:** Handle my job according to my own time schedule; no specific working hours required.

• •

Other Values: Add any other values that are particularly important to include in your future work.

_____

_____

_____

_____

_____

Once you have completed the Work Values Checklist, go back over it and select the values that are most important to you and write them in the following spaces.

My Most Important Work Values

1. _____

2. _____

3. _____

4. _____

5. _____

---

3. How much money do you want to make – or are willing to accept?

Earlier in this chapter, I presented some research that indicates that pay is not the most important thing for most people (see Table 10-4, for example). Even so, many people use pay rates as a primary criterion for selecting one career over another or one job over another.

The more you earn, the less important it becomes. . .

It's easy to say that money isn't important, but to someone struggling to get by economically, it would quite naturally be far more important than another work-related value, such as having a good work environment. I have made these trade-offs in my own working life and so have many others.

Decide the money issue in advance.

While money may not be everything, when planning your career or looking for a job, it is important to consider the money issue in advance. For example, a position like "I'll take any reasonable offer," is an invitation to trouble.

I remember a middle-aged executive who had made over $60,000 per year. He had been unemployed for some time and was quite depressed. When asked what he wanted to earn in his next job, he told me that he wanted to start at about $65,000 but that he really only needed $30,000 per year to maintain his lifestyle now that his kids were grown. I suggested he redefine his job objective to include jobs that he would really enjoy doing and not to screen out jobs paying less than $60,000 per year. He took a job paying $37,000 and loved it. He told me he would never consider going back to what he used to do—whatever the salary.

Pay is important, but relative. What you want to earn in your next job and in the future will affect your career choices. But some compromise is always possible.

You should know in advance what you would accept as well as what you would prefer.

Here are a few questions to help you define a salary range:

Your Acceptable Pay Range Worksheet

1. If you found the perfect job in all other respects (or were desperate), what would be the very least pay you would be willing to accept? (Hourly, weekly, or annual is okay.) _____

2. What is the upper end of salary that you could expect to obtain, given your credentials and other factors? _____

3. What sort of income would you need to pay for a desirable lifestyle? (However you want to define this.) _____

4. How much money do you hope to make in your next job?

Many people will take less money if the job is great in other ways – or to survive. Think about the minimum you would take as well as what you would eventually like to earn. Realistically, your next job will probably be somewhere between your minimum and maximum amount.

_____

Later in this book, I will show you how to find out how much various jobs pay, on the average, as well as tips for negotiating your salary to higher levels. But to be successful in your negotiations, you must start with a good idea of how much you want – and how much you are willing to accept.

4. How much responsibility are you willing to accept?

In most organizations, those who are willing to accept more responsibility are also typically paid more. There *is* typically a relationship between the two. Higher levels of responsibility often require you to supervise others or to make decisions that affect the organization. Some people are willing to accept this responsibility and others, understandably, would prefer not to. Decide how much responsibility you are willing to accept and write that below.

Here are some questions to help you consider how much responsibility you want (or are willing to accept) in your ideal job.

Your Preferred Level of Responsibility

1. Do you like to be in charge of things?

2. Are you good at supervising others?

3. Do you prefer working as part of a team?

4. Do you prefer working by yourself or under someone else's guidance?

Jot down where you see yourself, in terms of accepting responsibility for others, and in other ways within an organization.

_____

_____

_____

_____

5. Where do you want your next job to be located – in what city or region?

Narrowing down your job search as much as possible is a good thing to do. One of the factors to consider during your search for a job is where, geographically, you want to work. This could be as simple a decision as finding a job that allows you to live where you are now (because you want to live near your relatives, for example). But, if so, would you prefer to work in a particular area, close to a child care center, or what?

"Are you willing to relocate?" This is a very important question to answer now – before it comes up in an interview. There are often good reasons for wanting to stay where you now live, but certain jobs and career opportunities are limited unless you are willing to move.

For example, if you live in a small town, certain jobs exist only in small numbers, if at all. If you are willing to leave, you may be able to find jobs with higher overall wages, a larger and more varied job market, or some other advantage. Even if you decide to stay where you are, there are still geographic issues to consider. How far are you, for example, willing to commute? Would it be more desirable for you to work on one side of town than another?

When you've looked at all the options, you can make a more informed decision. If you prefer to stay but are willing to go, a good strategy is to spend a substantial part of your job search time looking locally. If you are willing to relocate, don't make the common mistake of looking for a job "anywhere." That sort of scattered approach is both inefficient and ineffective. It is preferable to narrow your job search to a few key geographic areas and concentrate your efforts there.

One strategy is to identify where the best job opportunities exist for the sort of job you want. A research librarian can help you find this information. But this should not be your sole criteria for relocating.

The right job in the wrong place is not the right job. A better course, before you get desperate, is to define the characteristics of the place you'd like to live. For example, suppose you would like to live near the ocean, in a midsize city, and in a part of the country that has mild winters but does have four seasons. That leaves out many places, doesn't it? Or it may be as simple as wanting to live near your mom. As you add more criteria, there are fewer and fewer places to look and your job search becomes more precise.

One way to do this is to consider the places you have already lived. Think about what you did and did not like about them. Use a sheet of paper to list the things you did like (on the left side) and did not like (on the right). This may help you identify the things you would like to have in a new place. You should also go to your library to research a particular location you are considering or just to learn about the options. The bibliography lists some excellent books that rate places to live and there are many other materials on this subject to browse through.

Preferred Geographic Location

Go ahead and write down your preferences for where you prefer your work to be located.

_____

_____

_____

_____

_____

---

6. What special knowledge or interests would you like to use or pursue?

You have all sorts of prior life experience, training, and education that can help you succeed on a new job. Chapter 9 reviewed these in detail, and you might want to review that material in considering your options.

Perhaps you know how to fix radios, keep accounting records, or cook food. You don't have to have used these skills in a previous job to include them. Write down the things you have learned from schooling, training, hobbies, family experiences, and other sources. Perhaps one or more of them could make you a very special applicant in the right setting. For example, an accountant who knows a lot about fashion would be a very special candidate if she just happened to be interviewing for a job with an organization that sells clothing.

Formal education, special training, and work experience are obviously important, but leisure activities, hobbies, volunteer work, family responsibilities, and other informal activities can also help define a previously overlooked job possibility.

To help you consider alternatives, use a separate sheet of paper to make a list of the major areas in which you:

> 1. Have received formal education or training
>
> 2. Are well-versed due to some prior work or nonwork experience
>
> 3. Are very interested, but don't have much practical experience

Once you have made your list, go back and select the areas that are most interesting to you. These could give you ideas for jobs that you might otherwise overlook.

Special Knowledge or Interest You Might Consider in Your Next Job

1. _____

2. _____

3. _____

4. _____

5. _____

If you already have a job objective and it does not include one of your top three choices, don't toss out that experience yet. For instance, if you are looking for a job as a warehouse manager, but you selected your hobby of making pottery as one of the three, can you think of a possible job combining the two? Perhaps distributing pottery supplies or managing some part of a pottery business would be more your cup of tea than just managing any sort of warehouse.

7. What sort of work environment do you prefer?

I don't like to work in a building without windows, and I do like to get up and move around occasionally. While most of us can put up with all sorts of less-than-ideal physical work environments, some things are more important than others.

Once again, defining the things that you did not like about previous work environments is a good way to help you define what you prefer. So think of all the places you've worked or gone to school and write down the things you didn't like about those environments. Then redefine them as positives, as in the following example. When you have completed the list for each job you've had (use extra sheets if necessary), go back and select the five environmental preferences that are really important to you. Here is one example of such a worksheet to help you get started.

Job: Accountant for the IRS

Things I Did Not Like About the Workplace	Environment I Would Like in My Next Job
too noisy	quiet workplace
no variety in work	lots of variety in work
no windows	my own window
parking was a problem	my own air strip (just kidding)
too much sitting	more activity
not people-oriented	more customer contact
indoors in nice weather	more outside work
too large a business	smaller business

Your Preferred Work Environment

Write those things that are most important to have on your next job on the lines below.

1. _____
2. _____
3. _____
4. _____
5. _____

8. What types of people do you prefer to work with?

An important element in enjoying your job is the people you work with and for. If you have ever had a rotten boss or worked with a group of losers, you know exactly why this is so important. But what someone else defines as a good group of people to work with might not be good for you.

You could argue that there is no way to know in advance the types of people you will end up having as coworkers. But then you have nothing but luck to help you if you haven't already given any thought to the subject. The following exercise will help you do just that.

Think about all your past jobs (work, military, volunteer, etc.) and your coworkers on those jobs. As in the previous sample worksheet, write down the things you didn't like about your coworkers, then redefine them into qualities you'd like to see in your workmates. When your list is complete, go back and identify the types of people you would really like to work with in your next job. Then select the three qualities that are most important to you.

Characteristics of the People You Would Prefer to Work With

Write those characteristics below that are particularly important to have in the people you work with:

1. _____
2. _____
3. _____
4. _____
5. _____

Now You Have a Basic Definition of Your Ideal Job

You may need to spend considerably more time in clarifying one or more of the eight issues I just presented. Any one of them, if left unresolved, can cause you problems during your search for a job. Even worse, accepting a job that is in major conflict with one or more of these issues can eventually lead to job failure or unhappiness.

I will help you pull together your definition of an ideal job at the end of this chapter through the use of a worksheet. It will summarize key factors to include in the job you want, and because it is short, you are more likely to remember what is most important to you.

Step II: Once You Know What You Want to Do, Then Define the Field and Industry Where You Want to Do It. . .

Most people jump into a job search without much consideration of the things I reviewed earlier in this chapter. Instead, they often begin with a job objective that is poorly formed and that excludes many possibilities. In most cases, they look for a job similar to one they had in the past. Rather than analyze what they really want to do, they stick to what they believe they are "qualified for."

While this may seem like a logical approach, few job seekers have a good knowledge of the jobs they seek and even fewer have spent time identifying job targets in other occupations or industries that use skills similar to those they already have. So, whether or not you believe you already have a clear job objective, what follows in this chapter will help you identify more options than you would likely consider otherwise.

Think of Jobs Within Clusters of Related Occupations

Most people overlook too many job opportunities. They often do this simply because they don't know about all the occupations that could use a person with their skills, interests, and experience. As I've mentioned, there are more than 12,000 jobs that are defined by the U.S. Department of Labor. This is entirely too large a number for anyone to comprehend in any meaningful way.

Most people simply go about their lives and careers with very little information about the universe of career and job possibilities that might suit them. They often end up in an educational program and, later, find jobs in a haphazard way. That is how it happened for me during my early years, and it was probably that way for you. Things simply happened.

But I think that most of us can do better. While I am not suggesting that the process of career planning is a simple one, I do think that there are a few simple things that we can do to help us make better decisions. And, in this chapter, I will present to you a few things that I think can be particularly helpful.

One of those things is to introduce you to several of the ways that labor market experts have organized jobs and information about jobs. Fortunately, the more than 12,000 job titles that exist are not arranged in random order. Someone has spent a lot of time arranging them into clusters of related jobs. Knowing these arrangements can help you in a variety of ways. For example, you might identify possible job targets, consider long-term career plans, write a better resume and, of course, prepare for interviews.

The Occupational Outlook Handbook (OOH)

Quick Tip

Begin with the *Occupational Outlook Handbook* – It's the very best source for descriptions of 250 major jobs.

I consider the *Occupational Outlook Handbook* (OOH) to be one of the most helpful books on career information available. I urge you to either buy one or arrange for frequent access to it throughout your job search because it is so useful in a variety of ways.

The OOH provides descriptions for about 250 of the most popular jobs in our workforce. While that may not sound like many – compared to the over 12,000 job titles that exist – these 250 jobs are the ones that about 85 percent of the workforce actually work in. Updated every two years by the U.S. Department of Labor, the OOH provides the latest information on salaries, projections for growth, related jobs, skills required, education or training needed, working

Quick Reference

conditions, and many other details. Each job is described in a readable and interesting format.

Reading any description will help you understand how useful the OOH job descriptions can be. Read it soon, while my comments on the OOH are fresh in your mind. . .

Some Ways to Use the OOH

The OOH is a helpful book to you in your job search, and I am an enthusiast of its virtues. Here are some ways you can use it:

✓ **1. To Explore Career Alternatives:** The jobs are arranged into logical clusters, so finding those that interest you is quite easy. You can quickly find out more about a job and also learn about others that you may have overlooked.

✓ **2. To Help Decide on Education or Training:** Too many people decide to obtain job-related training or education without knowing much about the job they will eventually seek. Reviewing the OOH descriptions of jobs that interest you is one place to learn more about an occupation **before** you enroll in an education or training program.

✓ **3. To Identify the Skills Needed in the Job You Want:** You can look up a job that interests you and the OOH will tell you the transferable and job-related skills it requires. Assuming that you have these skills, you can then emphasize them in your resume and interviews.

✓ **4. To Find Skills from Previous Jobs to Support Your Present Objective:** Look up OOH descriptions for jobs you have had in the past. A careful read will help you identify skills you used there that can be transferred and used in the new job. Even "minor" jobs can be used in this way. For example, if you waited on tables while going to school, you would discover that doing this requires the ability to work under pressure, good communications skills, the ability to deal with customers, work quickly, and many other skills. If, for example, you were now looking for a job as an accountant, you can see how transferable skills used in an apparently unrelated past job (such as waiting on tables) really can be used to support your ability to do another job.

✓ **5. To Identify Related Job Targets:** Each of the major jobs described in the OOH includes a listing of other jobs that are closely related to it. It also includes information on jobs that it often leads to through promotion or experience. And, since the jobs are listed within clusters of similar jobs, you can easily browse adjacent descriptions of similar jobs that you may have overlooked. All of this information gives you options to consider in your job search as well as information to include in your resume's job objective.

✓ **6. To Prepare for Interviews:** Before an interview, carefully review the OOH description for that job and you will be much better prepared to emphasize your key skills for that job. You should also study jobs you have held in the past and identify things you have done there that are needed in the new job.

✓ **7. To Find Out the Typical Salary Range, Trends, and Other Details:** The OOH will help you know what pay range to expect as well as many other details about the job and trends that are affecting it. But note that your local pay and other details can differ significantly from the national information provided in the OOH.

Most libraries will have the *Occupational Outlook Handbook,* but you probably won't be able to take it home. There is another book titled *America's Top 300 Jobs* that provides the very same information and that may be available for "circulation." You can also order either of these books through most bookstores, something I sincerely recommend based on how often they should be used as a reference tool during your job search and afterwards. Either book costs less than $20, and you can order them from the order form in the back of this very book.

The 250 Jobs in the *Occupational Outlook Handbook*

Following is a list of jobs in the current edition of the OOH. The jobs are arranged in clusters of related jobs and the listing will give you an idea of other jobs you might want to consider when writing your resume and conducting your job search.

One way to use this list is to check those jobs that you have held in the past as well as those that interest you now. Later, you can look these jobs up in the OOH and obtain additional information related to each.

Detailed Table of OOH Occupations
Within Clusters of Related Jobs

Executive, Administrative, and Managerial Occupations

Accountants and auditors
Administrative services managers
Budget analysts
Construction and building inspectors
Construction contractors and managers
Cost estimators
Education administrators
Engineering, science, and data processing managers
Financial managers
Funeral directors
General managers and top executives
Government chief executives and legislators
Health services managers
Hotel managers and assistants

Industrial production managers
Inspectors and compliance officers, except construction
Loan officers and counselors
Management analysts and consultants
Marketing, advertising, and public relations managers
Personnel, training, and labor relations specialists and managers
Property and real estate managers
Purchasers and buyers
Restaurant and food service managers
Retail managers
Underwriters

Professional Specialty Occupations

Engineers
Aerospace engineers
Chemical engineers
Civil engineers
Electrical and electronics engineers
Industrial engineers
Mechanical engineers
Metallurgical, ceramic, and materials engineers
Mining engineers
Nuclear engineers
Petroleum engineers

Architects and surveyors
Architects
Landscape architects
Surveyors

Computer, mathematical, and operations research occupations
Actuaries
Computer scientists and systems analysts
Mathematicians
Operations research analysts
Statisticians

Life scientists
Agricultural scientists
Biological scientists
Foresters and conservation scientists

Physical scientists
Chemists
Geologists and geophysicists
Meteorologists
Physicists and astronomers

Lawyers and judges
Social scientists and urban planners
Economists and marketing research analysts
Psychologists
Sociologists
Urban and regional planners

Social and recreation workers
Human services workers
Recreation workers
Social workers

Religious workers
Protestant ministers
Rabbis
Roman Catholic priests

Teachers, librarians, and counselors
Adult education teachers
Archivists and curators
College and university faculty
Counselors
Librarians

School teachers—Kindergarten, elementary, and secondary

Health diagnosing practitioners

Chiropractors
Dentists
Optometrists
Physicians
Podiatrists
Veterinarians

Health assessment and treating occupations

Dietitians and nutritionists
Occupational therapists
Pharmacists
Physical therapists
Physician assistants
Recreational therapists

Registered nurses
Respirator therapists
Speech-language pathologists and audiologists

Communications occupations

Public relations specialists
Radio and television announcers and newscasters
Reporters and correspondents
Writers and editors

Visual arts occupations

Designers
Photographers and camera operators
Visual artists

Performing arts occupations

Actors, directors, and producers
Dancers and choreographers
Musicians

Technicians and Related Support Occupations

Health technologists and technicians

Cardiovascular technologists and technicians
Clinical laboratory technologists and technicians
Dental hygienists
Dispensing opticians
EEG technologists
Emergency medial technicians
Licensed practical nurses
Medical record technicians
Nuclear medicine technologists
Radiologic technologists
Surgical technicians

Technologists, except health

Aircraft pilots
Air traffic controllers
Broadcast technicians
Computer programmers
Drafters
Engineering technicians
Library technicians
Paralegals
Science technicians

Marketing and Sales Occupations

Cashiers
Counter and rental clerks
Insurance agents and brokers
Manufacturers' and wholesale sales representatives
Real estate agents, brokers, and appraisers

Retail sales workers
Securities and financial services sales representatives
Services sales representatives
Travel agents

Administrative Support Occupations, Including Clerical

Adjusters, investigators, and collectors
Bank tellers
Clerical supervisors and managers
Computer and peripheral equipment operators
Credit clerks and authorizers
General office clerks
Information clerks
   Hotel and motel clerks

Interviewing and new accounts clerks
Receptionists
Reservation and transportation ticket agents and travel clerks
Mail clerks and messengers
Material recording, scheduling, dispatching, and distributing occupations
   Dispatchers

Stock clerks
Traffic, shipping, and receiving clerks
Postal clerks and mail carriers
Record clerks
  Billing clerks
  Bookkeeping, accounting, and auditing clerks
  Brokerage clerks and statement clerks
  File clerks
  Library assistants and bookmobile drivers

Order clerks
Payroll and timekeeping clerks
Personnel clerks
Secretaries
Stenographers and court reporters
Teacher aides
Telephone operators
Typists, word processors, and data entry keyers

Service Occupations

Protective service occupations
Correction officers
Firefighting occupations
Guards
Police, detectives, and special agents

Food and beverage preparation and service occupations
Chefs, cooks, and other kitchen workers
Food and beverage service occupations

Health service occupations
Dental assistants

Medical assistants
Nursing aides and psychiatric aides

Personal service and building grounds service occupations
Animal caretakers, except farm
Barbers and cosmetologists
Preschool workers
Flight attendants
Gardeners and groundskeepers
Homemaker-home health aides
Janitors and cleaners
Private household workers

Agriculture, Forestry, Fishing, and Related Occupations

Farm operators and managers
Fishers, hunters, and trappers

Forestry and logging occupations

Mechanics, Installers, and Repairers

Aircraft mechanics and engine specialists
Automotive body repairers
Automotive mechanics
Diesel mechanics
Electronic equipment repairers
  Commercial and industrial electronic equipment
    repairers
  Communications equipment mechanics
  Computer and office machine repairers
  Electronic home entertainment equipment
    repairers
  Telephone installers and repairers
Elevator installers and repairers

Farm equipment mechanics
General maintenance mechanics
Heating, air-conditioning, and refrigeration
  technicians
Home appliance and power tool repairers
Industrial machinery repairers
Line installers and cable splicers
Millwrights
Mobile heavy equipment mechanics
Motorcycle, boat, and small-engine mechanics
Musical instrument repairers and tuners
Vending machine servicers and repairers

Construction Trades and Extractive Occupations

Bricklayers and stonemasons
Carpenters
Carpet installers
Concrete masons and terrazzo workers
Drywall workers and lathers
Electricians
   Glaziers
Insulation workers

Painters and paperhangers
Plasterers
Plumbers and pipefitters
Roofers
Roustabouts
Sheetmetal workers
Structural and reinforcing ironworkers
Tilesetters

Production Occupations

Assemblers
Precision assemblers

Blue-collar worker supervisors

Food processing occupations
Butchers and meat, poultry, and fish cutters

Inspectors, testers, and gardners

Metalworking and plastics-working occupations

Boilermakers
Jewelers
Machinists and tool programmers
Metalworking and plastics-working machine operators
Tool and die makers
Welders, cutters, and welding machine operators

Plant and systems operators
Electric power generating plant operators and power distributors and dispatchers
Stationary engineers
Water and wastewater treatment plant operators

Printing occupations
Prepress workers

Printing press operators
Bindery workers

Textile, apparel, and furnishings occupations
Apparel workers
Shoe and leather workers and repairers
Textile machinery operators
Upholsterers

Woodworking occupations

Miscellaneous production occupations
Dental laboratory technicians
Ophthalmic laboratory technicians
Painting and coating machine operators
Photographic process workers

Transportation and Material Moving Occupations

Busdrivers
Material moving equipment operators
Rail transportation occupation

Taxi drivers and chauffeurs
Truckdrivers
Water transportation occupations

Handlers, Equipment Cleaners, Helpers, and Laborers
Job Opportunities in the Armed Forces

Quick Tip

The Complete Guide for Occupational Exploration (CGOE)

Explore 12,000 jobs in *The Complete Guide for Occupational Exploration* (CGOE). All jobs are organized into just 12 interest areas.

The *Occupational Outlook Handbook* provides excellent descriptions of the major jobs but does not cover more specialized ones. This can be a limitation if you have experience, education, or interest in a specific area and want to know the variety of jobs that area offers. In some cases, you may also want to know the variety of jobs you might consider in making a career change or in searching for a new job.

Unlike the OOH, *The Complete Guide for Occupational Exploration* (CGOE) is a book that does not provide descriptions of jobs. What it does do is arrange virtually every known job – more than 12,000 of them – in a very useful way.

All jobs are first organized within just 12 major interest areas. These areas are then divided into 64 groupings of related jobs and then divided into 348 additional subgroups of even more closely related jobs. Each of these groupings and subgroupings are described in an easy-to-understand way, including the types of training, skills required, and many other details.

If you are looking for other jobs to consider as job targets, the CGOE's arrangement will allow you to quickly identify groupings of jobs that are most closely related to what you want to do. All along the way, from major interest area to the various subgroupings, helpful information is provided related to each group of jobs. So, even if some of the jobs themselves are not familiar to you, there is enough information provided to help you understand the jobs within that grouping and what they require. In a quick and logical way, you can narrow down the thousands of job possibilities to the dozen or so that most closely match what you want to do and are good at.

Major interest areas in the CGOE

The CGOE's 12 major interest areas, along with brief definitions of each, follow. Typically, most of the careers that will interest you are within one or two of these major clusters.

The CGOE's 12 Major Interest Areas

1. **Artistic:** An interest in creative expression of feelings or ideas.

2. **Scientific:** An interest in discovering, collecting, and analyzing information about the natural world, and in applying scientific research findings to problems in medicine, the life sciences, and the natural sciences.

3. **Plants and Animals:** An interest in working with plants and animals, usually outdoors.

4. **Protective:** An interest in using authority to protect people and property.

5. **Mechanical:** An interest in applying mechanical principles to practical situations by use of machines or hand tools.

6. **Industrial:** An interest in repetitive, concrete, organized activities done in a factory setting.

7. **Business Detail:** An interest in organized, clearly defined activities requiring accuracy and attention to details, primarily in an office setting.

8. **Selling:** An interest in bringing others to a particular point of view by personal persuasion, using sales and promotional techniques.

9. **Accommodating:** An interest in catering to the wishes and needs of others, usually on a one-on-one basis.

10. **Humanitarian:** An interest in helping others with their mental, spiritual, social, physical, or vocational needs.

11. **Leading and Influencing:** An interest in leading and influencing others by using high-level verbal or numerical abilities.

12. **Physical Performing:** An interest in physical activities performed before an audience.

The more specific CGOE subgroupings

As mentioned earlier, each of the CGOE's 12 interest areas is further broken down into more specific groupings of related jobs. Each of these subgroups includes information related to that grouping as well as specific job titles that fit into each.

The chart below shows you how the Artistic interest area is broken down into its subgroups. The most specific groupings provide lists of jobs as well as some information regarding each job within the group.

This arrangement makes it easy to locate the types of jobs you want to explore by simply turning to the appropriate section of the CGOE. Once there, you can quickly see the specific jobs that are within that grouping and identify other jobs that may be suitable for job targets based on skills you already have.

Sample Section: CGOE Subgroupings Within the Artistic Interest Area

Literary Arts
Editing
Creative Writing
Critiquing
Visual Arts
Instructing and Appraising
Studio Art
Commercial Art
Performing Arts: Drama
Instructing and Directing
Performing
Narrating and Announcing

Performing Arts: Music
Instructing and Directing
Composing and Arranging
Vocal Performing
Instrumental Performing
Performing Arts: Dance
Instructing and
   Choreography
Performing
Craft Arts
Graphic Arts
   and Related Crafts

Arts and Crafts
Hand Lettering, Painting,
   and Decorating
Elemental Arts
Psychic Science
Announcing
Entertaining
Modeling
Personal Appearance

Quick Tip

While the CGOE is almost 1,000 pages long, it is very easy to use and will quickly help you identify the many specialized jobs that are related to the skills, education, and experiences you already have. Also, a variety of cross-referencing systems in the CGOE allow you to look up jobs based on education, hobbies and leisure interests, military experience, and many other factors.

The Dictionary of Occupational Titles (DOT)

While the CGOE can be very helpful in exploring career and job alternatives, it does not include descriptions of the more than 12,000 jobs it cross-references since doing so would require the CGOE to be almost 2,500 pages long. So, once you locate a job that interests you, the CGOE points you to a description for that job in another book, the *Dictionary of Occupational Titles* (DOT).

The DOT is the only book that lists virtually every job title in our labor force. Published by the U.S. Department of Labor, this enormous book (over 1,400 pages) provides brief descriptions for 12,741 jobs. Because of the difficulty in gathering accurate information on this many jobs, the government is the only source of such comprehensive information, and the DOT is the only book of its kind.

Last updated in 1991, the current edition of the DOT provides many new and changed jobs since the previous edition was published in 1977. For example, the many jobs created around new technologies and the use of computers are now included, and many descriptions have been changed to reflect changes in technologies.

Quick Tip

The DOT is considered a standard career reference book, and you should be able to find a current edition in most larger libraries. Because of the huge number of jobs and the complexity of organizing them, the DOT is not very easy to use and will require some study, but this effort can pay off.

The first several sections of the book describe how jobs are coded and organized. While the system is too complex to thoroughly describe here, the jobs are organized within major job categories and are assigned a nine digit code number. The first three numbers organize the job into categories of similar jobs, and the second three numbers provide information on how much skill the job requires in relation to Data, People, and Things. The last three numbers are assigned sequentially to jobs that fall within the same grouping. Each job has it own "DOT number," and all are arranged in numerical sequence.

The arrangement allows you to look up jobs in a variety of useful ways. For example, you can find a job that you have already held and look for other jobs in the same cluster as possible job targets. Or you can read the description of a job you are considering and identify skills you should emphasize in the interview. You can also learn more about jobs you might move up into or consider for the future. Appendices in the book also allow you to look up jobs by title and to identify jobs within specific industries that interest you.

The job descriptions themselves, while short, are packed with information including alternate job titles, industries where found, tasks and duties performed, skills required, strength and education levels, and other details. Since some of this information is in coded form, it will again require some study to understand, but most of it is quite clear.

While the DOT is not for everyone, it is a unique and valuable source of information on virtually all jobs in our workforce and can be an important source of information for career changers, job seekers, and many others.

Both the CGOE and DOT are valuable resources for finding job targets that would be overlooked otherwise. The information they provide can also help you identify skills and other details (such as the key skills needed in the jobs that interest you) to include in your interviews, resumes, or cover letters.

The Enhanced Guide for Occupational Exploration (EGOE)

There is one other book that might interest you, titled *The Enhanced Guide for Occupational Exploration* (the *EGOE*, of course). This book uses the same organizational structure as the CGOE *and* includes DOT descriptions for about 2,500 jobs. These descriptions cover over 95 percent of the workforce, including all but the most specialized or obscure jobs. Unless you are interested in highly specialized jobs, the EGOE will also help you locate a wide variety of jobs that are related to your interests.

Chapter 10

Additional Resources

In addition to the four book resources already discussed in this chapter (OOH, CGOE, DOT, and EGOE), there are several other resources to consider.

Besides the sources of career information I have mentioned in this chapter, I have included a variety of other information sources in this book:

✓ **In the appendices:** I have included various tables of information in the appendices including: a list of the 50 fastest growing jobs; data on self employment; a list of the fastest growing industries; resources for those with Armed Forces experience; fastest growing jobs for college graduates; the fastest growing types of jobs.

✓ **Other chapters:** Chapter 11 provides additional information on researching an occupation, industry, or a specific employer, and there is a list of average pay rates for several hundred jobs in Chapter 16.

✓ **The bibliography:** I have put together a very thorough bibliography that includes many resources for researching most things related to career planning and job seeking.

Other resources include the following.

Computer access to over 12,000 job descriptions is now possible

While the books I've just mentioned are very useful, they all have limitations. For example, you may need to refer to two or three big reference books to get all of the available information on a specific job. Another limitation is that some of the more detailed information is provided in coded form that is not easy to understand.

Part of the difficulty of using these books is the sheer number of jobs that need to be included. Providing details on all of them requires a massive number of pages. Fortunately, more powerful and less expensive computers with large data storage capabilities now are available to handle this.

JIST's Electronic Dictionary of Occupational Titles (on CD-ROM)

JIST now publishes several career information programs on CD-ROM that allow you to rapidly access substantial career information. For example, a program titled *JIST's Electronic Dictionary of Occupational Titles* allows you to quickly look up the over 12,000 job descriptions in the *Dictionary of Occupational Titles*. It provides a variety of simple ways to look up jobs such as CGOE clusters, DOT groupings and to even sort for jobs that meet your criteria. It then provides you access to a report that provides a brief description of the job, plus more than 60 details, including training requirements, abilities and skills required, strength needs, work environment measures, and many others – all in easy-to-understand language.

JIST's Electronic Occupational Outlook Handbook (on CD-ROM)

Another program on CD-ROM, titled *JIST's Electronic Occupational Outlook Handbook,* allows you to look up the complete text of any job listed in the OOH, plus another 7,700 more specific DOT job descriptions that are related to the more general OOH jobs.

What is particularly important is that the programs are very easy to use and very fast. They allow you to look up jobs by interest, occupational grouping, and several other ways. Check with your library to see if it has a copy of these programs or, if you have a CD-ROM reader on your computer, it may pay to have your own copy.

Chapter 11 has additional tips on looking up information on careers via computer as well as a variety of other career research tips.

Getting information on industries is also important

Deciding what industry you work in can also be an important issue, though it is another one of those things that most job seekers may not think much about. The pharmaceutical industry, for example, pays considerably better than many other industries, even though the jobs don't differ all that much.

I'll review several sources of information on various industries in the next chapter, and there are a variety of resources listed in the bibliography at the end of the book.

One book of particular value to you as a job seeker is titled the *Career Guide to America's Top Industries.* It provides descriptions of over 40 major industries and was specifically written to be of help to someone looking for a job or planning their career. It and other sources of industry information are reviewed in the next chapter.

Step III: Clarify and Refine Your Ideal Job Objective

While you will continue to examine options throughout your job search, I suggest that you be as clear as possible about your job objective before you go out looking for a job.

The Ideal Job Worksheet

I've provided the worksheet that follows as a way for you to gather your thoughts and to narrow down your job objective as much as is reasonable. Answer each question by including those things you identified as being most important to you in the activities earlier in this chapter. In some cases, such as the question on skills, you may need to review previous chapters to refresh your memory.

The Ideal Job Worksheet

In completing this worksheet, don't worry about being too practical: that can come later. Answer each question by including only those two or three things that are most important to you related to each question.

1. What skills do you want to use in your next job?

Adaptive skills:

_____

_____

_____

Transferable skills:

_____

_____

_____

Job-related skills:

_____

_____

_____

2. What values are particularly important for you to include or pursue in your next job?

_____

_____

_____

3. What range of earnings do you expect or would prefer?

_____

_____

4. What level of responsibility would you prefer in your work?

_____

_____

_____

5. What location or geographic preferences would you prefer?

_____

_____

_____

_____

6. What special knowledge or interests would you like to use or pursue?

_____

_____

_____

_____

7. What type of work environment do you prefer?

_____

_____

_____

_____

8. What types of people would you prefer to work with or for?

_____

_____

_____

_____

After you have completed the worksheet above, go back over all your responses and select the three things that are *most* important to include in your next job. Write those things on the following page.

The Three Most Important Things to Include in My Next Job

1. _____

2. _____

3. _____

Key Comment:

Once you have assembled the components of your ideal job, consider the possibilities. Your task in the job search is to find a job that comes as close as possible to meeting the criteria you have selected. If you conduct a creative job search, you won't be looking for *a* job but for *the* job. Of course, some compromise between the ideal and what you accept may be needed. But the closer you can come to finding a job that meets your preferences, the better job it will be for you.

The Job Objective Worksheet

Use this worksheet to create a draft of your job objective. Later, you can use it as a basis for writing a job objective for your resume.

The Job Objective Worksheet

1. What sort of position, title, and area of specialization do you seek? Write out the type of job you want just as you might explain it to someone you know.

_____

_____

_____

2. Define your "bracket of responsibility." Describe the range of jobs that you would accept at a minimum as well as those that you might be able to handle if given the chance.

_____

_____

_____

3. Name the key skills that you have that are important in this job. Describe the two or three key skills that are particularly important for success in the job that you seek. Select one or more of these that you are strong in and that you enjoy using and write it (or them) below.

_____

_____

_____

4. Name any specific areas of expertise or strong interests that you want to utilize in your next job. If you have substantial interest, experience, or training in a specific area and want to include it in your job objective (knowing that it may limit your options), what might it be?

_____

_____

_____

5. Is there anything else that is important to you? Is there anything else that you want to include in your job objective? This could include a value that is particularly important to you (such as "A position that allows me to affect families" or "Employment in an aggressive and results-oriented organization"); a preference for the size or type of organization ("A small-to mid-size business"); or some other thing.

_____

_____

_____

Write a Clear Job Objective Statement – Just as You Need to Do on a Resume

While it is important for you to consider what your ideal job might include, employers are a practical lot and you will have to communicate to them specifics of why they should hire you over another. The activities that follow can help you make the translation from the ideal (what you want) to the practical (what you have to offer the employer).

As I have mentioned before, employers are impressed if you are clear about why you want the particular type of job they have to offer. During the interview, you may be asked why you want the job and you need to have a good answer. For many, this can be more difficult to do than it might seem. It assumes, for example, that you have a good idea of the type of jobs that you want. And, even if you are not so certain, you will need to handle this issue in an interview.

One way to clarify your job objective is to write a job objective as if you were writing one for use in your resume. Doing this will force you to spend time researching various career alternatives and to select those that are most acceptable to you. You may end up settling for a broad job objective to cover a variety of jobs that you would qualify for, even if you are not sure that these are the ones that you want in the long term. In some cases, a broad job objective – or even multiple job objectives – will allow you to consider various options while you continue to research alternatives.

Tips for writing a good job objective

Although the job objective you write should meet your specific needs, here are some things to consider in writing it:

1. Avoid job titles

Job titles such as "Secretary" or "Marketing Analyst" can involve very different activities in different organizations. The same job can often have different titles in different organizations and using such a title may very well limit your being considered for such jobs as "Office Manager" or "Marketing Assistant." It is best to use broad categories of jobs rather than specific titles, so that you can be considered for a wide variety of jobs related to the skills you have. For example, instead of "Secretary" you could say "Responsible Office Management or Clerical Position" if that is what you would really consider – and qualify for.

2. Define a "bracket of responsibility" to include the possibility of upward mobility

While you may be willing to accept a variety of jobs related to your skills, you should include those that require higher levels of responsibility and pay. In the example above, it keeps open the option to be considered for an office management position as well as clerical jobs. In effect, you should define a "bracket of responsibility" in your objective that includes the range of jobs that you are willing to accept. This bracket should include the lower range of jobs that you would consider as well as those requiring higher levels of responsibility, up to and including those that you think you could handle. Even if you have not handled those higher levels of responsibility in the past, many employers may consider you for them if you have the skills to support the objective.

3. Include your most important skills

What are the most important skills needed for the job you want? Consider including one or more of these as being required in the job that you seek. The implication here is that if you are looking for a job that requires "Organizational Skills," then you have those skills. Of course, your interview (and resume) should support those skills with specific examples.

4. Include specifics if these are important to you

If you have substantial experience in a particular industry (such as "Computer Controlled Machine Tools") or have a narrow and specific objective that you *really* want (such as "Art Therapist with the Mentally Handicapped"), then it is OK to state this. But, in so doing, realize that by narrowing your alternatives down you will often not be considered for other jobs for which you might qualify. Still, if that is what you want, it just may be worth pursuing (though I would still encourage you to have a second, more general objective just in case).

Finalize Your Job Objective Statement

Look over the following sample job objectives to see how others have written their job objectives. Note that most do not include all the elements that are presented in the Job Objective Worksheet. That is perfectly acceptable. Some are very brief, providing just a job title or category of jobs, while others are quite long and detailed.

Some Sample Job Objectives

Copywriter/Account executive in Advertising or Public Relations Agency.

Program Development, Coordination, and Administration ... especially in a people-oriented organization where there is a need to assure broad cooperative effort through the use of sound planning, strong administration, skills of persuasion to achieve goals.

A responsible position in retail sales.

A middle/upper-level management position with responsibilities including problem solving, planning, organizing, and managing budgets.

Challenging position in programming or related areas that would best utilize expertise in the business environment. This position should have many opportunities for an aggressive, dedicated individual with the leadership abilities needed to advance.

To obtain a position as a financial manager in the health care industry, utilizing 16 years of demonstrating success and accomplishment.

To obtain a position as an Elementary School Teacher in which a strong dedication to the total development of children and a high degree of enthusiasm can be fully utilized.

An administrative position in the area of rehabilitation/geriatric health care utilizing my knowledge of clinical, community, and patient services.

Highly skilled Executive Secretary with outstanding professional experience including:
* Ability to communicate with all levels of management and employees
* International communication liaison with subsidiary companies
* Contract negotiation bargaining team member
* Use of word processing, Windows, Lotus 1-2-3

Some Sample Job Objectives

Seeking a position as a Registered Nurse where I can be most effective in helping other medical personnel assist patients and provide quality health care.

Obtain a challenging, entry-level position in Broadcast Journalism, with a special interest in reporting, anchoring, and producing with a commercial television station.

Position as a Word Processing Secretary that will utilize my computer knowledge, strong people skills, organizational abilities, and business experience.

Before you begin looking for a job, it is essential that you:

1. Can clearly state what sort of a job you want

2. Know what kinds of skills and experiences are needed to do well in that job

Even if you decide to change your job objective later, it is very important that you decide on a temporary one now. In my opinion, you should be able to answer each of the following questions before you begin your job search:

Questions You Should Be Able to Answer Before Beginning Your Job Search

1. What is the general type of job you want?

2. What specific job or job titles are most appropriate for you to look for now?

3. What top adaptive and transferable skills do you have that this job requires?

4. What specific job-related skills or knowledge do you have that directly relate to doing this particular job?

5. What special training or education do you have that directly supports your doing this job well?

6. Does the job require you to use any special tools or equipment? If so, what experience do you have in using them?

7. What specific work experiences, similar duties, tasks, responsibilities, etc., relate to your doing this job well?

8. What else can you offer that supports your doing this job well?

Unless you can answer all of the above items thoroughly, you are not ready to conduct a truly effective job search. If necessary, seek help from the other sources I've mentioned, but do settle on a job objective before you begin your job search.

Quick Summary

- ✓ There are over 20,000 job titles. Add to that the obvious variable of different work environments. You might be delighted to work in one and entirely miserable working in another. Yet both could *look* very much the same to a job seeker. And both could have the very same job title.

- ✓ Many people confuse a job objective with a job title, but they are not the same thing at all. A job objective is more complex and specific to you and your needs. It mentions skills and preferences without limiting the choices. This approach leaves open a variety of options, and it also provides more information on what the person wants and is good at doing. A sample job objective would clearly allow this person to do a wide variety of jobs.

- ✓ When surveyed, most people do not choose money as what they want most in a job. Many other factors rate higher in various studies of job satisfaction. Yet many people begin their job search without knowing what they really want.

- ✓ The eight components of an ideal job are 1) Skills required, 2) Personal values or interests, 3) Preferred earnings, 4) Level of responsibility, 5) Location, 6) Special knowledge, 7) Work environment, 8) Types of people you like to work with or for.

- ✓ Completing the worksheets in this chapter can help you determine the answers to questions relating to these eight components, thus helping you discover what it is that you really want in a job.

- ✓ There are many resources available to help you define the field and industry where you want to work: *Occupational Outlook Handbook* (OOH), *The Complete Guide for Occupational Exploration* (CGOE), *Dictionary of Occupational Titles* (DOT), *The Enhanced Guide for Occupational Exploration* (EGOE), CD-ROM titles, etc.

- ✓ Before beginning your job search, it is essential that you have a clear statement of what sort of job you want and that you know what kinds of skills and experiences are needed to perform that job well.

CHAPTER ELEVEN

Preparing for
the Job Search

Research Before
the Interview –

Print and Computer Resources

![Quick Overview]

≡Quick Overview

In this chapter, I review the following:

✓ Sources of industry information

✓ Occupational information resources

✓ How to gather information about organizations and interviewers

✓ People – another important information source

✓ Computer on-line services

There is an overwhelming amount of information available on jobs, specific organizations, job seeking, and many related topics. A good library will have hundreds of resource materials available to help you prepare for your interview. Bookstores also have helpful materials, and an increasing number of resources are becoming available via computer software and on-line services.

In this chapter, I review some of the most important of those resources, and I advise you on how best to use them. Note also that I have included hundreds of resources, both print and computer, in the bibliography, and you should refer to it for additional resources on specific topics.

Industry Information

I spent more time in the previous chapter showing you the major sources of career information, but having solid information about the industry is also very important.

Quick Alert

Many of you think you can skip this section because you've worked in your industry before and think you know enough about it. But veterans as well as new graduates need to research industry information when preparing for an interview.

For instance, do you know each of the following:

➤ How stable your industry is?

➤ How many people are in this industry in the country? In your area?

➤ What the average salary range is between entry level and upper level employees in your field?

➤ What the biggest challenges are facing that industry in the next five years?

This industry information you gather will be invaluable to you in the interview. For example, knowing that there are only 9,000 available certified property managers and 250,000 real estate firms needing agents allows you to present yourself as among the top three percent in the field – an excellent thing to know at salary negotiation time!

Highly Recommended Industry Information Resources

Of the many sources of information on industries, I want to emphasize a few that are of particular value to you in your search for a job.

The Career Guide to America's Top Industries

Based on information provided by the U.S. Department of Labor, the *Career Guide to America's Top Industries* was specifically written to help in career planning and job seeking. It provides information on over 40 major industries covering about 75 percent of the workforce.

Each industry description includes an overview of the industry, types of jobs it offers, employment projections, earnings, training required, working conditions, advancement opportunities, industry trends, sources of additional information, and more.

What is important about this book is that, for the first time, important information on industry trends and opportunities is provided in an easy-to-understand and readable format. The information is designed to help you make good career decisions and can be very helpful in preparing for an interview. For example, did you know that the construction industry is among the economy's largest employers; consists mostly of smaller businesses employing fewer than 10 people; has a very large number of self-employed people; and that good job prospects are projected in the construction trades for the future? Or did you know that three out of four people in the construction industry work for small employers – those with fewer than 500 employees? Or that people who work in the drug manufacturing industry earn almost twice as much as the average wage for all industries (which would make it a good industry to target)? Interesting.

While this information has been available in the past, it hasn't been readily available to most people, and few have used it to help them make career-related decisions. This new book should change that as it becomes better known and more widely available. I think it is good enough to be an essential part of a good career library and highly recommend it as a resource.

Listing of Industries in the *Career Guide to America's Top Industries*

Here is a list of major industries covered in the current edition of the *Career Guide to America's Top Industries.*

Agriculture, Mining, and Construction

Agricultural services
Construction
Mining and quarrying
Oil and gas extraction

Manufacturing

Aerospace manufacturing
Apparel and other textile products
Chemicals manufacturing, except drugs
Electronics
Food processing
Furniture and fixtures
Motor vehicle and
    equipment manufacturing
Printing and publishing
Steel manufacturing
Textile mill products

Transportation and Communication

Air transportation
Radio and television broadcasting
Telephone communications
Trucking and warehousing

Wholesale and Retail Trade

Department, clothing, and
    accessory stores
Eating and drinking places
Grocery stores
Motor vehicle dealers
Wholesale trade

Finance and Insurance

Banking
Insurance
Securities and commodities

Services

Advertising
Amusement and recreation services
Child-care services
Computer and data processing
    services
Educational services
Federal government
Health services
Hotels and other lodging places
Management and public relations
    services
Motion picture production and
    distribution
Personnel supply services
Social services
State and local government

The U.S. Industrial Outlook

The *U.S. Industrial Outlook* provides descriptions of 350 industries. Produced by the U. S. Department of Commerce, it provides an excellent overview of major trends within each industry, the effect of foreign competition, and other details that will be helpful in an interview. While an annual edition of this book has been published for many years, its future is now uncertain, and its publication may be dropped. If so, this will be a loss for job seekers, but the current edition of the book will provide useful information for several years to come. A good library should have a copy of this standard business reference book.

Other Sources of Industry Information

A good library will have lots of information on industries. Consider the following publications.

Industry trade magazines

Industry trade magazines such as *Advertising Age, Automotive News, Hotel and Motel Management, Modern Healthcare*, and *Supermarket News* are full of articles detailing trends and problems in their particular industries. Going over the last six months' issues will give you a good background on current issues.

While you have these publications in hand, photocopy and highlight facts that support your position in that industry, and scribble in the margins some questions you'd like your prospective employer to answer. You should also review the classified ads to get an idea of what is available, as well as pay rates.

The *Encyclopedia of Associations*

A good library should also have a current copy of the *Encyclopedia of Associations*. This lists the thousands of specialized associations and is sure to include some that relate to your occupation or industry interests. Listings are by category. For example, there are 63 listings alone for the general "employment" category, including the Career Planning and Adult Development Network, Tradeswomen Inc., and Uglies Unlimited ("dedicated to unattractive individuals who are vexed by discrimination against 'uglies'").

Each entry gives the address, contact name, phone and fax numbers, mission statement, newsletters, and conventions for that group. Pick the ones in your industry category that closely match your situation and give them a call. They will often send you copies of a recent newsletter or journal and provide other information.

Matthew Lesko's *Info-Power* book

Another good general resource is Matthew Lesko's *Info-Power* book, published by Information USA, Inc. It lists information sources ranging from the Epidemic Intelligence Service to Displaced Homemakers Job Network to Literature Translators Opportunities. There's a great section on how to research a company, too, that will give you ideas on how to get information on a specific organization.

Information About the Occupation

If you have done the activities in earlier chapters, you should have a good idea of the types of jobs you want as well as your skills and other details. Now your task is to determine how those traits translate into job positions within your field.

For example, let's say you have chosen to work in the history field. You've gathered information on the latest history theories and trends within the field. Now you need to determine if your personal skills and talents would be more conducive to market research, archiving and records management, preparing institutional histories, or teaching, to name a few. How are you going to determine that? Research!

Let's begin by reviewing several of the most important and basic sources of career information. While I mentioned these in the previous chapter, their importance bears repeating.

The *Occupational Outlook Handbook* (OOH)

Updated every two years by the U.S. Department of Labor, I strongly recommend this book. It is essential in preparing for an interview. It provides good information on the 250 or so top jobs in our economy and covers about 85 percent of our workforce. JIST publishes a bookstore version of this book titled *America's Top 300 Jobs*, available from most bookstores or libraries.

The Complete Guide for Occupational Exploration (CGOE)

This book cross-references 12,741 job titles into groupings of related jobs. The system is easy to use and allows you to locate jobs for which you might qualify that you may have previously overlooked. It also provides additional information about each of the job clusters, which may help you in an interview.

The Enhanced Guide for Occupational Exploration (EGOE)

Organized like the CGOE, this book includes descriptions for 2,500 jobs. Since these jobs are those held by over 95 percent of the population, this is a very useful book.

The *Dictionary of Occupational Titles* (DOT)

This enormous book is a standard occupational reference that provides brief descriptions for the more than 12,000 jobs that are cross-referenced in the CGOE. It is particularly helpful if you are interviewing for a very specific type of job and you are not that familiar with it.

Sample Job Reports

I have included occupational descriptions from two sources in this section. I decided to show you actual reports but in a reduced size, so please excuse the smaller-than-normal print size.

The first report is one of the over 7,500 occupational reports available from a software CD-ROM program titled *JIST's Electronic Occupational Outlook Handbook*. This program provides quick computer lookup of any of the 250 OOH jobs and then cross-references to over 7,500 more specific jobs that are related to those jobs.

I selected the JEOOH's one-page description for a job titled Public Relations Representative, which is one of the job titles covered by the OOH's more general Public Relations Specialists description. The report's description is based on the description in the *Dictionary of Occupational Titles,* and the information on training and other details is obtained from other governmental sources. As you can see, it is very different from the OOH description.

The second report comes from the *Occupational Outlook Handbook* (OOH). It presents information on Public Relations Specialists and will give you a good idea of what sorts of information to expect on the other 250 jobs described in the OOH. The OOH reports are very helpful in preparing for an interview because they include skills to emphasize, salary information, and other details that should be of great help to you.

PUBLIC-RELATIONS REPRESENTATIVE
PROFESSIONAL AND KINDRED OCCUPATIONS

Plans and conducts public relations program designed to create and maintain favorable public image for employer or client: Plans and directs development and communication of information designed to keep public informed of employees programs, accomplishments, or point of view. Arranges for public relations efforts in order to meet needs, objecbves, and policies of individual, special interest group, business concern, nonprofit organizabon, or governmental agency, serving as in-house staff member or **as** outside consultant. Prepares and distributes fact sheets, news releases, photographs, scripts, motion pictures, or tape recordings to media representatives and other persons who may be interested in learning about or publici;dng employees activities or message. Purchases adverbsing space and time **as** required. Arranges for and conducts public-contact programs designed to meet employees objectves, ubli2ing knowledge of changing atfitudes and opinions of consumers, clients, employees, or other interest groups. Promotes goodwill through such publicity efforts as speeches, exhibits, films, tours, and queston/answer sessions. Represents employer during community projects and at public, social, and business gatherings. May research data, create ideas, write copy, lay out artwork, contact media representatives, or represent employer directly before general public. May develop special projects such as campaign fund raisers or public awareness about political issues. May direct activities of subordinates. May confer with production and support personnel to coordinate production of television advertisements and on-air promotions. May prepare press releases and fact sheets, and compose letters, using computer. May disseminate facts and information about organizabon's activities or governmental agency's programs to general public and be known as Public Information Officer (profess. & kin.).

Strength - Sedentary Work
GED
Reasoning Development: - 5 (Hi=6, Lo=l)
Mathematical Development: - 4 (Hi=6, Lo=l)
Language Development: - 5 (Hi=6, Lo=l)
SVP
Specific Vocational Preparation - 7 (Hi=9, Lo=l)

Public Relations Specialists

(D.O.T. 165.017,.167)

Nature of the Work

An organization's reputation, profitability, and even its continued existence can depend on the degree to which its goals and policies are supported by its targeted "publics." Public relations specialists serve as advocates for businesses, governments, universities, hospitals, schools, and other organizations, and strive to build and maintain positive relationships with the public. As managers recognize the growing importance of good public relations to the success of their organizations, they increasingly rely on public relations specialists for advice on strategy and policy.

Public relations specialists handle such functions as media, community, consumer, and governmental relations; political campaigns; interest-group representation; conflict mediation; or employee and investor relations. Public relations is not only "telling the organization's story," however. Understanding the attitudes and concerns of consumers, employees, and various other groups also is a vital part of the job. To improve communications, public relations specialists establish and maintain cooperative relationships with representives of community, consumer, employee, and public interest groups and those in print and broadcast journalism.

Public relations specialists put together information that keeps the general public, interest groups, and stockholders aware of an organization's policies, activities, and accomplishments. Their work keeps management aware of public attitudes and concerns of the many groups and organizations with which it must deal.

Public relations specialists prepare press releases and contact people in the media who might print or broadcast their material. Many radio or television special reports, newspaper stories, and magazine articles start at the desks of public relations specialists. Sometimes the subject is an organization and its policies towards its employees or its role in the community. Often the subject is a public issue, such as health, nutrition, energy, or the environment.

Public relations specialists also arrange and conduct programs for contact between organization representatives and the public. For example, they set up speaking engagements and often prepare the speeches for company officials. These specialists represent employers at community projects; make film, slide, or other visual presentations at meetings and school assemblies; and plan conventions. In addition, they are responsible for preparing annual reports and writing proposals for various projects.

In government, public relations specialists – who may be called press secretaries, information officers, public affairs specialists, or communications specialists – keep the public informed about the activities of government agencies and officials. For example, public affairs specialists in the Department of Energy keep the public informed about the proposed lease of offshore land for oil exploration. A press secretary for a member of Congress keeps constituents aware of their elected representative's accomplishments.

In large organizations, the director of public relations, who is often a vice president, may develop overall plans and policies with other executives. In addition, public relations departments employ public relations specialists to write, do research, prepare materials, maintain contacts, and respond to inquiries.

People who handle publicity for an individual or who direct public relations for a small organization may deal with all aspects of the job. They contact people, plan and do research, and prepare material for distribution. They may also handle advertising or sales promotion work to support marketing.

Working Conditions

Some public relations specialists work a standard 35- to 40-hour week, but unpaid overtime is common. In addition, schedules often have to be rearranged to meet deadlines, deliver speeches, attend meetings and community activities, and travel out of town. Occasionally they may have to be at the job or on call around the clock., especially if there is an emergency or crisis.

Employment

Public relations specialists held about 98,000 jobs in 1992. About two-thirds worked in services industries – management and public relations **firms,** educational institutions, membership organizations, hospitals, social service agencies, and advertising agencies, for example. Others worked for a wide range of employers, including manufacturing firms, financial institutions, and government agencies. Some were self-employed.

Public relations specialists are concentrated in large cities where press services and other communications facilities are readily available, and where many businesses and trade associations have their headquarters. Many public relations consulting firms, for example, are in New York, Los Angeles, Chicago, and Washington, DC. There is a trend, however, for public relations jobs to be dispersed throughout the nation.

Training, Other Qualifications, and Advancement

Although there are no defined standards for entry into a public relations career, a college education combined with public relations experience, usually gained through an internship, is considered excellent preparation for public relations work. The ability to write and speak well is essential. Many beginners have a college major in public relations, journalism, advertising, or communications. Some firms seek college graduates who have worked in electronic or print journalism. Other employers seek applicants with demonstrated communications skills and training or experience in a field related to the firm's business – science, engineering, sales, or finance, for example.

In 1992, well over 200 colleges and about 100 graduate schools offered degree programs or special curricula in public relations, usually in a journalism or communications department. In addition, many other colleges offered at least one course in this field. A commonly used public relations sequence includes the following courses: Public relations principles and techniques; public relations management and administration, including organizational development; writing, emphasizing news releases, proposals, annual reports, scripts, speeches, and related items; visual communications, including desktop publishing and computer graphics; and research, emphasizing social science research and survey design and implementation. Courses in advertising, journalism, business administration, political science, psychology, sociology, and creative writing also are helpful, as is familiarity with word processing and other computer applications. Specialties are offered in public relations for business, government, or nonprofit organizations.

Many colleges help students gain part-time internships in public relations that provide valuable experience and training. The Armed Forces also can be an excellent place to gain training and experience. Membership in local chapters of the Public Relations Student Society of America or the International Association of Business Communicators provides an opportunity for students to exchange views with public relations specialists and to make professional contacts that may help them find a full-time job in the field. A portfolio of published articles, television or radio programs, slide presentations, and other work is an asset in finding a job. Writing for a school publication or television or radio station provides valuable experience and material for one's portfolio.

Creativity, initiative, good judgment, and the ability to express thoughts clearly and simply are essential. Decision making, problem solving, and research skills are also important.

People who choose public relations as a career need an outgoing personality, self-confidence, an understanding of human psychology, and an enthusiasm for motivating people. They should be competitive, yet flexible and able to function as part of a team.

Some organizations – particularly those with large public relations staffs – have formal training programs for new employees. In smaller organizations, new employees work under the guidance of experienced staff members. Beginners often maintain files of material about company activities, scan newspapers and magazines for appropriate articles to clip, and assemble information for speeches and pamphlets. After gaining experience, they may write news releases, speeches, and articles for publication, or design and carry out public relations programs. Similar to other occupations, public relations specialists in smaller firms generally get all-around experience, whereas those in larger firms tend to be more specialized.

The Public Relations Society of America accredits public relations specialists who have at least 5 years of experience in the field and have passed a comprehensive 6-hour examination (5 hours written, 1 hour oral). The International Association of Business Communicators also has an accreditation program for professionals in the communications field, including public relations specialists. Those, who meet all the requirements of the program earn the designation, Accredited Business Communicator. Candidates must have at least 5 years of experience in a communication field and pass a written and oral examination. They also must submit a portfolio of work samples demonstrating involvement in a range of communication projects and a thorough understanding of communication planning. Employers consider professional recognition through accreditation a sign of competence in this field, and it may be especially helpful in a competitive job market.

Promotion to supervisory jobs may come as public relations specialists show they can handle more demanding managerial assignments. In public relations firms, a beginner may be hired as a research assistant or account assistant and be promoted to account executive, account supervisor, vice president, and eventually senior vice president. A similar career path is followed in corporate public relations, although the titles may differ. Some experienced public rerations specialists start their own consulting firms.

Job Outlook

Keen competition for public relations jobs will likely continue among recent college graduates with a degree in communications – journalism, public relations, advertising, or a related field – as the number of applicants is expected to exceed the number of job openings. People without the appropriate educational background or work experience will face the toughest obstacles in finding a public relations job.

Employment of public relations specialists is expected to increase about as fast as the average for all occupations through the year 2005. Recognition of the need for good public relations in an increasingly competitive business environment should spur demand for public relations specialists in organizations of all sizes. However, corporate restructuring and downsizing, in an effort to cut costs, could limit employment growth. Employment in public relations firms should grow as firms hire contractors to provide public relations services rather than support full-time staff. The vast majority of job opportunities should result from the need to replace public relations specialists who leave the occupation to take another job, retire, or for other reasons.

Earnings

Median annual earnings for salaried public relations specialists who usually worked full time were about $32,000 in

1992. The middle 50 percent earned between $24,000 and $5 1,000 annually; the lowest 10 percent earned less than $17,000; and the top 10 percent earned more than $62,000.

A College Placement Council salary survey indicated new college graduates entering the public relations field were offered average starting salaries of about $21,000 in 1993.

According to a 1992 salary survey by the *Public Relations Journal*, the median entry level salary of public relations account executives was almost $21,000 a year. Median annual salaries of all public relations account executives ranged from $28,000 in public relations firms to about $36,000 in corporations. Manufacturers, utilities, and scientific and technical firms were among the highest paying employers; museums and miscellaneous nonprofit organizations, religious and charitable organizations, and advertising agencies were among the lowest paying employers. The survey indicated an annual median salary for all respondents, including managers, of about $44,000. Some highly successful public relations workers earn considerably more.

In the Federal Government, persons with a bachelor's degree generally started at $22,700 a year in 1993; those with a master's degree generally started at $27,800 a year. Public affairs specialists in the Federal Government in non-supervisory, supervisory, and managerial positions averaged about $45,400 a year in 1993.

Related Occupations

Public relations specialists create favorable attitudes among various organizations, special interest groups, and the public through effective communication. Other workers with similar jobs include fundraisers, lobbyists, promotion managers, advertising managers, and police officers involved in community relations.

Sources of Additional Information

A comprehensive directory of schools offering degree programs or a sequence of study in public relations, and a brochure on careers in public relations, are available for $10 and $2, respectively, from: Public Relations Society of America, Inc., 33 Irving Place, New York, NY 10003-2376.

Current information on the public relations field, salaries, and other items is available from: *PR Reporter*, P.O. Box 600, Exeter, NH 03833.

Career information on public relations in hospitals/health care is available from: The American Society for Health Care Marketing and Public Relations, American Hospital Association, 840 North Lake Shore Dr., Chicago, IL 60611.

Information About the Organization and Interviewer

According to experienced librarians, some of the best sources for information on local organizations are local newspaper articles, local directories, and area trade journals. Some libraries have clipping files of articles on area companies, CEOs, and industries. Ask your new library friends for ranked lists of local companies in your field. Depending on the library's size, you may even lay your hands on annual reports and various promotional literature, too. If the library doesn't carry copies of these materials, request them from the organization itself.

I have listed a variety of business references in the bibliography of this book that can help you track down information on a specific potential employer. If the organization is a small or privately owned company, this type of information may not be available at all. In that case, explore comparable companies and apply what you find. And don't forget – it's never a mistake to pick up the phone and talk with the organization's suppliers, customers, and current employees.

But now that you've gathered all this raw data, how do you apply it to the interview? Here are some questions your research should answer.

Questions to Ask About an Organization

1. Who are the prospective employers and what do they do?

2. What has the organization done in the last three years?

3. Where is the organization headed? What new products or services are on the horizon?

4. What/who is the competition? Where is this organization at an advantage or disadvantage?

5. What are the success factors?

6. How can the job you are pursuing contribute to the organization's success?

Quick Tip

Offer to drop by and pick up the organization's material in person rather than have it mailed to you. This fosters several positives: 1) It allows you to meet with the receptionist and make a positive impression with an insider (good news travels fast, especially when it concerns a future employee), 2) It strengthens an impression that you are well-organized and very interested, and 3)It forces you to travel the route in advance and scout out potentially slowing traffic patterns, confusing addresses, and so forth.

Ultimately, when it comes to finding out information about your specific interviewer, you may have to rely on the telephone once again. Politely and unobtrusively ask current employees about this person's style of work, how he or she spends the day, and other information that might help you in an interview.

People – Another Important Source of Information

While you can get an enormous amount of information from book and computer research, talking to people remains a very important source of information. So, pick up the telephone and contact people that work in the industry. Ask for their advice on where your skills could be best applied. Be sure to talk with people who work at a variety of levels, from association leaders to practitioners to technicians in satellite industries.

For instance, if you are interested in office management, get in touch with members of a local professional association that most closely relates to your interest, an office supplies firm, a temporary firm that specializes in placing office personnel, or actual office managers. Bring up anything you are curious about. For example, ask the office manager how often his or her position is needed in smaller businesses versus larger ones, what are the long-term advantages and disadvantages of full-time work as opposed to temporary assignments, how other members of a staff often treat this position, characteristics of successful office managers, etc. Continually compare this information to your situation.

Quick Reminder

Don't neglect to send a brief, sincere thank-you note to each person you talk to in this process. Since a job search is never completely linear, it's always possible that one of these contacts could evolve into a job interview; so you want to position yourself to take the early advantage.

Quick Case Study

I was recently told of a situation that illustrates how thank-you notes can work. A local magazine publisher had met with a freelance writer who had contacted her to explore business writing in general. Three days after the conversation, the writer's portfolio and a thank-you note arrived in the mail. That afternoon, the publisher's editor resigned, so she immediately called the writer to schedule an interview. The publisher told me she did this for two reasons: 1) the writer had impressed her with her professionalism, and 2) the writer's phone number was right in front of her. That's exactly how informal contacts can work out.

Computer On-line Services

Another place you can turn for information of all kinds is perhaps the most exciting advancement in the career industry – computer on-line services and bulletin boards. The debate over the advantages and disadvantages of Prodigy, CompuServe, America Online, and the Internet could fill another book, and all of these services have incredible networking capabilities. Post your occupational question here and you'll get replies from different levels and experiences across the country.

Much of what you want to know about an industry or organization may be available through a bulletin board system – and the number of bulletin board systems increases daily. And while the databases and articles are valuable, the assistance doesn't stop there. Executives, employees, and fellow job seekers freely share information, leads, and advice on a 24-hour basis – and it's all literally at your fingertips (no searching through library shelves!).

Quick Case Study

Already the business world is full of examples of job seekers who have landed positions through bulletin board systems. For instance, take Terry Carroll, a law student at Santa Clara University in California. According to *U.S. News and World Report*, the former computer designer caught the eye of two lawyers by responding to queries posted on CompuServe's legal forum. They promptly invited him to assist them on cases. Then when Carroll lost his computer job and decided to take up law full-time, he put the word out via electronic mail. Within 24 hours he had made six contacts and heard about six more job openings.

A Partial Listing of On-line Career Resources

Don't underestimate the fun of this newest job search tool. Candidates who skip the research stage because it's "too boring" will find themselves fascinated by the interactive, immediate-gratification format of bulletin board systems.

Although there is a tremendous amount of data and interactive advice available from the major on-line services, I've listed some of the career-specific services from America Online's Career Center. This is a special service set up to provide resources for career planning and job seeking. These services are impressive and always expanding.

The Career Resource Library

An excellent on-line career resource is the Career Resource Library.

Career development tasks

The Career Resource Library can be of value if you or someone you know requires assistance with any of the following career development tasks:

Selecting a career direction or goal

Conducting an effective job search

Selecting a vocational/technical program of study and institution

Selecting a college and major

Obtaining financial assistance to attend school or college

Finding work with your state or the federal government

Analyzing the future of a particular career field or industry

Researching potential employers

Starting and operating a small business

Working from home

Understanding your personality style and make-up

Enhancing your personal and social development

Dealing with job discrimination

Career planning after retirement

Diverse information sources and formats

The information available via this library includes information from diverse sources and in many formats including:

Audio cassettes

Books

CD-ROM and computer software programs

Conferences

Films

Magazines

Newsletters

Newspapers

On-line databases

Phone and fax services

Professional associations

Professional services

Videotapes

Workshops and seminars

On-line catalogs and ordering

You can even order career books and materials via this career center. Many JIST books (including this one) are available there via our on-line catalog, and we have a variety of career information resources available there as well. You can even download the latest JIST catalog in its entirety from the Career Resource Library and send orders via e-mail.

Company profiles

Hoover's handbooks database includes portfolios of more than 900 of the largest, most influential, and fastest growing public and private companies in the United States and the world. The Reference Press (Austin, Texas) creates and manages this database. Each profile includes:

Overview of operations and strategy

Founders' names and company history

Names, ages, and salaries of key officers

Headquarters address, telephone number, and fax number

Locations of operations

Lists of divisions, subsidiaries, products, services, and brand names

Names of key competitors

The Reference Press provides an alphabetical list of all companies in the database, so you can scroll through this or go directly to a company in which you are interested. You may also search for companies located in a particular state, region, or country. And if you don't know which company you are looking for, type in one or more search words. For instance, if you are interested in locating companies that make submarines, you can search for this word and discover that General Dynamics and Teneco are the two largest submarine makers in the country.

Employer contacts

Employer Contacts is a collection of information on more than 5,000 American employers, supplied by Demand Research Corp. (Chicago, Illinois). This service assists you in finding potential employers that match your occupational interests and goals.

Demand Research Corp. specializes in compiling and distributing information on every U.S. public company listed on the NYSE, the AMEX, and the NASDAQ National Market System. Each listing here includes:

The company's name, address, phone, and fax numbers

Ticker symbol

Exchange affiliation

Full name of the chief executive officer

Full name of the chief financial officer

Primary industry classification

Quick Summary

✓ Major sources of industry information include *Career Guide to America's Top Industries, U.S. Industrial Outlook,* industry trade magazines, *Encyclopedia of Associations,* and Matthew Lesko's *Info-Power* book.

✓ Among the most highly recommended occupational information resources are the *Occupational Outlook Handbook* (OOH), *The Complete Guide for Occupational Exploration* (CGOE), *The Enhanced Guide for Occupational Exploration* (EGOE), and *Dictionary of Occupational Titles* (DOT).

✓ According to experienced librarians, some of the best sources for information on local organizations are local newspaper articles, local directories, and area trade journals. Some libraries have clipping files of articles on area companies, CEOs, and industries.

✓ Much of what you want to know about an industry or organization may be available through electronic bulletin boards and computer on-line services, such as Prodigy, CompuServe, America Online, and the Internet. All have incredible networking capabilities. Post your occupational question here and you'll get replies from across the country. And while the databases and articles are valuable, the assistance doesn't stop there. Executives, employees, and fellow job seekers freely share information, leads, and advice on a 24-hour basis.

Section 3:
Quick Resumes,
Cover Letters, and
Thank-You Notes

Section 3 Introduction

You may have wondered why I did not include resumes in Section 1, where all the important stuff was supposed to be. The reason is simple: I think that resumes get entirely too much attention as a tool in the job search. Besides, I knew you'd look them up anyway.

The chapter on resumes will give you enough information to construct a basic resume and to do it in just a few hours. And that is precisely the point – a simple resume may be all that you need. I've also included information on more sophisticated resumes as well as a variety of examples. Most importantly, I provide you with some suggestions on how to most effectively use (and not use) your resume in your search for a job.

Chapter 13 provides tips on creating and using cover letters and a variety of other job search correspondence. If you want more information on resumes, there are a variety of good books on this topic listed in the bibliography at the end of the book, including my own, titled *The Quick Resume & Cover Letter Book.*

Chapters in This Section:

Chapter 12: Quick Tips on Writing and (More Importantly) Using Your Resume

Provides worksheets, tips, and sample resumes that can be completed in just a few hours as well as more advanced resume examples and tips.

Chapter 13: Cover Letters, Thank-You Notes, and Other Job Search Correspondence

Includes good examples of cover letters and how they can best be used as well as details on the often overlooked but effective thank-you note and other job search correspondence.

*Quick Resumes,
Cover Letters, and
Thank-You Notes*

Quick Tips on Writing and (More Importantly) Using Your Resume

There is entirely too much emphasis placed on the resume in the job search. If you are looking for a job where an employer will expect you to have a resume, write one. But the problem is that many people believe that a resume should be used to get interviews. That is a very old-fashioned idea.

Unfortunately, too many people write resume and job search books that provide bad advice. Their idea of the job search is the traditional one, where a job is advertised and people are screened in or out of an interview based on an application or a resume. In that context, the advice is to send out lots of great looking resumes (that will somehow stand out from the others) and get you an interview.

While that approach makes sense from the personnel manager's point of view, it is not a helpful mindset for you to adopt. It encourages you to be passive and completely dependent on someone else to evaluate your merits without ever meeting you. Since most people now work for smaller employers who don't have a personnel department, the passive and traditional approach of sending in an unsolicited resume just does not make good sense.

Even where there *is* a personnel office and a traditional interview/screening situation, you would be far better off calling up the person who is most likely to supervise you there and asking for an interview. How could it hurt? While others are dutifully (and passively) sending in their resumes to the personnel department, you have made direct contact and have a shot at an interview.

So a legitimate question might be "Why have a resume at all?" I cover this question by presenting both sides of the argument – as well as my own conclusions. I also give you guidelines you should use in writing your resume and tips on how it should be used in the job search.

Section I: What Is a Resume?

Let's examine what a resume is, and consider what it can and cannot do, as a first step in creating one.

A "resume" is the term most often used to describe a piece or two of paper summarizing your life's history. The idea is to select those specific parts of your past that support your doing a particular job well. Most often, the paper then presents you to prospective employers who, based on their response to the paper, may or may not grant you an interview. Along with the application form, it is the tool employers use most to screen job seekers.

So a resume is clearly a tool to use in getting a job, right? The answer to this is both yes and no. Many people who write resume books provide very bad advice. They confuse the purpose of a resume, and I think, put entirely too much emphasis on using it as a way to get interviews. But before I give you more of my own opinions on this matter, let me present what others are saying about resumes.

Do You Really Need a Resume?

Despite the popularity of resumes, some people say that you don't need one. Nonetheless, some apparent advantages of having a resume remain.

Some People Say You Don't Need a Resume

Trying to get an interview by sending out dozens of resumes is usually a waste of stamps.

For a variety of reasons, many career professionals suggest that resumes aren't needed at all. Some of these reasons make a lot of sense:

1. Resumes aren't good job search tools.

It's true, resumes don't do a good job of getting you an interview. When used in the traditional way, your resume is far more likely to get you screened out. There are better ways to get in to see people, and some of these ways will be reviewed elsewhere in this book.

2. Some jobs don't require resumes.

Employers of office, managerial, professional, and technical workers often want the details provided by a resume. But, for many jobs, particularly entry-level, trade, or unskilled positions, resumes aren't typically required at all.

3. Some job search methods don't use resumes.

Many people get jobs without using a resume at all. In most cases, they get interviews because they are already known to the employer or are referred to them by someone who does. While a resume might help in these situations, they are not required.

4. Some resume experts call a resume by another name.

Richard Lathrop, for example, advises you not to use a resume at all in his book, *Who's Hiring Who?* Instead, he advises you to use his "Qualifications Brief." Bernard Haldane, author of *Career Satisfaction and Success*, suggests that you use his "Professional Job Power Report" instead of a resume. And there are other names, including "Curriculum VITA," "Employment Proposal," and other terms. In all their forms, they are really various types of resumes.

Some Good Reasons Why You Should Have a Resume

In my opinion, all things considered, there are more good reasons to have a resume than not:

1. Employers often ask for resumes.

This alone is reason enough to have a resume. If an employer asks for one, why have excuses?

2. Resumes help structure your communications.

A good resume requires you to clarify your job objective, select related skills and experiences, document accomplishments, and get it all down in a short format. Doing these things are all very worthwhile activities for job seekers and are essential steps required in the job search, even if you don't use a resume at all.

3. If used properly, a resume can be an effective job search tool.

A well-done resume presents details of your experiences efficiently and in a way that an employer can refer to as needed. It can also be used as a tool to present the skills you have to support your job objective and to present details that are often not solicited in a preliminary interview. When used appropriately, a well-done resume can help you conduct an effective job search campaign.

How Do You Use a Resume?

"Send out your resume to lots of strangers and, if it is good enough, you will get lots of job offers" and other fairy tales

As I say at various times in this book, your objective should be to get a good job, not to do a great resume.

That's right. Contrary to the advice of many resume and job search "experts," writing a dynamite or perfect (or whatever) resume will rarely get you the job you want. THAT will happen only following an interview, with an occasional odd exception. So the task in the job search is to get interviews and to do well in them, and sending out lots of resumes to people you don't know – and other traditional resume advice – is a lot of BALONEY (or, if you prefer, bologna).

I hope this doesn't upset you. It's simply the truth. That is why I suggest that you do a *simple* resume early in your job search. This approach allows you to get on with getting interviews rather than sit at home working on a better resume.

And, for those of you who don't like to read (or are particularly anxious to get on with your job search without delay), following are some basic tips for using your resume that I have learned over many years.

Four Tips for Using a Resume Effectively

At best, a resume will help you get an interview. However, there are better ways of getting one – as you've learned in earlier chapters of this book. Here is a quick review of how to use your resume to its best effect:

1. Get the interview first.

Don't send an unsolicited resume. It is almost always better to directly contact the employer by phone or in person. Then send your resume after you schedule an interview, so that the employer can read about you before your meeting.

2. Send your resume after an interview.

Send a thank-you note after an interview and enclose a JIST Card (my preference) or resume. Or both. (JIST Cards are covered in Chapter 6.)

3. Give resumes to people you know.

Give copies of your resume (and JIST Card) to everyone in your growing job-search network. They can pass them along to others who might be interested.

4. If all else fails, use traditional techniques.

> If you can't make direct contact with a prospective employer, send your resume in the traditional way. An example would be answering a want-ad with only a box number for an address. But if that's all you do, don't expect much to happen.

Quick Reminder

Whatever you do, honesty is the best policy. Many people lie on their resumes and claim credentials they don't have, hoping that no one will find out. Many organizations now verify this information, sometimes long after a person is hired. I have always found that it is best to avoid lying, but that does not mean that you have to present negative information! Make sure that everything you put in your resume *supports your job objective* in some direct way! If you really can do the job that you want, someone will probably hire you because you can. And you will sleep better. . .

A Big Problem with Resumes Is That Everyone Is an Expert

A resume is one of those things that almost everyone seems to know more about than you do. If you were to show your resume to any three people, you would probably get three different suggestions on how to improve it. One person might tell you that you really only need a one-page resume ("And how come no references are listed?"). Another will tell you that, of course you should have listed all your hobbies plus the fact that you won the spelling bee in sixth grade, right in front of the whole school. And the third may tell you that your resume is boring and that the way to get attention is to print your resume, with red ink, on a brown paper bag.

So, one of the problems with resumes is that everyone is an expert but few agree. This means that *you* will have to make some decisions on how you do your resume. Fortunately, I'll help.

Guidelines for Writing a Superior Resume

There are some basic guidelines you should follow when you develop your resume. These aren't rules exactly, but you should carefully consider each of these suggestions since each is based on many years of experience and, I think, make good common sense.

Keep It Short

Opinions differ on this, but one or two pages is a good range. If you are seeking a managerial, professional, or technical position – where most people have lots of prior experience – two pages is the norm. In most cases, a resume any longer than two pages will not be read at all by a busy person. Shorter resumes are often harder to write but can be worth doing.

Chapter 12

Eliminate Errors

I am always amazed how often an otherwise good resume has typographical, grammatical, or punctuation errors. Don't have any! Find someone else who is good at proofreading and whom you can ask to review yours if necessary. Then review it again.

Make It Look Good

You surely know that your resume's overall appearance will affect an employer's opinion of you. Is it well laid out? Is it "crisp" and professional looking? Does it include good use of "white space"?

Use Word Processing

Computers are now often used to produce resumes, although output from a good quality typewriter is still acceptable. If you don't have access to a high quality computer laser printer or a typewriter with excellent type quality, have someone else print or produce your resume for you.

Most computer word processors can create very attractive resumes because you can use bold and different sizes and styles of type. You can also get two or more typed pages on one typeset page – or allow for more white space (a distinct advantage).

Microsoft Word for Windows and WordPerfect are excellent software packages (for word processing) that you can use to help create your resume. For help with WordPerfect, take a look at *Using WordPerfect in Your Job Search* by David Noble (JIST, 1995).

You can also have your resume word processed and "designed" at many smaller print shops. They will charge a modest fee for this service but can make your resume look quite professional by using a laser printer to give it a typeset look.

Use Good Photocopying and Printing

Some people dislike professionally typeset, word processed, or printed resumes because they present a mass-marketing image. They prefer an individually typed resume (the old-fashioned way) targeted to them. But, as I said earlier, you just can't please everyone, and good quality photocopies of your resume are now widely used and accepted. If you do have your own computer and high quality printer, individually prepared and printed resumes can present a better appearance and, of course, allow you to target your resume to a particular job.

You can also take your resume to most small print shops and have them print a few hundred copies for a reasonable cost. However you produce them, it is important that you have plenty of them on hand to use as needed. Important job targets can get an individually produced and targeted resume and cover letter as needed.

Use Quality Paper

A good quality paper is important. Never use cheap paper like those typically used for photocopies. Most copy machines will copy your resume content onto good quality paper, so get your own paper supply if necessary. Most print shops and office supply stores have a selection of papers, and you often can get matching envelopes. While most resumes are on white paper, I prefer an off-white (ivory) paper. You could use other light pastel colors such as light tan, blue, or gray, but I do not recommend red, pink, or green tints.

Papers also come in different qualities, and you can see the difference. Ones that include cotton fibers, for example, have a richer texture and a quality "feel" that is appropriate for the professional look you should use in a resume.

Stress Accomplishments and Use Action Words

Most resumes are boring. In yours, don't simply list what your duties were, emphasize what you got done! Make sure that you mention the specific skills you have to do the job, as well as any accomplishments and credentials. Even a simple resume can include some of these elements, as you will soon see. Look over the list of "Action Words and Phrases" and sample resumes in this chapter for ideas.

Don't Be Humble

Like an interview, your resume is no place to be humble. If you don't communicate what you can do, who will?

Make Every Word Count

Write a long rough draft and then edit, edit, edit. If a word or phrase does not support your job objective, consider dropping it.

Write It Yourself

While I expect you to use ideas and even words or phrases you like from the sample resumes in this book, *it is most important that your resume represent you, and not someone else.* Present your own skills in your resume, and support them with your own accomplishments. If you do not have good written communication skills, it is perfectly acceptable to get help from someone who does. Just make sure your resume ends up sounding like you wrote it.

Break Some Rules

This will be *your* resume, so you can do whatever makes sense to you. There are few rules that can't be broken in putting together your own resume. In this book, you will learn about the types of resumes and see a few basic examples. Remember that it is often far more useful to you to simply have an acceptable resume as soon as possible – and use it in an active job search – than to delay your job search while working on a better resume. A better resume can come later, after you have created a presentable one that you can use right away.

Chapter 12

Section II: Types of Resumes

To keep this simple, I discuss only three types of resumes. There are other, more specialized types, but these three are generally the most useful:

The Chronological Resume

The word "chronology" refers to a sequence of events in time, and the primary feature of this type of resume is the listing of jobs held from the most recent backwards. This is the simplest of resumes and can be a useful format if used properly.

The Skills or Functional Resume

Rather than listing your experience under each job, the skills resume style clusters your experiences under major skill areas. For example, if you are strong in "communication skills," under that major heading you could list a variety of supportive experiences from different jobs, school, or volunteer situations. Several other major skill areas would also be presented.

This approach would make little sense, of course, unless you had a job objective that *required* these skills. For this reason and others, a skills resume is harder to write than a simple chronological resume. If you have limited paid work experience, are changing careers, or have not worked for awhile, a skills resume may be a clearly superior approach to help you present your strengths and avoid displaying your weaknesses.

The Combination or Creative Resume

Elements of chronological and skills resumes can be combined in various ways to improve the clarity or presentation of a resume. There are also creative formats that defy any category but that are clever and have worked for some people. I've seen hand-written resumes (usually *not* a good idea); unusual paper colors, sizes, and shapes; resumes with tasteful drawings and borders; and lots of other ideas. Some were well done and well received, others were not.

Section III: The Basic One-Hour "Chronological" Resume

Keeping things simple has its advantages. This section shows you how to create a basic chronological resume in about an hour. While the resulting resume can certainly be improved, it has the distinct advantage of letting you get on with your job search right away. Later, as time permits, you can do a better one.

The big advantage of a chronological resume is that it is easy to do. It works best for those who have had several years of experience in the same type of job they are seeking now. This is because a chronological resume will clearly display your recent work experience. If you are wanting to change careers, have been out of the workforce recently, or do not have much paid work experience related to the job you want now, a skills resume, presented later in this chapter, might be preferable.

Most employers will find a chronological resume perfectly acceptable (if not exciting), providing it is neat and has no errors. You can use it early in your job search while you work on a more sophisticated resume. The important point here is to get an acceptable resume together quickly so that you won't be sitting at home worrying about your resume instead of out looking for a job.

Following is an example of a simple resume that uses a chronological format. The information and format are quite basic. Yet this approach works well enough in this situation because Judith is looking for a job in the same career field and has a good job history. The Instant Resume Worksheet later in this chapter will help you write the content for this type of basic resume in about an hour.

Judith's basic resume is then improved, adding a number of features, including a more thorough job objective; a "Special Skills and Abilities" section; and more details regarding her accomplishments and skills in the Education and Experience section. Although the improved resume would take most people longer than an hour to create, it still uses the basic chronological approach and could be completed by most people in one day or less.

Samples of Simple and Improved Chronological Resumes

Judith J. Jones

115 South Hawthorne Avenue
Chicago, Illinois 46204
(317) 653-9217 (home)
(317) 272-7608 (message)

JOB OBJECTIVE

Desire a position in the office management, secretarial, or clerical area. Prefer a position requiring responsibility and a variety of tasks.

EDUCATION AND TRAINING

Acme Business College, Indianapolis, Indiana
Graduate of a one-year business/secretarial program, 1996.

John Adams High School, South Bend, Indiana
Diploma, business education.

U.S. Army
Financial procedures, accounting functions. Other: Continuing education classes and workshops in Business Communication, Scheduling Systems, and Customer Relations.

EXPERIENCE

1995 - 1996 - Returned to school to complete and update my business skills. Learned word processing and other new office techniques.

1993 - 1995 - Claims Processor, Blue Spear Insurance Company, Indianapolis, Indiana. Handled customer medical claims, used a CRT, filed, miscellaneous clerical duties.

1991 - 1993 - Sales Clerk, Judy's Boutique, Indianapolis, Indiana. Responsible for counter sales, display design, and selected tasks.

1989 - 1991 - E4, U.S. Army. Assigned to various stations as a specialist in finance operations. Promoted prior to honorable discharge.

Previous jobs - Held part-time and summer jobs throughout high school.

PERSONAL

I am reliable, hardworking, and good with people.

Judith J. Jones

115 South Hawthorne Avenue
Chicago, Illinois 46204
(317) 653-9217 (home)
(317) 272-7608 (message)

JOB OBJECTIVE

Seeking position requiring excellent management and secretarial skills in office environment. Position should require a variety of tasks, including typing, word processing, accounting/bookkeeping functions, and customer contact.

EDUCATION AND TRAINING

Acme Business College, Indianapolis, Indiana
Completed one-year program in Professional Secretarial and Office Management. Grades in top 30 percent of my class. Courses: word processing, accounting theory and systems, time management, basic supervision, and others.

John Adams High School, South Bend, Indiana
Graduated with emphasis on business and secretarial courses. Won shorthand contest.

Other: Continuing education at my own expense (Business Communications, Customer Relations, Computer Applications, other courses).

EXPERIENCE

1995 - 1996 - Returned to business school to update skills. Advanced course work in accounting and office management. Learned to operate word processing and PC-based accounting and spreadsheet software. Gained operating knowledge of computers.

1993 - 1995 - Claims Processor, Blue Spear Insurance Company, Indianapolis, Indiana. Handled 50 complex medical insurance claims per day - 18 percent above department average. Received two merit raises for performance.

1991 - 1993 - Assistant Manager, Judy's Boutique, Indianapolis, Indiana. Managed sales, financial records, inventory, purchasing, correspondence, and related tasks during owner's absence. Supervised four employees. Sales increased 15 percent during my tenure.

1989 - 1991 - Finance Specialist (E4), U.S. Army. Responsible for the systematic processing of 500 invoices per day from commercial vendors. Trained and supervised eight employees. Devised internal system allowing 15 percent increase in invoices processed with a decrease in personnel.

1985 - 1989 - Various part-time and summer jobs through high school. Learned to deal with customers, meet deadlines, work hard, and other skills.

SPECIAL SKILLS AND ABILITIES

Type 80 words per minute and can operate most office equipment. Good communication and math skills. Accept supervision, able to supervise others. Excellent attendance record.

The Major Sections of a Chronological Resume

An "Instant Resume Worksheet" follows these tips. Use it to complete each section of a basic chronological resume. You may find it helpful to complete each section of the worksheet after you read the tips related to each of the sections covered below.

The heading

Often, at the very top of a resume, the word "RESUME" is typed, just in case the reader didn't know what it was. For this reason, the heading is, in my opinion, optional. If you are employed now and don't want your employer to know of your job search, put "CONFIDENTIAL RESUME" at the top and hope the reader honors it.

Identification

Name

This one seems obvious enough, but there are some things to avoid. Don't use a nickname – you want to present a professional image. Even if you have to modify your name a bit from the way you typically introduce yourself, it may be appropriate to do so.

Address

Don't abbreviate things such as "Street" to "St." and do include your zip code. If you may move during your job search, ask a relative, friend, or neighbor if you can temporarily use their address to handle your mail. As a last resort, arrange for a P.O. Box at the post office. Forwarded mail will be delayed and can cause you to lose an opportunity. If you plan to move to a new city during your job search, get a local address at the new location so that you appear to be settled there.

Phone numbers

An employer is most likely to phone rather than write to you. For this reason, it is essential that you can be reached, or that a message can be taken for you, during the day. Unless you use an answering machine, one phone number is not usually enough. You *could* try to be home at all times, but that is hardly a good way to get a job.

Provide the number of a friend or relative in *addition* to your home number. Type "home" for your home number and "message" for the other one. That way, an employer will know you probably won't be there, but to leave a message. It works. If you can use your business phone number for your job search, put it on the resume and identify it simply as "business," but still provide one or more alternative phone numbers!

While I (and many others) dislike telephone answering machines, it is better than not answering the phone at all. Consider using one during your job search or, better yet, use an answering service. Look in the *Yellow Pages* under "Telephone Answering Service" for sources. If you use one, type "answering service" next to that phone number. And don't forget to include your area code when you provide a phone number. You never know who will be calling you – or from where.

At this point, complete the identification section in the Instant Resume Worksheet following this section.

Job objective

You could put together a simple resume without a job objective; in most cases, though, it is wise to include it. If possible, avoid using a narrow job title (such as "secretary"), but don't try to include everything either. You want to have a job objective that will not exclude you from jobs that you would consider, without sounding like you would be willing to do just anything.

I see lots of objectives that emphasize what the person wants but that do not provide information on what the person can do. For example, an objective that says "Interested in a position that allows me to be creative and that offers adequate pay and advancement opportunities" is NOT a good objective at all. Who cares? This objective (a real one that someone actually wrote) displays a self-centered, "gimme" approach that will turn off most employers.

Refer to the following examples of simple, but useful job objectives. Most provide some information on the type of job that is sought as well as the skills that person offers. The best ones avoid a narrow job title and keep options open to a wide variety of possibilities within a range of appropriate jobs.

Sample Job Objectives

A responsible, general office position in a busy, medium-sized organization.

A management position in the warehousing industry. Position should require supervisory, problem-solving, and organizational skills.

Computer programming and/or systems analysis. Prefer an accounting-oriented emphasis and a solution-oriented organization.

Medical assistant or secretary in a physician's office, hospital, or other health services environment.

Responsible position requiring skills in public relations, writing, and reporting.

An aggressive and success-oriented professional, seeking a sales position offering both challenge and growth.

Desire position in the office management, secretarial, or clerical area. Position should require flexibility, good organizational skills, and an ability to handle people.

I've included a Job Objective Worksheet later in this chapter. Go ahead and complete it now if you want to include a job objective on your basic resume. Then complete the job objective section on the Instant Resume Worksheet.

Education and training

Recent graduates can put their educational credentials toward the top of their resume because it represents a more important part of their experience. But, for more experienced workers, your education typically is placed towards the end of your resume.

This section can also be dropped if it doesn't help support your job objective, or if you don't have the educational credentials that are typically required by those seeking the same type of position. This is particularly true if you have lots of work experience in your career area. Usually, though, you should emphasize the most recent and/or highest level of education or training that relates to the job.

Look at the sample resumes in this chapter for ideas. Then, on a separate piece of paper, rough out your section on education and training. After you edit it to its final form, write it on the Instant Resume Worksheet following this section.

Quick Tip

If you have received any formal recognition or awards that support your job objective, consider mentioning them. A separate section can be used, or they can be put in the work experience, skills, education, or personal sections.

Work, military, and volunteer experience

This section of your resume provides the details of your work history. If you have had significant work history, list each job along with details of what you accom-

---

Use Action Words and Phrases

Use active rather than passive words and phrases throughout your resume. The following list includes many good examples. Also, look at the sample resumes in this chapter for additional ideas.

Administered	Expanded	Planned
Analyzed	Implemented	Presented
Controlled	Improved	Promoted
Coordinated	Increased productivity	Reduced expenses
Created	Increased profits	Researched
Designed	Initiated	Scheduled
Developed	Innovated	Solved
Diagnosed	Instructed	Supervised
Directed	Modified	Trained
Established policy	Negotiated	
Established priorities	Organized	

plished and any special skills you used. Emphasize any skills that directly relate to the job objective you have stated on your resume.

List your most recent job first, followed by each previous job. Use additional sheets to cover *all* your significant jobs or unpaid experiences. Any significant volunteer or military experience can be treated the same as a job.

Whenever possible, provide numbers to support what you did: number of people served over one or more years, number of transactions processed, percent of sales increase, total inventory value you were responsible for, payroll of the staff you supervised, total budget you were responsible for, etc. As much as possible, mention results using numbers, too. These can be very impressive when mentioned in an interview or resume!

Emphasize accomplishments! Think about the things you accomplished in jobs, school, military, and other settings. Make sure that you emphasize these things, even if it seems like bragging or unconventional to do so. Many of the sample resumes include statements about accomplishments to show you how this can be done. In writing about your work experience, be sure to use action words. Quantify what you did and provide evidence you did it well. Take particular care to mention skills that would directly relate to doing well in the job you want.

Use separate sheets of paper to write rough drafts of what you will use in your resume. Edit it so that every word contributes something and, when done, transfer your statements to the Instant Resume Worksheet.

Previous job titles

Remember that you can modify the title you had to more accurately reflect your responsibilities. For example, if your title was "Sales Clerk" but you frequently opened and closed the store and were often left in charge, you might use the more descriptive title of "Night Sales Manager." Check with your previous supervisor if you are worried about this, and ask if they would object. If you were promoted, you can handle the promotion as a separate job and, if so, make sure that you mention that you were promoted.

Previous employers

Provide the organization's name and city, state or province in which it was located. A street address or supervisor's name is not necessary – you can provide those details on a separate sheet of references.

Employment dates

If you have large gaps in your employment history that are not easily explained, just use full years as a way to avoid displaying them. If you do have a significant period of time where you did not work, did you do anything else during that time that could explain it in a positive way? School? Travel? Raise a family? Self-employment? Even if you mowed lawns and painted houses for money while you were unemployed, that could count as self-employment. It's much better than saying you were unemployed.

Professional organizations

If you belong to job-related professional groups, it may be worth mentioning, particularly if you were an officer or were active in some other way. Mention any accomplishments or awards.

Personal information

The tradition is that somewhere on a resume you put things such as height, weight, marital status, hobbies, leisure activities, and other trivia. My advice is to not include this sort of information. Earlier I advised you to make every word count – if it does not support your job objective, delete it. Same here.

There are situations where including relevant extracurricular activities, hobbies, or leisure activities do help you; if so, go ahead and use them. Look at the sample resumes later in this chapter and decide for yourself.

While a personal section is optional, I sometimes like to end a resume on a personal note. Some of the sample resumes provide a touch of humor or playfulness as well as selected positives from outside school and work lives. This is also a good place to list significant community involvements, a willingness to relocate, or personal characteristics an employer might like. Keep it short.

Turn now to the Instant Resume Worksheet and list any personal information you feel is appropriate.

References

It is not necessary to include the names of your references on a resume. There are better things to do with the precious space. It's not even necessary to state "references available upon request" at the bottom of your resume, since that is obvious. If employers want them, they know they can ask you for them.

It *is* helpful to line up your references in advance. Pick people who know your work as an employee, volunteer, or student. Make sure they will say nice things about you by asking them just what they would say. Push for any negatives and don't feel hurt if you get some. Nobody is perfect, and it gives you a chance to get them off your list before they do you any damage. Once you know who to include, type up a clean list on a separate sheet. Include name, address, phone number, and details of why they are on your list.

Be aware that some employers are not allowed by their procedures to give references. I have refused to hire people who probably had good references but about whom I could not get information. If this is the case with a previous employer, ask them to write a letter of reference for you to photocopy as needed. This is a good idea anyway, so you may want to ask them for one even if it's not a problem to give phone references.

Quick Advice

Keep copies of the list and any letters of recommendation and provide them when asked or as needed. Do not attach them to your resume unless you are asked to do so.

The "Instant Resume" Worksheet

Directions: *This worksheet will help you organize the information needed to complete a simple chronological resume as well as the basis for a skills resume. Write out rough drafts for each of the more complicated sections that follow, then complete the form with content close to that you want to use in your resume.*

Identification

Name: _____

Home address: _____

_____ Zip: _____

Phone number and description (if any): ( ) _____

Alternate phone number and description: ( ) _____

Job Objective

_____

_____

_____

_____

_____

Education and Training

(Beginning with highest level/most recent)

Institution name: _____

City and state/province (optional): _____

Degree or certificate earned: _____

Relevant courses, awards, achievements, and experiences:

_____

_____

_____

Chapter 12

Relevant courses, awards, achievements, and experiences:

_____

_____

_____

_____

_____

_____

College/Post High School

Institution name: _____

City and state/province (optional): _____

Degree or certificate earned: _____

Relevant courses, awards, achievements, and experiences:

_____

_____

_____

_____

_____

_____

_____

_____

High School

(Optional if attended college)

Institution name: _____

City and state/province (optional): _____

Degree or certificate earned: _____

Relevant courses, awards, achievements, and experiences:

_____

_____

_____

_____

_____

_____

_____

_____

_____

Armed Services Training and Other Training or Certification

_____

_____

_____

_____

_____

Specific things you can do as a result:

_____

_____

_____

_____

_____

Work, Military, and Volunteer Experience

(Begin with most recent job.)

Name of organization: _____

Address: _____

Phone number: _____

Dates employed: _____

Job title(s): _____

Supervisor's name: _____

Details of any raises or promotions: _____

_____

_____

_____

_____

Machinery or equipment you handled: _____

_____

_____

_____

Special skills this job required: _____

_____

_____

_____

_____

List what you accomplished or did well: _____

_____

_____

_____

_____

_____

(Next most recent job)

Name of organization: _____

Address: _____

Phone number: _____

Dates employed: _____

Job title(s): _____

Supervisor's name: _____

Details of any raises or promotions: _____

_____

_____

_____

_____

Machinery or equipment you handled: _____

_____

_____

_____

_____

Special skills this job required: _____

_____

_____

_____

_____

_____

List what you accomplished or did well: _____

_____

_____

_____

_____

_____

_____

(Next most recent job)

Name of organization: _____

Address: _____

Phone number: _____

Dates employed: _____

Job title(s): _____

Supervisor's name: _____

Details of any raises or promotions: _____

_____

_____

_____

_____

Machinery or equipment you handled: _____

_____

_____

_____

_____

Special skills this job required: _____

_____

_____

_____

_____

_____

List what you accomplished or did well: _____

_____

_____

_____

_____

(Next most recent job)

Name of organization: _____

Address: _____

Phone number: _____

Dates employed: _____

Job title(s): _____

Supervisor's name: _____

Details of any raises or promotions:_____

_____

_____

_____

_____

Machinery or equipment you handled: _____

_____

_____

_____

_____

Special skills this job required: _____

_____

_____

_____

_____

_____

List what you accomplished or did well: _____

_____

_____

_____

_____

Professional Organizations

_____

_____

_____

_____

Personal Information

_____

_____

_____

_____

Write Your Basic Resume Now

At this point, you should have completed The "Instant Resume" Worksheet. Carefully review dates, addresses, phone numbers, spelling, and other details of the information it contains. The Worksheet can now be used as a guide for preparing a better-than-average chronological resume.

Use the examples of simple chronological resumes in this chapter as the basis for creating your own chronological resume. Additional examples of skills resumes are included later in this chapter, and you should look them over for ideas for writing and formatting your own.

Quick Reminder

Remember that your initial objective is not to do a wonderful, powerful, or creative resume at all. That can come later. You first need to have an acceptable resume, one that can be used tomorrow to begin an active job search. So keep it simple and set yourself a tight deadline for having a simple resume together so that the lack of one does not become a barrier for your job search.

If you have access to your own computer, go ahead and put the information you have collected into the form of a resume. Make sure that you edit each section carefully and that the resume has no errors at all. If you do not have a computer or are not a good typist, I suggest that you have someone else type or word process your resume for you. But whether you do it yourself or have it done, CAREFULLY REVIEW IT ONCE MORE for typographical or other errors that may have slipped in. Then, when you are certain that everything is correct, have the final version prepared.

Section IV: Write a "Skills" Resume in Less Than One Day

Even though it does take a bit longer to do a skills resume, it has some advantages that may make it worthwhile to consider.

Considering a Skills Resume

Quick Alert

In its simplest form, a chronological resume is little more than a list of job titles and other details. Many employers look for those with a successful history in a job similar to the one they have. If you are a recent graduate or have little prior experience in the career you now want, you will find that a simple chronological resume emphasizes your lack of related experience rather than your ability to do the job. If you want to change your career or increase your level of responsibility, this style of resume can often be an obituary.

A skills resume avoids these problems by highlighting what you have done under the heading of your specific skills rather than jobs you have held.

If you hitchhiked across the country for two years, a skills resume won't necessarily display this as a gap in your employment record. Instead, you could now say, "Traveled extensively throughout the country and am familiar with most major market areas." That could be a very useful experience for certain positions.

Because it is a tool that can hide your problem areas, some employers do not like a skills resume. But many do, and we've already discussed how you can't please everyone. Besides, if you do have a problem that a traditional chronological resume highlights, a skills resume may help get you the opportunity to meet with a prospective employer (who doesn't like your resume) rather than get screened out. Who wins?

Even if you don't have anything to hide, a skills resume can let you emphasize key skills and experiences more clearly. And you can always include a chronological listing of jobs as one part of your skills resume, as some of the examples in this book do.

So a skills resume should be considered by anyone, though it does take a bit more work to create a good one.

A Sample Skills Resume

Following is an example of a basic skills resume. The example is for a recent high school graduate whose only experience has been in a hamburger place. A skills resume is a good choice here since it allows her to emphasize her strengths without emphasizing that her work experience is limited.

While the sample format is simple, it presents her in a positive way. Since her employment will be at the entry level in a nontechnical area, an employer will be more interested in her basic skills that can transfer from things she has done in the past rather than her job-specific experiences. What work experience she has is a plus. And notice how she presented her gymnastics experience under "Hardworking."

Chapter 12

Lisa M. Rhodes
813 Evergreen Drive
Littleton, CO 81613
Home: (413) 643-2173   Message: (413) 442-1659

Position

Sales-oriented position in a retail or distribution business.

Skills and Abilities

Communications: Good written and verbal presentation skills. Use proper grammar and have a good speaking voice.

Interpersonal: Able to accept supervision and get along well with co-workers. Received positive evaluations from previous supervisors.

Flexible: Willing to try new things and am interested in improving efficiency on assigned tasks.

Attention to Detail: Like to see assigned areas of responsibility completed correctly. Am concerned with quality, and my work is typically orderly and attractive.

Hard Working: Have previously worked long hours in strenuous activities while attending school full-time. During this time, maintained above-average grades. At times, I was handling as many as 65 hours a week in school and other structured activities.

Customer Contacts: Have had as many as 500 customer contacts a day (10,000 per month) in a busy retail outlet. Averaged lower than a .001% rate of complaints, and was given the "Employee of the Month" award in my second month of employment.

Cash Sales: Handled over $2,000 a day ($40,000 a month) in cash sales. Balanced register and prepared daily sales summary and deposits.

Education

Franklin Township High School. Took advanced English and other classes. Member of award-winning band. Excellent attendance record. Superior communication skills. Graduated in top 30% of class.

Other

Active gymnastics competitor for four years – taught me discipline, team work, and following instructions. I am ambitious, outgoing, and willing to work.

Constructing a Skills Resume

The skills resume uses a number of sections that are similar to those in a chronological one. Here I will discuss only those sections that are substantially different – *the job objective and skills sections.* Refer back to comments related to the chronological resume for information on sections that are common to both.

Tips on combination and creative resume formats are provided later in this chapter, followed by sample resumes. These samples will give you ideas on resume language, organization, layout, and how special problems are handled.

Don't be afraid to use a little creativity in writing your own skills resume, since you are allowed to break some rules in this format if it makes sense to do so.

If you have ready access to a computer *and* are familiar with word processing software, go ahead and write your draft resume content on a computer. But, if computers are new to you, this is probably not the time to learn. It might be far better to take your handwritten resume content to a professional typist or word processor and have them complete your resume.

The Job Objective

Although a simple chronological resume does not absolutely require a career objective, a skills resume does. Without a reasonably clear job objective, it is not possible to select and organize the key skills you have to support that job objective. It may be that the job objective you wrote for the chronological resume is good just as it is; but for a skills resume, your job objective statement should be more carefully constructed.

Tips for writing a good job objective

While the job objective you write should meet your specific needs, here are some things to consider in writing it:

1. Avoid job titles.

Job titles such as "Secretary" or "Marketing Analyst" can involve very different activities in different organizations. The same job can often have different titles in different organizations and using such a title may very well limit you in being considered for such jobs as "Office Manager" or "Marketing Assistant." It is best to use broad categories of jobs rather than specific titles, so that you can be considered for a wide variety of jobs related to the skills you have. For example, instead of "Secretary" you could say "Responsible Office Management or Clerical Position" if that is what you would really consider – and qualify for.

Chapter 12

2. Define a "bracket of responsibility" to include the possibility of upward mobility.

While you may be willing to accept a variety of jobs related to your skills, you should include those that require higher levels of responsibility and pay. In the example above, it keeps open the option to be considered for an office management position as well as clerical jobs. In effect, you should define a "bracket of responsibility" in your objective that includes the range of jobs that you are willing to accept. This bracket should include the lower range of jobs that you would consider as well as those requiring higher levels of responsibility, up to and including those that you think you could handle. Even if you have not handled those higher levels of responsibility in the past, many employers may consider you for them if you have the skills to support the objective.

3. Include your most important skills.

What are the most important skills needed for the job you want? Consider including one or more of these as being required in the job that you seek. The implication here is that if you are looking for a job that requires "Organizational Skills," then you have those skills. Of course, your interview (and resume) should support those skills with specific examples.

4. Include specifics if these are important to you.

If you have substantial experience in a particular industry (such as "Computer Controlled Machine Tools") or have a narrow and specific objective that you *really* want (such as "Art Therapist with the Mentally Handicapped"), then it is OK to state this. But, in so doing, realize that by narrowing your alternatives down you will often not be considered for other jobs for which you might qualify. Still, if that is what you want, it just may be worth pursuing (though I would still encourage you to have a second, more general objective just in case).

The Job Objective Worksheet

Directions: If you are not clear about what you want to do, you should review other chapters in this book as needed to help you identify your ideal job. But, for the purposes of writing a skills resume, completing the items that follow will help you write a job objective.

1. What sort of position, title, and area of specialization do you seek? Write out the type of job you want just as you might explain it to someone you know.

_____

_____

_____

2. Define your "bracket of responsibility." Describe the range of jobs that you would accept at a minimum as well as those that you might be able to handle if given the chance.

_____

_____

_____

3. Name the key skills that you have that are important in this job. Describe the two or three key skills that are particularly important for success in the job that you seek. Select one or more of these that you are strong in and that you enjoy using and write it (or them) below.

_____

_____

_____

4. Name any specific areas of expertise or strong interests that you want to use in your next job. If you have substantial interest, experience, or training in a specific area and want to include it in your job objective (knowing that it may limit your options), what might it be?

_____

_____

_____

5. Is there anything else that is important to you? Is there anything else that you want to include in your job objective? This could include a value that is particularly important to you (such as "A position that allows me to affect families" or "Employment in an aggressive and results-oriented organization"); a preference for the size or type of organization ("A small-to mid-size business"); or some other thing.

_____

_____

_____

_____

Finalize your job objective statement

Most employers will be impressed with someone who is very clear about the job they want and why they want it. Few interviews end well unless the interviewer is convinced that you want the job available and have the skills to do it reasonably well.

For this reason, it is essential to have a clear job objective. Then, once you've settled that, go out and get interviews for jobs that closely approximate what you want. In the interview, support your interest in the job by presenting the skills and experiences you have and the advantages you present over others they may be considering. It sounds simple enough – and can be – as long as you are clear about what you want to do and are well organized about finding it.

The Skills Section

This section can also be headed as "Areas of Accomplishment" or "Summary of Qualifications" or "Areas of Expertise and Ability" or by other terms as used in various sample resumes. Whatever you choose to call it, this section is what makes a skills resume. To construct it, you must carefully consider which skills you want to emphasize. You should feature those skills which are essential to success on the job you want *and* those skills which are your particular strengths. You probably have a good idea of which skills meet both criteria but you may find it helpful to review Chapter 3, as needed, to help you identify these skills.

Note that many skills resumes emphasize skills that are not specific to a particular job. For example, the skill of being "well organized" is important in *many* jobs. In your resume, you will provide specific examples of situations or accomplishments that show that you do have that skill and this is where you can often bring in examples from previous work or other experiences.

Key skills list

Here is a short list of skills that I consider to be key skills for success on most jobs. If you have to emphasize some skills over others, these are ones to consider (if you have them, of course). Recall from Chapter 3 that *transferable skills* can be used in a variety of jobs (i.e. they transfer from one job to the next).

The Basics:	Key Transferable Skills:
Accept supervision	Instructing others
Get along with coworkers	Managing money and budgets
Get things done on time	Managing people
Good attendance	Meeting deadlines
Hard worker	Meeting the public
Honest	Negotiating
On time	Organizing/managing projects
Productive	Public speaking
	Written communication skills

In addition to these types of skills, most jobs require skills specific to that particular job. For example, an accountant would need to know how to set up a general ledger, use accounting software, develop an income and expense report, and other tasks typically required in this type of job. These skills are called job content skills and can also be quite important in qualifying for a job.

Identifying your key skills

Review Chapter 3 to identify the skills you have that you should emphasize in your skills resume. Emphasize skills that you have *and* that are particularly important for the job you want. Also include any other job content or other skills you have that you think are important to communicate to an employer regarding the job you want. Write at least three, but no more than six, of these most important skills below:

1. _____

2. _____

3. _____

4. _____

5. _____

6. _____

Proving your key skills

Now, write down each of the skills you wrote above on a separate piece of paper. For each one, write any particularly good examples of when you used that skill. If possible, you should use work situations, but you can also use other situations such as volunteer work, school activities, or any other life experience. Whenever possible, quantify the example by including numbers such as money saved, increased sales, or other measures to support those skills. Emphasize results you achieved and accomplishments.

An example of what one person wrote for one of their key skills follows and may give you an idea of how you can document your own skills.

An Example of a Key Skill

Key Skill: Meeting Deadlines

I volunteered to help my social organization raise money. I found out about special government funds, but the proposal deadline was only 24 hours away. I stayed up all night and submitted it on time. We were one of only three whose proposals were approved, and we were awarded over $100,000!

Editing your key skills proofs

Go over each "proof sheet" from the previous exercise and select those proofs that you feel are particularly valuable in supporting your job objective. You should have at least two proofs for each skills area. Once you have selected your proofs, rewrite them using action words and short sentences. Delete anything that is not essential. For example, here is a rewrite of the example I provided earlier. Do a similar editing job on each of your own proofs until they are clear, short, and powerful. You can then use these statements in your resume, modifying them as needed to fit that format. Here is an edited version of the previous skill statement in a form appropriate for use in a resume.

Key Skill Rewrite

Key Skill: Meeting Deadlines

On 24-hour notice, submitted a complex proposal that successfully obtained over $100,000 in funding.

Tips for Fine-tuning Your Resume

Before you make a final draft of your skills resume, look over the sample resumes at the end of this chapter for ideas on content and format. Several of them use interesting techniques that may be useful for your particular situation. Also, keep in mind the following tips.

✓ If you have a good work history, providing a very brief chronological listing of jobs can be a helpful addition to your skills resume.

- ✓ If you have substantial work history, beginning the resume with a summary of total experience can provide the basis for details that follow.

- ✓ Remember that this is your resume, so do with it what you think is best.

- ✓ Trust your own good judgment and be willing to break a few rules if you think that it can help you.

- ✓ Write out the draft content for your resume on separate sheets of paper or on a computer, if you have access to one.

- ✓ Rewrite and edit until the resume communicates what you really want to say about yourself.

- ✓ If you are doing your resume on a computer, print out the "final" copy and ask someone else to very carefully review it for typographical and other errors.

- ✓ Even if you are having someone else prepare your resume, have their "final" copy reviewed by someone other than yourself for any errors you have overlooked.

- ✓ After you are certain that your resume contains no errors (and only then), have the final version prepared.

Section V: A Gallery of Sample Skills Resumes

Quick Reference

Look over the sample resumes that follow to see how others have adapted the basic skills format to fit their own situation. These examples are based on real resumes (though their names and other details are not real), and I have included comments to help you understand details that may not be apparent.

The formats and designs of the sample resumes in this chapter are intentionally basic and can be done by virtually any word processor, or even a good typewriter. If you want to see more resume examples, you can refer to another book I wrote titled *The Quick Resume & Cover Letter Book.*

I have also included a sample JIST Card to accompany the first resume example. This is a nifty job search tool that is covered in more detail in Chapter 6.

Darrel Craig's Resume and JIST Card

Comments on Darrel's Resume

This is a resume of a career changer. After working in a variety of jobs, Darrel went to school and learned computer programming. The skills format allows him to emphasize the business experiences in his past to support his current job objective. There is no chronological listing of jobs and no dates are indicated related to his education, so it is not obvious that he is a recent graduate with little formal work experience as a programmer.

Darrel does a good job of presenting his previous work experience and includes numbers to support his skills and accomplishments. Even so, the relationship between his previous work and current objective could be improved. For example, collecting bad debts requires discipline, persistence, and attention to detail – the same skills required in programming. And, while he is good at sales, how does this relate to programming?

To correct this, he might consider modifying his job objective to include the use of his sales skills (such as selling technological services) or emphasizing other skills from his previous work experience. Still, his resume is reasonably effective and does a decent job of relating past business experience to his ability to be an effective programmer in a business environment. He did get a job as a programmer and is doing just fine in his new career.

Darrel's JIST Card

Darrel Craig   (412) 437-6217
                                       Message: (412) 464-1273

Position Desired: PROGRAMMER/SYSTEMS MANAGEMENT

Skills: Over 10 years combined education and experience in data processing, business, and related fields. Programming ability in COBOL, RPG, BASIC, and FORTRAN. Knowledge of various database and applications programs in networked PC, Mac, and mainframe environments. Substantial business experience, including accounting, management, sales, and public relations.

Dedicated, self-starter, creative, dependable, and willing to relocate

---

Darrel Craig

Career Objective
Challenging position in programming or related areas which would best utilize expertise in the business environment. This position should have many opportunities for an aggressive, dedicated individual with leadership abilities to advance.

Programming Skills
Include functional program design relating to business issues, including payroll, inventory and data base management, sales, marketing, accounting, and loan amortization reports. In conjunction with design would be coding, implementation, debugging, and file maintenance. Familiar with distributed network systems, including PCs and Macs, and working knowledge of DOS, UNIX, COBOL, Basic, RPG, and FORTRAN. Also familiar with mainframe environments including DEC, Prime, and IBM, including tape and disk file access, organization, and maintenance.

Areas of Expertise
Interpersonal communication strengths, public relations capabilities, innovative problem-solving and analytical talents.

Sales
A total of nine years experience in sales and sales management. Sold security products to distributors and burglar alarm dealers. Increased company's sales from $16,000 to over $70,000 per month. Creatively organized sales programs and marketing concepts. Trained sales personnel in prospecting techniques while also training service personnel in proper installation of burglar alarms. Result: 90% of all new business was generated through referrals from existing customers.

Management
Managed burglar alarm company for four years while increasing profits yearly. Supervised office, sales, and installation personnel. Supervised and delegated work to assistants in accounting functions and inventory control. Worked as assistant credit manager, responsible for over $2 million per month in sales. Handled semi-annual inventory of five branch stores totaling millions of dollars and supervised 120 people.

Accounting
Balanced all books and prepared tax forms for burglar alarm company. Eight years experience in credit and collections, with emphasis on collections. Collection rates were over 98% each year, and was able to collect a bad debt deemed "uncollectible" by company in excess of $250,000.

Education
School of Computer Technology, Pittsburgh, PA
Business Application Programming/TECH EXEC - 3.97 GPA

Robert Morris College, Pittsburgh, PA
Associate degree in Accounting, Minor in Management

2306 Cincinnati Street, Kingsford, PA 15171 (412) 437-6217
Message: (412) 464-1273

Susan Smith's Resume

Comments on Susan's Resume

This is a two-page resume that is based on one included in a book by Richard Lathrop titled Who's Hiring Who? *It originally was squeezed onto one page. While he calls it a "Qualifications Brief," it is a pure form example of a skills resume.*

This resume is unconventional in a variety of ways. It clearly takes advantage of the skills format by avoiding all mention of a chronology of past jobs. There are no references to specific employers, to employment dates, or even to job titles. If you read it carefully, you may figure out that Susan's job history has been as a housewife. This is a clever example of how a well-done skills resume can be used to present a person effectively in spite of a lack of formal paid work experience – or to cover other problems. Students, career changers, and others can benefit in similar ways.

SUSAN SMITH
1516 Sierra Way
Piedmont, California 97435
Telephone: (416) 486-3874

OBJECTIVE

Program Development, Coordination, and Administration

...especially in a people-oriented organization where there is a need to assure broad cooperative effort through the use of sound planning and strong administrative and persuasive skills to achieve community goals.

MAJOR AREAS OF EXPERIENCE AND ABILITY

Budgeting and Management for Sound Program Development

With partner, established new association devoted to maximum personal development and self-realization for each of its members. Over a period of time, administered budget totaling $285,000. Jointly planned growth of group and related expenditures, investments, programs, and development of property holdings to realize current and long-term goals. As a result, holdings increased twenty-fold over the period, reserves invested increased 1,200%, and all major goals for members have been achieved or exceeded.

Purchasing to Assure Smooth Flow of Needed Supplies and Services

Made purchasing decisions to assure maximum production from available funds. Determined ongoing inventory needs, selected suppliers, and maintained a strong continuing line of credit while minimizing financing costs. No significant project was ever adversely affected by lack of supplies, equipment, or services on time.

Personnel Development and Motivation

Developed resources to assure maximum progress in achieving potential for development among all members of our group. Frequently engaged in intensive personnel counseling to achieve this. Sparked new community progress to help accomplish such results. Although arrangements with my partner gave me no say in selecting new members. (I took them as they came), the results produced by this effort are a source of strong and continuing satisfaction to me. (See "specific results.")

Transportation Management

Determined transportation needs of our group and, in consultation with members, assured specific transportation equipment acquisitions over a broad range of types (including seagoing). Contracted for additional transportation when necessary. Assured maximum utilization of limited motor pool to meet often-conflicting requirements demanding arrival of the same vehicle at widely divergent points at the same moment. Negotiated resolution of such conflicts in the best interest of all concerned. In addition, arranged four major moves of all facilities, furnishings, and equipment to new locations.

Other Functions Performed

Duties periodically require my action in the following additional functional areas: Crisis management; proposal preparation; political analysis; nutrition; recreation planning and administration; stock market operations; taxes; building and grounds maintenance; community organization; social affairs administration (including VIP entertaining); catering; landscaping; (two awards for excellence); contract negotiations; teaching and more.

Some Specific Results

Above experience gained in 10 years devoted to family development and household management in partnership with my husband, Harvey Smith, who is equally responsible for results produced. Primary achievements: Daughter Sue, 12, leading candidate for the U.S. Junior Olympics team in gymnastics. A lovely home in Piedmont (social center for area teenagers). Secondary achievements: Vacation home at Newport, Oregon (on the beach) and a cabin in Big Sur. President of Piedmont High School PTA for two years. Organized successful citizen protest to stop incursion of Oakland commercialism on Piedmont area. Appointed by Robert F. Kennedy as coordinator for this campaign in Oakland.

PERSONAL DATA AND OTHER FACTS

Often complimented on appearance. Bachelor of Arts (Business Administration), Cody College, Cody, California. Highly active in community affairs. Have learned that there is a spark of genius in everyone which, when nurtured, can flare into dramatic achievement.

Peter Neely's Resume

Comments on Peter's Resume

Peter lost his factory job when the plant closed in the early 1990s. He had picked up a survival job as a truck driver and now wants to make this his career because it allows him to earn good money and he likes the work.

Notice how his resume emphasizes skills from previous experiences that are essential for success as a truck driver. This resume uses a "combined" format since it includes elements from both the skills and chronological resume formats. The skills approach allows him to emphasize specific skills that support his job objective and the chronological listing of jobs allows him to display his stable work history.

The miscellaneous jobs that Peter had before 1977 are simply clustered together under one grouping, since they are not as important as more recent experience – and because doing this does not display his age. For the same reasons, he does not include dates for his military experience or high school graduation, nor does he separate them into different categories such as "Military Experience" or "Education." They just aren't as important in supporting his current job objective as they might be for a younger person.

An unusual element here is Peter's adding comments about his not smoking or drinking, although it does work, as do his comments about a stable family life.

Peter also has another version of this resume that simply changed his job objective to include supervision and management of trucking operations and added a few details to support this. When it made sense, he used the other version.

He got a job in a smaller long-distance trucking company driving a regular trip, and now he supervises other drivers.

Peter Neely

203 Evergreen Road

Houston, Texas 39127

Messages: (237) 649-1234   Beeper: (237) 765-9876

POSITION DESIRED: Truck Driver

Summary of Work Experience:	Over twenty years of stable work history, including substantial experience with diesel engines, electrical systems, and truck driving.

SKILLS

Driving Record/ Licenses:	Chauffeur's license, qualified and able to drive anything that rolls. No traffic citations or accidents for over 20 years.
Vehicle Maintenance:	I maintain correct maintenance schedules and avoid most break downs as a result. Substantial mechanical and electrical systems training and experience permits many breakdowns to be repaired immediately and avoid towing.
Record Keeping:	Excellent attention to detail. Familiar with recording procedures and submit required records on a timely basis.
Routing:	Knowledge of many states. Good map reading and route planning skills.
Other:	Not afraid of hard work, flexible, get along well with others, meet deadlines, responsible.

WORK EXPERIENCE

1994 - Present	CAPITAL TRUCK CENTER, Houston, Texas Pick up and deliver all types of commercial vehicles from across the United States. Am trusted with handling large sums of money and handling complex truck purchasing transactions.
1984 - 1994	QUALITY PLATING CO., Houston, Texas Promoted from Production to Quality Control. Developed numerous production improvements resulting in substantial cost savings.
1982 - 1984	BLUE CROSS MANUFACTURING, Houston, Texas Received several increases in salary and responsibility before leaving for a more challenging position.
1978 - 1982	Truck delivery of food products to destinations throughout the South. Also responsible for up to 12 drivers and equipment maintenance personnel.
Prior to 1978	Operated large diesel-powered electrical plants. Responsible for monitoring and maintenance on a rigid schedule.

OTHER

Four years experience in the U.S. Air Force operating power plants. Stationed in Alaska, California, Wyoming, and other states. Honorable discharge. High school graduate, plus training in diesel engines and electrical systems. Excellent health, love the outdoors, stable family life, nonsmoker and nondrinker.

Andrea Atwood's Resume

Comments on Andrea's Resume

This resume uses few words and lots of white space. It looks better, I think, than more crowded resumes. I would like to see more numbers used to indicate performance or accomplishments. For example, what was the result of the more efficient record keeping system she developed? And why did she receive the Employee-of-the-Month awards?

Andrea does not have substantial experience in her field, having had only one job. For this reason, this skills format allows her to present her strengths better than a chronological resume. Because she has formal training in retail sales and is a recent graduate, she could have given more details about specific courses she took or other school-related activities that would support her job objective. Even so, her resume does a good job of presenting her basic skills to an employer in an attractive format.

ANDREA ATWOOD
3231 East Harbor Road
Grand Rapids, Michigan 41103

Home:(303)447-2111   Message:(303)547-8201

Objective: A responsible position in retail sales.

**Areas of
Accomplishment:**

Customer Service	• Communicates well with all age groups. • Able to interpret customer concerns to help them find the items they want. • Received six Employee of the Month awards in 3 years.
Merchandise Display	• Developed display skills via in-house training and experience. • Received Outstanding Trainee award for Christmas Toy Display. • Dress mannequins, arrange table displays, and organize sale merchandise.
Stock Control and Marking	• Maintained and marked stock during department manager's 6-week illness. • Developed more efficient record-keeping procedures.
Additional Skills	• Operate cash register and computerized accounting systems. • Willing to work evenings and weekends. • Punctual, honest, reliable, and hard-working

Experience:

Harper's Department Store
Grand Rapids, Michigan
1992 to present

Education:

Central High School
Grand Rapids, Michigan
3.6/4.0 grade point average
Honor Graduate in Distributive Education

Two years retail sales training in Distributive Education. Also courses in Business Writing, Computerized Accounting, and Word Processing.

Linda Marsala-Winston's Resume

Comments on Linda's Resume

Linda's resume is based on one included in a book by David Swanson titled The Resume Solution, *and it shows the type of resume style that he prefers. It uses lots of white space, short sentences, and brief but carefully edited narrative.*

The format for this resume is based on a resume template provided with a popular word processing program. That program offers several predetermined design options that include various typefaces and the use of other simple but effective format and design elements. Other resumes in this book also have used similar templates as a basis for their designs, and this approach makes formatting a resume much easier.

Linda's resume is short but does present good information to support her job objective. I have included other examples of resumes from The Resume Solution *later in this book, and they all share the same principles of less being more. Of course, they are being used with Dave's permission.*

Linda Marsala-Winston
6673 East Avenue
Lakeland, California, 94544
(415) 555-1519 (leave message)

Objective: Copywriter, Account Executive in Advertising or Public Relations Agency
Professional Experience

Copywriter
Developed copy for direct mail catalogs featuring collectible items, for real estate developments, and for agricultural machinery and equipment.

Writer
Wrote for Habitat magazine. Specialized in architecture, contemporary lifestyles, and interior design.

Sales Promotion
Fullmeris Department Store, Detroit. Developed theme and copy for grand opening of new store in San Francisco Bay area.

Fabric Designer
Award-winning textile designer and importer of African and South American textiles.

Other Writing and Promotion
News bureau chief and feature writer for college newspaper, contributor to literary magazine. Script writer for fashion shows. Won creative writing fellowship to study in Mexico. Did public relations for International Cotton Conference. Summer graduate fellow in public information, United Nations, New York City.

Education
University of California, Berkeley
Bachelor of Arts Degree in English. Graduate study, 30 credits completed in Journalism.

California State University, Fresno
Master of Arts Degree in Guidance and Counseling

Professional Membership
San Francisco Women in Advertising

Thomas Marrin's Resume

Comments on Thomas' resume

This is one of those resumes that is hard to put into a category since it is neither a skills nor a chronological resume – but combines elements of both. Remember that I have suggested that you can break any rule that you want in putting together your own resume if you do so for a good reason. Thomas' resume does break some rules but he does so for good reasons, and the resume presents him well.

Thomas has kept his job objective quite broad and does not limit it to a particular type of industry or job title. Because he sees himself as a business manager, it does not matter to him much just what kind of business, though he prefers to work in a larger organization, as his job objective indicates.

His education is towards the top of his resume because he thought it would be a strength. His military experience, while not recent, is also listed towards the top because he also felt that would help him. Note how he presented his military experience using civilian language such as annual budgets and staff size, things that are easy to relate to a business environment.

Thomas has work experience with one employer for many years, but he presents each job he held there as a separate one. This approach allows him to provide more details about his accomplishments within each job and also clearly points out that these were promotions. This shows a progression of increasingly responsible jobs nicely.

This resume could easily have been a two-page resume, and doing so would allow him to provide additional details on his job at Hayfield Publishing and in other areas. The extra space could also be used to provide more white space and a less crowded look, though it works fine as it is.

Thomas got a job in a smaller company (50 employees) as a vice president of operations and is as happy as a clam.

THOMAS P. MARRIN
80 Harrison Avenue
Baldwin L.I., New York 11563
Answering Service: (716) 223-4705

OBJECTIVE:
A middle/upper-level management position with responsibilities including problem solving, planning, organizing, and budget management.

EDUCATION:
University of Notre Dame, B.S. in Business Administration. Course emphasis on accounting, supervision, and marketing. Upper 25% of class. Additional training: Advanced training in time management, organization behavior, and cost control.

MILITARY:
U.S. Army – 2nd Infantry Division, 1985 - 1988. 1st Lieutenant and platoon leader – stationed in Korea and Fort Knox, Kentucky. Supervised an annual budget of nearly $4 million and equipment valued at over $40 million. Responsible for training, scheduling, and activities of as many as 40 people. Received several commendations. Honorable discharge.

BUSINESS EXPERIENCE:
Wills Express Transit Co., Inc. – Mineola, New York

Promoted to Vice President, Corporate Equipment – 1993 to Present
Controlled purchase, maintenance and disposal of 1100 trailers and 65 company cars with $6.7 MM operating and $8.0 MM Capital expense responsibilities.

- Scheduled trailer purchases, 6 divisions
- Operated 2.3% under planned maintenance budget in Company's second best profit year while operating revenues declined 2.5%
- Originated schedule to correlate drivers' needs with available trailers.
- Development systematic Purchase and Disposal Plan for company car fleet.
- Restructured Company Car Policy, saving 15% on per car cost.

Promoted to Assistant Vice President, Corporate Operations – 1992 to 1993
Coordinated activities of six sections of Corporate Operations with an operating budget over $10 million.

- Directed implementation of zero base budgeting.
- Developed and prepared Executive Officer analyses detailing achievable cost reduction measures. Resulted in cost reduction of over $600,000 in first two years.
- Designed policy and procedure for special equipment leasing program during peak seasons. Cut capital purchases by over $1 million.

Promoted to Manager of Communications – 1990 to 1992
Directed and Managed $1.4 MM communications network involving 650 phones, 150 WATS lines, 3 switchboards, 1 teletype machine, 5 employees.

- Installed computerized WATS Control System. Optimized utilization of WATS lines and pinpointed personal abuse. Achieved payback earlier than originally projected.
- Devised procedures that allowed simultaneous 20% increase in WATTS calls and a $75,000/year savings.

Hayfield Publishing Company, Hempstead, New York.

Communications Administrator – 1987 - 1990

Managed daily operations of a large Communications Center. Reduced costs and improved services.

≡≡≡Quick Summary

✓ A "resume" is the term most often used to describe a piece or two of paper summarizing your life's history. The idea is to select those specific parts of your past that support your doing a particular job well. Most often, the paper then presents you to prospective employers who, based on their response to the paper, may or may not grant you an interview. Along with the application form, it is the tool employers use most to screen job seekers.

✓ Your objective should be to get a good job, not to do a great resume. Trying to get an interview by sending out dozens of resumes is usually a waste of stamps. Do a *simple* resume early in your job search. This approach allows you to get on with getting interviews rather than sit at home working on a better resume. Contrary to the advice of many resume and job search "experts," writing a perfect resume will rarely get you the job you want. Interviews (not resumes) get jobs.

✓ For a variety of reasons, many career professionals suggest that resumes aren't needed at all. Resumes don't do a good job in getting you an interview. When used in the traditional way, your resume is far more likely to get you screened out.

✓ Some resume experts call a resume by another name, such as "Qualifications Brief," "Professional Job Power Report," "Curriculum VITA," "Employment Proposal," and other terms. In all their forms, they are really various types of resumes.

✓ All things considered, there are more good reasons to have a resume than not: Employers often ask for resumes. Resumes help structure your communications. A well-done resume presents details of your experiences efficiently and in a way that an employer can refer to as needed. It can also be used as a tool to present the skills you have to support your job objective and to present details that are often not solicited in a preliminary interview.

✓ Four Tips for Using a Resume Effectively: 1. Get the interview first. (Don't send an unsolicited resume. It is better to directly contact the employer by phone or in person. Then send your resume after you schedule an interview, so that the employer can read about you before your meeting.) 2. Send your resume after an interview. 3. Give resumes to people you know. 4. If all else fails, use traditional techniques.

✓ **Types of Resumes:**

1. The Chronological Resume: The primary feature of this type of resume is the listing of jobs held from the most recent backwards. This is the simplest of resumes and can be a useful format if used properly. The big advantage of a chronological resume is that it is easy to do. It works best for those who have had several years of experience in the same type of job they are seeking now. This is because a chronological resume will clearly display your recent work experience.

2. The Skills or Functional Resume: Rather than listing your experience under each job, the skills resume style clusters your experiences under major skill areas. This approach would make little sense, of course, unless you had a job objective that required these skills. For this reason and others, a skills resume is harder to write than a simple chronological resume. If you have limited paid work experience, are changing careers, or have not worked for awhile, a skills resume may be a clearly superior approach to help you present your strengths and avoid displaying your weaknesses.

3. The Combination or Creative Resume: Elements of chronological and skills resumes can be combined in various ways to improve the clarity or presentation of a resume. There are also creative formats that defy any category but that are clever and have worked for some people.

✓ Most employers will find a chronological resume perfectly acceptable (if not exciting), providing it is neat and has no errors. You can use it early in your job search while you work on a more sophisticated resume. The important point here is to get an acceptable resume together quickly so that you won't be sitting at home worrying about your resume instead of out looking for a job.

✓ In writing about your work experience, use action words and emphasize what you accomplished. Quantify what you did and provide evidence that you did it well. Take particular care to mention skills that would directly relate to doing well in the job you want. Think about the things you accomplished in jobs, school, military, and other settings.

✓ Use The "Instant Resume" Worksheet in this chapter to create a usable resume quickly. Use the examples of simple chronological resumes in this chapter as the basis for creating your own chronological resume. Follow the "Guidelines for Writing a Superior Resume" presented in this chapter, to keep it short, simple, positive, and professional.

✓ If you do not have a computer or are not a good typist, have someone else type or word process your resume for you. If computers are new to you, this is probably not the time to learn.

✓ While a simple chronological resume does not absolutely require a career objective, a skills resume does. Without a reasonably clear job objective, it is not possible to select and organize the key skills you have to support that job objective.

✓ While the job objective you write should meet your specific needs, here are some tips to consider in writing it: Avoid job titles. Define a "bracket of responsibility" to include the possibility of upward mobility. Include your most important skills. Include specifics if these are important to you.

✓ The Job Objective Worksheet in this chapter can help you construct a well-stated, clear, accurate job objective. This is important because most employers will be impressed with someone who is very clear about the job they want and why they want it. Few interviews end well unless the interviewer is convinced that you want the job available and have the skills to do it reasonably well.

✓ Before you make a final draft of your skills resume, look over the sample resumes at the end of this chapter for ideas on content and format. Several of them use interesting techniques that may be useful for your particular situation. Also, keep in mind the tips presented in this chapter for fine-tuning your resume before submitting it.

*Quick Resumes,
Cover Letters, and
Thank-You Notes*

Cover Letters, Thank-You Notes, and Other Job Search Correspondence

Quick Overview

In this chapter, I review the following:

✓ When and how to write a good cover letter

✓ Guidelines for writing superior cover letters

✓ How to write cover letters to people you know

✓ How to write cover letters to people you don't know

✓ Tips on when and why to send thank-you notes

✓ Sample cover letters, thank-you notes, etc.

During the course of an active job search, you will probably send out a variety of types of correspondence. Resumes are often sent along with a "cover" letter which provides details that may not be included in the resume.

As with resumes, a big mistake with cover letters is to use them as part of a passive job search campaign that sends out lots of unsolicited resumes. I suggest that cover letters are best used *after* you have made some personal contact with a potential employer by phone or in person rather than as a replacement for direct contact.

A variety of other written communications that are used during a job search are often overlooked in most job search books. Thank-you notes are an example of correspondence that can make a big difference to you if used well during your search for a job. These and similar forms of written communications are the focus of this chapter.

When and How to Write a Good Cover Letter

It is not appropriate to send a resume to someone without an introductory letter or note attached to it. The traditional way this is handled is to provide a letter *along with* your resume – a cover letter. Depending on the circumstances, the letter would explain your situation and ask the person who receives it for some specific action, consideration, or response.

Some authors of books on the art of writing a cover letter go into great detail on how to construct a "powerful" cover letter. Some suggest that a cover letter can actually be used to replace the resume by providing similar information but targeting the content specifically to the person who is receiving it. While there are merits to these ideas, my objective here is to provide you with *a simple and quick* review of the basics of writing and using cover letters that will meet most needs.

Quick Tip

While many situations require writing a formal cover letter, there are many others where a simple note will do. Additional information on notes will be provided later in this chapter.

Eight Guidelines for Writing Superior Cover Letters

No matter what the situation, virtually every good cover letter should follow these guidelines:

1. Write to Someone in Particular

NEVER send a cover letter to "To whom it may concern" or some other impersonal opening. We all get enough junk mail; if you don't send your letter to someone by name, it *will* be treated like junk mail.

2. Make Absolutely NO Errors

One way to offend someone quickly is to misspell a name or use an incorrect title. If there is any question, call and vilify hte corectly spalding of of their nime and other detales before you send the latter. (Hey! did you catch those erears?) Review your letters carefully to be sure that they do not contain any typographical, grammar, or other errors of any kind.

3. Personalize Your Content

I've never been impressed by form letters of any kind, and you should not use them. Those computer-generated letters that automatically insert your name ("yes, Jim Furn, you have won one of the following useless and cheap prizes...") never fool me at all, and I find cover letters done this way a bit offensive. While I know that lots of job search books recommend sending out lots of "broadcast letters" to people you don't know, I suggest that doing so is a waste of time and money. If you can't personalize your letter in some way, don't send it.

4. Present a Good Appearance

Your contacts with prospective employers should always be professional. Buy good quality stationery and matching envelopes. The standard 8 1/2 -by- 11 inch paper size is typically used but you can also use the smaller "Monarch" size paper with matching envelopes. Use only good quality paper – I prefer a white, ivory, or light beige-colored paper. This is business correspondence, so don't handwrite a cover letter. A typewriter with excellent type quality or a computer word processor with letter quality or laser output (not dot-matrix) is a must.

5. Use an Appropriate Format

Any standard business correspondence format is acceptable. Look at the sample cover letters in this chapter for ideas.

6. Provide a Friendly Opening

Begin your letter with a reminder of any prior contacts and the reason for your correspondence now. The examples will give you some ideas on how this can be handled.

7. Target Your Skills and Experiences

To do this well, you must know something about the organization or person with whom you are dealing. Present any relevant background that may be of particular interest to the person you are writing to.

8. Define the Next Step

Don't close your letter without clearly identifying what you will do next. I do not recommend that you simply leave it up to the employers to contact you, since that really isn't their responsibility.

The Only Two Groups of People Who Should Get Your Cover Letters

If you think about it, there are only two groups of people you might send a resume and cover letter. They are:

1. People you know

2. People you don't know.

While I realize that this sounds simple, it's true. And this observation makes it easier to understand how you might handle a letter to each of these groups.

Writing Cover Letters to Someone You Know

It is always best if you are already known to the person you are writing. Any written correspondence is less effective than personal contact, and it is always better to send a resume and cover letter after already having spoken with the person directly.

For example, it is far more effective to first call someone who has advertised in the paper than to simply send a letter and resume. There are also the *Yellow Pages*, personal referrals, and so many other ways of coming to know someone. So I assume you have made some sort of personal contact before sending your resume. Within this assumption there are hundreds of variations, but I review the most important ones and let you adapt them to your own situation. (See sidebar.)

The Four Situations for Sending Cover Letters to People You Know

There are four basic situations you can consider when sending out a cover letter, and each one requires a different approach. Each situation presents an approach that can be used in getting interviews. Getting interviews and job offers is the real task in the job search – not sending out resumes and cover letters. Look at the samples for each type of cover letter and see how, in most cases, they assume that a personal contact has been made before the resume was sent. The situations are presented below, along with some explanation of each.

Situation #1. An interview is scheduled, and there is a specific job opening that may interest you.

In this case, you have already arranged an interview for a job opening that interests you, and the cover letter should provide some details of your experience that relate to that specific job.

Situation #2. An interview is scheduled, but no specific job is available.

This is a letter you will send for an interview with an employer who does not have a specific opening for you now but who might in the future. This is fertile ground for finding job leads where no one else may be looking.

Situation #3. After an interview takes place.

Many people overlook the importance of sending a letter after an interview. This is a time to say that you want the job (if that is the case, say so) and to add any details on why you think you can do the job well.

Situation #4. No interview is scheduled, yet.

There are situations where you just can't arrange an interview before you send in a resume and cover letter. In these cases, a good letter can allow you to follow up more effectively.

Sample cover letters addressed to people you know

I've included a sample cover letter covering each of the four situations involving people you know. Note that they use different formats and styles as a way to show you the range of styles that are appropriate. Each letter addresses a different situation, and each incorporates all of the cover letter guidelines presented earlier in this chapter.

Sample Cover Letter: Pre-Interview, for a Specific Job Opening

Comments: This writer called first and arranged an interview – the best approach of all. Note how this new graduate included a specific example of how he saved money for a business by changing its procedures. While it is not clear, his experience with lots of people was while working as a waiter. Note also how he included skills such as "hard worker" and "deadline pressure" that I reviewed in Chapter 9 of this book.

Richard Swanson
113 So. Meridian Street
Greenwich, Connecticut 11721
March 10, 19XX

Mr. William Hines
New England Power and Light Company
604 Waterway Blvd.
Parien, Connecticut 11716

Mr. Hines,

I am following up on the brief chat we had today by phone. After getting the details on the position you have open, I am certain that it is the kind of job I have been looking for. A copy of my resume is enclosed providing more details of my background. I hope you have a chance to review it before we meet next week.

My special interest has long been in the large-volume order processing systems that your organization has developed so well. While in school, I researched the flow of order processing work for a large corporation as part of a class assignment. With some simple and inexpensive procedural changes I recommended, check-processing time was reduced by an average of three days. For the number of checks and dollars involved, this one change resulted in an estimated increase in interest revenues of over $35,000 per year. Details do count!

While I have recently graduated from business school, I do have considerable experience for a person of my age. I have worked in a variety of jobs dealing with large numbers of people and deadline pressure. My studies have also been far more "hands-on" and practical than those of most schools, so I have a good working knowledge of current business systems and procedures. This includes a good understanding of various computer spreadsheet and applications programs, the use of automation, and experience with cutting costs and increasing profits. I am also a hard worker and realize I will need to apply myself to get established in my career.

I am most interested in the position you have available and am excited about the potential it offers. I look forward to seeing you next week.

Sincerely,

Richard Swanson

Sample Cover Letter: Pre-Interview, No Specific Job Opening

Comments: This letter indicates that the writer first called and set up an interview as the result of someone else providing the employer's name. The writer explains why she is moving to the city and asks for help in making contacts there. While there is no job opening here, she is wise in assuming that there might be one in the future. Even if this is not the case, she asks the employer to think of others who might have a position for someone with her skills. Assuming that the interview goes well and the employer gives her names of others to call, she can then follow up with them.

ANNE MARIE FURN
616 Kings Way • Minneapolis, MN 54312

February 10, 19XX

Mrs. Francine Cook
Park-Halsey Corporation
5413 Armstrong Drive
Minneapolis, Minnesota 54317

Dear Mrs. Cook,

When Steve Marks suggested I call you, I had no idea you would be so helpful. I've already followed up with several of the suggestions you made and am now looking forward to meeting with you next Tuesday. The resume I've enclosed is to give you a better sense of my qualifications. Perhaps it will help you think of other organizations with people who may be interested in my background.

The resume does not say why I've moved to Minneapolis, and you may find that of interest. My spouse and I visited the city several years ago and thought it a good place to live. He has obtained a very good position here, and based on that, we decided it was time to commit ourselves to a move. As you can see from my work experience, I tend to stay on and move up in jobs, so I now want to more carefully research the job opportunities here before making a commitment. Your help in this task is greatly appreciated.

Feel free to contact me if you have any questions; otherwise, I look forward to meeting with you next Tuesday.

Sincerely,

Anne Marie Furn

Sample Cover Letter: After an Interview

Comments: This letter shows you how you might follow up after an interview and make a pitch for solving a problem – even when no job formally exists. In this example, the writer suggests that she can use her skills to solve a specific problem that she uncovered during her conversations with the employer. While it never occurs to many job seekers to set up an interview where there appears to be no job opening, many jobs are created in just these situations. I have often enough done it myself, just to accommodate a good person. . .

Sandra A. Kijeh
115 So. Hawthorn Drive
Port Charlotte, Florida 81641

April 10, 19XX

Christine Massey
Import Distributors, Inc.
417 East Main Street
Atlanta, Georgia 21649

Dear Ms. Massey,

I know you have a busy schedule, so I was pleasantly surprised when you arranged a time for me to see you. While you don't have a position open now, your organization is just the sort of place I would like to work in. As we discussed, I like to be busy with a variety of duties, and the active pace I saw at your company is what I seek.

Your ideas on increasing business sound creative enough to work. I've thought about the customer service problem and would like to discuss with you a possible solution. It would involve the use of a simple system of color-coded files that would prioritize older correspondence to give them a priority status. The handling of complaints could also be speeded up through the use of simple form letters similar to those you mentioned. I have some thoughts on how this might be done, too. I will work out a draft of procedures and sample letters if you are interested. It can be done on the computers that your staff members already have and would not require any additional costs to implement.

Whether or not you have a position for me in the future, I appreciate the time you have given me. An extra copy of my resume is enclosed for your files – or to pass on to someone else. Let me know if you want to discuss the ideas I presented earlier in the letter. I will call you next week as you suggested to keep you informed of my progress.

Sincerely,

Sandra Kijeh

Sample Cover Letter: No Interview Is Scheduled

Comments: This letter explains why the person is looking for a job and presents additional information that would not normally be included in a resume. Note that the writer had obtained the employer's name from the membership list of a professional organization, one excellent source of job leads. Also note that the writer stated that he would call again to arrange an appointment. While this letter is assertive and might turn off some employers, many others would be impressed with his assertiveness and be willing to see him when he finally reaches them. (Note: Look at Chapter 6 for an example of a JIST Card.)

January 5, 19XX

Pam Nykanen
Nykanen Clothing
8661 Parkway Blvd.
Phoenix, AZ 27312

Ms. Nykanen,

As you may know, I phoned you several times over the past week while you were in meetings. I hope that you got the messages. Since I did not want to delay contacting you, I decided to write.
I got your name from the American Retail Clothing Association membership list. I am a member of this group and wanted to contact local members to ask their help in locating a suitable position. I realize that you probably don't have a position open now for someone with my skills, but I ask you to do two things on my behalf.

First, I ask that you consider seeing me at your convenience within the next few weeks. Though you may not have a position available for me, you may be able to assist me in other ways. And, of course, I would appreciate any consideration for future openings. Second, you may know of others who have job openings now or may have in the future.

While I realize that this is an unusual request and that you are quite busy, I do plan on staying in the retail clothing business in this area for some time and would appreciate any assistance you can give me in my search for a new job.

My resume is attached for your information, along with a "JIST Card" that summarizes my background. As you probably know, Allied Tailoring has closed, and I was one of those who stayed on to shut things down in an orderly way. In spite of their regrettable business failure, I was one of those who was responsible for Allied's enormous sales increases over the past decade and have substantial experience to bring to any growing retail clothing concern, such as I hear yours is. I will contact you next week and arrange a time that is good for us both. Please feel free to contact me at any time regarding this matter.

Sincerely,

Cornell Morley

Writing Cover Letters to Someone You Don't Know

If it is not practical to directly contact a prospective employer via phone or some other method, it is acceptable to send a resume and cover letter. This approach makes sense in some situations such as if you are moving to a distant location or responding to a "blind" ad offering only a post office box number.

The approach of sending out "To Whom It May Concern" letters by the basketful is not recommended. However, there are ways to modify this "shotgun" approach to be more effective. Try to find something you have in common with the person you are contacting. By mentioning this link, your letter then becomes a very personal request for assistance. Look at the letters that follow for ideas.

Sample Cover Letters Addressed to People You Don't Know

I've included two sample cover letters that address unfamiliar people. Note that both writers "zeroed in" on location as the common link.

Sample Cover Letter: John Andrews

Comment: Responding to a want ad puts you in direct competition with the many others who will read the same ad, so the odds are not good that this letter would get a response at all. The fact that the writer does not yet live in the area is another negative. Still, I do believe that you should follow up on any legitimate lead you find. In this case, the position will likely be filled by someone who is available to interview right away, but there is always the chance that, with good follow-up, another position will become available – or the employer can give them the names of others to contact.

John Andrews
12 Lake Street
Chicago, Illinois 60631

January 17,19XX

The Morning Sun
Box N4317
2 Early Drive
Toronto, Ontario R5C 1S3

re: Receptionist/Bookkeeper Position

As I plan on relocating to Toronto, your advertisement for a Receptionist/Bookkeeper caught my attention. Your ad stated yours is a small office, and that is precisely what I am looking for. I like dealing with people and in a previous position had over 5,000 customer contacts a month. With that experience, I have learned to handle things quickly and pleasantly.

The varied activities in a position combining bookkeeping and reception sound very interesting. I have received formal training in accounting methods and am familiar with accounts receivable, accounts payable, and general ledger posting. I am familiar with several computerized accounting programs and can quickly learn any others that you may be using.

My resume is enclosed for your consideration. Note that I went to school in Toronto, and I plan on returning there soon to establish my career. Several of my family members also live there, and I have provided their local phone number should you wish to contact me. Please contact that number soon, since I plan on being in Toronto in the near future and would like to speak with you about this or future positions with your company. I will call you in the next few weeks to set up an appointment should I not hear from you before then.

Thank you in advance for your consideration in this matter.

Sincerely,

John Andrews

Sample Cover Letter: John B. Goode

Comments: Another example of a person conducting a long distance job search using names obtained from a professional association. This one also explains why he is leaving his old job and includes positive information regarding his references and skills that would not normally be found in a resume. This one also asks for an interview even though there may not be any jobs open now, as well as for names of others to contact.

John B. Goode
321 Smokie Way
Nashville, Tennessee 31201

July 10, 19XX

Paul Resley
Operations Manager
Rollem Trucking Co.
I-70 Freeway Drive
Kansas City, Missouri 78401

Mr. Resley,

I obtained your name from the membership directory of the Affiliated Trucking Association. I have been a member for over 10 years, and I am very active in the Southeast Region. The reason I am writing is to ask for your help. The firm I had been employed with has been bought by a larger corporation. The operations here have been disbanded, leaving me unemployed.

While I like where I live, I know that finding a position at the level of responsibility I seek may require a move. As a center of the transportation business, your city is one of those I have targeted for special attention.

A copy of my resume is enclosed for your use. I'd like you to review it and consider where a person with my background would get a good reception in Kansas City. Perhaps you could think of a specific person for me to contact?

I have specialized in fast-growing organizations or ones that have experienced rapid change. My particular strength is in bringing things under control, then increasing profits. While my resume does not state this, I have excellent references from my former employer and would have stayed if a similar position existed at their new location.

As a member of the association, I hoped that you would provide some special attention to my request for assistance. Please call my answering service collect if you have any immediate leads. I plan on coming to Kansas City on a job-hunting trip within the next six weeks. Prior to then, I will call you for advice on whom I might contact for interviews. Even if they have no jobs open for me now, perhaps they will know of someone else who might!

Thanks in advance for your help on this.

Sincerely,

John B. Goode
Treasurer, Southeast Region
Affiliated Trucking Association

A Powerful and Often Overlooked Job Search Tool – The Thank-You Note

While resumes and cover letters get the attention, thank-you notes often get results. That's right – sending thank-you notes makes both good manners and good job search sense. When used properly, they can help you make a positive impression with employers that more formal correspondence often can't.

So here are the basics of writing and using thank-you notes – that often overlooked but surprisingly effective job search tool.

Thank-You Notes Get Results. Here are Some Tips on When to Send Them – And Why

Thank-you notes have a social tradition that is more intimate and friendly than more formal and manipulative business correspondence. I think that is one of the reasons they work so well – people respond well to those who show good manners and say thank you. Here are some situations when you should use them, along with sample notes to show you how it's done.

Send a note before an interview

An informal note sent before the interview is often appropriate. In some cases, you can simply thank someone for being willing to see you. You could also enclose a note with a copy of your resume, but if so, keep your note informal and friendly. Remember, this is supposed to be a sincere thanks for help and not an assertive business situation.

Quick Tip

Enclose a JIST Card with your thank-you notes (see Chapter 6 for an example). JIST Cards fit well into a thank-you-note-sized envelope and they provide key information (such as a phone number) that an employer can use to contact you. They also provide key skills and other credentials that will help you create a good impression. And, of course, they could always forward the card to someone else who might have a job opening for you.

Sample Thank-You Note #1

Cynthia Kijek,

Thanks so much for your willingness to see me next Wednesday at 9:00 a.m. I know that I am one of many who is interested in working with your organization and appreciate the opportunity to meet you and learn more about the position.

I've enclosed a small JIST Card that presents the basics of my skills for this job and will bring a copy of my resume to the interview. Please call me if you have any questions at all.

Sincerely,

Bruce Vernon

Send a note after an interview

One of the best times to send a thank-you note is right after an interview. There are several reasons for this, in my opinion.

Three Good Reasons for Sending a Thank-You Note After an an Interview

1. Sending a note creates a positive impression that you have good follow-up skills – to say nothing of good manners.

2. Their receiving a note creates yet another opportunity for you to remain in their consciousness at an important time.

3. Should they have buried, passed along, or otherwise lost your resume and previous correspondence, sending a thank-you note and a corresponding JIST Card provides one more chance for them to find your number and call you.

For these reasons, I suggest you send a thank-you note right after the interview and certainly within 24 hours. Next is an example of such a note.

Sample Thank-You Note #2

Dear Mr. O'Beel,

Thank you for the opportunity for interviewing for the position you have available in the production department. I want you to know that this is the sort of job that I have been looking for, and I am enthusiastic about the possibility of my working for you.

I am not just saying this either, since I have been searching for just such a position and believe that I have both the experience and skills to fit nicely into your organization and be productive quickly.

Thanks again for the interview, I enjoyed the visit.

Sara Hall

**Quick
Tip**

Send a thank-you note as soon as possible after an interview or other event. This is when you are freshest in the mind of the person who receives it and are most likely to create a good impression.

Send a note whenever anyone helps you in your job search

Send a thank-you note to anyone who helps you during your job search. This includes those who give you referrals, people who provide advice, or simply those who are supportive of you during your search for a new job. I suggest you routinely enclose one or more JIST Cards in these notes since the recipient can then give them to others who may be in a better position to help you. You just never know. . .

Sample Thank-You Note #3

October 31, 1999

Debbie Childs
2234 Riverbed Avenue
Philadelphia, PA 17963

Ms. Helen A. Colcord
Henderson and Associates, Inc.
1801 Washington Blvd., Suite 1201
Philadelphia, PA 17963

Dear Ms. Colcord,

Thank you for sharing your time with me so generously yesterday. I really appreciated talking to you about your career field.

The information you shared with me increased my desire to work in such an area. Your advice has already proven helpful as I have an appointment to meet with Robert Hopper on Friday.

In case you think of someone else who might need a person like me, I'm enclosing another JIST Card.

Sincerely,

Debbie Childs

A Few Tips for Writing Superior Thank-You Notes

Paper and envelope

Use a good quality note paper with matching envelope. Most stationery stores have thank-you note cards and envelopes in a variety of styles. Select a note that is simple and professional – avoid cute graphics and sayings. A simple "Thank You" on the front will do.

I suggest off-white and buff colors. You can also use a simple but excellent quality stationery paper with matching envelopes, although I prefer the printed cards.

Typed vs. handwritten

The tradition with thank-you notes is that they are handwritten. If your handwriting is good, it is perfectly acceptable to write them. If not, they can be typed but they should never appear formal.

Salutation

Unless you already know the person you are thanking, don't use their first name. Write "Dear Mrs. Pam Smith" or "Ms. Smith" or "Dear Mrs. Smith" rather than the less formal "Dear Pam." Include the date.

The note itself

Keep it short and friendly. This is not the place to write "The reason you should hire me is . . ." Remember, the note is a thank-you for what *they* did, not a hard-sell pitch for what *you* want.

As appropriate, be specific about when you will next contact them. If you plan to meet with them soon, still send a note saying you look forward to the meeting and thanking them for the appointment. And make sure you include something to remind them of who you are as your name may not be enough for them to recollect you.

Your signature

Use your first and last name. Avoid initials and make your signature legible.

Send it right away

Write and send your note no later than 24 hours after you make your contact. Ideally, you should write it immediately after the contact while the details are still fresh in your mind. Always send a note after an interview, even if things did not go well. It can't hurt.

Enclose a JIST Card

Depending on the situation, a JIST Card is often the ideal enclosure to include with a thank-you note. It's small, soft-sell, and provides your phone number, should the person wish to reach you. It will remind them of you (should any jobs open up) or give them a tool to pass along to someone else. Make sure your thank-you notes and envelopes are big enough to enclose an unfolded JIST Card.

Other Job Search Correspondence

There are a variety of miscellaneous types of correspondence that you can send to people during the course of your job search, and I've included some brief comments about a few of them in the section that follows.

Follow-up Letters – After an Interview, to Solve a Problem, or to Present a Proposal

I have already shown examples of letters and notes that were sent following an interview. In some cases, a longer or more detailed letter would be appropriate. The objective here would be either to provide additional information or to present a proposal. The Sandra Kijeh sample cover letter is an example of a follow-up letter that suggests a specific proposal.

In some cases, you could submit a more comprehensive proposal that would essentially justify your job. If there were already a job opening available, you could submit an outline of what you would do if hired. And if there were not a job available, you could create a proposal that would create a job and what you would do to make it pay off for the employer.

In writing such a proposal, it is essential that you be specific in detailing what you would do and what results these actions would bring. For example, if you felt that you could increase sales, how would you do it and how much might they increase? It is not that unusual for a job to be created as a result of this approach.

Enclosures

In some cases, you may want to include something along with other correspondence, such as a sample of your writing. This can be appropriate, although I advise against sending too much material unless it is asked for. And never send originals of anything unless you are willing to lose them. Assume, in all cases, that the employer will keep what you send.

Post-It Notes

You have surely seen and used those little notes that stick on papers, walls, and other things. These can be useful when used to point out specific points on attachments, to provide additional details, or simply to indicate who the materials are coming from.

Letters to People Who Help You in Your Network

As I mentioned in the thank-you note section, you should consider sending notes or letters to anyone who helps you in your job search. This includes those who simply give you the name of someone else to contact or who spoke with you on the phone. Besides being good manners, it provides you with an opportunity to do three other things:

1. Give them additional information about you via an enclosed resume and JIST Card

2. Help to keep your needs in their consciousness

3. Give them something (A resume or JIST Card) that they can pass along to others

While this list of advantages should look suspiciously like those I presented in the section on cover letters, it's worth repeating here. Anyone can become part of the group of people who can help you during your job search. Staying in touch – and giving them tools such as a JIST Card – allows them to help you in ways that are difficult to know in advance.

A List of References

Once an employer begins to get serious, the person doing the hiring may want to contact your references as part of a final screening process. To make this easier for the employer, I suggest that you prepare a list of references. This list should include the complete name, title, organization, address, and phone number for each person. You should also include information about how each one knows you. For example, that someone was your immediate supervisor for two years.

Be careful to inform those on your list that they may be contacted and asked to provide references. In some cases, you should take the time to prepare them by sending them information on the types of jobs that you now seek, a current resume, and other details. If there is any question whether they would provide you with a positive reference, discuss this in advance so that you know what they are likely to say about you. If it is not positive, consider dropping them from your list.

Letters of Reference

Many organizations fear lawsuits as the result of giving out negative information regarding an ex-employee. For this reason, it can often be difficult for a prospective employer to get meaningful information over the phone. This is one reason I recommend that you request previous employers and other references to write you a letter that you can submit to others if asked to do so. If the letters are positive, the advantages should be clear. Even if the letter is negative, at least you now know that there is a problem with this reference and have the opportunity to contact them and negotiate what they will tell prospective employers. Of course, you should not volunteer a negative letter of reference.

Unsolicited Letters

Once more, I want to discourage you from sending unsolicited letters requesting an interview or other assistance as a primary technique. Even though many job search books recommend sending out lots of unsolicited letters and resumes, the evidence is overwhelming that this does not work for most people. The exception is if your skills are very much in demand, but in most cases, you would still be far better off to simply pick up the phone and ask for an interview.

I do think that sending a letter to people with whom you share a common bond – such as alumni or members of a professional group – can be reasonably effective. This is particularly so if you are looking for a job in another city or region and send a letter asking them to help you by giving you names of contacts. Several of the sample cover letters provide examples of those using this very technique, and it can work, particularly if you follow up by phone.

≡≡≡Quick Summary

✓ As with resumes, a big mistake with cover letters is to use them as part of a passive job search campaign that sends out lots of unsolicited resumes. Cover letters are best used *after* you have made some personal contact with a potential employer by phone or in person rather than as a replacement for direct contact.

✓ The eight guidelines for writing superior cover letters are

1. Write to someone in particular
2. Make absolutely no errors
3. Personalize your content
4. Present a good appearance
5. Use an appropriate format
6. Provide a friendly opening
7. Target your skills and experiences
8. Define the next step

✓ Base your cover letters on the samples in this chapter, taking into account whether you know the recipient or not.

✓ While resumes and cover letters get the attention, thank-you notes often get results. Sending thank-you notes makes both good manners and good job search sense. When used properly, they can help you make a positive impression with employers that more formal correspondence often can't.

✓ In this chapter, you learn the basics of writing and using thank-you notes – that often overlooked but surprisingly effective job search tool. Send a thank-you note 1) before an interview, 2) after an interview, and 3) any time someone helps you in your job search.

✓ There are a variety of miscellaneous types of correspondence, (including follow-up letters, letters of reference, proposals, etc.) that you can send to people during the course of your job search. These types of communication can help you to make a good impression, and most importantly, can help you find (or create) the job you want.

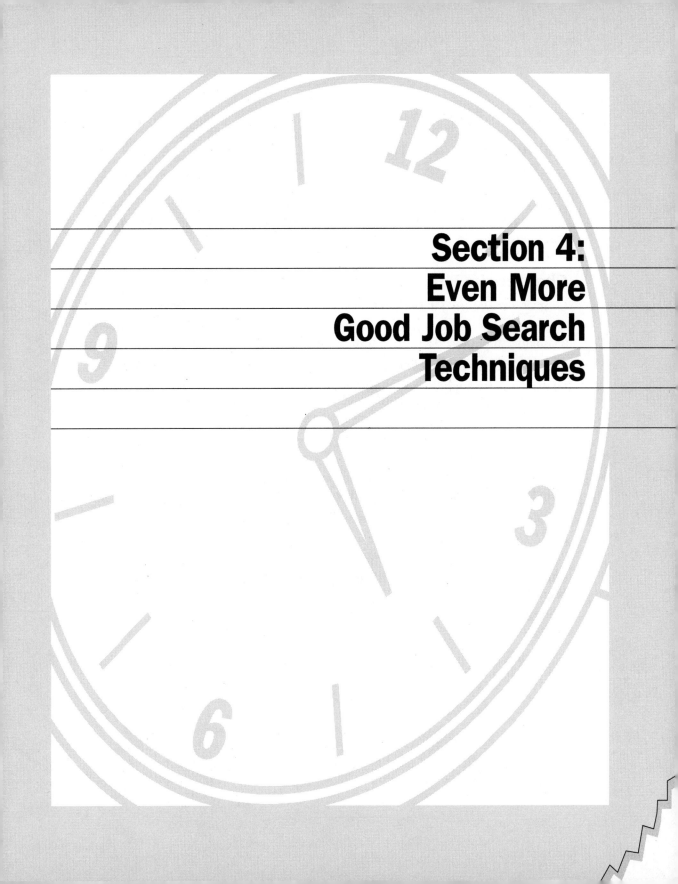

Section 4:
Even More
Good Job Search
Techniques

Section 4 Introduction

I've included a variety of information in this section and, while some of it may not interest you, some will. For example, effective telephone techniques should be of interest to most job seekers while "how to complete an application" or "using a computer in your job search" may not. I suggest you select the chapters that interest you most and review those first, coming back to the others at another time.

Chapters in This Section

Chapter 14: Dialing for Dollars – Using the Phone to Get Interviews

The phone is an important tool to use in your job search and this chapter covers techniques that have been proven to work in getting interviews.

Chapter 15: The Truth About Job Applications

I'll explain how applications are often used to screen people out and that there are often better ways to get interviews – as well as how to complete an application without damaging your chances for employment.

Chapter 16: More Answers to Specific Problem Interview Questions – And a List of 94 Frequently Asked Questions

This chapter reviews some interviewing methods covered in Section 1 and includes dozens of answers to specialized questions.

Chapter 17: Changing Technologies – Using a Computer in the Job Search

If you are computer literate, there are many resources available to you that you may not be aware of and this chapter reviews some of those options.

Chapter 18: Tips for Coping with Job Loss – And Other Things You Might Want to Know

Managing your money, emotions, time, and interpersonal relationships are some of the topics covered in this chapter.

CHAPTER FOURTEEN

*Even More
Good Job Search
Techniques*

Dialing for Dollars –

Using the Phone to Get Interviews

Quick Overview

In this chapter, I review the following:

✓ Why using the telephone can be both a very effective and very efficient job search method

✓ How to use your JIST card as a basis for a phone interview

✓ The five parts of an effective phone script

✓ Tips for completing your phone script

✓ Tips for making cold contacts – Calling people you don't know

✓ Tips for making warm contacts – Calling people you know

✓ How to get the interview

✓ How to overcome phone phobia

The telephone is a wonderful invention, and if used correctly, it is the most effective job search tool. In fact, many job seekers get more interviews by using the phone than with any other method.

Using the phone is also one of the most efficient ways of looking for work. You don't spend any time traveling, and you can talk to lots of people in a very short time. In one morning, you can easily talk to more than 20 employers once you learn how.

For example, you can:

➤ Call people you already know to get interviews or referrals

➤ Follow up with leads you get from want ads

➤ Stay in touch with prospective employers and with people in your network who might hear of openings

➤ Contact employers whose names you get from the *Yellow Pages*

In this chapter, I show you some very effective ways to use the telephone to find job openings and set up interviews. I present a variety of simple-to-use techniques that can make a big impact on how many job leads you get. Many people have used these methods to get two or more job interviews in just a few hours of work.

A Review of Some Key Concepts

In reading this chapter, there are two key concepts that you need to keep in mind. First, it is essential that you remember the new definition of an interview. I presented this concept in an earlier chapter, and here it is again:

Quick Reminder

> ## An interview can now be any face-to-face contact with a person who might use a person with your skills – whether or not they have a job opening.

This concept is important since you will often be calling people who don't have a job opening when you call, or who may not even know of any job openings for someone with your skills. Even so, there are opportunities you can find in these situations, and you must train yourself to be alert to them.

The second important point to remember is that there are a variety of ways to find job leads. Back in Chapters 1 and 2, I reviewed basic strategies for finding job leads. Some of the methods I covered included making contacts with people you know (or *warm contacts*) and techniques for making contacts with people you don't know (or *cold contacts*).

The *Yellow Pages* was one of the sources of cold contacts that I reviewed, and it should be pretty obvious that this is a good source of leads for making phone calls. Go back over that material to refresh your memory if you need to.

Use Your JIST Card as the Basis for a Phone Script

It just so happens that the content of your JIST Card makes a very nice basis for a presentation that you can make by phone. JIST Cards were covered in Chapter 6, and if you've written one, it will help you greatly in getting the most out of this chapter.

The Transformation of John Kijek

Read the following example to see how John Kijek (the person presented in the sample JIST Card in Chapter 6) used his JIST Card to develop a phone script. As you read the phone script that follows, imagine that you are an employer who hires people with these skills. Would you be interested in interviewing this person?

John Kijek **Home:** (219) 232-9213
Message: (219) 637-6643

Position Desired: Management position in a small- to medium-size organization.

Skills: B.A. in business plus over five years experience in increasingly responsible management positions. Have supervised as many as 12 staff and increased productivity by 27 percent over two years. Was promoted twice in the past three years and have excellent references. Started customer follow-up program that increased sales by 22 percent within 12 months. Get along well with others and am a good team worker.

Willing to travel and can work any hours

Hardworking, self-motivated, willing to accept responsibility

"Hello, my name is John Kijek. I am interested in a management position in a small- to medium-size organization. I have a B.A. in business, plus over five years experience in increasingly responsible management positions and have supervised as many as 12 staff members whose productivity increased by 27 percent over two years. During a three year period, I was promoted twice, and I have excellent references. I initiated a customer follow-up program that increased sales by 22 percent within 12 months. I also get along well with others, am a good team worker, and am willing to travel or work any hours as needed.

"I am hardworking, self-motivated, and willing to accept responsibility. When may I come in for an interview?"

If you were an employer that supervised people with skills similar to John's, how might you react to his calling you in this way? If you needed someone like this, would you give John an interview?

Yes _____ Maybe _____ Definitely Not _____

Quick Fact

Most employers respond well to a short phone contact – and good phone techniques result in more interviews. . .

Using the Telephone to Get Interviews

Most people say they *would* or might give John Kijek an interview if they had an opening. Not everyone, but most. For this reason, reading a phone script based on your JIST Card is a very effective way to use the telephone.

You should also notice that the script used above takes most people 30 seconds or less to read. And, once you get to the prospective employer, that is about how long it would take to say it out loud. In just that short time, you present a great deal of information. Based on many years of experience, the JIST Card/ phone script approach has been carefully constructed to reduce the opportunity for an employer to interrupt you (remember, it is only 30 seconds) and it does not allow for a "no" response.

I have run job search programs where phone scripts based on JIST Cards were used. Thousands of people have used this technique, and their experience has been that it takes from 10 to 15 cold-contact phone calls to get one interview. That may sound like a lot of rejection, but most people can make that many calls in less than an hour. In two hours of making phone calls, most people in those programs got two or more interviews. And how many job search methods are you aware of with that kind of a track record?

As I will show you, you can adapt your phone script for use in calling people you know, as well as in making cold contacts to employers. In both situations, the telephone can be used as a time-efficient tool for finding jobs in the hidden job market.

The Five Parts of an Effective Phone Script

The phone script I will show you assumes that you will contact a person who does not know you and who may or may not have a job opening. An example of this situation would be if you were making cold calls to organizations listed in the *Yellow Pages*. Later, you can adapt your script to the situation, but for now, I suggest that you begin by writing a script in the specific way I outline below. This approach has been carefully crafted based on years of experience, and it *is* effective.

I have divided the script into five sections. As I review each section, complete the related section in the Phone Script Worksheet found later in this chapter.

1. The Introduction

This one is easy. Just add your name to the blank space on the Phone Script Worksheet. Write your name as if you were introducing yourself.

2. The Position

Always begin your statement with "I am interested in a position as. . . " and write in your job objective.

It takes you only about 30 seconds to read your phone script, and you don't want to get rejected before you begin. So don't use the word "job" in your first sentence. If you say you are "...looking for a job..." or anything similar, you will often be interrupted. Then you will be told there are no openings. For example, if you say "Do you have any jobs?" the person you are talking to will often say "No." And your presentation will come to a screeching halt in less than 10 seconds.

Remember that, in the new definition of an interview, you are not looking for a job opening, you simply want to talk to people who have the ability to hire a person with your skills – even if they don't have a job opening now.

If the job objective from your JIST Card sounds good spoken out loud, then add it to your worksheet. If it doesn't, change it around a bit until it does. For example, if your JIST Card says you want a "management/supervisory position in retail sales," your phone script might say "I am interested in a management or supervisory position in retail sales."

3. The Hook

The skills section of your JIST Card includes length of experience, training, education, special skills related to the job, and accomplishments. Rewriting the content from this part of your JIST Card for use in your phone script may take some time. Make sure that the sentences in your phone script sound natural when spoken. You may find it helpful to write and edit this section on a separate piece of paper before writing the final version on your script worksheet. Then read the final version out loud to hear how it sounds. Also, read it to others and continue to make improvements until it sounds right.

4. The Clincher

Simply take the last section of your JIST Card, containing your key adaptive skills, and make these key traits into a sentence. For example, "reliable, hard working, and learn quickly" from a JIST Card might be written in a phone script as "I am reliable, hard working, and I learn quickly." These are some of your most important skills to mention to an employer and putting them last gives them the most power.

5. The Goal

The goal of the phone script is to get an interview. In the example I used earlier in this chapter, the final statement was "When can I come in for an interview?" and that is what I suggest you write on your own script. The reason is that it tends to work. If you said, for example, "May I come in for an interview?" (or "Could you please, please, let me come in to talk with you?"), that allows the employer to say "No." And you don't want to make it easy for the employer to say no. They can, of course, do that on their very own, without your assisting them.

Tips for Completing Your Phone Script

Use the Phone Script Worksheet to write out your final draft, but write rough drafts out on separate sheets of paper until you are satisfied with your script.

In writing your phone script, consider the tips that follow.

✓ Write exactly what you will say on the phone

A written script will help you present yourself effectively and keep you from stumbling around for the right word. If you have not already completed your own JIST Card, you really ought to do so before you write your phone script. Avoid the temptation (I know that you are resisting this) to "wing it" without a script. It just won't work as well. Trust me.

✓ Keep your telephone script short

Just present the information an employer would want to know about you, then ask for an interview.

✓ Write your script the way you talk

A well-written JIST Card uses short sentences and phrases, and you probably wouldn't talk that way. So add some words to your script to make it sound natural when you say it out loud.

✓ Use the words I use

As you write your phone script, avoid being too creative. Over the years, I refined the words used in the examples, and to avoid specific problems, I suggest you use them as they are presented.

For example, do not write or say "Good morning, my name is _____" because that will build a bad habit, which you will realize all too late on one overcast afternoon. Really, I have learned the best words to use through years of making mistakes, and there is no need for you to make the same ones. Start my way, you can change it to your way after you have mastered mine.

✓ Practice saying your script out loud

I know that your neighbors may think you are nuts, but reading your script out loud etches it into your soul in a way that reading it to yourself cannot do. It has something to do with neural pathways and brain stuff. Or maybe something more spiritual, having to do with the way we define ourselves. Or both. But the fact is, reading an honestly prepared phone script out loud helps you accept that all the good stuff our phone script says about you is true. Later, having this information etched into your subconscious, will help you in an interview.

Phone Script Worksheet

· ·

Complete this worksheet with your final script content.

1. Introduction

Hello, my name is _____

2. The Position

I am interested in a position as _____

_____

_____

3. The Hook

_____

_____

_____

_____

_____

4. The Clincher

_____

_____

5. The Goal

When can I come in for an interview?

Making Effective Phone Contacts

Now that you have developed your phone script, you need to know how to use it effectively. Following are some tips that I have gathered over many years that should help.

Tips for Making Cold Contacts – Calling Someone You Don't Know

Calling a prospective employer directly can be very effective. For example, let's say that you are calling employers listed in the *Yellow Pages* under a category of businesses or organizations that need people with your skills. This is a type of cold contact that many people have used to obtain interviews that would have been most difficult to obtain any other way. Here are some guidelines to follow.

✓ Get to the hiring authority

You need to get directly to the person who is most likely to supervise a person with your skills. Unless you want to work in the personnel department, you wouldn't normally ask to talk to someone there. Depending on the type and size of the organization you're calling, you should have a pretty good idea of the title of the person who would likely supervise you. For example, in a small business you might ask to speak to the manager or the "person in charge." In a larger one, you would ask for the name of the person who is in charge of a particular department.

✓ Get the name of a specific person

If you don't have the name of the person you need to speak to, ask for it. For example, ask for the name of the person in charge of the accounting department or warehouse if that is where you want to work. Usually, you will be given the name, and your call will be transferred to him or her immediately. When you do get a name, get the correct spelling and write it down right away. Then you can use their name in your conversation.

✓ Get past the secretary (dragon)

In some cases, secretaries or receptionists will try to screen out your call. Be nice to them, it's their job. If they find out you are looking for a job, they may transfer you to the personnel department (if they have one) or ask you to send an application or resume. Here are two things you can do to avoid getting screened out in these situations:

1. **Call back:** If you get screened out on your first try, call back a day later and say you are getting ready to send some correspondence to the person who manages such and such. You want to use the correct name and title and request that they give you this information. This is true since you will be sending them something soon. And this approach usually gets you what you need. Say thank-you and call

back in a day or so. Then ask for the manager by name and you will often get right through.

2. **Call when the dragon is out:** You are likely to get right through if you call when that secretary is out to lunch. Other good times are just before and after normal work hours. Less experienced staff members are likely to answer the phones and transfer your call to the boss – who is often there early or is working late.

Tips for Making Warm Contacts – Calling Someone You Know

Quick Fact

The best phone calls are ones to people you know.

Up to this point in the chapter, I have used examples of phone calls made to strangers. I did this to help prepare you to make these kinds of calls. These cold contacts are more difficult for most people, so preparing to do them makes calls to those you know less threatening.

I hope you forgive me for having done this since I truly believe that making calls to people you know is far easier for most people. I figure that once you accept the idea of making cold contacts, making warm contacts is a lot less threatening. While using the phone to make cold contacts is clearly an effective job search technique, it is always preferable to call someone you know. This includes calling people whose name you have been given by someone else. Here are a few tips for warm contacts.

✓ Chat informally, give the reason for your call, and then follow your script

Sometimes, using your telephone script just as it is written on your worksheet will not make sense. For example, if you are calling someone you know, you would normally begin with some friendly conversation before getting to the purpose of your call. Once you have chatted informally for awhile, you can then get to the purpose of your call by saying something like this:

> *"The reason I called is to let you know I am looking for a job, and I thought you might be able to help. Let me tell you a few things about myself. I am looking for a position as..." (From here on you continue with the rest of your phone script.)*

✓ When calling referrals, begin by saying who referred you

I covered the concept of developing a network of contacts from names given to you by people you know in Chapter 2. Even though you don't know these referrals directly, most will be willing to talk to you if you approach them in the right way.

In making a call to a referral, immediately give the name of the person who suggested that you call. For example, say:

"Hello, Mister Rhodes, Joan Bugsby suggested I give you a call."

If the receptionist asks why you are calling, say:

"A friend of Mister Rhodes' suggested I give him a call."

When a friend of the employer recommends that you call, you usually get right through. Not always, but often.

Getting the Interview!

The primary goal of a phone contact is to get an interview. This is important to remember at all times when making phone calls. To succeed, you must be ready to get past the first and even the second rejection.

Here are some suggestions that will help you meet your objective.

Ask three times for the interview

To increase your chances of getting an interview, you need to practice **asking** for the interview. This often requires you to overcome initial rejections, but you must learn how to handle this by asking again. Here is an example:

Persistence Pays

Ask once:

> *You:* When may I come in for an interview?
>
> *Employer:* I don't have any positions open now.

Ask again:

> *You:* That's OK, I'd still like to come in to talk to you about the possibility of future openings.
>
> *Employer:* I really don't plan on hiring within the next six months or so.

Be prepared to ask again:

> *You:* Then I'd like to come in and learn more about what you do. I'm sure you know a lot about the industry, and I am looking for ideas on getting into your field and moving up.

Although such a persistent approach does not always work, asking the third time works more often than most people would believe. It is essential that you learn to keep asking after the first time you are told no. Of course, you should be sensitive to the person you are speaking to and not push too hard, but it is more often a question of not being persistent enough than being too aggressive.

Arrange for an interview time or ask for other help

If the employer agrees to an interview, arrange a specific time and date. If you are not sure of his or her complete name or address, you can always call back later and ask the receptionist.

In some cases you will decide not to ask for an interview. The person may not seem helpful or you may have caught him or her at a busy time. If so, there are alternative things you can do:

1. **Get a referral:** Ask for names of other people who might be able to help you and find out how to contact them. Then add these new referrals to your job search network. When you call them, remember to tell them that you were referred by so and so.

2. **Ask to call back:** If your contact is busy when you call, ask if you can call back. Get a specific time and day to do this, and add the call to your to-do list for that day. When you do call back (and you must), the employer will likely be positively impressed – and may give you an interview for just that reason.

3. **Ask if it is okay to call back from time to time:** Maybe your contact will hear of an opening or have some other information for you. Many job seekers get their best leads from a person they have checked back with several times. Every two to three weeks seems like an interval that works well.

Quick Reminder

Always follow up with anyone you contact via phone, especially anyone who is helpful to you. This effort can make a big difference. The best way to follow up is with a thank-you note. Send it right after the phone call.

If you arranged for an interview, send a note saying you look forward to your meeting. If that person gave you a referral to someone else, send another note, later, telling how things turned out. Or send a thank-you note telling how you followed up on any suggestion he or she gave you. And notice how nicely a JIST Card fits into a thank-you note-sized envelope.

Overcoming Phone Phobia

Quick Reminder

Phone contacts only get you interviews if you use them.

You may find it hard to use the phone in the way I suggest. Many people do. They think it is "pushy" to call someone and ask for an interview. Before you decide this technique is not for you, think about why you are afraid. What is the worst thing that can happen to you? Most calls take only a minute or so. And most employers don't mind talking to a person they might be interested in hiring.

These calls do require you to overcome some shyness, but they are really quite easy to do. Soon you will find that most people are happy to help you. Even people you just picked from the *Yellow Pages* will typically treat you well.

Quick Tip

The experience of thousands of job seekers is that very few people will be rude to you. And you probably wouldn't want to work for someone who is rude anyway.

Many people dread making phone contacts, so if you count yourself among them, try the following:

➤ Begin by calling people you know, then the people they refer you to. That will improve your confidence and give you practice in getting better.

➤ Role-play your phone contacts, too – if at all possible. Have another person be the employer, and see if you can overcome their resistance to seeing you by asking three times for an interview.

➤ Contact the organizations in the phone book that you rated a "3" (indicating you were not at all interested in working there) as described in Chapter 2. That way you can't screw things up too badly.

There are many other situations where you will need to adapt your basic script. Use your own judgment on this. With practice, it becomes easier.

Quick Alert

Don't practice too long, though, before making real phone contacts.

Making phone calls is work, and that is how you should approach it – as a job. It is easiest if you plan to make your calls at a certain time each day and continue this throughout your job search. With just two hours of making phone calls a day, most people learn to get at least two interviews. That's two interviews each day – 10 interviews a week – about twice what the average job seeker gets in a *month*. Which is a pretty good way to let your fingers do the walking.

Quick Summary

✓ The telephone is the most effective job search tool. In fact, many job seekers get more interviews by using the phone than with any other method.

✓ JIST Cards make a very nice basis for phone interview scripts. A script takes 30 seconds or less to read. In two hours of making phone calls (while using this technique), many people get two or more interviews.

✓ The five parts of an effective phone script are: 1) Introduction, 2) The Position, 3) The Hook, 4) The Clincher, and 5) The Goal.

✓ The best phone calls are ones to people you know. However, by following tips given in this chapter, you can make effective phone contacts to people you don't know as well. And you'll have the interviews to show for it.

✓ Most employers respond well to a short phone contact. The experience of thousands of job seekers is that very few people will be rude to you when you call.

✓ Many people dread making phone contacts, so tips in this chapter help you to overcome your phone phobia. For example: Begin by calling people you know, then the people they refer you to. That will improve your confidence and give you practice in getting better.

CHAPTER FIFTEEN

Even More Good Job Search Techniques

The Truth About
Job Applications

▰▰▰Quick Overview

In this chapter, I review the following:

✓ Why applications are not an effective job search tool

✓ Why you still need to know how to complete applications

✓ How to avoid being screened out by sloppy, incomplete applications

✓ How to handle troublesome application questions and issues

Applications are not a job seeker's best friend. In this chapter, I explain to you why this is so. And since you may be required to complete applications during your search for a new job, I also provide you with tips on doing so in a more effective way.

Hardly anyone I know enjoys rejection. One way job seekers avoid it (at a place of possible employment) is by asking if they can fill out "an application." Most employers will say "Yes," since it doesn't cost them much to do so. And they know exactly what to do after you're gone: File it.

Why Applications Are Not an Effective Job Search Tool

While most job seekers assume that filling out applications is part of the job search process, you need to know that they have considerable limitations as a job search tool. Here are some things to consider about their limited value.

Applications Are Designed to Screen You Out

Think about it. An "Application for Employment" creates a barrier between you and anyone who would actually hire or supervise you. In larger organizations, there may be hundreds – sometimes thousands – of applications submitted for each job opening. The chance is slim that yours will jump out and be *THE* one.

Let me tell you what the director of a large organization's personnel department recently told me.

"I've worked in personnel departments for over 15 years and am now in charge of the personnel functions of a FORTUNE 500 company. We get many thousands of applications per year. I estimate that most of them get less than 60 seconds of attention before getting filed. And we rarely go back and look through filed applications.

If someone walks in today who meets the criteria of a job opening, they may be referred for an interview. The ones who came in yesterday probably won't. The truth is, most of our new employees are referred by our own employees. Maybe 15 percent or so are hired as the result of filling out an application. We accept applications because we are expected *to – not because we need to.*"

Applications Are Usually Used by Personnel Departments

The people who work in personnel departments are usually very nice. I even have a few as friends. But, unless you want to work in a personnel department, they can't hire you. They can only screen you out – and applications are the primary tool they use to screen out applicants.

Quick
Fact

About 70 percent of all workers in the private sector are employed by businesses with fewer than 250 employees and the most rapid growth of new jobs has been in businesses with fewer than 50 staff.

Most smaller businesses don't have a personnel department and often don't even have applications. So, if you think of the job search as a process of dealing with personnel offices and their forms, you will miss out on most of the jobs in our new economy.

A growing number of larger companies also now don't have personnel departments because they have decided that spending money to accept, file, and forget applications isn't worth it. Instead, they refer you to the local, state, or provincial employment office which will do their screening for them. Many large corporations also have smaller branch offices and the hiring is done right there, where they don't have a personnel office.

So, you see, the changes in our economy make the concept of filling out applications even less effective than it was in the past.

Applications Allow for Limited Information

Have you ever seen an application that asks you to list your strengths or why you think you would be a good employee? There are a few that do, but 99 percent do not.

Applications Encourage You to Reveal Your Flaws

If you have limited work experience, do not have ideal credentials, have gaps in your job history, want to change careers, are unemployed or underemployed, have ever been fired, or have anything other than a near-perfect work history, the application will encourage you to reveal it. It was designed to do just that. The reason is that applications are a tool that employers developed to collect details that can be used to quickly screen out those whose qualifications are not what they want.

Why You Still Need to Know How to Complete Applications

There *are* some advantages in knowing how to complete applications well.

Applications Are Often Required

Some employers may ask you to complete an application before they interview you so they don't have to waste time with the details of your background. Larger companies sometimes have a policy requiring you to go through personnel before being formally hired or considered. You may also be asked to complete an application after the job offer but before you begin. In all these cases, knowing what to do is important.

Quick
Fact

Recent research into how people find jobs indicates that filling out applications is a more effective technique for younger people than for more experienced workers.

Many of the jobs that young people get are low-paying, entry-level jobs where there is relatively high turnover and relatively low skill or training requirements. Employers in these situations use applications as an initial screening process to weed out those who clearly are unsuited for these jobs.

Even though the application completion process works better for youth looking for these sorts of jobs, I still would suggest that getting to talk with the manager is still the most effective approach – and that applications create a barrier to doing this.

Applications Force You to Deal with Your Flaws

An application is designed to collect negative information. Learning how to deal with this gracefully is important preparation for handling tough interview questions and writing resumes.

Quick Advice

The Best Way to *Use* an Application

Like a resume, many job seekers assume that the function of an application is to help them get an interview. I hope you now see that the actual function is to provide an employer with a tool that can be used to quickly screen most people out. So using either a resume or an application as a means for getting interviews is often a frustrating experience.

A better approach, as I have been encouraging you to consider throughout this book, is to find out about openings through people you know and to make direct contact with those within an organization who are most likely to use someone with your skills. Applications and resumes won't work well in getting you interviews, and their best use is *after* you have set up an interview. Then you can send a resume or fill out an application.

In fact, when I worked in large organizations, I often hired someone before they ever went to personnel. I sent them there to fill out the necessary paperwork, including the application form. From the point of view of the job seeker, that is the best time to complete one – after you get the job. Consider it.

Completing Your Application

Step 1: Master the Basics

An application form is designed to uncover negatives so that the employer can quickly screen you out. Here are some basic tips for completing an application form so that you don't get screened out without a second glance.

1. **Read and follow directions carefully**

   Don't write if it says print, and don't put your year of birth where the month should have been. Employers notice this carelessness and assume that you will be similarly careless on the job. Work slowly and do it right.

2. **Use an erasable pen, not a pencil**

   Blue or black ink ball-point pens present a more professional appearance. Most stationery stores carry erasable pens and you should carry two such pens in case one stops working.

3. **Be neat and thorough**

   Appearance counts. If your paperwork is messy, the negative impression will get you screened out – fast. So, print if your writing is hard to read, and make your entries as legible and neat as you can. And be complete. Don't leave blank spaces. If the question does not apply to you, write "N/A," draw a line through it, or make some other response. However, in some cases, it is better to write "will explain in interview" or leave it blank than to volunteer negative information.

4. **Be positive, but honest**

   Although you always want to present yourself in the most positive light, I recommend honesty throughout your job search and do not advise you to falsify your application or anything else. This is very important. For more details, read the sidebar "Tell the Truth on Your Application" on the next page.

5. **Add positive information wherever you can**

   Since most applications don't ask you for your strengths and accomplishments, you should look for a place to mention them anyway. In the work experience section, mention that you were promoted, trained new staff, or any other positives wherever you can fit them in. Mention any extracurricular school activities, volunteer work, or other accomplishments or proof that would support your ability to do the job. Even if an application does not provide space for positive information, write in positive information in any available spaces on the application.

Step 2: Get Past Troublesome Questions and Issues

In the old days, applications often asked information that had nothing to do with your ability to do the job. Questions such as your age, your parents' occupations, and your marital status were common. With the change in laws, you are much less likely to find these sorts of questions today.

Quick Alert

Generally, issues that don't relate to your ability to perform the job should not be considered in the employment process. Even so, some applications (usually by smaller employers) still ask "illegal" questions and even allowed questions can create problems for the unwary.

Here are some of the potentially troublesome questions you might get asked along with suggestions for handling each.

Position desired

Applications often ask what sort of a job you want, what hours and days you want to work, the salary you expect, and other details. How you handle this can be very important. If you know of a specific job opening with this employer, you could use that job title. A safer approach would be to use the general career area or department that job is in. For example, if you were looking for a position as a warehouse manager, you might write "business or shipping/receiving management or related tasks." That approach would leave your options open to be considered for other jobs that might interest you. Saying "anything," however, indicates you don't know what you want to do and will not impress an employer.

Whatever job objective you do write down defines how and what you emphasize on the rest of your application. If you want to work in the accounting department of a hospital, for example, you would emphasize your accounting related training and education, experience with computerized accounting systems and software, previous work and military experience that was related to accounting, and anything else that directly supported your stated job objective.

Quick
Tip

Tell the Truth on Your Application

It is easy to lie on an application (or on a resume or in an interview, for that matter) but it is not a good idea. Many employers will fire you if they find out you lied about any important item on your application. A better approach is to consider the following options:

Leave a sensitive question blank.

I cover a variety of answers to problem questions in Chapter 5 and you may find some of them useful in answering certain questions on an application. But the test is this: If your truthful response to an application question could be interpreted as a negative by an employer, consider leaving that section blank. You can explain that item later in an interview or after being offered a job, if it is important.

Look for jobs that don't require an application.

If you would be screened out of a job by providing an honest response to an application question, you may want to avoid using applications as a job search tool altogether. It can be done and often is. If you have a serious problem that an application would reveal, you'll be better off looking for job openings that don't require an application. For less serious situations, such as being fired, the words you choose to explain what happened are very important. Always look for a way to express yourself that puts you in a positive light.

The fact is, an application is more likely to do you harm than good. If you *do* fill one out, be sure that it is as good as you can make it (while still being truthful) and that it has nothing in it that could eliminate you from consideration.

Health information

Health-related absences and accidents are expensive to an employer, so you may be screened out if you've had a history of either. The issue here is whether or not your health will keep you from doing a good job and being a dependable worker. Unless you have a problem that will keep you from doing the job, you should say your health is "excellent." Don't mark "fair" or even "good" without a good reason. Such responses will usually get you screened out.

Some applications have a checklist to screen for all sorts of specific medical problems. If the application doesn't ask, you may be asked in a pre-employment medical screening. If you do have a medical problem that limits your ability to do the job, or if the problem is long-term and/or can get worse, you have a problem that is not easily resolved.

Quick Reminder

If you lie on the application, you could be fired later for lying.

Some conditions, such as chronic back pain, dizzy spells and seizures, or various physical and emotional disabilities, make it very difficult to find employment, and the very nature of an application makes it even harder. One solution here is to get good career counseling in the preparation for and selection of a job objective. If the job does not require what you can't do, there is no longer a problem, is there? If your condition does not affect your ability to do the job, you could write "I have no limitations that affect my performance on this job." And that should be that.

Quick Tip

The Americans With Disabilities Act (ADA) is legislation that is designed to protect the rights of workers with disabilities. A good library should have information on what this law covers, should you be interested in learning more about it.

Attendance

If you have a good attendance record, state it. For example "only two days absent out of the past year." If you have a good long-term record but were ill recently and have now recovered, you could say something like this:

"Over the past five years, I have had an excellent attendance record, missing fewer than three days a year for four of the past five years."

Workers' compensation

Workers' compensation is pay you get for a job-related injury or illness that prevents you from working. Some employers assume that those who received this pay in the past are accident-prone or unwilling to work. If you did receive this pay, consider leaving this section blank and discussing it in an interview if it comes up.

Unemployment compensation

Unemployment compensation is money you receive after leaving one job and before finding another. Employers pay for these expenses and do not like to hire people who have misused these payments in the past. If you did receive it, say so and write in a good reason. For example, "company closed, am willing to relocate."

Education and formal training

Present any education and training that supports your job objective in as positive a way as possible. Since the spaces on an application are often small, you can't write much, so use whatever space you can to your advantage.

If you received formal training in a setting other than a traditional school (the military is one good example), consider including it in the education section of the application. This would be particularly true if the training you received supports the job you now seek. Before completing the education section, first look over the rest of the application. If there are small or no sections for training you received in technical, trade, business, military, or other programs, look for ways to squeeze it into the education section.

If you attended but did not complete high school, college, or some training program, do not emphasize that fact. Indicate that you "attended" and mention the job-related courses or major you took. If you went to three schools but graduated from only one, acknowledge just that school you graduated from if space is limited. Of course, mention anything you did while in school that might create a positive impression such as "kept grades in top half of class while working part-time to support myself," or "practiced in school band 10 to 20 hours a week in addition to class work."

Military experience

Military experience is just as important as any civilian job, schooling, or training. The military has the largest training and education program in the world and the levels of responsibility held are often much higher than anything available to civilians of equal age and training.

If the military section of an application does not let you present your training and experience well, use the education, work experience, and other sections of the application to present this. Present the information in civilian terms and emphasize those things that support your job objective.

Salary and working conditions

Do not state a specific salary. Write "open" or "salary negotiable," since you do not yet want to be screened out from consideration on this factor. If forced to, write in a very wide salary range, such as "mid-teens to low twenties," "low to mid-thirties," or "$7 to $10 per hour."

Are you willing to work evenings if necessary? Weekends? The best response is to write (if asked) "will consider" or, if you do have a strong preference write something like "prefer daytime hours but will consider other shifts." The same approach applies to questions about relocation, travel, and other issues. While you don't have to take a job you don't want, you do not want to be screened out early either.

Previous work experience

Employers look at what you have done on previous jobs to support what you want to do now. This is a section that troubles many job seekers. It is unusual for anyone to have an "ideal" work history, yet you must learn to present yourself as a person who has a good chance of succeeding on the job you seek.

Following are some common problems job seekers have and tips to help deal with them.

Gaps in employment

If you have gaps between jobs, the odds are that you did something constructive during that time. If you went to school, did part-time jobs (self-employed), raised children, got career counseling, or did anything else, mention it. It provides a reason for the gap. If the gap was short, looking for a job is an acceptable reason. You can also avoid using specific employment dates if they display gaps in your history. For example, put "Summer 1995 to Spring 1996" for one job followed by "Spring 1996 to Present." For larger gaps, you can simply use the years, such as "1995 to 1996" or "1994 to Present."

Job titles

If the job title you had does not accurately describe your responsibilities or duties, consider changing it. For example, if you were a "Customer Service Representative" but supervised a department of people, you could use the more generic and descriptive "Department Head, Customer Service and Support." Use judgment on this and select new titles that would be helpful in communicating what you did but that do not misrepresent your actual responsibilities. Consider checking first with a previous employer to see if they would object to this.

Job descriptions

Some applications provide a tiny space to describe your job. In these cases, select statements indicating your responsibility or achievements like: "supervised staff of seven in a three-state area," or "served over 3,000 people a month," or "opened and closed store, deposited $10,000 per week in bank." You don't have many words, so don't waste them.

Getting fired

Most people get fired over what could be called a "personality conflict." Whatever the reason, *never* write "fired" on an application. Is there any way you could express, in a more positive way, your reason for leaving? If, after you left, you went to school or took a job paying more money, mention those things under "reason for leaving past jobs." If you are currently unemployed, think of some way to avoid saying you were fired. If all else fails and you did nothing criminal, what does the truth sound like? For example, "The job I left just did not work out the way I wanted. My boss wanted to do everything herself, and I could not use my own ideas," could be reworded on an application as "looking for a more responsible and demanding position."

Previous supervisors and what they might say about you

If you worry about what your ex-supervisor would say about you, there are two things you should do:

1. **Find out. Call up and/or go see your old boss.** Tell him or her you are looking for a new job and are concerned about what he or she

would say to a prospective employer wanting a reference. You can usually negotiate what, exactly, the boss will say. Make sure both you and the boss are clear what will be said to reference inquiries, and say thanks. You could then follow up your visit with a letter reviewing what was discussed and enclose a draft letter of recommendation that they could modify to their satisfaction, sign, and return to you as a signed original.

2. **Get an alternate source.** If your ex-boss will say harmful things about you, consider giving the name of another responsible person in your old organization who will say good things about your performance.

Too little or "no" experience

If you have had no or limited paid work experience, you must fall back on what experience you do have. Look carefully at volunteer, education, training, hobbies, and other experiences. Some of these could count as jobs or provide the equivalent experience. Note something positive in the available application space, even if it is not requested. For example, write "I worked in a variety of part-time jobs while going to school," or "My studies allowed little free time, and I concentrated my spare time on homework and family responsibilities," or "I am new to the job market but am now ready to put my complete energy into the career I have carefully chosen," or whatever else you might say that is positive.

If you have received job-related training, mention this again. For example, you could say "I have over 18 months of intensive job-related training, including over 150 hours of hands-on experience with equipment similar to yours."

Too much experience

If you feel you have too much experience, perhaps you should be looking for a more responsible job. The true issue is the employer's concern that you will not be satisfied with the job and the pay they have and you will leave. But if you have good reasons for seeking lower pay or responsibility levels, explain why. You could write, for example, "My children are grown, and I now want a creative and challenging position that does not require relocation," or "I am very interested in positions paying from the mid-twenties (or whatever) and above."

If you have had many jobs, cluster the older ones under a heading like: "1989 to 1990 – A variety of increasingly responsible jobs in the sales and service areas." If you received any promotions on the job, say "Customer Service Supervisor, promoted to Director of Operations" under job title or wherever it's appropriate.

Arrest record

Applications can ask if you have ever been convicted of a felony. The key word here is "convicted." Employers have a need to know of a convicted embezzler, for example, who is applying for a job as a bank teller. If you were charged but not convicted, our legal system defines you as innocent. Only you, of course, can know the truth, but if you were not convicted you don't have to say you are guilty of anything. The files of juveniles are usually closed and you do not have to reveal any arrest records from that time in your life.

If the application asks if you've ever been arrested, and you have, you might leave this section blank as you are not required to answer it in most situations. If the arrest was minor, you could write "minor traffic violations," or whatever is appropriate.

If your arrest record is more serious, consider using job search techniques that do not let you get screened out based on an application. Also, depending on your offense, you should realistically avoid looking for certain jobs. People who were convicted of theft should not look for jobs handling money, for example. You may want to (and be qualified) to do such work, but it is unwise to seek it.

Transportation

Some jobs require you to have your own car or have a valid driver's license. If you don't have what is requested, write "I will obtain a car if hired," or another appropriate comment.

Certification, licenses, and registration

If you have job-related credentials, mention them somewhere, even if the information is not requested.

Volunteer activities

If asked, list those that support the job objective and mention specific skills used, responsibilities, or achievements that support your job objective. If these activities are an important part of your experience, consider putting them in the work experience section of an application.

Hobbies and recreational activities

List those that support your job objective in some way. If these activities made money or received recognition, mention that. For example, "I designed and developed prototype craft items now sold throughout the state," (which indicates good sales skills and self-motivation) or "I competed and coached an average of 20 hours a week on various gymnastics teams for over six years while maintaining a B average," (indicating you are a hard worker with good time management skills).

Future plans

Emphasize your interest in doing a better job through specific education, training, career advancement, hard work, and superior performance.

References

The best references are those who know your work, who like you, and who are responsible people. Consider such people as your coach, teachers, managers from other departments you know from previous jobs, heads of organizations for which you do volunteer work, or professionals with whom you have worked on prior jobs. Friends and relatives won't be objective about you and employers don't usually contact them for that reason. Whomever you select, be sure to ask them if it is okay to list them and find out what they would say about you. You just can never be sure.

Often, previous employers will not give references over the phone due to company policy, or fears of legal action being brought against them. For this reason, it is often helpful to ask a previous employer to write you a letter of recommendation in advance. You can then make copies of it for prospective employers when asked. You may want to tell your previous employer the kinds of things you would appreciate being included in the letter such as your attendance record, hard work, certain skills or achievements, or other positives. The worst thing they can say is no.

Quick Summary

✓ Applications are not a very effective job search tool because:

They are designed to screen you out.

They are usually used by personnel departments. Most smaller businesses don't have a personnel department and often don't even have applications. So, if you think of the job search as a process of dealing with personnel offices and their forms, you will miss out on most of the jobs in our new economy. Most personnel departments serve as a barrier between you and the prospective hiring manager or employee.

They allow for only limited, mostly negative information.

They encourage you to reveal your flaws, not your strengths.

✓ Recent research into how people find jobs indicates that filling out applications is a more effective technique for younger people than for more experienced workers.

✓ It is still important to know how to fill out an application effectively because:

They are often required.

They force you to confront your flaws and learn how to deal with them effectively.

✓ When completing an application form, be sure to keep the following basics in mind:

1. Read and follow directions carefully

2. Use an erasable pen, not a pencil

3. Be neat and thorough

4. Be positive, but honest

5. Add positive information, wherever you can

✓ Follow the countless tips for dealing with difficult application questions and issues presented in this chapter.

✓ Above all, be truthful in filling out the application. Dishonesty will most likely only get you fired eventually. Besides, your integrity is far more important than any job.

Chapter 15

CHAPTER SIXTEEN

*Even More
Good Job Search
Techniques*

More Answers to Specific Problem Interview Questions –

And a List of 94 Frequently Asked Questions

≡Quick Overview

In this chapter, I review the following:

✓ How to answer problem interview questions

✓ Legal and illegal questions

✓ Answers to many specific problem questions relating to work history and personal situations

✓ 94 interview questions to prepare for (i.e. think about and practice answering) before interviewing

As mentioned in Part I, about 80 percent of all people who get interviews do not, according to employer surveys, do a good job in answering one or more interview questions. This is a very big problem in the job search and has kept many, many good people from getting jobs that they are perfectly capable of handling. However, they didn't get those jobs because they failed to convince the employer that they had the needed skills and other characteristics to do the job.

So, at issue here is not your ability to *do* the job, it is your need to improve your ability to communicate clearly that you *can* do the job. In this chapter, I cover the basic techniques used to answer most interview questions. This is a very important topic, particularly if you already know that you have a "problem" that will be an issue for an employer.

A Quick Review of How to Answer Problem Interview Questions

Employers are people, just like you, and they want to make a good decision in hiring someone. Think about it – hiring the wrong person will cause them much extra work and grief. If the person does not perform well, they will have to spend extra time supervising that person. If the employee does not stay very long, the employer will lose lots of training time and have to hire and train all over again. And if the person they hire does not work out and has to be replaced, this creates a situation that most employers desperately want to avoid – firing someone.

So employers are very much motivated to hire a "good" person. They want someone who has the skills to do the job and usually base this on the applicant's past work experience and education. These "credentials" are very important in considering one person over another, and if you don't meet the minimum criteria, often you just won't be considered.

Assuming that you have done your homework (as presented in Part II of this book) and know your skills and the types of jobs that you are best suited for, then you are seeking jobs for which you do have the necessary skills and, at least, the minimum credentials. This being the case, how well you perform in the interview will often be the key factor in an employer giving you a chance over someone else who has better credentials. You see, it is not always the best person who gets the job, it is often the one who has the best communication skills.

Quick Tip

To be considered, you must meet an employer's expectations.

Recall from Chapter 4 the discussion of employer expectations. They are an important element in understanding what an employer will be looking for during an interview. The three major employer expectations cited were 1) Appearance, 2) Dependability, and 3) Credentials.

Notice that I put credentials third? This is because I assume that you have the minimal credentials to be considered for the job in question. Appearance is first, because if you do create a negative impression (as about 40 percent of all job seekers do) you are unlikely to be considered at all. That leaves Expectation #2 as the one that most employers will focus on during the interview.

The 10 Most Frequently Asked Problem Questions

Way back in Chapter 5, I provided detailed answers to 10 interview questions, which I have carefully selected because I feel that they are representative of the types of questions that most often create problems for people in an interview. Often, the actual question will not be phrased in the same way, but the employer is usually asking one of those questions in a different form. That is why I proposed in Chapter 5 that, if you can provide a good and honest response to each of the 10 questions, you will be better prepared to answer most other interview questions.

Since I provided detailed answers in Chapter 5 to each of the questions that follow, I won't repeat them here. The list of questions may help you recollect them, though.

Ten Most Frequently Asked Problem Questions

1. Why don't you tell me about yourself?

2. Why should I hire you?

3. What are your major strengths?

4. What are your major weaknesses?

5. What sort of pay do you expect to receive?

6. How does your previous experience relate to the jobs we have here?

7. What are your plans for the future?

8. What will your former employers (or teachers, if you are a recent student) say about you?

9. Why are you looking for this sort of position and why here?

10. Why don't you tell me about your personal situation?

A Quick Review of the Three-Step Process

In answering any interview question, it is essential that you understand what the employer really wants to know. In some cases, this will be quite obvious and you can answer directly. Questions regarding credentials and job-related skills often have no hidden agenda and can be answered in a forthright manner – though some answers are clearly better than others.

But the big problem for most job seekers is that many interview questions are not what they seem to be at all. Some questions, like "Why don't you tell me about yourself?" don't seem to have a direct answer. And others, such as "Do you come from this area?" often have hidden agendas (in this case, the employer is probably trying to find out if you are likely to remain in this area due to family or other ties).

To help you answer these less-than-direct questions, I have developed a simple technique that you can use to answer most interview questions. The technique, called the Three-Step Process for Answering Interview Questions, is covered in detail in Chapter 4. A quick review follows here.

> ## The Three-Step Process for Answering Interview Questions
>
> ➤ **Step #1: Understand What Is Really Being Asked** (Most questions relate to the Three Major Employer Expectations mentioned above.)
>
> ➤ **Step #2: Answer the Question Briefly, in a Nondamaging Way**
>
> ➤ **Step #3: Answer the Real Question by Presenting Your Related Skills**

To perform Step #3 effectively, recall the "Prove It" technique from Chapter 5, in which you identify key statements and accomplishments to use. Briefly, the steps of the technique are 1) Present a Concrete Example, 2) Quantify, 3) Emphasize Results, and 4) Link It Up.

Together, the Three-Step Process and "Prove It" techniques form the basic approach to answering problem questions, and it is most important that you understand and use these techniques to improve your interviewing skills.

Legal and Illegal Questions

Technically, this is a free country, and interviewers can *ask* whatever they wish. Dumb questions, questions in poor taste, and personal questions can all be asked. It's what employers *do* that can get them in trouble with the law. It is illegal to hire or not hire someone based on certain criteria. It is also very difficult to prove that someone actually does that.

As a job seeker, the more important issue might be whether or not you want the job. If you want to insist that you do not have to answer a certain question, fine. But also realize that the question was probably intended to find out whether you will be a good employee. That *is* a legitimate concern for an employer, and you have the responsibility, if you want the job, to let them know you will be a good choice.

There are situations (thankfully, very rare) where an interviewer's questions are offensive, either in the way they are asked or in the types of questions asked. If that is the case, you could fairly conclude that you would not consider working for such a person. Ever. You just might, in this sort of situation, tell that employer just what you think of them. Or you might report them to the authorities. Yes, this would be a situation where a thank-you note would not be required.

Some laws that protect you from discrimination

Thanks to a variety of national and local laws, there are a host of ways to phrase a question that are off-limits to interviewers. Notice I said "phrase" a question – the illegality is not in what they want to know as much as how they go about discovering that information.

Two major laws present real problems for employers who can be proven to illegally discriminate against protected groups in their hiring:

➤ Title VII of the Civil Rights Act (enacted in 1964 and still very much in effect) makes discrimination on the basis of race, sex, religion, or national origin illegal in hiring discussions.

➤ The more recent Americans With Disabilities Act requires that an employer provide an equal opportunity for an individual with a disability to participate in the job application process and to be considered for a job.

There are situations where a specific job might require an answer to some questions that might appear to be illegal for other jobs. For example, a firefighter would need to be in good physical condition and health-related questions are acceptable. But, in general, interview questions should focus only on your ability to do the job. If a question doesn't seem right to you, it probably isn't.

This does take some creative thinking but, if you handle it well in interviews, will help you get job offers that might not come otherwise.

Quick Fact

According to the U.S. Equal Employment Opportunity Commission (EEOC), in a recent year some 270,000 allegations were filed with the commission and its 82 state and local counterparts. *Inc.* magazine reports that complainants numbered just over 150,000 – some had lodged more than one charge. The number of complaints has been rising sharply – up about 30 percent in just two years and 2,200 percent in the past two decades.

Many people now sue simply for being terminated, even though the employer did nothing wrong. But it can cost employers between $5,000 and $20,000 just to defend themselves through the charge-filing stage, where claims are brought before the EEOC or a state agency. Defending these suits also costs time and results in substantial loss of revenue even when there is no valid basis for a complaint. As a result, many employers are becoming increasingly careful when they hire, screening people far more thoroughly so that they are less likely to have to terminate someone later. Other employers are simply hiring fewer people.

What to do about "illegal" questions

Just like anyone else, some employers are jerks. I know for a fact that some base their hiring decisions on things that should not be an issue at all – things such as age, religious affiliation, weight, family status, race or ethnic background, and many others. I also know that my suggestions on dealing with this are controversial to some.

Let's begin by saying that this is a free country. People have the freedom to say or believe almost anything. It is their actions that most often can get them in trouble. What this means is that employers can ask almost anything they want in an interview or on an application. Some people would disagree, saying that an employer does not have this right, but I believe that the constitution gives all of us the right of free speech. This includes the right of an employer to ask inappropriate questions. The problem arises when that information is used to hire one person over another based on certain considerations.

There are a variety of laws that provide punishment for employers who base hiring decisions on certain criteria. And that is how it should be. But employers still have legitimate concerns about the people they hire and want to be as certain as they can be that the one they hire can and will be productive in the job to be filled.

So let's assume that your concern is that you might be unfairly discriminated against because of your status. Let's also assume that you are reasonably well-qualified for the jobs you seek. Given this, you need to understand that highly-qualified people with no apparent "problems" often are unable to obtain jobs after many interviews. The labor market can be very competitive and others may get the jobs simply because they have better qualifications. But I also know that less-qualified people often get offers simply because they do well in the interview. Since you can't easily change your situation, you need to improve your interview skills to give you an edge.

Begin by considering how an employer might be legitimately concerned about you or your situation. Might they think that you would be less reliable, less productive, or in some other way less capable of doing the job? If so (and the answer here is usually yes), practice an answer that indicates that, in your particular case, that will not be an issue. For example, if you have young children at home (an issue, by the way, that men are rarely asked about), it is to your advantage to mention that you have excellent child care and don't expect any problems over this. Then look for a way to present your "problem" as an advantage. Perhaps you could say that your additional responsibilities make it even more important for you to be well-organized, a skill that you have developed over many years and fully expect to be applied in the new job. In other words, turn your disadvantage into an advantage.

Smart interviewers use open-ended questions to avoid problems – and still get the information they want

Employers want to get the information they need to make a safe, profitable decision. You, the candidate, want some privacy and a fair chance to be considered based on your merits. Open-ended interview questions generally achieve both goals.

For instance, instead of asking "Are you living with anyone?" interviewers can phrase the question as "Do you foresee any situations that would prevent you from traveling or relocating?" This allows you to decide what information about your private life applies to the job at hand. Of course, if you are not prepared for such a question, you can provide information that might damage your chances.

So, you see, employers will often want to know details of your personal situation for legitimate reasons: they want to be sure that you can be depended on to stay on the job and work hard. That, if you remember, is Employer Expectation # 2 and is of great concern to most employers. Your task in the interview is to provide information indicating that, yes, you can be counted on to do the job. Often, if you don't get that idea across, you simply will not be considered.

Answers to Specific Problem Questions

I have divided the questions that follow into two sections. The first deals with issues that most people experience and that are often legitimate issues for an employer to explore. This includes things such as gaps in your employment or being fired from a previous job. The second section presents issues that many consider inappropriate areas for an employer to consider when making a decision to hire, such as age, race, and gender.

Many of the questions may not relate to you at all. For example, if you are young and just entering the workforce, you won't be interested in answering questions directed to those who are "old." So review only those issues or questions that relate to your situation – and skip over those that don't.

Many of the questions I review here are those that most workers experience. They are not sins, and you will find that, if you learn to handle them well, they will not become a major problem in being considered for a job.

Most of these questions are more likely to be an issue in a traditional interview. You may remember that I defined a traditional interview (way back in Chapter 2) as one where there is a job opening and you are just one of several candidates for the position. Traditional interviews are not a lot of fun for most people, but preparing for the types of concerns an employer is likely to raise will improve your ability to handle less formal meetings as well.

One good thing about the traditional interview is that you can accurately guess – and prepare for – the questions most likely to be asked. In fact, that's one of the biggest complaints human resource personnel have about this style. They, too, can predict what type of answers applicants will give to their routine questions. Yet, because it is the most straightforward way of getting information, this interviewing approach lives on at organizations of all sizes across the country.

Even mentioning that some of the things in this chapter might be regarded as "problems" by an employer will make some people angry. For example, some would object to any mention that someone over 50 might experience discrimination in the labor market – although anyone over 50 knows that their age makes it harder to get a good job. Others will resent that employers would even consider such things as race, religion, native origin, child care, and other "politically sensitive" matters in evaluating people for employment. But some do, although unfairly.

Employers, as I have said before, are simply people. They want to be assured that, yes, you will stay on the job for a reasonable length of time and do well. Sometimes, you just need to get this message across.

You also have to realize that very, very few interviewers have had any formal interview training. They are merely trying to do their best and may, in the process, bumble a bit. They may ask questions that, technically, they should not. But you should consider forgiving them in advance for this, if their intent is simply to find out if you are likely to be reliable. That is a legitimate concern on their part, and you will often have to help them find out that, in your case, their concerns are unwarranted.

In that context, I suggest you consider your situation in advance and be able to present to the employer that, in your case, being "overqualified," or having children, or being over 50, or whatever your situation, is simply not a problem at all, but an advantage.

So, at the risk of offending someone, I have included questions that are a bit sensitive. But I think that you, as a job seeker, need to accept reality and look for ways to overcome problems. It can be done. It is true that some employers are unfair. Some do consider things in making hiring decisions that should not be a factor. In the interview, learn to be candid and present your problems as potential advantages. But do note that, in most cases, you should try to answer the question using the Three-Step Approach.

Quick Case Study

You just can't ever be sure what will concern an employer. Like all people, some will have concerns that just will not make sense to others. And some will make assumptions that may or may not be true. For example, I once had a boss who did not believe in hiring managers who had college degrees. His position was that those without degrees were often just as good or better – and would be happy being paid less money. I'm not at all sure that he was right, but I do know that he had that attitude and few managers with college degrees were on his staff. As you might guess, he did not himself have a degree, and I suspect that his real concern was to avoid hiring someone who had better credentials that he did...

Typical problem areas

Following are brief reviews of some of the problem areas you are most likely to run into.

Gaps in your work history

Some of the most accomplished people I know have been out of work at one time or another, and one out of five people in the workforce experiences some unemployment each year. It's really not a sin, and many bosses have experienced it themselves, as have I.

The traditional resume technique is to write "19xx to Present" when referring to your most recent job, which makes it look as if you are still employed. If you use this trick, however, realize that it puts you in an uncomfortable position right off the bat. One of the first things you will have to do in the interview is explain that this is not actually the case.

Many people have gaps in their work history. If you have a legitimate reason for major gaps, such as going to school or having a child, tell the interviewer in a matter-of-fact tone. By all means, don't apologize or act cagey about it. You could, however, add details about an alternative, related activity you did during that period that would strengthen your qualifications for the job at hand. This reinforces that you aren't out-of-touch with what that employer needs – you merely chose not to actively practice it for a while.

During the conversation, it may help to refer to dates in years rather than months. For example, if asked when you worked in the restaurant business, reply, "from '92 to '93" rather than "from November 1992 to June 1993." Of course, if pressed, give the exact dates without hesitation.

Being fired!

I remember looking for a new job after having been "fired" from my previous one. Actually, I was "replaced" as a result of internal politics. I hadn't done anything wrong other than be associated to the wrong boss – one who had lost favor. Still, I feared that the people that remained behind would not give me good references. And it was awkward explaining to potential employers just why I wasn't still working there.

Lots of people get "fired," and it often hurts their chances of getting some jobs. In some cases, employers are afraid that you will be a problem to them as well. And, of course, if you were fired for just cause, you need to learn from the experience and either change or consider another career. But in most cases, we harm our own chances of finding a new job more than being fired requires.

Because we don't know how to explain our situation, we don't do a good job in interviews. We too often leave the potential employer wondering just what happened and, not knowing more, assuming the worst. Leaving an employer with the thought that you are hiding something is a bad way to make a good impression. So, as a result, you don't get job offers.

Many employers tell me they will not hire someone unless and until they know why the person left their last job. They want to be sure that you are not a big problem. It is clear that you will have to deal with this issue if you want to get hired. The good news here is that many employers have been fired themselves. Normally, people in charge rock the boat and have had interpersonal conflicts or other situations. If you have a reasonable explanation, many will understand because they have had similar experiences.

So if you have lost a job, the best policy is usually to tell the truth. Avoid saying negative things about your last employer. Get used to putting a positive spin on what happened. If you are NOT a big problem, say so – and explain how you are very good at the things that *this* job requires. Tell the truth of what happened in an objective way and quickly turn to presenting the skills you have to do the job now.

One other thing – make sure that you negotiate with a previous employer on what they will say in giving you a reference. Ask for a written letter of reference too. You can often negotiate this so that you won't be harmed as much as you might fear. You may also be able to use as a reference someone else in the organization who feels positively about you. Ask them for a written reference, too. All of this can help offset a negative person who just may have a simple personality conflict with you. It happens a lot, and it doesn't have to hurt you as much as you may think. Since almost everyone will lose their job once, you are in good company – including mine.

Get an alternate reference. While you may have had conflict with a previous boss, there are often others at your previous place of employment who thought well of you. If so, it is often wise to get written recommendations from them in advance. You should also contact those people to find out how they might help if asked to provide a reference.

Job history unrelated to your current job objective/ Changing careers

Chances are this isn't as important an issue as you may assume. Sure, the interviewer is curious and wants to get to know you better, but if it were a real barrier, you wouldn't have been invited for an interview in the first place. Stick to a planned schedule of emphasizing your skills and how they relate to the job you are discussing. For instance, a teacher who wants to become a real estate sales agent could point to her hobby of investing in and fixing up old houses. She could cite superior communication skills and an ability to motivate students in the classroom.

Sensitive questions having to do with your personal situation or status

"Turtling" – A Basic Technique for Turning a Negative into a Positive

Like a turtle on its back, a problem is a problem only if you leave it that way. By turning it over ("turtling" is what I have come to call this), you can often turn a perceived disadvantage into an advantage. For example:

Too Old: "I am a very stable worker requiring very little training. I have been dependable all my life, and I am at a point in my career where I don't plan on changing jobs. I still have 10 years of working until I plan on retiring. How long has the average young person stayed here?"

Too Young: "I don't have any bad work habits to break, so I can be quickly trained to do things the way you want. I plan on working hard to get established. I'll also work for less money than a more experienced worker."

You can use the Turtling technique on most problem questions to turn what some may see as a negative into, in your case, a positive.

Most employers are wise enough to avoid making decisions based on things that should not matter and they will try to hire someone who convinces them that they can do the job well. So, a good interview allows you to discuss your strengths without lying about them. It also assures the interviewer that you are not a stereotype – but in order to prevent misconceptions you must know what they are and subtly address them.

For this reason, even if your "problem" does not come up in the interview – because the law forbids the question or the interviewer is too uncomfortable to ask – it may be to your advantage to bring it up and deal with it. This is particularly so if you think that an employer might wonder about the issue or that it might hurt you if you don't answer it. However you handle the interview, the ultimate question you have to answer is "Why should I hire you?" – so provide a good answer, even if the question is not asked quite so clearly.

"Too old"

Older workers – particularly those over 50 – have a harder time finding new jobs in the labor market. Anyone who is over 50 and has looked for a job, knows that their age can work against them. There are a lot of highly qualified managers, technicians, and professionals out there who have lost jobs due to layoffs. And there have been huge numbers of blue-collar workers who have lost jobs due to "downsizing" of large companies and other reasons. About a third end up getting even better jobs, another third about the same, and the last third end up much worse. By age, older workers do the worst, with many of those remaining unemployed or dropping out of the labor market.

What is going on? There are some commonsense reasons that few people seem to want to talk about – and some ways to overcome them. For many, they had not kept up with the latest technologies, and their skills are no longer in demand. Younger workers have better training and win jobs over older workers without it. But I think that there are two other reasons that have to do with money and assumptions about being "overqualified."

People with more experience tend to be paid more. And, as anyone knows who has been in the labor market recently, the competition for higher-paying jobs is often intense. The data indicates that the more you make, the longer your job search. In making a new hire, most employers will try to avoid hiring someone who was paid more in the previous position. Why? Because they fear that the person earning less than he or she is used to will be unhappy and will leave. It is one of the reasons an employer will hire a person with less experience – they figure that they will be more satisfied with the pay they get. Added to this fact is that many of the new jobs being created in the last decade are in smaller companies who just can't pay as much as many more established firms.

But there are some things to do:

1. **First, realize that many of the growing small businesses are run by "older workers" who know what they are doing.**

Experienced older workers started businesses and consultancies in droves over the last decade. If you're not ready to start your own business, put your experience to work by approaching larger and smaller businesses and telling how you can help them do even better.

2. **Be specific.**

If you know how to develop product, manage, sell, or make any significant contribution, go to the places that need your skills and tell the person in charge what you can do. If you can convince them you can help them make more money than you cost, they may just create a job for you. And make sure that you present your substantial experience and good work history as an advantage. For example, you can probably be immediately productive and are likely to be more reliable than a younger worker.

3. **And don't give up.**

Someone out there needs what you can do, but you will have to go out and find them.

According to a 1993 survey cosponsored by the Research Committee of the Society for Human Resource Management (SHRM) and the Commerce Clearing House, when employers face an older person across the interviewing desk, they are afraid the person won't be able to adjust to changes in the business environment. Among the specific concerns and comments:

➤ Older employees have created the greatest challenges for us. Employees hired 15 or more years ago may not have the education or technical skills to move forward.

➤ Attempts to increase accountability and employ more team-oriented strategies have met with resistance.

➤ Older workers have not adapted to drastic changes in procedures and technology.

A big problem with the "too old" category is figuring out if you truly belong in it. The over-65 growth rate in our country is slowing, and the biggest group taking over the job market is the aging Baby Boomers – those between the ages of 35 and 54. In fact, according to a Small Business Administration report, workers in the 45 to 54 age range are expected to increase by an amazing 72.2 percent by the year 2000. And the Hudson Group reports: Everyone who will be working in the year 2000 has already been born, and two-thirds of them are at work today. So what is "too old?"

Don't let these negative preconceptions discourage you – there are plenty of ways to combat them effectively during the job interview. For starters, understand that the flood of younger workers is slowing to a trickle, so employers eventually will have no option but to fight over the qualified older workers.

To push the interviewer along that path, present your wealth of experience and maturity as an advantage rather than a disadvantage. Older workers often have some things going for them that younger workers do not. Emphasize your loyalty to previous employers, and highlight accomplishments that occurred over a period of time. If you encounter hesitation after the first interview, meet the fear head-on with a question such as "Are you concerned about compensation?" or "If I could reduce your costs significantly, would you be willing to keep me in consideration?"

If you have more than 15 years of work experience, draw upon your more recent work for examples of work habits and successes. Select activities that best support your ability to do the job you are now seeking and put the emphasis on them. You don't automatically have to provide many details on your work history from earlier times – unless it is clearly to your advantage.

To avoid sounding "too old," mention something topical (like the fact that you own a notebook computer, would welcome the refreshing opportunity to operate in a self-directed team situation, or that you have enrolled in a technology course related to the job). Your background research on the organization should reveal a host of ways to plug your up-to-date knowledge and current worthiness.

"Too young"

Young people need to present their youth as an asset rather than a liability. For example, perhaps you are willing to work for less money, accept less desirable tasks, work longer or less convenient hours, or do other things that a more experienced worker might not. If so, say so. Emphasize the time and dedication you put into school projects, and activities you gave up to reach your goals. Above all, conduct yourself with maturity, show some genuine enthusiasm and energy, and you'll leave the interviewer with the impression you need a chance, not a guidance counselor.

If you are turned down in favor of a more experienced worker, don't despair. Despite the major layoffs that continue to besiege American companies, 72 percent of executives polled in a national survey conducted by Accountemps fear there will be a shortage of skilled labor between now and the year 2000. Keep hammering away at your particular skills, your trainability, and your available years of dedication – and some employer will be happy to snag you.

Overqualified/Too much experience

It doesn't seem to make sense that you could have too much experience, but some employers may think so. They may fear you will not be satisfied with the job that is available and that, after awhile, you will leave for a better one. So, what they really need is some assurance of why this would not be the case for you. If, in fact, you are looking for a job with higher pay – and if you communicate this in some way during the interview – it is quite likely that the company will not offer you a job for fear that you will soon leave.

This may not be far from the truth. After a period of unemployment, most people become more willing to settle for less than they had hoped for. If you are willing to accept jobs where you may be defined as overqualified, consider not including some of your educational or work-related credentials on your resume – though I do not necessarily recommend doing this. Be prepared to explain, in the interview, why you *do* want this particular job and how your wealth of experience is a positive and not a negative.

Employers are afraid, of course, that you will become bored by the job duties and take the next job offer that comes your way. It's a legitimate fear, and one you should resolve in your own mind before you push for the position.

If you do want to continue pursuing the job for whatever reason, go out of your way to assure the interviewer that you aren't a job gypsy. Maintain high enthusiasm for the organization's future, and present ways you could grow in this position. Suggest how you could assist other departments, solve long-term problems, build profit, and use your experience to help out in other ways.

Remember, the interviewer is also mentally calculating salary requirements during this time. Unfortunately, the very secrecy surrounding the figure has him or her worried that the interview time will be ultimately wasted. Your goal is to raise your desirability to the point where the organization is willing to chip in the extra money it thinks it takes to get you.

New graduate/Not enough experience

Every spring, newspapers across the country blast headlines about how difficult it is for today's graduates to find a job in their areas of study. Before you start believing the bad press too much, keep in mind that such articles only show one side of the story. Yes, it is difficult to find a position with a skinny resume. But a well-rounded one is not guaranteed to magically unlock doors either.

Quick Reminder

Remember that small employers are where the action is. The current Lindquist-Endicott Report from Northwestern University reports that small- to mid-sized companies tend to be the most active recruiters and large companies are doing less hiring. For your part, companies outside the FORTUNE 500 ranks can be more open to letting you take on new projects and directions. Take a secretarial position to get in the door of a smaller firm and you are less likely to be railroaded into that line of work for years.

Students are recognizing that they must take control of their careers and make their own decisions. More than 8 out of 10 (83 percent) students surveyed in a recent Right Associate's Career Expectations and Attitudes Comparison cited their own interests and skills as the major influence on their career choice. Other traditional influences – family pressure, anticipated salary, and luck/chance – have dropped significantly in popularity. When you interview for a position that matches your personality and talents, your natural enthusiasm for that job goes a long way in impressing interviewers.

Labor Secretary Robert Reich has noted that "employers have more incentive to train," because the young labor force is much smaller than it was during the Baby Boomer years. About 17 percent of all workers now get formal, on-the-job skills training (up from 11 percent 10 years ago). Computer literacy is the key – and young people are more computer-smart than their elders were.

So if you fall into the "not enough experience" category, emphasize the adaptive skills you identified in Chapter 3 that would tend to overcome a lack of experience.

Again, consider expressing a willingness to accept difficult or less desirable conditions as one way to break into a field and gain experience. For example, indicating that you are willing to work weekends and evenings or are able to travel or relocate may appeal to an employer and open up some possibilities.

Quick
Case Study

Howard W. Scott, Jr., president of Dunhill Personnel System, likes to tell the story of his first job search back in 1959. The broadcast major from Northwestern University ran into walls at almost every turn. Finally, a station manager in Roswell, New Mexico, offered Scott a position at $50 a week. "But I have a degree from Northwestern!" he cried. To which the station manager replied, "I know – otherwise it would have been $40 a week." And that's the one thing about interviewing that hasn't changed since our parents' days: The same sacrifices are necessary to break into nearly any field.

Don't overlook acceptable experiences such as volunteer work, family responsibilities, education, training, or anything else that you might present as legitimate activities in support of your ability to do the work you feel you can do.

Quick
Fact

Issues related to being a woman

Gaining equality and acceptance for women in the workplace is still a challenge. Several issues continue to pose a threat to women's success, including those related to child care, sexual harassment, discrimination, prejudice, and so on.

As the cigarette commercial used to drone: "You've come a long way, baby." But although the numbers of women in the workforce have increased rapidly, employers still imagine problems. According to the comments expressed in a recent survey conducted by the Society of Human Resource Management:

> *"Working women with children have difficulties finding adequate child care in our area. Time off and absenteeism are big issues for our working mothers."*

> *"Gaining coworker acceptance of women in nontraditional roles is a serious problem. Many of our executives are uncertain how to manage women."*

> *"We have more women managers, but few women officers, and only one percent on the board of directors. The glass ceiling is a reality."*

Interestingly enough, women employers are often just as concerned as male employers are about a woman's family status. In both cases, they assume that a

Quick
Fact

woman may, for example, have child-related problems and want to be certain that this will not become a work-related problem.

Arthur Bell points out that approximately 90 percent of all working women are in their child-bearing years; fully 80 percent of that number can be expected to have one or more children. More than half (54 percent) of all working mothers now care for one or more children under age 5. The stress, not to mention the financial hardships of paying for full-time child care can create potential disruptions for women in the workplace.

Bell refers to a *Harvard Business Review* study documenting that "on average, working mothers put in an 84-hour work week between their homes and their jobs; working fathers put in 72 hours, and married people with no children put in 50." Those numbers are staggering: a mother essentially holds down two full-time jobs plus overtime. And that's not taking into account the fact that elder care generally falls on the shoulders of women in our country, too. So, your number one task is to assure the interviewer that, although you don't intend to abandon your children, you do intend to devote the necessary time to the job.

Again, it's simply a matter of turning the situation into a positive. Why not present your resourceful nature by giving an example of how you secured reliable child care? Or illustrate your management skills by describing how you handled work responsibilities when your child was ill and you needed to be at home. Be prepared to back up your loyalty claims with actual numbers of days missed from previous jobs.

Quick
Tip

Don't make the mistake of assuming that just because a woman interviews you, it isn't necessary to bring up the child care issue. Even though she may be in the same boat herself, empathy rarely plays a role in landing you a position in today's tough competition. I've personally discussed candidates with other women who mentioned that child care could pose a huge attendance problem with some of the potential hires. An interviewers' main focus is hiring someone who can do the job – regardless of whether they are a man or a woman.

It seems almost laughable that with the number of women in today's workplace, some interviewers would still be uncertain how to manage women. Yet sensational headlines of sexual harassment and discrimination have trickled down to all levels of an organization.

According to Carol Price, an educator and lecturer with Career Track who specializes in teaching women power presentations, it's best to begin establishing your equal status the second you walk in the room. "Once you do that, I really believe gender issues go away," she says.

OK, so how do you "establish equal status" without appearing like a militant on a mission – another image that frightens employers? Simply look like you belong at the interview. "That means my head is held up, my shoulders are back, I walk in without hesitation, and I put my hand out," says Price. The handshake in particular is crucial. "A handshake was originally devised to prove we were weaponless.

In a job interview, that translates to 'you and I are equal in value' when my hands goes out," Price says.

During the interview itself, do not complain – or even mention – the lack of opportunity for women at your current or last job as the reason you are seeking new employment. In fact, don't bring up the fact that there may be questions about your sex's competency at all. Assume you are accepted and you will be, Price advises. "I don't live in an ivory tower," she adds.

> *"I know there are jerks out there who won't see you as worthwhile if you have ovaries. But the bottom line, at minimum, is that they set up an appointment with you. At worst, they have to see you for quota purposes. At best, they are interested in your skills. So if you go in with the attitude 'He won't think I'm as good as Bill simply because I'm female,' you act that way. You start believing your own press and then you're in serious danger."*

In a book titled *Managing a Diverse Work Force*, the author John P. Fernandez asked people to respond to a series of statements regarding women in the workplace. They were asked to either agree or disagree with each of the following statements:

1. The increasing employment of women has led to the breakdown of the American family.

2. Many women obtained their current position only because they are women.

3. Pluralism will force us to lower our hiring and promotion standards.

4. Many women use their gender as an alibi for difficulties they have on the job.

5. Many women are not really serious about professional careers.

6. Many women are too emotional to be competent employees.

The results:

➤ 35 percent of the women surveyed and 27 percent of the men did not agree with any of these statements

➤ 46 percent of the women and 45 percent of the men agreed with one to two statements

➤ 16 percent of the women and 22 percent of the men agreed with three to four of the questions

➤ 3 percent of the women and 7 percent of the men agreed with five to six of the statements

Issues related to men

While it is seldom brought up, there are certain biases that tend to be held against men, just because of their gender. Men are expected to have steady employment and not take time off for raising a family. Those who do not aspire to higher status can be quickly branded as losers. And, just as for women, you will find few males in certain occupations dominated by women, such as grade school teacher, clerical worker, and nurse. While some would argue that this condition is because these jobs pay poorly and have low status, that is clearly not always the case.

In the recent past, many men have been frustrated in their inability to move up in pay and stature. A big reason is the large number of baby boomers who are competing for the limited number of management jobs – and the greater number of educated and qualified women in the workforce who want the same things. Perhaps unexpectedly, the competition has become tough.

Even so, there are few situations where being a man will work against you, particularly if you have a good work history. For example, how many men get questions about their plans to have or care for children?

Sexual preference

You may be astounded to find this category in this chapter. However, these days unmarried men and women can create suspicion as to their sexual preference in some interviewers' minds.

The fears are twofold. The first is that their departments will become a stage for airing social concerns to the detriment of producing products or services. The Society of Human Resource Management reveals that its respondents said, "We have not encountered any pressures from gay/lesbian groups directly. However, employees continue to voice their concerns about having to work with these groups and the potential risk – real or perceived – that they pose," and "In our traditional, conservative culture, managers have deeply ingrained biases and fears of gay and lesbian employees."

And with health-care costs a serious issue in most companies, the potential cost for employees at greater risk to become HIV-positive plays a factor. True, homosexuals are not the only group infected, and most interviewers readily acknowledge that. But while I have advocated attacking stereotypes head-on in the other categories, here I advise you adopt the military's "don't ask, don't tell" policy. The risks of divulging such personal information are too great to broach this subject in an interview.

Military career

The military has long had a reputation among the youth of this country as an excellent job-training ground. Indeed, this is correct in many cases; the law enforcement field usually welcomes this experience with open arms. However, military service can work against you if you aren't aware of the misperceptions interviewers may form before you ever walk into their offices.

Some people perceive military personnel as dangerously aggressive.
Recent media reports of increased cases of spouse and child abuse in military families have added to the perception. "But they don't take into account that the population is generally younger, newly married, concentrated, and away from home," says Bob Stein, director of transition supports and services at the Department of Defense. "If you took a similar population in the private sector, the numbers might be the same." So, make a conscious effort to counteract the stereotype by remaining calm and pleasant at all times during the interview.

The second common misperception is that military personnel are too likely to follow orders rather than be creative. In some jobs this is not necessarily a problem. However, even factory positions are evolving into self-directed teams that require creative input from each member of the team. Be sure to mention ideas you have for growing within your position and interacting with others to overcome this liability.

Third, the number of people exiting the military every year causes concern with some interviewers. "People assume there are hundreds of thousands of persons being fired," Stein confirms. "That's not the case at all. Because we are such a large organization, for the past 10 years we've averaged 354,000 separations a year."

Quick Tip

Be sure to bring up why you left the military to put the interviewer's mind at rest that it had nothing to do with the private concept of being "fired." As one Air Force colonel expresses it, "If I were in business, I'd look at the military cuts as a godsend. People just don't understand what today's military is like. We're talking about the cream of the crop." So convey that to the interviewer in no uncertain terms!

Stanley Hyman, a 69-year-old counselor in Crystal City, Virginia, who teaches interviewing skills to military personnel, suggests not using military badges of honor such as service-academy rings and anchor tie clips when dressing for the interview. As for the language you use, avoid the excessive jargon that is common in military life.

Do emphasize that your experience in the military marks you as a leader, and has taught you discipline, responsibility, and dependability.

Minorities

The good news is that a majority of interviewers are aware that they shouldn't care about another person's race, religion, or skin color – and most do not. The bad news is the issue continues to impact the business environment and its needs.

Take a look at what employers said in a recent survey conducted by the Society of Human Resource Managers:

> *"Finding African-Americans with education and experience for advancement in our industry is difficult."*

"African-American workers interpret managerial actions as having a racial bias. Managers find it very challenging to convey constructive criticism and direction without being accused of bias."

"Asians have encountered language and cultural difficulties. Some are not willing to disagree with the boss, which hinders continuous improvement."

On the upside, the survey also reveals that the last decade has introduced more African-Americans, Hispanics, and Asians into the employee populations of many organizations that participated in the study. This increase is expected to continue due to the shrinking numbers of young people, the rapid pace of industrial change, and the ever-rising skill requirements of the emerging economy. These trends make the task of fully utilizing minority workers' skills particularly urgent between now and 2000.

Quick Advice

My advice to women holds true for minorities as well. Assume you are equal. Shake hands firmly and look the interviewer in the eye. Then present the skills and abilities you have to do the job.

Recent graduate

If you have recently graduated, you probably are competing against those with similar levels of education *and* more work experience. If you don't have a lot of work experience related to the job you want, you will obviously want to emphasize your recent education or training. This might include specific mention of courses you took and other activities that most directly relate to the job you now seek.

New graduates need to look at their school work as the equivalent of work experience. Indeed, it *is* work in that it required self-discipline, the completion of a variety of tasks, and other activities that are similar to those required in many jobs. You also may have learned a variety of things that are directly related to doing the job you want. You should present these during the interview in the same way you might present work experiences.

If you can, you should also play up the fact that you are familiar with the latest trends and techniques in your field and can apply these skills right away. And, since you are experienced in studying and learning new things, you will be better able to quickly learn the new job.

No degree/Too little education

If you want a job that is often filled by someone with more education, you must emphasize the experience and skills you have to do the job, as well as provide assurance that your lack of degree will not be a hindrance. You can simply avoid mentioning that you do not have a degree or less education than typically required.

Quick Alert

Note that I do not suggest that you misrepresent yourself here by overstating your qualifications or claiming a degree you do not have. That would result later in your being fired and is clearly not a good idea. But again, there is no law that says you need to mention your weaknesses.

Recently moved

Employers may sometimes be concerned that someone who has recently moved to an area may soon leave. If you are new to the area, make sure that the employer knows you are here to stay. Provide a simple statement that presents you as a stable member of the community rather than someone with a more transient lifestyle.

Have a disability

Biases against those with disabilities is real enough that the government has passed laws to prevent unfair discrimination – the Americans With Disabilities Act. But no one will ever successfully pass a law against stereotypes. That's the true barrier you are up against in the interview, no matter how many government agencies exist to back up your eligibility.

According to a Society of Human Resource Management survey, many respondents indicated that accommodating employees with disabilities presents difficulties for their organizations. Among the specific comments: "We are a small organization and accommodation of physical requirements for disabled workers and time off for illness and medical treatment cause disruption to work and schedules." "Some disabled workers are looked upon with disdain by their managers and peers. We have to overcome these attitudes."

I assume you will not seek a job that you can't or should not do. That, of course, would be foolish. So that means you are seeking a job that you are capable of doing, right? And, that being the case, you don't have a disability related to doing this job at all. But, as I said, the employer will still use his or her judgment in hiring the best person for the job, and that means people with disabilities have to compete for jobs along with everyone else. That is fair, so you need to present to an employer a convincing argument for why they should hire you over someone else.

Most importantly, don't assume that the person chatting with you understands the technical details of your handicap. I see nothing wrong in casually mentioning how you have worked around your disability in other positions. Just remember to remain matter-of-fact in your explanation – avoid a defensive tone at all costs – and you will not only put the interviewer at ease but also assure him or her that your future colleagues will admire your abilities and attitude, too.

Quick Case Study

I once worked a temporary job taking inventory at a department store. My partner that first day was a young woman who had an artificial arm. My first reaction was an inner groan: I assumed she wouldn't be able to write, so I automatically would have to keep the tally sheets. Furthermore, with only one "real" hand, she would be too slow in reaching for and reading the tags. Fortunately, she had the confidence to smile, introduce herself, and proceed to tell me how the artificial arm worked. It took less than two minutes to put my doubts to rest and less than five to prove I had been a clod, even if I had kept my prejudices to myself. The two of us teamed up the entire week and received much praise for our quick work.

Negative references

Most employers will not contact your previous employers unless you are being seriously considered as a candidate for the job. If you fear that one of your previous employers may not give you a positive reference, here are some things you can do:

✓ 1. List someone other than your former supervisor as a reference, someone who knew your work there and who will put in a good word for you.

✓ 2. Discuss the issue in advance with your previous employer and negotiate what they will say. Even if not good, at least you know what they are likely to say and can prepare potential employers in advance.

✓ 3. Get a written letter of reference. In many cases, employers will not give references over the phone (or negative references at all) for fear of being sued. Presenting a letter in advance assures that you know what is said about your performance.

Criminal record

It should be obvious that a resume or application should not include negative information about yourself. So if you have ever been "in trouble" with the law, you would certainly not mention it there. Newer laws even limit an employer from including such general questions on an application as "Have you ever been arrested?" and limit formal inquiries to "Have you ever been convicted of a felony?"

In this country, we are technically innocent until proven guilty, and that is why employers are no longer allowed to consider an arrest record in a hiring decision. Being arrested and being guilty are two different things. Arrests for minor offenses are also not supposed to be considered in a hiring decision. The argument has been that minorities tend to be more likely to have arrest records and consideration of arrest records in a hiring decision is, therefore, discriminatory.

A felony conviction is a different matter. These crimes are more serious and current employment laws do allow an employer to ask for and get this information – and to use it in making certain hiring decisions. For example, few employers would hire an accountant who had been convicted of stealing money from a previous employer. Certain types of arrest records, such as those for child molesting, are also allowed to be considered by an employer in making certain hiring decisions. For example, few would place a person with this kind of record in charge of children's programs.

If you have an arrest or conviction record that an employer has a legal right to inquire about, my advice is to avoid looking for jobs where your record would be a big negative. The accountant in the example above should consider changing careers. Even if the applicant did get a job by concealing his or her criminal history, that person could be fired at any time in the future. Instead, I might suggest they consider selling accounting software, starting their own business, or getting into a completely different career unrelated to accounting.

As always, your interview should emphasize what you can do rather than what you can't. If you chose your career direction wisely and present a convincing argument that you can do the job well, many employers will, ultimately, overlook previous mistakes. As you prove yourself and gain good work experience, your distant past becomes less important.

16 Tricky But Legal Questions

Following are examples of legal questions you may run into. Be prepared!

What can you tell me about yourself?

I've mentioned this question before, and repeat it now because it is probably the number one question on the popularity scale, and it almost always kicks off the interview. Again, don't be tempted to go back to childhood and talk about your hard-working parents, your dog, and whatnot. Describe yourself in terms of what the interviewer wants to hear: your work ethic, your skills that apply to this job, your educational background, etc.

What is your greatest strength?

Overall, this is such a positive question that few people have a problem coming up with an answer. Where they trip up is in not supporting that answer. So if you want to emphasize your people skills, for instance, back it up with a short example of how that translates in the workplace. Then brace yourself for its counter question:

What is your greatest weakness?

I talked about this question back in Chapter 5, and mention it here to remind you to choose something that isn't overtly negative. Being a workaholic or a perfectionist or too critical of your own work isn't necessarily a strike against you.

What would you like to accomplish during the next ten (or five) years?

Talk about what you want to do for that employer, not for yourself. "I'd like to cut production costs by at least 5 percent and find ways to streamline the layout procedure so that we can add publications without adding staff," is a much better answer than "I'd like to be making 25 percent more in salary and own my own magazine."

How long have you been looking for another job?

Never give an actual time frame! Casually reply, "Time isn't a factor because I'm searching for the position that best matches my skills and goals."

What type of person would you hire for this position?

Flashback: You're casting your ballot for class president and mark the box for your opponent out of modesty. You lost then and you'll lose now if you don't choose yourself! "I'd hire someone who, beyond a shadow of a doubt, has the skills and people experience to handle this job. I would definitely hire myself."

Are you willing to take a pay cut from your present position?

You aren't willing to discuss salary yet, so politely say so. "I feel we are still in the process of getting to know one another – I'd feel more comfortable talking about salary once we agree on employment" (or something to that effect).

Note that a section of this book, part of Chapter 18, is devoted to helping you answer questions related to salary.

Why do you want to work for our organization?/Why should we hire you?

These questions, which are really one and the same, are at the heart of every question in any interview. Appropriate responses are covered in some detail in Chapter 5.

Why do you want to leave your present job?

Note: Do not, under any circumstances, give into complaints about the atmosphere at your current position!

Acceptable answers include this being a step in your career plans and wanting a better job location. "After introducing a more nutritious menu plan to the day care center and establishing a fun yet informative healthy lifestyle program for the after-school crowd, I've reached the top of the ladder at this smaller firm. I want the opportunity to use my expertise and continue to grow in a larger organization."

Be prepared to answer why you left all of the jobs listed on your résumé.

How do you normally handle criticism?

Aah, an easy question if you take it on the chin well. But, because most of us aren't that admirable, we have to put a twist on this common question. "Obviously, criticism comes from not doing the job properly, and I'm eager to correct any mistakes or misunderstandings the minute they arise. I'm grateful to the person who cares enough to help me out in that respect."

How do others view your work?

Just who are "others"? Colleagues, supervisors, clients, subordinates – the ability to see yourself from all perspectives is a plus in this situation. "The people I manage know that I will set the example before I ask them to make sacrifice of time or convenience. My colleagues understand that I am sympathetic to how our departments must work together for the common good. My supervisors are

Why Did You Leave?

To help you form an acceptable answer to the "Why did you leave?" question, use the acronym CLAMPS:

C = Challenge. You weren't able to grow professionally in that position.

L = Location. The commute was unreasonably long.

A = Advancement. There was nowhere to go. You had the talent, but there were too many people ahead of you.

M = Money. You were underpaid for your skills and contribution.

P = Prestige. You wanted to be with a better organization.

S = Security. The organization was not financially stable.

impressed with my dedication and realize that if I promise something, I will deliver it. And clients view the product that my department produces as a symbol of quality."

How do you feel about working overtime and on weekends?

Even if this prospect does not appeal to you, this question can be answered so that your response does not harm you. "I have no problem devoting evening hours and Saturdays to getting a special project done. I also believe that a balanced life leads to a fresh, energetic employee who is less likely to burnout, so I try to pace myself for a consistent, dependable job performance over the long term, too."

What do you do for fun in your spare time?

This question has a dual motivation. First, the interviewer is confirming your response to the "Will you work overtime?" question. If you replied yes to that question but then outline a lifestyle that involves weekends at a cabin, evenings at the gym, and commitments to various nonprofit and community events, it's unlikely you'll cancel those plans to work overtime.

On the other hand, this is also an opportunity for the interviewer to confirm those things he or she can't legally ask, such as if you have a family, if you attend church, etc. "My in-laws have a cabin by a nearby lake, and the children enjoy going there on weekends. I accompany them when I can, but sometimes projects prevent that. Of course, the grandparents welcome those times so they can spend one-on-one time with Jim and Sally."

Describe your typical day.

Naturally, leave out the fact that you aren't a morning person or you start winding down at 4:30 P.M. to hit the parking lot by 5 P.M. This is your opportunity to advertise how well you can organize yourself and conceptualize long-term projects. "I keep a calendar on my desk with appointment times recorded on the left side and tasks to accomplish that day on the right. I allot time each day to stay in touch with other departments and to return any missed phone calls promptly. Overall, my entire day is focused on providing customers with a top-notch product."

What do you like most about your present boss?

For most candidates, it's not to hard to find something nice to say in response to this question. Do frame your answer on the type of supervision your boss provides and not necessarily on a personality type. "I appreciate the regular feedback," is a more useful response than "I enjoy the fact that he/she always has an upbeat attitude," even though both are certainly positive answers.

What do you like least about your present boss?

You knew this was coming based on the previous question. Again, stick to management principles and skip the personality conflicts.

Interviewers also like to pose the "What do you like best/least about your present job?" set of questions as well. As I have advised before, continue to look at your current job's opportunities rather than specific tasks. "I don't like to type my own memos," is honest but short-sighted.

94 Interview Questions

Here is a list of questions most often asked by recruiters who interview new graduates at college campuses. While some of the questions may not apply to your situation, they will give you a good idea of the types of questions a trained interviewer might ask. Look over the list and identify any that you will need practice in answering. Then, practice!

1. What are your future vocational plans?
2. In what school activities have you participated? Why? Which did you enjoy the most?
3. How do you spend your spare time? What are your hobbies?
4. In what type of position are you most interested?
5. Why do you think you might like to work for our company?
6. What jobs have you held? How were they obtained?
7. What courses did you like best? Least? Why?
8. Why did you choose your particular field of work?
9. What percentage of your school expenses did you earn? How?
10. How did you spend your vacations while in school?
11. What do you know about our company?
12. Do you feel that you have received a good general training?
13. What qualifications do you have that make you feel that you will be successful in your field?
14. What extracurricular offices have you held?
15. What are your ideas on salary?

16. How do you feel about your family?

17. How interested are you in sports?

18. If you were starting school all over again... ?

19. Can you forget your education and start from scratch?

20. Do you prefer any specific geographic location? Why?

21. Do you have a girl (boy) friend? Is it serious?

22. How much money do you hope to earn at age _____?

23. Why did you decide to go to the school you attended?

24. How did you rank in your graduating class in high school? Other schools?

25. Do you think that your extracurricular activities were worth the time you devoted to them? Why?

26. What do you think determines a person's progress in a good company?

27. What personal characteristics are necessary for success in your chosen field?

28. Why do you think you would like this particular type of job?

29. What is your father's occupation?

30. Tell me about your home life during the time you were growing up.

31. Are you looking for a permanent or temporary job?

32. Do you prefer working with others or by yourself?

33. Who are your best friends?

34. What kind of boss do you prefer?

35. Are you primarily interested in making money?

36. Can you take instructions without feeling upset?

37. Tell me a story!

38. Do you live with your parents? Which of your parents has had the most profound influence on you?

39. How did previous employers treat you?

40. What have you learned from some of the jobs you have held?

41. Can you get recommendations from previous employers?

42. What interests you about our product or service?

43. What was your record in military service?

44. Have you ever changed your major field of interest? Why?

45. When did you choose your major?

46. How did your grades after military service compare with those previously earned?

47. Do you feel you have done the best work of which you are capable?

48. How did you happen to go to post secondary school?

49. What do you know about opportunities in the field in which you are trained?

50. How long do you expect to work?

51. Have you ever had any difficulty getting along with fellow students and faculty? Fellow workers?

52. Which of your school years was most difficult?

53. What is the source of your spending money?

54. Do you own any life insurance?

55. Have you saved any money?

56. Do you have any debts?

57. How old were you when you became self-supporting?

58. Do you attend church?

59. Did you enjoy school?

60. Do you like routine work?

61. Do you like regular work?

62. What size city do you prefer?

63. When did you first contribute to family income?

64. What is your major weakness?

65. Define cooperation.

66. Will you fight to get ahead?

67. Do you demand attention?

68. Do you have an analytical mind?

69. Are you eager to please?

70. What do you do to keep in good physical condition?

71. How do you usually spend Sunday?

72. Have you had any serious illness or injury?

73. Are you willing to go where the company sends you?

74. What job in our company would you choose if you were entirely free to do so?

75. Is it an effort for you to be tolerant of persons with a background and interests different from your own?

76. What types of books have you read?

77. Have you plans for further education?

78. What types of people seem to rub you the wrong way?

79. Do you enjoy sports as a participant? As an observer?

80. Have you ever tutored another student?

81. What jobs have you enjoyed the most? The least? Why?

82. What are your own special abilities?

83. What job in our company do you want to work toward?

84. Would you prefer a large or a small company? Why?

85. What is your idea of how industry operates today?

86. Do you like to travel?

87. How about overtime work?

88. What kind of work interests you?

89. What are the disadvantages of your chosen field?

90. Do you think that grades should be considered by employers? Why or why not?

91. Are you interested in research?

92. If married, how often do you entertain at home?

93. To what extent do you use liquor?

94. What have you done that shows initiative and willingness to work?

Practice, Practice, Practice

It is not enough to read and think about problem questions. As I have said before in this book, interviewing is an art of conversation and interaction. In order to get better at answering problem questions, you do need to think about responses in advance. This is particularly true for those problem questions that you fear will hurt you if you are asked them in an interview.

You need to practice your interviewing skills *out loud*. If possible, get someone to act as an interviewer and have them throw problem questions at you. Use the Three-Step Approach to answer most questions and your interviewing skills will surely improve.

Pay Rates for the Top 250 Jobs

Bonus

The information that follows provides median weekly earnings for over 250 occupations as a reported by the U.S. Department of Labor in 1994. The occupations cover over 85 percent of the workforce and the information is a useful starting point for salary negotiations.

It is important, however, to understand the limitations of these figures. For one thing, remember that the median means that one half of all workers in these occupations earned more and one half earned less. Workers with less experience, for example, will tend to earn less than the median – and some earn significantly more than the listed rate.

The pay rates are also based on national surveys, and your local rates can differ significantly. Even so, this table should provide you with a good starting point for your research into pay for jobs that interest you – and ammunition for salary negotiations.

The occupations are arranged into groupings of related jobs. This allows you to quickly locate jobs that are most closely related to your interests and to identify other jobs (requiring similar skills) that may pay somewhat more. You should look through the entire list for jobs that you may be able to do with your present skills but that you may have previously overlooked.

Most of the jobs listed here are described in considerable detail in the *Occupational Outlook Handbook*. I have described this publication elsewhere in this book on several occasions, and I again encourage you to refer to it for more detailed information on the job as well as the pay and other details.

Managerial and Professional Specialty — 675

<u>Executive, Administrative, and Managerial</u> — 664

Administrators and officials, public administration	724
Administrators, public services	733
Financial managers	776
Personnel and labor relations managers	723
Purchasing managers	773
Managers, marketing, advertising, and public relations	851
Administrators, education and related fields	778
Managers, medicine and health	692
Managers, food serving, logging, and establishments	407
Managers, properties and real estate	511
Management-related occupations	597
Accountants and auditors	612
Underwriters	595
Other financial officers	670
Management analysts	775
Personnel, training and labor relations specialists	598
Buyers, wholesale and retail trade except farm products	495
Construction inspectors	588
Inspectors and compliance officers, except construction	671

<u>Professional Specialty</u> — 682

Engineers, architects and surveyors	902
Architects	694
Engineers	911
Aerospace engineers	1,008
Chemical engineers	996
Civil engineers	867
Electrical and electronic engineers	941
Industrial engineers	861
Mechanical engineers	895
Mathematical and computer scientists	816

Chapter 16

Chapter 16

Chapter 16

Quick Summary

✓ Employers are very much motivated to hire a "good" person. They want someone who has the skills to do the job (usually based on the applicant's past work experience and education).

✓ How well you perform in the interview will often be the key factor in an employer giving you a chance over someone else who has better credentials. It is not always the best person who gets the job, it is often the one who has the best communication skills. To be considered, you must meet an employer's expectations.

✓ Together, the Three-Step Process and "Prove It" techniques form the basic approach to answering problem questions, and it is most important that you understand and use these techniques to improve your interviewing skills.

✓ Technically, interviewers can *ask* whatever they wish. It's what employers *do* that can get them in trouble with the law. It is illegal to hire or not hire someone based on certain criteria. It is also very difficult to prove that someone actually does that.

✓ Title VII of the Civil Rights Act makes discrimination on the basis of race, sex, religion, or national origin illegal in hiring discussions. The more recent Americans With Disabilities Act requires that an employer provide an equal opportunity for an individual with a disability to participate in the job application process and to be considered for a job. In general, interview questions should focus only on your ability to do the job.

✓ Begin by considering how an employer might be legitimately concerned about you or your situation. Then look for a way to present your "problem" as an advantage ("turtling"). Your task in the interview is to provide information indicating that, yes, you can be counted on to do the job. Often, if you don't get that idea across, you simply will not be considered.

✓ In this chapter, answers to specific problem questions are given. Most of these questions are more likely to be an issue in a traditional interview, and many are a bit sensitive. One good thing about the traditional interview is that you can accurately guess – and prepare for – the questions most likely to be asked. Keep in mind that very few interviewers have had any formal interview training.

✓ By preparing and practicing answers to the many questions presented in this chapter, you considerably improve your chances of performing well in an interview.

CHAPTER SEVENTEEN

*Even More
Good Job Search
Techniques*

Changing Technologies –
Using a Computer in the Job Search

⟩⟩⟩ *Quick Overview*

Unless you have been living in a cave for the past ten years, you have probably
noticed that computers are everywhere. About a third of all homes now have a computer in them, and many, many jobs require their use or are affected by their pres-
ence. In spite of this, computers have not affected how most people go about planning
their careers or looking for a job, with the exception of the use of word processors for
resumes and correspondence.

Well, computers are becoming increasingly helpful now in career planning and in job
seeking, although few people are yet using a computer's full potential in these tasks. I
mention some of these uses in this chapter, and if you are computer literate, you may
be able to make use of some of my suggestions.

But even if you are not computer literate, you probably can benefit from the new uses
of computer technologies in various ways throughout your job search. For example,
most libraries now provide access to computerized databases of various kinds that
allow you to search for newspaper and magazine articles by topic. More and more
also provide access to computers and software such as for word processing and resume
preparation. Some also have more sophisticated services or programs like those I mention later in this chapter.

What to Do If You Don't Have a Computer

Even if you don't have your own computer or modem, you may be able to get access to one through a library, university student or friend, or someone else you know who does have access. And having someone help you who already knows how to find things on-line can be a big time saver as well.

You should also realize that there is an enormous amount of information available in a good bookstore or library and that a computer is not yet an essential tool for the job search, although computer literacy is increasingly important.

The Electronic Job Search

Over the past several years, many millions of people have gained regular access to computers at work and at home. Virtually any computer can create a resume, and they are often used in the job search for this task and for other word-processing activities. Specialized software to help create resumes, organize the job search, and even help with career planning have been available for some time. But none of these computerized tasks have been truly revolutionary – although I predict that a revolution is coming.

The difference is that many new computers now come "packaged" with a modem and communications software. This allows you to connect your computer via phone to other computer users, sources of data, and much more.

A recent article in *Time* magazine mentioned that about 25 million people now use the Internet, one of these communications networks, and its use is expected to double in the years to come. America Online, CompuServe, and Prodigy are several of the larger commercial networks, and millions of people subscribe to them. It seems obvious to me that the new communications technologies offer opportunities for improved access to career information as well as for finding jobs. (See box "The Electronic Age.")

While all of this sounds great – and can work for some people – I believe that job seeking via computer will have its limitations. If you are computer literate and can access the computer networks, it is worth the time to see what is available there. But most people agree that face-to-face interviews will still be important for the future. And, if you are not computer literate yet, you may better use your time in getting a new job than trying to learn how to use a computer in your job search.

There is far more information on using computers in the job search than I could begin to include here, so consider what follows as an introduction. If you want to know more, there are several good books on the subject listed in the bibliography, including JIST's book titled *Using the Internet in Your Job Search* by Fred Jandt and Mary Nemnich.

The Electronic Age – Some of the Things That Are Coming (or Already Here)

Access to career information: A good library has lots of good career information, but some of it is hard to find and its sheer volume makes it difficult to find just what you need. Computer sorting by subject, topic, or key words will allow you to get to more information in less time.

Information about employers: It can be difficult to get specific information on a particular employer, yet computer access to large databases of news stories, business reports, and other detailed information will make this much simpler.

Electronic resumes: There are already services that, for a fee, will make your resume available for employers to access via their computers. Special formats allow them to electronically sort through thousands of resumes to find those with the key skills they seek.

Want ad sorts: You can now get lists of newspaper ads from specific cities and for certain types of jobs. Special services also allow employers to list openings for people to respond to via computer.

Government jobs: Federal job descriptions and lists are already available on-line, and local government jobs will come.

Employer databases: Sort through lists by region, size, industry, product or other criteria to get a custom list of contacts.

E-mail ads: Although controversial, it is possible to place an ad saying you are available for hire. And you can send electronic mail (e-mail) looking for job leads to almost anyone on the system.

Networking and interview chats: You can "talk" to someone else via computer by typing comments as another reads and responds. This allows you to interact with others who might want more information about you or who may know of job openings. Some employers are already doing initial "interviews" this way.

The Internet and Other On-Line Computer Services

This section lists the major on-line services, along with a few comments related to each. Some of these services have been around for quite some time. They used to provide somewhat distinct services, but now the differences between them are dimming. Most of them now provide a full range of categories of information, including business, financial, sports, weather, entertainment, etc. The Internet, however, is a distributed system (meaning, not run from a centralized place by a particular company) and therefore is in a class by itself.

The Internet

You have surely heard of the Internet by now, because it has been a trendy news topic. The Internet is an informal collection of thousands of computer systems that are accessible via phone lines. Host computers can be anywhere in the world and can provide information or services of almost endless variety. While it was originally developed for national defense and scientific information sharing, it has expanded rapidly and now can be accessed by anyone with an account number and a service provider.

There are few rules on the Internet, and almost anything you can think of is out there somewhere. This is not a place for novice on-line users, so I suggest that you get initial access to the Internet via one of the major commercial on-line services mentioned below.

America Online

The fastest growing on-line service, America Online, includes full Internet access and an excellent Career Center that provides a range of helpful services for job seekers. Call 800-827-6364 for details.

CompuServe

CompuServe is the oldest of the on-line services and has excellent access to an enormous number of databases of information. Call 800-848-8990 for information.

Prodigy

Prodigy is jointly run by IBM and Sears and has about 2 million users. It is targeted primarily to home users. Call 800-766-3449 for information.

Other commercial services and freenets

There are numerous commercial providers of information and Internet access that are too many to mention here. Some of these are operated as "free" services to designated groups such as members of a university, or those who live in the community.

An Example of What's Available from One On-line Service

There is a tremendous amount of data and interactive advice available from all of the major on-line services, but I've selected America Online for this example. I've listed some of the career-specific services available there in an area called the *Career Center*. This is a special service set up to provide resources for career planning and job seeking, and the services are impressive – and expanding.

The Career Resource Library

The Library can be of value if you, or someone you know, requires assistance with any of the following career development tasks:

- Selecting a career direction or goal
- Conducting an effective job search
- Selecting a vocational/technical program of study and institution
- Selecting a college major and institution
- Obtaining financial assistance to attend school or college
- Finding work with your state or the federal government
- Analyzing the future of a particular career field or industry
- Researching potential employers
- Starting and operating a small business
- Working from home
- Understanding your personality style and make-up
- Enhancing your personal and social development
- Dealing with job discrimination
- Career planning after retirement

The information available via this library includes information from diverse sources and in many formats including:

- Audio cassettes
- Books
- CD-ROM and computer software programs
- Conferences
- Films
- Magazines
- Newsletters
- Newspapers
- On-line databases
- Phone and fax services
- Professional associations
- Professional services
- Videotapes
- Workshops and seminars

You can even order career books and materials via this career center. Many JIST books (including this one) are available there via our on-line catalog, and we have a variety of career information available there as well. You can even download the latest JIST catalog in its entirety from the Library and send orders via e-mail.

Company Profiles – Hoover's Handbooks

The company profiles – Hoover's Handbooks database includes portfolios of over 900 of the largest, most influential, and fastest-growing public and private companies in the United States and the world. The Reference Press out of

Austin, Texas, creates and manages this assistance database. Each profile includes:

Overview of operations and strategy

Founders' names and company history

Names, ages, and salaries of key officers

Headquarters address, telephone number, and fax number

Locations of operations

Lists of divisions, subsidiaries, products, services, and brand names

Names of key competitors

The Reference Press provides an alphabetical list of all companies in the database, so you can scroll through this or go directly to a company in which you are interested. You may also search for companies located in a particular state, region, or country. And if you don't know which company you are looking for, type in one or more search words. For instance, if you are interested in locating companies that make submarines, you can search for this word and discover that General Dynamics and Teneco are the two largest submarine makers in the country.

Employer Contacts

Employer Contacts is a collection of information on over 5,000 American employers, supplied by Demand Research Corp. out of Chicago, Illinois. This section, too, assists you in finding potential employers that match your occupational interests and goals.

Demand Research Corp. specializes in compiling and distributing information on every U.S. public company listed on the NYSE, the AMEX, and the NASDAQ National Market System. Each listing here includes:

- The company's name, address, phone and fax numbers
- Ticker symbol
- Exchange affiliation
- Full name of the chief executive officer
- Full name of the chief financial officer
- Primary industry classification

Career Guidance Services

For some lucky folks, their skills and interests point to one definite career direction. For the other 99 percent of us, figuring out how to translate our talents into job positions can be an agonizing process. The on-line Career Center offers three unique areas to help you set your feet in the right direction.

Career Focus 2000

The Career Focus 2000 service consists of a series of four "workbook" exercises that you may download and complete at your leisure. CF 2000 is designed to guide you in selecting a career direction in line with your personality style, and in developing a plan for reaching your career goal. It is appropriate for anyone who is undecided about a career direction or unsure about how to reach a career goal.

The heart of the CF 2000 is an interest inventory. This inventory allows you to sample 225 work activities and then compare your strongest interests to approximately 1,000 occupations as a means of finding occupations that match your interests.

Career Analysis Service

This is a very comprehensive, computer-assisted analysis service designed to identify occupations that match your interests, abilities, and work preferences. This service is appropriate for individuals who wish a more thorough analysis of career options than what is possible with the Career Focus 2000 program.

A questionnaire form allows you to indicate your preference for various work activities and situations. You then e-mail your answers back to the Career Center, where a professional career counselor enters your answers into an occupational database produced by the U.S. Department of Labor and compares them to over 10,000 occupations. Within 48 hours, you receive a listing of occupations (by job title) that best match your interests, abilities, and work preferences. At the time of this writing, there is a one-time charge of $39.95 to use the Career Analysis Service.

Individual Career Counseling

Here you may meet privately with an experienced, professional career counselor on-line – in real time – to discuss your career needs and problems. Counseling is available on an appointment basis, and there is no additional fee for this service other than your normal America Online fees.

Some of the Things You Can Do On-Line

Once again, I can only begin to mention here the many resources available to you on line. Check the bibliography for additional resources and note that many of the business information resources I mention there are also available on-line.

Access Bulletin Boards and Interest Groups

Local computer bulletin boards (BBS) have been available via modem for years. They are typically run by a group or individual based on a shared interest (such as a computer club) or topic (such as flying radio-controlled model airplanes).They provide information to a group of users typically including e-mail, information files, answers to FAQs (frequently asked questions), free software, on-line interaction with other members, and other services.

Some of these bulletin boards are quite large and provide many services, while others are very small and run by one person after their regular work hours. Join any local computer club and you can get a list of local bulletin boards. Most are free but some have a charge to help support it.

You can also get to bulletin boards of all kinds via the Internet or the various commercial on-line services. Anything you can imagine has a *special interest group (SIG),* or *newsgroup,* somewhere.

Perform Electronic Networking and Job Seeking

It should be pretty obvious that an electronic gathering place like an interest group or bulletin board would have at least some people either looking for jobs or looking to hire people. Sure enough, that has become one of the many things that are discussed electronically in these forums.

At its simplest level, some people leave e-mail messages for others to read, saying they are looking for openings of certain kinds. Anyone who reads that message may respond with a lead or advice. This is a form of networking, and it works precisely the same way as other networking processes except in an electronic forum.

Some bulletin boards have more sophisticated or organized mechanisms for job seekers and employers to use. It may be as simple as a separate subgroup for leaving messages or "meeting" with others interested in this. There may also be information or established procedures for handling this situation. Larger bulletin boards can have extensive services available for job seekers in addition to e-mail networking.

Get Information on Companies

An enormous amount of information is available out there on specific companies and organizations. You can get basic information from various databases such as that offered by Biz*File, an on-line directory of 11 million U.S. and Canadian businesses that includes information assembled from various sources (including phone books, annual reports, press releases, newspapers and magazines, and the millions of calls they make each year to verify the data). You can also do on-line key word sorts for newspaper or journal stories mentioning a specific organization, and there are many other sources of information.

Find Information on People

A variety of on-line resources can help you get information on people, too. Let's say you want to know something about the people who interview you: maybe they are listed in Marquis Who's Who covering key North American professionals. This is available via several commercial on-line services, as is access to newspaper data searches that mention their names, etc.

Find Out About Government Jobs

CompuServe has a resource available providing information on a variety of government services (GO INFOUSA), including a list of hundreds of government run BBSs (GOVBBS.TXT), with some that provide details on federal job openings. You can also call the federal, state, or local government personnel offices in your area and ask for the BBS phone numbers listing openings or providing employment information. Then log in and browse.

Research Newspapers, Journals, and Magazines

You can find out about virtually anything by searching through databases of general information. For example, IQUEST provides a service (available through various commercial on-line services) that provides reference to over 800 publications, databases, and indices of business, government, research, and other information. A research librarian will help you focus your question and then begin an automated search for information on, say, a company you will interview with tomorrow. The results may knock their socks off...

Access Want Ad Databases

Many large city newspapers now advertise a service offering you a print out of want ads to meet your specifications. This might include key words such as "Engineer" and cover only specific regions, such as "California." This is a cooperative program between cooperating major newspapers who already have their want ad listings on computers. Selling access to this database, for a fee, makes sense, and I expect to soon see direct computer access to this sort of database (it may already be available but I just haven't seen it).

Fax Broadcasting of Resumes

If you have a fax machine, you have probably already received unsolicited junk fax. There are various sources of directories listing fax numbers now, and anyone who has access to the numbers can send stuff. A computer having access to a fax-phone list can send pages automatically, fax after fax.

Just as in the old-fashioned idea of sending unsolicited resumes, sending unsolicited faxed resumes is not recommended, though it could work occasionally if you got lucky (and, unlike the mail, local faxes are "free"). A better approach would be targeted faxing. For example, you could fax your resume to members of your local computer group, asking them for help in finding any leads. Or you could fax resumes and a request for help to members of a related professional organization (which you should join, if you are not already a member).

Submit Electronic Resumes

Some large employers are already scanning resumes and putting them in a database, throwing away the paper resumes. When looking for a new hire, they can then scan the database for key words such as "operations engineer" and "Master's Degree" and "computer science" or any combination or criteria. You can see how such a system can work against you because the searcher will only look at resumes that meet specific criteria. So, if you don't just happen to use the right words or have the perfect combination of words on your resume, you will never be considered.

The scanning process also removes any design from your resume, typically reducing its content to a bland character-only format. So what they actually see is words rather than any particular design or format. Everyone is presented in olive green.

Commercial and public resume databases

There are now several commercially available databases of resumes. America Online has one of them available through its career center. For a fee, you can have your resume scanned and included in the database for potential employers to find (often for a fee as well). While at least one of these commercial resume database services has failed in the past year, I suspect that more will be created in the months to come.

Some Universities provide free listings of student or alumni resumes in a school sponsored resume database. Employers can then access these resumes and, hopefully, interview and hire some of those listed. There are other similar computerized resume databases available from a variety of sources including local government programs, bulletin boards, employment programs, and others.

The problem with computerized resume databases

I have no problem if you want to try these things, unless they cost you more than $10 or so. But don't hold your breath. Just like answering want ads and sending unsolicited resumes, this technique does not work well for most people because it is passive rather than active. Only the most qualified tend to be selected out and the emphasis is on those with advanced technical or computer skills.

Multimedia resumes

I have even seen computer accessible resumes that included video clips of the job seeker, voice, music, and other multimedia elements. They are attention-getting and make sense for someone looking for a job using multimedia programming skills. Most interesting...

A Selection of Computer Software and CD-ROMs Useful for Job Seeking

A few categories of software, such as those for word processing and contact management, were not specifically developed for job seeking but have obvious applications to this task. In addition, more and more software and information is becoming readily available that is intended to be used for career planning and job seeking. I've selected a few examples of software and information databases that can be helpful to you in your job search, but there are many others available. I review categories of readily available software and CD-ROM products in this section that you may find of use.

Word Processing Software

Virtually any word processing program will help you handle the basic writing tasks needed in the job search. This includes writing resumes and correspondence. These tasks do not require advanced computer systems, although a letter-quality laser printer is a must.

Newer versions of the full-featured word processing programs often include special capabilities that can be very helpful. For example, newer versions of both WordPerfect and Microsoft Word include resume templates that help you create a variety of professional looking resumes by filling in the blanks. These programs have similar templates for formatting letters.

Check out the features of a word processing program you are already familiar with and you may find useful features that you have not previously used. For example, most full-featured word processors allow you to enter names of contacts and later automatically enter those names in a letter going out to a group of them. (Look up terms such as "template," "mailmerge," and "form letter" in your software's manual or help system for further information.)

Quick Reference

If you are a WordPerfect User, you may be interested in a very good book titled *Using WordPerfect in Your Job Search* by David Noble. It does a thorough job of showing you how to use the program to create superior resumes, letters, JIST Cards, follow up forms, daily schedules, as well as do a variety of other job search tasks using WordPerfect. It's an impressive book and will teach you things you could do with a good word processor that can help you tremendously in your search for a job.

Resume Preparation Software

If you go into any retail computer software outlet, you are likely to find at least several resume preparation software packages. Even though some are not at all good, others are now quite helpful. Many include other features that can be helpful in your search for a job.

One example is *PFS: Resume Pro.* It helps you with easy-to-use templates for a variety of resume styles. It includes seven print styles, a simple word processor for cover and follow up letters, a spell checker, a database for entering your contacts for follow up, an automated calendar, and other features.

Another program that is readily available is *The Perfect Resume.* Based on the resume book with the same title by Tom Jackson, it provides good advice on resume writing as well as lots of format options.

While these programs can be helpful, I do have several cautions. Many resume programs have the same problem as many resume books – they provide bad job search advice. Keep in mind that creating fancy resumes and sending them out is, in my opinion, a very outdated approach, and I caution you not to fall into that trap even though many resume programs foster this underlying assumption. You should also be aware that many resume programs encourage you to take a fill-in-the-blank approach to your resume that may produce a good looking resume with mediocre content.

Contact Management Programs

Sales people use these programs to keep track of people they have contacted. If you have a computer, I recommend that you use this type of program to help you in your job search. A widely available example is called *ACT!* It keeps names and addresses, keeps notes regarding contacts, reminds you to follow up as you want to, automates correspondence, handles scheduling of appointments, and has many other useful functions.

While you can do all of this with a card file and a few simple paper systems, contact management software can save you time and help you be more disciplined in following up with your contacts on a regular basis. And that *does* make a difference.

Career Exploration and Planning

Some programs are now available that have been designed to guide you through a career planning process. One impressive one is titled *Career Design.* Based on the concepts of John Crystal, it covers skills identification, resumes, career planning, and even some job seeking skills. You should be able to find it in a well-stocked software store, along with other programs that claim to do similar things.

Information on Occupations: Quick Access to Information on over 12,000 Job Titles

I have mentioned a publication titled the *Occupational Outlook Handbook* (OOH) earlier in this book, and software versions of it are available. Since the OOH provides good information on about 250 jobs, browsing through clusters of related occupations is an excellent way to explore career alternatives. A software program titled *JIST's Electronic Occupational Outlook Handbook* (OOH), *Enhanced* is very easy to use and allows you to sort for jobs using various criteria. A multimedia version of this program is also available on CD-ROM that includes photos of people in each occupation, voice commentary, and a variety of other features.

While I highly recommend the career information in the OOH, some software programs based on it really don't give you more information than the book itself. CD-ROMs allow for much larger databases and, as a result, more sophisticated databases of occupational information are coming out.

Quick Computer Access to Over 12,000 Job Descriptions

I have been in the career counseling field for over 20 years and a big problem continues to be helping people narrow down the jobs that best meet their interests or qualifications. For example, what sorts of jobs might fit a laid off factory worker who likes to work with kids, or a displaced engineer who needs to change careers, or a college student trying to figure out a major, or a person who likes to work with their hands but who can't lift more than 20 pounds because of a back injury – and many other individual situations.

Much of the information is there but the problem has always been in getting to it in a simple and direct way. For example, the U.S. Department of Labor keeps lots of information on over 12,000 job titles. The information includes descriptions for each as well as details such as training required, work environment factors, aptitudes and skills required, strength factors, and over 60 other data elements. But you would have to use at least three large reference books to get the information on just one job and much of the information is in hard-to-understand codes. Looking up the details on multiple jobs has simply been impractical.

But things are changing. With the availability of inexpensive and powerful computers and CD-ROM storage disks, all of the data can now be accessed electronically. The possibility now exists to put this enormous amount of information into an easy-to-retrieve-and-use form.

This is an exciting prospect to me. Over the past several months, I've been working on a computer program to quickly get to that information in a useful way. Titled *JIST's Electronic Dictionary of Occupational Titles and Guide for Occupational Exploration,* it creates a six-page report on each of over 12,000 jobs. To give you some idea of the magnitude of information involved, it would take over 13 miles of paper to print those reports. Yet it all can fit on one CD-ROM storage disk. This information is also now easy to get to via groups of similar jobs that can be accessed by interest, job type, and other criteria.

The information is now finally easy to get to and the program is very fast. It will be of great help to job seekers looking for alternative job targets, students considering career options, and many others who have needed – but never had ready access to – this information. While the program is quite new, you may be able to find it at a library that includes CD-ROMs in its collection, and a bookstore version is planned for the future.

Federal Form SF-171 Software

If you plan on applying for federal jobs, you will have to deal with a complex application form called the SF-171. It is an important document and quite complex, including sections where you are required to write things of paragraph length. If your handwriting is as awful as mine, you might not want to handwrite this, and typing it will result in erasures and errors. To the rescue: a program titled *Quick and Easy for the SF-171*. It automates the process and prints the results neatly.

Education and College Selection

There are now programs to help you sort through thousands of colleges and select those that meet your criteria. For example, *Lovejoy's College Counselor CD-ROM* includes substantial information on all major colleges, technical, trade, and business schools plus information on college majors, over 2,500 scholarships, and even video clips of many of the schools. You can sort by region, college major, price, and other criteria to get the schools that best meet your requirements.

Computerized Yellow Pages

Select Phone is an example of a CD-ROM program that provides almost all U.S. residential and business phone numbers. It allows you to identify employers by *Yellow Pages* heading in a specific area of the country, for example, or sort by other criteria. The implication for making cold contacts in another city are obvious. Cheapskates can get a similar CD-ROM that includes all the toll free 800 phone numbers, allowing you to make free calls to all sorts of potential employers and information sources throughout the country.

Employer Databases and Information Sources

A number of the business and other information sources mentioned in the bibliography and elsewhere in this chapter are available as data in CD-ROMs. If you have access to the information (via CD-ROM just as via modem), you can typically sort through it in a variety of ways to get what you want. A big library will have a variety of sources of these databases, and I expect to see more of them available in bookstores in the coming months as CD-ROMs.

Job Search Books on CD-ROM

Examples of CD-ROMs that contain a collection of books in digital form are already available. You can sort them for key words, find information via a table of contents, or simply read the text. I know of at least one such collection that includes a few "career" books, and more will surely follow.

While I often prefer a book in printed form over digital, I can see some uses for putting the content of some books on CD-ROM. For example, sorting through a good collection of resumes by occupation, college major, and other criteria might be quite useful. I've even been approached to include one or more of my books on CD-ROM, and I'd consider it if and when that medium made sense to me for this use. Stay tuned.

Video Interviewing and Video Conferencing

Some organizations videotape their interviews. They do this for a variety of reasons, including avoiding lawsuits for discrimination (because the video can prove what was said by the interviewer). But there are more compelling reasons for employers to decide to record an interview on video, including:

> ➤ The playback button allows them to zero in on specific answers where the interviewer may not have taken specific notes (or scrap note-taking altogether).

> ➤ They may compare different candidates' answers on the same questions.

> ➤ They can watch the tapes whenever and wherever they want.

> ➤ They can evaluate all interviewees the same day.

> ➤ They can send the tapes to managers at another location.

While video offers some advantages to an employer, it offers little advantage to you because it will make your verbal or nonverbal habits more noticeable. Poor answers, ill-conceived attempts to dodge questions, nervous gestures, and the like don't have a chance to fade in importance in the interviewer's mind. They live over and over in full-color.

Fortunately, there are things you can do to prepare for a videotaped interview. Videotaped interviewing lends itself well to structured interviews, so if you know in advance about the set-up, concentrate on preparing for likely questions. It's always a good idea to videotape yourself privately to check for annoying verbal habits and work on changing them. Above all, don't let the mechanics of the camera sidetrack you from focusing on your job at hand: answering the questions and establishing a relationship with the interviewer.

The use of video is not restricted just to traditional interview settings. Some employers ask potential employees to demonstrate how they would handle specific job and management situations. In a study of Colgate-Palmolive employees screened in this way, turnover in those hires averaged 5 to 10 percent compared with 20 to 25 percent for the rest of the company, and promotions were three times more common than for employees hired using more conventional methods.

Similarly, employers no longer have to rely on a face-to-face meeting to interview you. Videoconferencing is making inroads in the interviewing process as well. Videoconferencing uses images and audio transferred via phone lines to television screens, and in some cases, computer screens.

While large companies are more likely to use this technology, video teleconferencing is available for a fee from some hotels and training centers and can be used by smaller employers to interview someone at a distant site. You might even suggest a video interview for a distant employer who seems reluctant to schedule an interview with you because they are not yet convinced that your skills are worth the dollars to fly you to them. In this case, videoconferencing is a cost-effective alternative to suggest.

If you are set up for an interview via video teleconferencing, do not assume the session is merely a preliminary chat before the "real" interview. Some employers use them to screen applicants and, if you do well in this last screening phase, they may make an offer right there.

Computer Testing Can Supplement the Interview

Some employers now use a computer to ask a variety of questions and to then record the job applicant's responses. Those who do well enough on this computer interview then may get a person-to-person interview. The approach saves an employer time and offers other advantages as well. This approach can also be combined with video or telecommunications to help screen out applicants and is more likely to be used by larger employers. An example is the Pic'n Pay shoe stores that require applicants to dial an 800 number and answer a 100-question interview via phone mail.

Employers have found that applicants will often be more honest with a computer than with another human. Researchers Dennis Nagoa and Christopher Martin discovered that students will more accurately confess their true grade averages and SAT scores to a computer than a person. Duke University documented that people would admit to drinking significantly higher amounts of alcohol when a computer asked them about it than when a person made the same inquiry.

In the business field, corporate users report that job applicants display similar candor with the computer. In fact, one retailer discovered that approximately 15 percent of its applicants actually tell a computer that, if hired, they intend to quit that job in less than a year. It appears that many people believe that the computer somehow "knows" the right answer and will catch them in a lie. Others simply relax when dealing with the computer's nonjudgmental approach.

Quick Alert

Some computers are programmed to time how long you paused before answering, record when you changed your mind, canceled an answer in favor of another, and compile contradictory responses between similar questions. All of this information may be interpreted by the program to be either positives or negatives. And because a computer is effective in getting negative information, employers tend to use them to ask the more delicate and personal questions. So, if you are confronted by a computerized screening system, do take it seriously and try to avoid providing personal information that you would not be willing to share in a face-to-face interview.

CHAPTER EIGHTEEN

18

Even More Good Job Search Techniques

Tips for Coping with Job Loss –

And Other Things You Might Want to Know

Quick Overview

This chapter includes a variety of topics that didn't fit neatly into other chapters, such as the brief information I have provided on self-employment. In some cases, I give additional details that were not included earlier but that you should find of interest. I don't assume you will read through the material in this section from front to back. I encourage you to simply find what interests you and focus on that.

Hardly Anyone Dies from Unemployment – Some Tips on Surviving and Coming Back from Unemployment

Being out of work is not fun for most people and is devastating to some. It may help you to know that you are not alone in this experience, and I've included some information here on what to expect and some suggestions for getting through it.

Some Problems You May Experience

Here are some feelings and experiences that you may have after losing your job.

Loss of professional identity: Most of us identify strongly with our careers, and unemployment can often lead to a loss of self-esteem. Being employed brings respect in the community and in the family. When a job is lost, part of your sense of self may be lost as well.

Loss of a network: The loss may be worse when your social life has been strongly linked to the job. Many ongoing "work friendships" are suddenly halted. Old friends and colleagues often don't call because they feel awkward or don't know what to say. Many don't want to be reminded of what could happen to them.

Emotional unpreparedness: If you have never before been unemployed you may not be emotionally prepared for it and devastated when it happens. It is natural and appropriate to feel this way. You might notice that some people you know don't take their job loss as hard as you have taken it. Studies show that those who change jobs frequently, or who are in occupations prone to cyclic unemployment, suffer far less emotional impact after job loss than those who have been steadily employed and who are unprepared for cutbacks.

The Emotional Stages to Expect

Losing your job can be similar in its emotional impact to the loss of a close friend or family member. I can tell you from personal experience that strong feelings are not easy to avoid or control. There have been a lot of studies done on how to deal with loss, and it may help you to know in advance that your emotional response to job loss is normal.

Psychologists have found that people often have an easier time dealing with loss if they know what feelings they might experience during the "grieving process." Grief doesn't usually overwhelm us all at once; it usually is experienced in stages.

Possible Stages of Loss or Grief

Shock: You may not be fully aware of what has happened.

Denial: Denial usually comes next – you cannot believe that the loss is true.

Relief: Then relief enters the picture for some, and you feel a burden has lifted and opportunity awaits.

Anger: Anger often follows – you blame (often without cause) those you think might be responsible, including yourself.

Depression: Depression may set in some time later, when you realize the reality of the loss.

Acceptance: Acceptance is the final stage of the process – you come to terms with the loss and get the energy and desire to move beyond it. The "acceptance" stage is the best place to be when starting a job search, but you might not have the luxury of waiting until this point to begin your search.

Knowing that a normal person will experience some predictable "grieving" reactions can help you deal with your loss in a constructive way. The faster you can begin an active search for a new job, the better off you will be.

Keeping Healthy

Unemployment is a stressful time for most people, and it is important to keep healthy and in shape. Try to do the following on a regular basis:

Eat properly. How you look and your sense of self-esteem can be affected by your eating habits. It is very easy to snack on junk food when you're home all day. Take time to plan your meals and snacks so that they are well-balanced and nutritious. Eating properly will help you keep the good attitude you need during your job search.

Exercise. Include some form of exercise as part of your daily activities. Regular exercise reduces stress and depression and can help you get through those tough days.

Allow time for fun. When you're planning your time, be sure to build fun and relaxation into your plans. You are allowed to enjoy life even if you are unemployed. Keep a list of activities or tasks that you want to accomplish, such as volunteer work, repairs around the house, or hobbies. When free time develops, you can refer to the list and have lots of things to do.

Facing Family Issues

Unemployment is a stressful time for the entire family. For them, your unemployment means the loss of income and the fear of an uncertain future, and they are also worried about your happiness. Here are some ways you can interact with your family to get through this tough time.

Do not attempt to "shoulder" your problems alone. Be open with family members even though it is hard. Discussions about your job search and the feelings you have allow your family to work as a group and support one another.

Talk to your family. Let them know your plans and activities. Share with them how you will be spending your time.

Listen to your family. Find out their concerns and their suggestions. Perhaps there are ways they can assist you.

Build family spirit. You will need a great deal of support from your family in the months ahead, but they will also need yours.

Seek outside help. Join a family support group. Many community centers, mental health agencies, and colleges have support groups for the unemployed and their families. These groups can provide a place to let off steam and share frustrations. They can also be a place to get ideas on how to survive this difficult period. More information about support groups is presented later in this chapter.

Helping Children

If you have children, realize that they can be deeply affected by a parent's unemployment. It is important for them to know what has happened and how it will affect the family. However, try not to overburden them with the responsibility of too many of the emotional or financial details.

Keep an open dialogue with your children. Letting them know what is really going on is vital. Children have a way of imagining the worst, so the facts can actually be far less devastating than what they envision.

Make sure your children know it's not anybody's fault. Children may not understand about job loss and may think that you did something wrong to cause it. Or they may feel that somehow they are responsible or financially burdensome. They need reassurance in these matters, regardless of their age.

Children need to feel they are helping. They want to help, and having them do something like taking a cut in allowance, deferring expensive purchases, or getting an after-school job can make them feel as if they are part of the team.

Also, some experts suggest that it can be useful to alert the school counselor to your unemployment so that they can watch the children for problems at school before the problems become serious.

Coping with Stress

Here are some coping mechanisms that can help you deal with the stress of being unemployed:

Write down what seems to be causing the stress. Identify the "stressors," and then think of possible ways to handle each one. Can some demands be altered, lessened, or postponed? Can you live with any of them just as they are? Are there some that you might be able to deal with more effectively?

Set priorities. Deal with the most pressing needs or changes first. You cannot handle everything at once.

Establish a workable schedule. When you set a schedule for yourself, make sure it is one which can be achieved. As you perform your tasks, you will feel a sense of control and accomplishment.

Reduce stress. Learn relaxation techniques or other stress-reduction techniques. This can be as simple as sitting in a chair, closing your eyes, taking a deep breath and breathing out slowly while imagining all the tension going out with your breath. There are a number of other methods, including listening to relaxation tapes, which may help you cope with stress more effectively. Check the additional source material books which offer instruction on these techniques. (Many of these are available at your public library.)

Avoid isolation. Keep in touch with your friends, even former coworkers, if you can do that comfortably. Unemployed people often feel a sense of isolation and loneliness. See your friends, talk with them, socialize with them. You are the same person you were before unemployment. The same goes for the activities that you may have enjoyed in the past. Evaluate them. Which can you afford to continue? If you find that your old hobbies or activities can't be part of your new budget, perhaps you can substitute new activities that are less costly.

Join a support group. No matter how understanding or caring your family or friends might be, they may not be able to understand all that you're going through. And you might be able to find help and understanding at a job-seeking support group.

These support groups consist of people who are going through the same experiences and emotions you are. Many groups also share tips on job opportunities, as well as feedback on ways to deal more effectively in the job search process. *The National Business Employment Weekly,* available at major newsstands, lists support groups throughout the country. Local churches, YMCAs, YWCAs, and libraries often list or even facilitate support groups. A list of self-help clearinghouses, some of which cover the unemployed, is available from the National Self-Help Clearinghouse, 25 West 43rd St., Room 620, New York, NY 10036. The cost is $3, plus a self-addressed, stamped envelope.

Forty Plus is a national non-profit organization and is an excellent source of information about clubs around the country and on issues concerning older employees and the job search process. The address is 15 Park Row, New York, NY 10038. Their telephone number is (212) 233-6086.

Keeping Your Spirits Up

Here are some ways you can build your self-esteem and avoid depression:

List your positives. Make a list of your positive qualities and your successes. This list is always easier to make when you are feeling good about yourself. Perhaps you can enlist the assistance of a close friend or caring relative, or wait for a sunnier moment.

Replay your positives. Once you have made this list, replay the positives in your mind frequently. Associate the replay with an activity you do often; for example, you might review the list in your mind every time you go to the refrigerator!

Use the list before performing difficult tasks. Review the list when you are feeling down or to give you energy before you attempt some difficult task.

Recall successes. Take time every day to recall a success.

Use realistic standards. Avoid the trap of evaluating yourself using impossible standards that come from others. You are in a particular phase of your life; don't dwell on what you think society regards as success. Remind yourself that success will again be yours.

Know your strengths and weaknesses. Know your strengths. What things are you good at? What skills do you have? Do you need to learn new skills? Everyone has limitations. What are yours? Are there certain job duties that are just not right for you and that you might want to avoid? Balance your limitations against your strong skills so that you don't let the negatives eat at your self-esteem. Incorporate this knowledge into your planning.

Picture success. Practice visualizing positive results or outcomes and view them in your mind before the event. Play out the scene in your imagination and picture yourself successful in whatever you're about to attempt.

Build success. Make a "to do" list. Include small, achievable tasks. Divide the tasks on your list and make a list for every day so you will have some "successes" daily.

Surround yourself with positive people. Socialize with family and friends who are supportive. You want to be around people who will "pick you up," not "knock you down." You know who your fans are. Try to find time to be around them. It can really make you feel good.

Volunteer. Give something of yourself to others through volunteer work. It will help you to feel more worthwhile, and may actually give you new skills.

Overcoming Depression

Are you very depressed? As hard as it is to be out of work, it also can be a new beginning. A new direction may emerge which will change your life in positive ways. This may be a good time to re-evaluate your attitudes and outlook.

Live in the present. The past is over and you cannot change it. Learn from your mistakes and use that knowledge to plan for the future – then let the past go. Don't dwell on it or relive it over and over. Don't be overpowered by guilt.

Take responsibility for yourself. Try not to complain or blame others. Save your energy for activities that result in positive experiences.

Learn to accept what you cannot change. However, realize that in most situations, you do have some control. Your reactions and your behavior are in your control and will often influence the outcome of events.

Keep the job search under your own command. This will give you a sense of control and prevent you from giving up and waiting for something to happen. Enlist everyone's aid in your job search, but make sure you do most of the work.

Talk things out with people you trust. Admit how you feel. For example, if you realize you're angry, find a positive way to vent it, perhaps through exercise.

Face your fears, and try to pinpoint them. "Naming the enemy" is the best strategy for relieving the vague feeling of anxiety. By facing what you actually fear, you can see how realistic your fears are.

Think creatively, stay flexible, take risks, and don't be afraid of failure. Try not to take rejection personally. Think of it as information that will help you later in your search. Take criticism as a way to learn more about yourself. Keep plugging away at the job search despite those inevitable setbacks. Most important, forget magic – what lies ahead is hard work!

Seeking Professional Help

If your depression won't go away, or leads you to self-destructive behaviors such as abuse of alcohol or drugs, you may wish to consider asking a professional for help. Many people who have never sought professional assistance before find that in a time of crisis it really helps to have someone who can listen and who can give needed aid.

Consult your local mental health clinics, social services agencies, religious organization, or professional counselors for help for yourself and family members who are affected by your unemployment. Some assistance may be covered by your health insurance or, if you do not have insurance, counseling is often available on a "sliding scale" fee based on income.

Managing Your Finances While Out of Work

As you already know, being unemployed has financial consequences. (Note: While I have made substantial changes to this material, it is also based on content from *Job Strategies for Professionals.*) While the best solution to this is to get a good job in as short a time as possible, you do need to manage your money differently during the time between jobs. Following are some things to think about.

Apply for benefits without delay

Don't be embarrassed to apply for unemployment benefits as soon as possible, even if you're not sure you are eligible. This program is to help you make a transition between jobs, and you helped pay for it by your previous employment. Depending on how long you have worked, you can collect benefits for up to 26 weeks and sometimes even longer. Contact your state Labor Department or Employment Security Agency for further information. Their addresses and telephone numbers are listed in your phone book.

Prepare now to stretch your money

Being out of work means lower income and the need to control your expenses. Don't avoid doing this, as the more you plan, the better you can control your finances.

Examine your income and expenses

Create a budget and look for ways to cut expenses. The worksheet that follows can help you isolate income and expense categories, but your own budget may be considerably more detailed. I've included several columns in the expense category. The "Normal" column is for entering what you have been spending in that category during the time you were employed. The "Could Reduce To" column is for an estimate of a lower number that you will strive for by cutting expenses in that category. The "Comments" column is for your comments on how you might cut expenses.

Monthly Income and Expense Worksheet

INCOME

Unemployment benefits _____

Spouse's income _____

Severance pay _____

Interest/Dividends _____

Other income _____

Total _____ _____

EXPENSES	Normal	Could Reduce To	Comments
Mortgage/Rent	_____	_____	
Maintenance/Repairs	_____	_____	
Utilities:	_____	_____	
Electric	_____	_____	
Gas/Oil heat	_____	_____	
Water/Sewer	_____	_____	
Telephone	_____	_____	
Food	_____	_____	
Restaurants	_____	_____	
Groceries	_____	_____	
Car payment	_____	_____	
Fuel/Maintenance/Repairs	_____	_____	
Insurance	_____	_____	
Other loan payments	_____	_____	
Health insurance	_____	_____	

EXPENSES	Normal	Could Reduce To	Comments
Other medical/ dental expenses	_____	_____	
Tuition, other school costs	_____	_____	
Clothing	_____	_____	
Entertainment	_____	_____	
Taxes	_____	_____	
Job hunting costs	_____	_____	
Other expenses	_____	_____	
_____	_____	_____	
_____	_____	_____	
_____	_____	_____	
_____	_____	_____	
TOTALS	_____	_____	

Tips on conserving your cash

While unemployed, it is likely that your expenses will exceed your income, and it is essential that you be aggressive in managing your money. Your objective here is very clear: You want to conserve as much cash as possible early on so you can have some for essentials later on. Here are some suggestions on doing this:

Begin right away to cut all nonessential expenses. Don't put this off! There is no way to know how long you will be out of work, and the faster you deal with the financial issues, the better.

Discuss the situation with other family members. Ask them to get involved by helping you identify expenses they can cut.

Look for sources of additional income. Can you paint houses on weekends? Pick up a temporary job or consulting assignment? Deliver newspapers in the early morning? Can a family member get a job to help out? Any new income will help, and the sooner the better.

Contact your creditors. Even if you can make full payments for awhile, work out interest-only or reduced-amount payments as soon as possible. When I was unemployed, I went to my creditors right away and asked them to help. They were very cooperative, and most are, if you are reasonable with them.

Register with your local consumer credit counseling organization. Many areas have free consumer credit counseling organizations that can help you get a handle on your finances and encourage your creditors to cooperate.

Review your assets. Make a list of all your assets and their current value. Money in checking, savings, and other accounts are the most available, but you may have additional assets in pension programs, life insurance, and stocks that could be converted to cash if needed. You may also have an extra car that could be sold, equity in your home that could be borrowed against, and other assets that could be sold or used if needed.

Reduce credit card purchases. Try to pay for things in cash to save on interest charges and prevent overspending. Be disciplined; you can always use your credit cards later, when you are getting desperate for food and other basics.

Consider cashing in some "luxury" assets. For example, sell a car or boat you rarely use to generate cash and to save on insurance and maintenance costs.

Comparison shop. Try to lower costs for home/auto/life insurance and other expenses.

Deduct job hunting expenses from your taxes. Some job hunting expenses may be tax deductible as a "miscellaneous deduction" on your federal income tax return. Keep receipts for employment agency fees, resume expenses, and transportation expenses. If you locate work in another city and you must relocate, some moving expenses are tax deductible. Contact an accountant or the IRS for more information.

Review your health coverage

You already know that it is dangerous to go without health insurance, so there is no need to lecture you on this, but here are some tips:

➤ You can probably maintain coverage at your own expense, under the COBRA law, if you worked for an employer that provided medical coverage and had 20 or more employees. To continue your health coverage under this law, you must tell your former employer within 60 days of leaving the job.

➤ Contact professional organizations you belong to; they may provide group coverage for their members at low rates.

➤ Speak to an insurance broker, if necessary, to arrange for health coverage on your own or join a local Health Maintenance Organization (HMO).

➤ Practice preventive medicine. The best way to save money on medical bills is to stay healthy. Try not to ignore minor ills. If they persist, phone or visit your doctor.

> ➤ Investigate local clinics. Many local clinics provide services based on a sliding scale. These clinics often provide quality health care at affordable prices.

> ➤ In an emergency, most hospitals will provide you with services on a sliding scale, and most areas usually have one or more hospitals funded locally to provide services to those who can't afford it.

Self-Employment and Consulting as an Alternative to a Conventional Job Search

As many as 40 percent of unemployed managers consider self-employment as an option for earning a living. While I definitely do not recommend that you start a business *because* you are unemployed, more and more people do work out of their homes, and being a freelance "consultant" can help you earn some money while you look for a full-time position.

For example, you could paint houses on weekends or pick up freelance work that you can do at home from previous employers or even competitors. Doing these things can help you create some income and pay the rent. It is an honorable activity, and you should be open to this possibility, particularly if it appears you may be unemployed for a long period of time.

While I warn you against forming a business out of desperation, it may be a sensible alternative for you if you have the right skills and motivations. Though I can't cover this topic in detail in this book, I have included a few things for you to consider in the material that follows.

The Self-Employed Are an Important Part of Our Workforce

Quick Fact

Of the approximately 123 million people who work, 8.3 percent – over 10 million workers – are self-employed. The number of self-employed is projected to grow by 15 percent over the next 12 years. Let's take a closer look at who they are and what they do.

More than half of the self-employed are in the services and retail trade industries, and most of the growth has been in this group. The most rapidly growing jobs include those in construction, finance, insurance, and real estate. About one third of the projected increase is expected among the executive, managerial, and administrative occupations. This is partly due to the large numbers of managers who have left large companies to start their own business. The next largest increase is projected in service jobs, such as child care workers, janitors and cleaners, housekeepers and maids, hairdressers, and cosmetologists. Other opportunities include those in craft and repair, sales and marketing, gardening and groundskeeping, and other areas.

There are hundreds of jobs where people are self-employed. Over half of all workers in some jobs are self-employed, including commercial artist, physician, real estate appraiser, real estate sales agent, farmer, and tailor. But there are at least some who have found ways to be self-employed in many jobs that would not be typically considered – such as librarian, retail sales person, chefs, mechanics, secretaries, and many others. And there are self-employed consultants in virtually every field.

Being self-employed has its advantages, but it is not for everyone. For example, you have to be disciplined enough to schedule your own time and handle financial record keeping – and no one will pay your fringe benefits for you.

Are You Likely to be Self-Employed Sometime in the Future?

The answer is "probably yes." Even if you don't plan on being self-employed as a career, you may become so once or more during your working years. I am a good example of this when, years ago, I put together enough consulting work to make ends meet for over a year when I was between "real" jobs. I've done this twice during my career, and many others have (or will), too.

Older and more experienced workers often have specialized skills that can be valuable to businesses or other organizations. And, if they lose their jobs, they often have difficulty finding jobs at similar levels of pay as in the past. So they try "consulting" as a way to make ends meet while they continue to look for a job. While I can't recommend consulting as an alternative to conventional employment, many people have made this transition either willingly or unwillingly. Some have done quite well at it.

Of course, you may also find self-employment an attractive alternative to working for someone else – and you may *want* to be self-employed. In either case, you need to approach this as you would if starting any small business venture. It is not for the faint of heart. I believe that the best way to find out if self-employment is for you is to gain some of the necessary skills while employed or to seek a job that allows you to develop the skills you need. You should also seek out people who are self-employed doing things similar to those that interest you and find out as much as you can about their work. This includes learning about the things they like as well as those things they do not like about being self-employed.

Some Futurists Predict That Fewer of Us Will Have Conventional Jobs

You've probably read about the growing numbers of people who work for someone else out of their homes. The wide and cheap availability of computers and electronic communications have made this much easier to do, though few employers seem yet willing to let go of the conventional workplace. There are also some indications that many workers *prefer* to come to a regular place of work instead of working out of their homes.

But what does the future hold? Clearly, the technology to allow people to do office work from home exists now for many jobs. And more and more people do work from home, often as self-employed workers. These "freelancers" do everything from graphics design and desktop publishing to engineering and technical writing. They have joined the traditional freelancers (such as attorneys, accountants, and architects) to make up a sizable and growing part of our workforce.

But there are other forces in our economy that may "force" more and more of us to be freelancers. While this is controversial, I and many others believe that new labor laws and increasing demands on employers provide real disincentives to hiring. Some studies have indicated that states with more employee rights regulations have decreased job growth. Employers simply decide that hiring employees is too expensive once you figure in all the costs such as health insurance, training, unemployment compensation, Social Security, retirement benefits, and much more.

And then there is the risk of lawsuits for terminating an employee and the related legal costs to defend against sometime ridiculous lawsuits – an unpredictable cost that has literally forced some businesses out of existence. So, many employers are using new technologies to reduce costs (and staff) and looking for ways to do more with less.

While we continue to create new jobs in our labor market, some believe that more and more of these jobs will be providing project-specific services to businesses. And many of these services will be provided by freelancers. Most will be self-employed or work in small groups of people who share projects as it makes sense to. They will work for various employers as their efforts are needed. Employers can avoid the long-term costs of an employee and gain people with specialized skills to work on specific problems.

Temporary employment agencies have grown rapidly and are one sign of the increased demand for project-specific workers over permanent ones. If this trend lasts, more and more of us may end up being self-employed. One implication for all of us is to continue to develop our job-related skills, particularly those involving new technologies – the demand for these advanced skills will surely increase, whether or not you work for yourself or someone else...

Sources of Additional Information on Self-Employment

A variety of excellent books on being self-employed are available, and you should read as much as you can before taking the plunge. While the libraries are full of titles on this topic, here are a couple that are published by JIST:

Mind Your Own Business – Getting Started as an Entrepreneur by LaVerne Ludden and Bonnie Maitlen. It covers self-employment as well as starting a small business – options that should often be considered together as alternatives. The book will help you understand whether self-employment is appropriate for you and, if it is, will show you how to develop a business plan and get started.

Franchise Opportunities Handbook lists over 1,500 franchise operations in businesses you have never considered as well as many you have. Originally compiled by the U.S. Department of Commerce, it has been revised to include advice on evaluation franchise opportunities and developing a business plan. Edited by LaVerne Ludden.

Information on Salary Ranges and Benefits

I've covered salary negotiation techniques earlier in this book, but thought it important enough to provide you with a quick review as well as some sources of information on pay ranges in the previous chapter that provides the pay for several hundred major jobs.

A Quick Review of the Salary Negotiation Process

"How much do you expect to be paid?"

There is big money at stake in how you handle salary negotiations. If you don't handle yourself well at a critical moment, it can cost you thousands of dollars and, perhaps, a job offer.

Let's examine what is going on here. In most cases, an employer does have a salary range in mind before an interview. In government jobs and some larger organizations, this range could be quite firm but in many situations there is often quite a bit of flexibility. You, on the other hand, should also know the salary range for jobs that interest you. This information is readily available from most libraries, professional associations, or by talking to people in similar jobs.

So let's say that they have in mind a range of $25,000 to $30,000 a year (you can insert any numbers here that make sense to you since the principles will be the same). The employer has the same range in mind. Let's try a few answers in response to the question I began with.

1. You answer that you are willing to accept no less than $26,000. That seems like a good answer but, now that the employer knows this, do you think it likely that they will offer you more? No. If you get the job, you are likely to get paid less than you might have. So your answer could cost you thousands of dollars over the years.

2. You cleverly ask for $32,000 figuring that you will let them know that you will not be pushed around. Wrong. In this instance, many employers would tend to screen you out of consideration, figuring that you would not be happy with their offer. They keep looking and you are out of the picture.

A better approach is to avoid talking about salary early in the screening process, because your response is often designed to screen you out if not in line with what the employer wants. So a good answer is one like "What range do you typically pay for this position?" or, if that does not work, "I am open to any reasonable offer, and I'm sure that you pay a competitive rate." While these delaying responses don't always work, they often do – and that allows you to avoid being screened out too early.

Your objective is to get a job offer, not to be screened out. If the employer pushes for an answer or if you are truly negotiating an offer, discuss salary *ranges* instead of specific numbers. For example, if you know that employers in your area pay between $26,000 and $32,000 for similar jobs (a big range but not unusual), you might say that you would accept offers from the mid-twenties to mid-thirties. Think about it. When stated this way, your range would cover from about $23,000 to $37,000 – an enormous range.

While you might not really be willing to accept the low end of this, you should at least go for an offer.

Stick to your guns and avoid mentioning a number early in the negotiations. The best move is to let the employer make the first offer, *then* negotiate. But don't ever refuse an initial offer as being too low. Ask for time to consider it. If it is not enough, thank them for the offer after a day's consideration and, if you want the job, state your minimum. Of course, they may go to another person, so this is not a game you should play unless you are willing to lose the job. If the offer is much too low, ask them to consider creating a new job for you or to consider you for future openings with higher levels of responsibility.

Like I said, good negotiations could be worth thousands of dollars to you over the years. If so, please consider sending me some part of your windfall...

What Fringe Benefits Do Others Get?

You may find it interesting to know what other people receive as fringe benefits from their employers since this is an important issue for you to consider in deciding to take a job. Details published in a book titled *Career Guide to America's Top Industries* (published by JIST and based on information provided by the U.S. Department of Labor) provide information on this and many other topics.

According to the data from government sources, benefits vary – with factors such as the type of industry and job, full- or part-time status, region of the country, union status, and size of the employer. This should come as no surprise because some employers clearly provide more benefits than others.

Following is data from the *Career Guide to America's Top Industries* that provides some interesting insights. It presents the percentage of full-time workers who receive various benefits for small employers (with fewer than 100 employees) and larger employers.

Table 17-1	Percentage of Full-Time Workers Who Receive Various Benefits	
	Small employers	*Medium & large Employers*
Paid holidays	83%	97%
Paid vacations	88	97
Health insurance	69	92
Life insurance	64	92
Retirement plan	36	81

From this information, larger employers are more likely to offer better benefits, although many smaller employers do as well. When paid leave was provided, the annual averages for all employers was 9 or 10 holidays, 3 days of funeral leave, and 11 or 12 days of military leave per year.

Fewer paid vacation days were offered in small establishments than in larger ones. After 1 year of service, small organizations gave 8 days while larger organizations gave 9 days. After 10 years of service, it was 14 vacation days in small and 17 days in larger and, after 20 years, 15 and 20 days in small and larger organizations. Part-time workers, as expected, fared much worse. Even in larger organizations, only 28% got paid holidays, 29% paid vacation days, and a very low 6% got health or life insurance benefits.

With 7 of every 10 workers in the private sector working for small- and medium-sized businesses, getting good fringe benefits such as heath insurance is more important than ever. Health insurance is an expensive benefit that adds thousands of dollars to an employer's cost for each worker. While this brings up complex economic and national issues that are being widely discussed, it is clear that individuals should consider benefits in their career planning and job search.

Employers who offer good health insurance and retirement programs pay considerably more for their workers than those who do not and will often expect higher levels of skills and productivity as a result. If getting a job with good benefits is a problem for you, it may be just one more reason to upgrade your skills to make you more attractive to those employers with superior benefits.

Sources of additional information on salary and wages

There are a variety of good sources of information on the pay ranges for various jobs and I present a variety of them here.

Reference books

Your local library or bookstore have a number of references to use to find out the salary ranges for the occupation which you are considering. Those marked with an asterisk are most likely to be available through a library or bookstore. Others are more specialized and may only be available through larger libraries. Ask your librarian for assistance as most libraries provide a variety of references that may not be listed here.

➤ The *Occupational Outlook Handbook* and *America's Top 300 Jobs*.

Both books contain the same information and are updated every two years based on information from the U.S. Department of Labor. I've mentioned these books elsewhere as an important source of information on jobs and both include starting and average pay rates for most larger jobs. For example, the current editions indicate that the middle half of earnings for engineering technicians ranged from $18,900 to $22,600 for entry-level positions to $28,800 for those with more experience and the ability to work with little supervision. Those in supervisory and senior-level jobs earned over $40,000 a year.

It also indicates that federal government pay begins at $14,600 to $18,300 depending on training and experience but that the average pay for all engineering technicians working for the federal government was $37,337. This higher average rate is due, apparently, to the higher pay received by the more experienced and supervisory employees. As you can see, this detailed information would be very helpful in your ability to know what pay to expect for various jobs at differing levels of experience.

➤ *Career Guide to America's Top Industries*.

This book includes information on about 60 major industries. Written for job seekers, it provides a description of each industry, employment projections, working conditions, typical occupations, training and advancement, outlook for industry growth, and earnings information.

For example, earnings information for those in the drug manufacturing industry indicates that workers there have higher than average earnings, averaging $831 a week ($43,000 a year) compared to $454 a week ($23,672 a year) for all industries. Production workers there earned an average of $540 a week ($28,157 a year) compared to $346 ($18,041 a year) for all industries. As you can see, there can be substantial earnings differences among industries, even for the same types of work. So it is important to know this in advance so that you are not unpleasantly surprised. On the other hand, you can also benefit from your industry research by looking for jobs in industries that tend to pay better – if you know which ones they are...

➤ *Career Connection to College Education* and the *Career Connection to Technical Education*.

Both books are by Fred Rowe, and each allows you to look up jobs related to major courses of study. Information on the average earnings for each of these jobs is included and this provides a useful starting point for those considering additional education – as well as information that can used in salary negotiations.

➤ *America's Federal Jobs*.

This book provides information on all major divisions of the federal government, including the types of positions available, college training sought, and pay ranges for each job, plus many additional details.

State and Metropolitan Area Data Book.

A specialized book published by the U.S. Department of Commerce. Compiles statistical data from many public and private agencies. Includes unemployment rates, rate of employment growth, and population growth for every state. Also presents a vast amount of data on employment and income for metropolitan areas across the country.

White Collar Pay: Private Goods-Producing Industries.

Produced by the U.S. Department of Labor's Bureau of Labor Statistics. Good source of salary information for white collar jobs in manufacturing.

AMS Office, Professional and Data Processing Salaries Report. (Administrative Management Society, Wash. DC)

Salary distributions for 40 different occupations, many of which are professional. Subdivided by company size, type of business, region of the country, and by 41 different metropolitan areas.

American Salaries and Wages Survey. (Gale Research, Detroit)

Detailed information on salaries and wages for thousands of jobs. Data is subdivided geographically. Also gives cost-of-living data for selected areas, which is very helpful in determining what the salary differences really mean. Provides information on numbers employed in each occupation, along with projected changes.

➤ *American Almanac of Jobs and Salaries.* (Avon Books, NY)

Information on wages for specific occupations and job groups, many of which are professional and white collar. Also presents trends in employment and wages.

Professional associations

There are associations for virtually any occupation or industry you can imagine – and some that you can't imagine. Most of the larger ones conduct salary surveys on an annual basis, and this information is available to members and, sometimes, in one of their publications. If you can get back issues of their journals or newsletters, they can provide excellent information on trends, including pay rates. Consider joining to get access to this information as well as access to local members for networking.

Local information

Local pay rates can differ substantially from national averages; starting wages are often substantially under those for experienced workers; some industries pay better than others; and smaller organizations often pay less than larger ones. For these reasons, it is important for you to find out prevailing pay rates for jobs similar to those you seek. Following are some additional sources of this information.

Professional associations: Once again, joining one or more professional associations related to your field will often allow you to obtain salary information they collect for their members. More importantly, it also gives you sources of local contacts. You can ask these people for help in determining local pay rates – and they can also often help you with job leads as well.

Your network: Talk to colleagues in your professional network. Although people frequently don't want to tell you what they personally are making, usually they are willing to talk about salary ranges. Ask colleagues, based on their experience, what salary range you might expect for the position.

Job search centers: These centers (which can be found in schools, libraries, community centers, or as part of federal, state, or local government programs) frequently keep salary information on hand.

Your past experience: If you are applying for a job in a field in which you have experience, you probably have a good idea of what someone with your skills and abilities should be paid. Think about your past salary. Unless the job you are applying for requires dramatically different responsibility than your former position, your previous salary is definitely a starting point for salary negotiation.

When stuck for local sources to determine salary ranges, try calling these sources:

➤ Chamber of Commerce, especially the economic development division, which may have statistics on what individual companies are paying

➤ Area business organizations such as Women in Communications or Society for Retired Executives

➤ Area government assistance programs such as the Small Business Association

Working for the Government

Way back in Chapter 8, I presented a chart of data on employment growth in various industries. Well, you may not have noticed that one of these "industries" was the government. And you also may have missed that government jobs are a very important part of our workforce.

Look at the chart that follows and you will see that the various government entities at the federal, state, county, city, town township, and other levels employ enormous numbers of people.

Government Employment Compared to Total Employment

Employment (in millions):	1950	1960	1970	1980	1990	2005
Total Labor Force (in millions):	62.2	69.6	82.8	106.9	124.8	151
# Govt. Employees (in millions):	13.3	15.4	17.7	18.0	16.7	22
% of Workforce Employed by the Government:	21.4	22.1	21.4	16.8	13.4	14.6

Trends in Government Employment

A few trends in government employment are worth considering. As you can see from the previous graph, both the number and percent of people employed by the government has been going down in recent years. While some have found it more difficult to get government jobs as a result, millions of new hires are being made each year by the various government entities. These hires are to replace retiring workers or those who leave government employment as well as to fill new positions requiring skills that are in short supply.

The projections through 2005 are for an increase in both the numbers and percentage of people working for government at various levels, though not at as fast a rate as the labor market as a whole. This means that competition for the more desirable government jobs will remain keen, although large numbers of people will be hired, with an emphasis on those with good training, education, and technical skills.

Advantages and Disadvantages of Government Jobs

There are a variety of things to like about working for the government, such as fair pay, equal employment and affirmative action hiring programs, security, retirement, and other benefits. And, of course, government workers tend to get more holidays per year, such as Mother Goose Day and Creative Redundancy Day, as well as half-day work days on summer Fridays and other strange things. But there are also disadvantages: sometimes the very things that are advantages to some become problems for others. For example, while various regulations make it hard to get fired from many government jobs, this practice tends to lead to some incompetent people remaining on the job, and their coworkers carrying a heavier load as a result.

Although I am not going to attempt to help you decide whether or not to seek a government job, you should certainly consider them as one option. There are, however, several realities that you need to know in looking for these jobs.

1. Civil service requirements: Most government jobs have objective requirements, such as tests, education, experience, and other credentials. These hiring guidelines have been created to avoid unfair hiring practices and force most hiring decisions to be justified based on the applicant's meeting objective criteria.

2. Bureaucratic hassles: One result of the many hiring rules is that you can't easily get hired informally and are more likely to have to play the game of going through the complete and correct application procedures.

3. An uneven playing field: While the rules appear to create a fair process for being considered, things are not as they appear. Government departments often have hidden agendas and don't really hire the best qualified. Instead, they may assign "points" to applicants based on their status rather than qualifications. For example, veterans, people with disabilities, minorities, women, and other groups may be given preferential treatment. And, of course, many government hires are not covered by the civil service rules and can be filled by political appointees or at the discretion of the employer.

4. Keen competition: There have traditionally been far more applicants for government jobs than there are openings, so do expect keen competition.

5. Long delays: While I encourage you to consider government jobs during your job search, you do need to realize that it may take months to work through their hiring procedures. If you need a job quickly, don't count on a government job unless your skills are very much in demand or you have special contacts.

As with all job search leads, don't ignore any opportunity but keep your options open.

The Long Distance Job Search – Looking for a Job in Another City or Area

Looking for a job in another area is a special issue that requires some special job search methods. Fortunately, it is fairly easy to build on the basic approach that I have provided throughout this book, with some adaptations. Here are some tips to consider in looking for a job in another location.

Decide, in Advance, Where You Want to Go

My point here is that looking for a job "anywhere" is just as dangerous as looking for "any" job. This is a big country, and you will be far better off in focusing your job search to specific regions and specific types of jobs than just "shotgunning" everywhere.

One of the criteria I presented in Chapter 10 of this book was to consider some of the criteria you have for the ideal location for your job. Go back and review that content and get more specific on just where it is you want to go. In some cases, looking at the things that you would prefer will narrow down your options. For example, you may prefer to work in a mid-sized city, near the ocean, in a warmer climate. By excluding things, you narrow down your options and the more you do so, the better off you will be.

Don't Just Go There, Set Up Interviews in Advance

I have seen too many people simply fly out to some place and hope to get interviews once there. That is a very bad idea, because there is much you can do in advance that will save you precious time and money. Your task is to set up interviews before you go anywhere and, fortunately, this can be done easily enough.

Adapt the Standard Networking Techniques to Establish Contacts in Your Targeted Location

I reviewed the basics of networking back in Chapters 2 and 14, and these can be readily adapted for use in identifying contacts virtually anywhere. Let me give you a few examples of how this might be done.

Let's say that you are looking for a job as a ceramics engineer, a narrow and specialized occupation that would seem to have few employment opportunities. And let's say that you live on the West Coast but would like to live in the mountain states, including Montana and Colorado.

You could begin by considering the groups of people that might form a basis for your networking efforts. For example, what about alumni from the college you went to, particularly those who were in your specialty of engineering? Get the list from the alumni office for all past graduates from that program. Get the names of current and past professors from that program, too. Then get the membership list from the professional association or associations that ceramics engineers are most likely to belong to (a good librarian can help you get this). Next, begin contacting these people who live in the mountain states and ask them to help you in your job search, as outlined in Chapters 2 and 14 – or ask them if they have any contacts in the mountain regions. While most of them will not know you or of any specific job opening, many will be willing to help you out by giving you names of people to contact. And some will be employers or work for companies that hire people with similar skills – or can give you the name of one or more other people to contact.

You make these contacts by phone – or by fax, on-line, or mail followed up by personal contact via phone. Once you make enough contacts, you can plan a trip to promising locations (like Denver) during a specific time in the future. Set up interviews during those days with those who seem most promising and work hard to fill your schedule while you are there with interviews. Then and only then should you spend the money to travel.

You can adapt this same basic approach to virtually any job sought in any area. Be creative and you will often find that your local contacts know people all over the place, if you simply ask them. Members of your local religious group have affiliations all over the world, and the same is true of many schools, fraternal organizations, clubs, hobby groups, professional associations, and other contact groups. You just have to be persistent and ask for assistance.

The New Graduate

There are far more graduates of post-secondary institutions now than in the past, and the recent job market has been a tight one for many of them. While the earnings of college graduates are far above those of the average high school graduate, the averages can be misleading.

New graduates face a variety of problems that have made it difficult for some to get professional jobs quickly. In some cases, the "quality" is not there, and a poorly educated college graduate is of little value to most employers. I know from personal observation that many college grads can't write a simple business letter without displaying their ignorance. I believe that, with more and more graduates, the standards for getting a degree are lower than they once were, and employers know this, too. As a result, a new graduate may not be able to do anything particularly well, yet they may have high expectations for pay and status.

Quick Reminder

You do have to remember that the "average" pay for a job is considerably higher than a new entrant to that occupation will typically be paid.

If you want more information on the fate of graduates from college and technical training, I refer you to several books I have written on those topics including *America's Top Jobs for College Graduates*, *America's Top Technical and Trade Jobs*, and other books in the *America's Top Jobs* series as mentioned in the bibliography.

If you are a new graduate, following are a few things that may help you in your job search.

1. Be clear about what you want to do: Many new graduates do not know what they want to do, and this lack of commitment and direction is often obvious to employers. As a result, they have to wonder just why they *should* hire you over other candidates who do know what they want to do, particularly if the other persons want to do what the employer has available. So do your homework and look for something specific – and be able to say why you want to do it.

2. Emphasize your experience and strengths: Since you probably don't have good work experience related to what you want to do now, you must be able to present what you do have to offer as alternatives. For example, what skills did you learn in previous jobs that can apply to this one? Even if your previous work experience is not directly related, you can often find transferable skills that will be used in the new job. Emphasize courses, extra-curricular activities, volunteer work, and any other activities as work equivalents.

3. Work harder to get interviews: Goofing off will not help you get interviews, yet that is how many recent grads spend their time. Working at your job search everyday is the only way to assure that you get a good job in less time.

4. Focus on smaller organizations: Larger organizations do hire new grads, but they often seek the ones with the best grades, most rounded backgrounds, and those from the best schools. Smaller organizations, as I pointed out in Chapter 2, now employ about 70 percent of the private sector workforce and are clearly the place that most new graduates will most likely work – yet they are often overlooked...

4. Be a particularly good interviewer: New graduates have to overcome their lack of work experience credentials, and superior interviewing skills can help considerably in convincing an employer to give you a chance. Plan on taking more time on practicing your interviewing skills, answering difficult questions, and doing as good an interview as you can learn to do. It will make a difference.

5. Be flexible: With any company, you might have to start out doing what appears to be routine tasks, not worthy of your advanced credentials. Relax, your expectations might have been inappropriate but, once you have some experience related to what you want to do, you can be in a good position to move up – or to move on to more responsible jobs.

It may occur to you that the advice for new grads is really very much like the advice I have provided throughout this book. I have found that job seekers are far more alike than they realize, in spite of differences in age, experience, earnings, education, or other factors. The basics seem to remain pretty much the same for everyone.

Over 40 and Unemployed

These are the most productive years of a person's career and are also traditionally the years that have the highest earnings. But anyone who has experienced unemployment when they are over 40 knows that it can be a cold and cruel world out there. And it gets even worse for those over 50. Anyone who doesn't believe this just hasn't looked at the data or experienced it themselves.

Part of the problem is that older workers tend to get paid more, and higher pay is often related to a longer job search. Older workers may also not have kept up with the computer and technological skills that are owned by many younger workers who are competing for the same jobs, often with lower salary expectations. Older workers also may not have looked for a job for some time and are often poorly prepared for an active job search – particularly after the trauma of losing a long-held job. And then there is age discrimination, something that I believe is quite real, even if it is related to the higher earnings I have already mentioned.

To combat these factors, older workers need to work harder on getting interviews, presenting themselves particularly well in interviews, and following up. Like all job seekers, they need to convince an employer to hire them over someone else.

BIBLIOGRAPHY

Annotated Bibliography

Annotated Bibliography –
Sources of Additional Information

Overview

This is not a conventional bibliography. My comments are informal and admittedly biased at times, and I've only included materials I like in some way.

I've been looking at career materials for over 20 years now, and it still amazes me that there is so much junk out there. I guess someone buys it simply because they don't know better. A good example of this is in the category of resume books, where many still suggest that the way to get a job is to send out lots of good-looking resumes. While the advice on creating a resume may be good, the advice on *using* it is too often not.

Since there are thousands of materials that might be mentioned here, I have only selected those that I think are particularly good or useful. I've

also emphasized materials you are most likely to find in a good library. Materials published or distributed by JIST are among those listed as some that I have written. Of course, I tend to be enthusiastic about materials I have been involved in, though I do try to be objective.

So now that you have been sufficiently warned, browse the resource materials that follow. I have organized them into categories and have provided comments on many of them. Since materials are often revised periodically, I have not provided dates of publication nor have I always provided the author's or publisher's name, and some may be out of print. This in an informal list rather than a formal bibliography, but I hope you find it helpful.

Job Search and Career Planning Books by Yours Truly

I have written a variety of career planning and job search books over the years and have included those you are most likely to find in a bookstore or library.

I feel strongly that there are only two main issues in the career planning and job search field that really matter. The first is that it is essential to select a career that will satisfy you. This involves knowing yourself well enough to select "THE" job rather than "a" job. The second issue is, if you need to

find a job, you might as well find a good one and do it in as little time as possible. All of my books include these simple principles. They tend to be practical and results-oriented.

The Very Quick Job Search: Get a Good Job in Less Time: This is my most thorough job search book, and it includes lots of information on career planning and, of course, job seeking. This is the book I would recommend to a friend who was out of work, if I had to recommend just one book. While written as a "bookstore" book, it is widely used in schools and colleges. There is an accompanying activities book, curriculum, and transparency set that are also available. Published by JIST.

The Quick Resume and Cover Letter Book – Write and Use an Effective Resume in Only One Day: The first section shows you how to quickly create a basic resume and then use it in an active job search. Other sections provide much greater detail on creating sophisticated resumes. There are over 60 sample resumes, including many selected from submissions by professional resume writers. Practical advice on career planning, job seeking, and letter writing is also emphasized. JIST.

The Quick Interview and Salary Negotiation Book – Dramatically Improve Your Interviewing Skills and Pay in a Matter of Hours: While this is a substantial book with lots of information, I arranged it so that you can read the first section and go out and do better in interviews later that day. Also covers career planning, job seeking, resumes, and other topics of importance for a job seeker. JIST.

Getting the Job You Really Want: Covers career planning and job seeking topics in a workbook format with lots of activities. Very popular in schools and job search programs and is available in bookstores. An instructor's guide is available. JIST.

America's Jobs Books: I have created a series of books providing information on a cluster of related jobs. Each one features similar elements, including a review of job market trends, 50 to 60 thorough job descriptions, career planning and job search advice, summary information on hundreds of additional jobs, useful appendices. The job descriptions are based on those used in the *Occupational Outlook Handbook* and include details on pay, education required, working conditions, and more. JIST.

Titles in this series include:
➤ *America's 50 Fastest Growing Jobs*
➤ *America's Top Jobs for College Graduates*
➤ *America's Top Medical and Human Services Jobs*
➤ *America's Top Office, Management, and Sales Jobs*
➤ *America's Top Technical and Trade Jobs*

The Right Job for You: A thorough career planning book that includes lots of information and worksheets. JIST.

The Work Book: Getting the Job You Want: This is my first job search book. Originally published in 1981, it has been revised several times and has now sold over 300,000 copies. It remains popular in post-secondary schools and programs. An instructor's guide is available. JIST.

Job Finding Fast: A thorough book that includes sections on career decision making as well as job seeking. It was written to support a full course or program at the post-secondary or college level. An instructor's guide is available. JIST.

The JIST Career Planning and Job Search Course: For instructors, a complete curriculum I wrote to support the use of *The Very Quick Job Search*. It includes lesson plans, over 50 overhead transparencies, and reproducible handout masters. JIST.

The JIST Course: The Young Person's Guide to Getting and Keeping a Good Job: Co-authored by Marie Pavlicko for use by high school students. It was field tested with thousands of students. Good graphics, easy to follow narrative, and a good accompanying instructor's guide and transparency set. JIST.

The Quick Job Search: A 32-page booklet covering the essentials needed for a successful job search. Very short but covers the basics. JIST.

Career Books Published by JIST

JIST publishes many books, but I've listed those that are career-related and that are most likely to be found in a bookstore or library. Some are listed elsewhere in this appendix under appropriate sections.

America's Federal Jobs: Reviews over 150 major departments in the federal government, including information on each department's mission, divi-

sions, available jobs, application procedures, and sources of additional information.

America's Top 300 Jobs: This is a version of the *Occupational Outlook Handbook* (mentioned later in this list) that is published for the bookstore and library market. Describes the top jobs in our labor market, covering about 85 percent of the workforce.

America's Top Military Careers: Reviews about 200 military jobs, including type of work performed, employment, related jobs, and other details. Useful in finding skills that transfer from military jobs to civilian counterparts.

Career Guide to America's Top Industries: Designed to help job seekers identify alternative job targets and to prepare for interviews. Provides trends and other information on over 40 major industries and summary data on many others. Excellent for getting information on an industry prior to an interview. Includes details on employment projections, advancement opportunities, major trends, and a complete narrative description of each industry.

Complete Guide for Occupational Exploration (CGOE). A major career reference book that arranges over 12,000 jobs into 12 major Interest Areas and increasingly specific clusters of related jobs. Useful for career exploration or identifying job targets. Includes a self-assessment section, a variety of useful cross references, narrative descriptions for each group of jobs, and other information.

Dictionary of Occupational Titles (DOT): JIST publishes a clone of this Department of Labor publication. It provides brief descriptions for over 12,000 jobs. Useful for identifying skills used in past jobs, preparing for interviews, and identifying job targets. While it is a bit hard to use, there is simply no other source of information like it.

Enhanced Guide for Occupational Exploration (EGOE), revised edition: Provides descriptions for 2,800 jobs arranged within 12 major Interest Areas and increasingly specific work groups. These jobs cover 95 percent of the job market, and the book is useful for career exploration, identifying skills used in previous jobs, researching new job targets, and preparing for interviews.

Job Doctor – Good Advice on Getting a Good Job: Phil Norris. A short and popular book that covers the basics of getting a good job. Phil ran a large and successful job search program and has a gift in making things simple and easily understood. JIST.

Occupational Outlook Handbook: JIST publishes a clone of this important career reference book published by the U.S. Department of Labor. It provides excellent descriptions of the 250 most popular jobs and covers about 85 percent of the workforce. I consider it one of the most helpful books on occupational information available. Very good for helping prepare for interviews, identifying skills needed on various jobs, and targeting possible opportunities.

The Resume Solution – How to Write (and Use) a Resume That Gets Results, revised edition: David Swanson. Provides a step-by-step approach to producing superior resumes. Good sample resumes and worksheets.

U.S. Industrial Outlook: U.S. Department of Commerce. Revised each year, provides business forecasts for over 300 industries. Good source of information to review prior to interviews. JIST publishes a clone.

Work in the New Economy: Robert Wegmann, Robert Chapman, and Miriam Johnson. This is a well-researched and well-written book that reviews the research on labor market trends and how a job seeker is affected. I admire the work of Bob Wegmann and consider him THE expert on this topic. He died early in 1991, and no one has replicated the quality of this information. JIST.

Career Connection for College Education – A Guide to College Education and Related Career Opportunities, revised edition: Fred Rowe. Provides information on over 100 college majors and 1,000 occupations that are related to them. Includes information on salaries, course requirements, related high school courses, and other details useful in planning a college major.

Career Connection for Technical Education – A Guide to Technical Training and Related Career Opportunities: Fred Rowe. Similar to the above but providing information on 70 technical training majors and 450 related occupations.

Career Satisfaction and Success – How to Know and Manage Your Strengths, revised edition: Bernard Haldane. This is a complete revision of a "classic" by an author many consider to be one of the founders of the modern career planning movement. It presents you with techniques for succeeding on the job and concepts that have changed many lives for the better, including defining your "motivated skills" and using them as a basis for career planning.

Dictionary of Occupational Terms – A Guide to the Specific Language and Jargon of Hundreds of Careers: Nancy Shields. Over 3,000 definitions, including descriptions of major jobs and the language used within various occupations.

Bibliography

Directory of Franchise Opportunities: U.S. Department of Commerce, edited by LaVerne Ludden. Provides details on over 1,500 franchise opportunities in every field, plus advice on starting a franchise business.

Exploring Careers – A Young Person's Guide to Over 300 Careers, revised edition: A revision of the original, published by the U.S. Department of Labor. An excellent resource for young people, providing details on over 300 jobs in an interesting format.

Gallery of Best Resumes – A Collection of Quality Resumes by Professional Resume Writers: David Noble. An excellent resource book providing over 200 sample resumes from experts across North America. Good advice on job seeking and cover letters, too.

Helping Your Child Choose a Career: Luthor Otto. Good advice to parents to help guide their children in selecting their career paths. Includes advice on vocational activities at various ages, including values and interests in career planning, outlook for industries, and choosing a college.

Job Savvy – How to Be a Success at Work: LaVerne Ludden. A workbook covering basic on-the-job behaviors for surviving on a new job and getting ahead. Includes lots of activities and worksheets.

Job Strategies for Professionals: Job search advice for the millions of professionals and managers who have lost their jobs. Based on material developed by the U.S. Employment Service and edited by JIST staff.

Mind Your Own Business: LaVerne Ludden and Bonnie Maitlen. Good advice for anyone who is considering starting their own business, including self assessment activities, funding sources, business plan tips, and other good advice.

PIE Method for Career Success – A New Job Search Strategy: Daniel Porot. The PIE method (Pleasure, Information, and Employment) uses a visual and creative format to present career planning and job search techniques. The author is one of Europe's major career consultants, and this book presents his powerful career planning and job seeking concepts in a visual and memorable way. JIST.

Ready, Set, Organize!: Pipi Peterson. Time management strategies for your personal and work lives. Good advice and a fun read.

Revised Handbook for Analyzing Jobs: A technical book describing various coding systems used to quantify and categorize jobs. JIST reprints the DOL version.

Secrets to Getting Better Grades: Brian Marshall and Wendy Ford. Teaches students to study smart, with lots of practical tips for notes, tests, papers, memory, and other techniques.

Standard Industrial Classification Manual: A JIST reprint of a government technical book that codifies all industries and assigns a "SIC" code. For accountants and others.

Young Person's OOH: JIST editorial staff. For grades 6-10. Provides information on career clusters and specific jobs listed in the *Occupational Outlook Handbook*. Also Includes career exploration advice.

Using the Internet in Your Job Search: Fred Jandt and Mary Nemnich. This is the first book available on this subject, and it is full of information on getting career information, finding job listings, creating electronic resumes, networking with user groups, and other interesting techniques for the high tech job search.

Using WordPerfect in Your Job Search: David Noble. A thorough book that will teach you things about using various versions of WordPerfect (the popular word processing software) to help you in your job search. A strong resume section plus techniques to schedule your time, organize you follow ups, create superior cover letters, use advanced resume design features, create JIST Cards, and more job search tricks than you could imagine.

Worker Trait Data Book: A technical book that provides coded information on over 12,000 jobs. Much of this information is not available elsewhere.

The Library as a Source of Career Information

Many of the resource materials I mention in this bibliography can be found in a good library. And they often have more than I can list here, including journals, newspapers, books, CD-ROM databases, and other resources. So here are some tips for using the library as your job search friend.

The librarian: That's right, your friendly librarian can be one of your best sources of specific information during your job search. If you can ask the question, he or she can probably give you some ideas on where to find an answer. JIST publishes many books, but I've listed those that are career-related and that are most likely to be found in a bookstore or library. Some are listed elsewhere in this appendix under appropriate sections.

America's Federal Jobs: Reviews over 150 major departments in the federal government, including information on each department's mission, divisions, available jobs, application procedures, and sources of additional information.

America's Top 300 Jobs: This is a version of the *Occupational Outlook Handbook* (mentioned later in this list) that is published for the bookstore and library market. Describes the top jobs in our labor market, covering about 85 percent of the workforce.

America's Top Military Careers: Reviews about 200 military jobs, including type of work performed, employment, related jobs, and other details. Useful in finding skills that transfer from military jobs to civilian counterparts.

Finding Facts Fast: Todd. Perhaps the best book on finding out about anything at the library or elsewhere. Great research aid.

Trade magazines and journals: Most libraries will have one or more professional journals related to a variety of major career areas. Staying current on the publications in your field will help you in the interviewing process, and they sometimes have job listings.

Career Planning & Job Search

There are now innumerable job search and career planning books, and more are published all the time. Most are written by corporate recruiters, headhunters, social workers, academics, and personnel experts who are well intentioned but have little practical experience in determining whether the job search methods they recommend actually work. Many books provide advice that would, if followed, slow down the job search process. Generally, I discard books that suggest sending out resumes or answering want ads as good job search methods – or that do not include methods appropriate for approaching smaller businesses. The research clearly indicates the relative importance of these issues, and anyone who is not aware of this should not be considered an expert. So, in my humble opinion, here are some of the better books.

Highly Recommended General Career Planning and Job Search Books

Complete Job Search Handbook: Howard Figler. Solid source for new ideas. Exercises to assess skills, values, needs. Procedures for exploring careers and developing a job objective. Innovative job search and interviewing techniques. An excellent book that is loaded with innovative ideas.

Job-Hunters & Career-Changers: Richard N. Bolles. This is the all-time best-selling, career-changing book ever. Well written and entertaining, it is updated each year and includes a useful self-assessment section, "The Quick Job Hunting Map." Bolles is fun to read, and the book is highly recommended.

Very Quick Job Search: Get a Good Job in Less Time: J. Michael Farr. This is the book we would recommend to a friend who is out of work. Proven techniques to plan careers and to reduce the time needed to find a job. Thorough. JIST.

Work in the New Economy: Robert Wegmann, Robert Chapman, & Miriam Johnson. A very well-researched book. Covers where our economy is going and how we should adapt our career planning and job search methods to get better results. Considered by many to be essential reading for any well prepared job seeker. Published by JIST.

Who's Hiring Who: Richard Lathrop. Solid, practical information for job seekers. Good self-assessment sections and excellent resume advice (he calls them "qualifications briefs"). I particularly like this book and respect Lathrop's work.

Bibliography

Other Good Career Planning and Job Search Books

Alternative Careers for Teachers: Pollack and Beard. Good ideas on getting a job in another field using transferable skills.

Big Splash in a Small Pond – Finding a Great Job in a Small Company: Resnick and Pechter.

Book of U.S. Government Jobs

Careers in Local and State Government: Zehring. Where they are, how to apply, how to take tests, internships & summer jobs. Job search tips.

Change Your Job, Change Your Life: Krannich. Reviews job trends and job search methods.

Complete Guide to Public Employment: Krannich. Reviews opportunities with federal and local governments, associations, nonprofits, foundations, research, international, and many other institutions. Well done.

Complete Job and Career Handbook: Feingold.

Do What You Love, The Money Will Follow: Sinetar. For those among us who seek meaning as our first priority, there is hope that we can also make a living doing the things we really want to do.

Doing Well by Doing Good: The First Complete Guide to Careers in the NonProfit Sector: McAdam.

Electronic Job Search Revolution: Kennedy and Morrow. Tips on using your computer and on-line services to get jobs.

Find a Federal Job Fast!

Finding A Job In Your Field: A Handbook for Ph.D.'s & M.A.'s

Foreign Jobs: The Most Popular Countries: Casewit. Profiles most desirable countries and how to get jobs there.

Getting a Job After 50: Morgan. Age discrimination is real, and people over 50 need better-than-average job seeking skills to overcome this.

Go Hire Yourself an Employer: Richard Irish. Lots of good stuff in this new revision. Covers skills identifi-cation, job search, resumes, interviews, the unemployment "blahs," succeeding on the next job, and other topics.

Government Job Finder

Guerrilla Tactics in the New Job Market: Tom Jackson.

Hardball Job Hunting Tactics: Dick Wright. From a trainer with lots of experience with the hard-to-employ. Excellent sections on completing applications (a topic not often covered well) and resumes. Brief but good section on job search. Tips for people with various "problems" on how to overcome them.

The High-Tech Career Book: Collard.

How to Create Your Ideal Job or Next Career: Richard N. Bolles, Ten Speed Press, 1989.

How to Get a Better Job in This Crazy World: Robert Half.

How to Get Interviews from Classified Job Ads: Elderkin.

How to Make a Habit of Success: Bernard Haldane. Originally published many years ago, it was a best-seller and is still available. Many consider Haldane one of the founders of the career planning movement that began in the 1950s. This is an important book that has much good advice.

Information Interviewing: What It Is and How to Use It in Your Career: Martha Stoodley.

Job & Career Building: Richard Germann & Peter Arnold. A good choice for laid-off professionals, managers, and others with more experience and training.

Job Doctor: Phil Norris. A very popular book that provides a quick review of the job search process. Provides practical advice that gets right to the point. The author has taught thousands of people to find jobs and has written a column titled "Ask the Job Doctor." Published by JIST.

Job Hunters Sourcebook: Where to Find Employment Leads and Other Job Search Sources: Michelle LeCompte.

Job Hunting for the 40+ Executive: Birsner. Provides good advice on the personal and job search needs of middle-aged executives.

Job Power: The Young People's Job Finding Guide: Haldane & Martin. One of our favorite books for group process ideas on skills identification and selecting a job objective. Simple, direct, useful for any age.

Job Search for the Technical Professional: Moore. For programmers and engineers.

Job Sharing Handbook: Smith. Provides guidelines for setting up a shared job, case histories, etc. Good.

Jobs for English Majors and Other Smart People: Good tips for liberal arts grads.

Joyce Lain Kennedy's Career Book: Kennedy & Laramore. Joyce writes a column on careers that appears regularly in many newspapers. This is a very thorough book for young people and their parents, covering just about everything that a young person would need to know about career – and life – decisions. Highly recommended.

Marketing Yourself: The Ultimate Job Seeker's Guide: Dorothy Leeds.

The MBA's Guide to Career Planning: Ed Holton

Moving Out Of Education: A Guide to Career Management & Change: Krannich & Banis. Good tips for this special situation from an ex-educator who moved out.

New Network Your Way to Job and Career Success: Ron & Carol Krannich.

Non-Profit Job Finder

Part-Time Professional: Good information on finding part-time jobs, benefits, negotiating with employers, converting full-time to part-time jobs, and other tips.

Professional Careers Sourcebook, an Informational Guide for Career Planning: K. Savage and C. Dorgan

Re-Careering in Turbulent Times: Ronald Krannich. Lots of good material, including employment trends, selecting a career, getting training and education, communication skills, sources of job leads, interviewing, resumes, relocation, public employment opportunities, and career advancement.

Robert Half on Hiring: Robert Half. Written to help employers select better employees. Most of the advice is based on a series of employer surveys providing unique insight into how employers make hiring decisions.

Selling on the Phone: Porterfield. Self-teaching guide for telemarketing and other sales approaches. Good ideas for reinforcing effective phone skills in the job search.

Starting Over: You in the New Workplace: Jo Danna.

Temp Track: Justice. Reviews the many opportunities for temporary jobs.

The 100 Best Companies to Work for in America: Robert Levering and Milton Moskowitz.

The Complete Job Search Book: Richard Beatty.

The Complete Job Search Handbook: All the Skills You Need to Get Any Job, and Have a Good Time Doing It: Howard Figler. A very good book.

The Job Bank Guide to Employment Services: Bob Adams.

The Only Job Hunting Guide You'll Ever Need: Kathryn Ross Petras.

The Right Place at the Right Time: Finding a Job in the 1990s: Robert Wegmann and Robert Chapman.

Three Boxes of Life and How to Get Out of Them: Richard Bolles. Introduces the concepts of "life/work planning" and provides many good activities and concepts. Very thorough.

VGM's Handbook of Government and Public Service Careers.

Where Do I Go from Here with the Rest of My Life?: John Crystal & Richard Bolles. This book presents the innovative career planning process of John Crystal as written by Richard Bolles. John has since died but his techniques and insights into the career planning process helped to start an important movement that came to be called "Life/Work Planning."

Wish Craft: Barbara Sher. An upbeat book that provides activities and advice on setting goals and reaching your full potential.

Information on Occupations

There are hundreds of books providing information on jobs, and most libraries will have a selection. I suggest you begin with the general references I suggest, then look for more specific information.

Recommended Sources of General Information

America's Top 300 Jobs: This is a "bookstore" version of the *Occupational Outlook Handbook*. It provides thorough descriptions for about 250 jobs plus summary information on hundreds more.

Career Discovery Encyclopedia: Six-volume set providing career information for youth, grades 4-8.

Dictionary of Occupational Titles (DOT): While the GOE allows you to locate thousands of job titles in a variety of helpful ways, it does not describe these jobs. The DOT does and is the only book to do so. Also published by the U.S. Department of Labor, the DOT can be found in most large libraries. It is a very large book (over 1,400 pages) and is not particularly easy to use but, combined with the GOE, provides the most thorough system of organizing jobs available.

Encyclopedia of Careers: Ferguson Publishing. A series of books providing useful information on all major occupations.

Enhanced Guide for Occupational Exploration: This book combines useful elements of both the GOE and the DOT. It uses the GOE's structure for organizing jobs into major interest areas and cross-references jobs in similarly helpful ways. But it also provides descriptions for each of the jobs it lists. It can do this within one book by excluding the many jobs that employ few people or are highly specialized. The 2,500 jobs it does include cover 95 percent of the jobs in the workforce, and few people will miss those that are not listed. In fact, I think that the excluded 10,000 jobs tend to get in the way of finding the ones that most people actually work in. This book is published by JIST, the same people who published the book you are reading.

Exploring Careers: This is an important career exploration book for young people that was originally published by the U.S. Department of Labor and revised and republished by JIST.

Guide for Occupational Exploration: The "GOE" provides a method of narrowing down broad interests to the many specific jobs within each major category. It lists over 12,000 jobs by occupational cluster, interests, abilities, and traits required for successful performance. In addition, each job is cross-referenced in useful ways. You can look up jobs by industry, types of skills or abilities required, values, related home/leisure activities, military experience, education required, or related jobs you have had. The U.S. Department of Labor published the earlier edition of this book, and a later edition was published by a private source.

Occu-facts: Provides one-page descriptions for over 500 jobs in an easy to read format. Jobs are arranged into groups of similar occupations which encourages its use as a career exploration tool.

Worker Trait Group Guide: A simpler version of the *Guide for Occupational Exploration* providing information on clusters of similar jobs.

More Career Information Books

There are hundreds of books that provide information on specific careers. I've selected representative titles, but you will find many others in a good library.

Career Finder – Pathways to Over 1,500 entry-Level Jobs: Schwartz and Breckner.

Opportunities in . . . Series: A series of books published by VGM Career Horizons. Each covers related jobs in that field, skills required, working conditions, pay, education required, and jargon. Some of the careers covered are Secretarial; Health & Medical Careers; Office Occupations; Data Processing; Computer Science; Travel Careers; Hotel & Motel Management; Cable Television; Accounting; and many others.

Professional Careers Series: Another series of books on a variety of professional jobs, including finance, medicine, law, computers, accounting, business, and others.

Careers Without College Series: A series of 11 books for those not planning on a 4-year college degree. Topics on health care, fashion, cars, office, sports, and others.

Great Careers: The 4th of July Guide to Careers, Internships, and Volunteer Opportunities in the Non-Profit Sector: An enormous reference of books and programs covering jobs with a social cause.

Peterson's Engineering, Science and Computer Jobs: An annual update of 900 employers, types of jobs, and more.

High Paying Jobs in 6 Months or Less: For jobs requiring brief training.

High Tech Jobs for Non High Tech Grads: O'Brien. Good ideas for those without technical training.

Real Estate Careers: Jamic & Rejnis.

Outdoor Careers: Shenk.

Choosing an Airline Career: March.

Information on Industries

While most people focus their career planning time on choosing an occupation, it would be wise to give more thought to the industry where you want to work. The same job can pay much more in some industries and less in others. Here are a few of the best sources of information on industries.

Career Guide to America's Top Industries: Information on over 40 major industries. Designed to help job seekers identify alternative job targets and to prepare for interviews. This is a very special book that is easy to read and loaded with helpful information. Written specifically to assist in career planning and job seeking, this is a JIST published clone of material developed by the U.S. Department of Labor.

U.S. Industrial Outlook: U.S. Department of Commerce. Provides business forecasts for over 300 industries. Good source of information to review prior to interviews. JIST publishes a clone.

Business/Employer References

A good library has many good sources of information on specific businesses and other organizations. While many of these resources were not specifically developed for use by job seekers, they can work just fine for that use.

There are several ways to use these resource materials. The first is to get information on a specific organization as background for an interview. You can also get names of organizations as well as background information to use in making direct contact lists. Because there are so many potential sources of information, ask a librarian to help you once you have a good idea of what you are looking for.

Newspapers, business periodicals, and professional journals: Review these sources for articles mentioning your target companies. Look for information on new products, expansions, consolidations, relocations, promotions, articles by executives in the companies, annual company earnings, and current problems.

Check back issues of newspapers for old want ads. They can provide important information on job duties, salary, and benefits. There may even be a want ad for a job in which you are interested. Perhaps the job was never filled or the person previously hired has already moved on.

Specialty newspapers such as *The National Business Employment Weekly* have a compilation of the previous week's want ads from the regional editions of *The Wall Street Journal,* plus its own want ads. *National Ad Search* is a weekly tabloid that has a compilation of want ads from 75 key newspapers across the U.S. Expect major competition for jobs listed this widely.

Newspapers not only contain want ads but also much other useful employment information. Articles about new or expanding companies can be valuable leads for new job possibilities.

If relocating is a possibility, look at newspapers from other areas. They can serve as a source of job leads as well as indicate some idea of the job market. The major out-of-town newspapers are sold in most large cities and also are available in many public libraries.

Back issues of major newspapers can be accessed by computer, allowing you to sort by key words.

Business Newsbank, Newsbank, Inc.: This service provides the narrative of articles from newspapers and business journals from 400 cities. It cross references information by company name, individual's name, industry, or product category.

The New York Times Index: A thorough index of all stories that appear in the *Times*.

The Wall Street Journal Index: This is an important source of information on larger businesses and business trends.

Contact the organizations themselves: If a larger organization, call the human resources or public relations department. In smaller organizations, the receptionist or manager may be able to help. Get brochures, an annual report, description of relevant jobs, and anything else that describes the organization.

Books

100 Best Companies to Work for in America: Levering and Moscowitz.

900,000 Plus Jobs Annually: Feingold & Winkler. Reviews 900+ periodicals which list openings and positions wanted in hundreds of fields.

America's Corporate Families, The Billion Dollar Directory: Describes the relationships of 2,500 large corporate "families" and their 28,000 subsidiaries. Also provides information on each and cross referencing by location, business or product type, and other methods.

America's Corporate Families, The Billion Dollar Directory: Describes the relationships of 2,500 large corporate "families" and their 28,000 subsidiaries. Also provides information on each and cross referencing by location, business or product type, and other methods.

America's Fastest Growing Employers: Bob Adams. Lists more than 700 of the fastest growing companies in the country.

Annual Reports

All publicly owned and many smaller organizations provide annual reports detailing earnings, trends, strategies, and other information. If one is available, it can provide an excellent source of information.

Bay Area 500: Hoover. An example of a regional listing, this one providing profiles of the largest companies in the San Francisco area.

Business Newsbank, Newsbank, Inc.: This service provides the narrative of articles from newspapers and business journals from 400 cities. It cross references information by company name, individual's name, industry, or product category.

Business Organizations and Agencies Directory, Gale Research Company: Provides a number of useful ways to look up business organizations – by name, types of business activity, and others. It then provides information on each organization, including address, phone number, contact person, and a brief description of the organization.

Business Periodicals Index: Cross references business articles from over 300 periodicals by subject and company name.

Chambers of Commerce: Most are not staffed to provide specific information to job seekers but many do provide some useful information, such as new businesses in the area, larger employers, and other details

Contacts Influential: A series of directories providing information on many smaller businesses. The directories allow you to look up organizations by name or by type of organization and learn various details of its operations and size.

Directories Listing Employers Within Industries

There are many directories which give information about firms in a particular industry, for example:

The Blue Book of Building and Construction

Directory of Advertising Agencies

Directory of Computer Dealers

McFadden American Bank Directory

American Business Information Inc. of Omaha, Nebraska, publishes business directories for many different industries. They can be reached by phone at (402) 593-4600.

The Chamber of Commerce and local business associations may also publish directories listing companies within a specific geographic area. These are available in libraries or by writing to the individual associations. And, of course, the telephone *Yellow Pages* provides local listings of governmental and business organizations for every section of the country.

Directory of Executive Recruiters: Joyce Lain Kennedy

Directory of Executive Search Firms: Lists and cross-references hundreds of these businesses.

Dun & Bradstreet Million Dollar Directory: Provides information on 180,000 of the largest companies in the country. Gives the type of business, number of employees, and sales volume for each. It also lists the company's top executives. An abbreviated version of this publication also exists, which gives this information for the top 50,000 companies.

Encyclopedia of Associations: Gale Research Company. Lists the over 19,000 associations representing more issues than you can imagine. It cross references them in various helpful ways. Find out the professional organization that people in the occupation you are interested in are likely to belong to, then read their journal and get their list of members to contact during your network. And consider joining one or more.

Hidden Job Market: A Guide to America's 2000 Little-Known Fastest Growing High-Tech Companies: Peterson's Guides. Concentrates on high-tech companies with good growth potential.

Hoover's Handbook of American Business: Hoover, Campbell, Spain. Profiles of 500 major corporations.

Hoover's Handbook of Emerging Companies: Spain, Campbell, Talbot. Profiles of 250 entrepreneurial companies.

Little Known, Fastest Growing High-Tech Companies: Peterson's Guides.

Macrae's State Industrial Directories: Published for 15 Northeastern states. Similar volumes are produced for other parts of the country by other publishers. Each book lists thousands of companies, concentrating almost exclusively on those that produce products, rather than services. They include a large number of small firms, in addition to the larger ones listed in many other guides.

Million Dollar Directory, Dun's Marketing Services: Provides general information on over 115,000 businesses.

Moody's Industrial Manual: Provides detailed information on over 3,000 larger organizations.

Moody's Industrial News Reports: Provides articles related to each of the businesses listed in the related directory.

National Business Telephone Directory: Gale Research. An alphabetical listing of companies across the United States, with their addresses and phone numbers. It includes many smaller firms (20 employees minimum).

Out of town Yellow Pages: Some libraries have out of town copies of phone books. If they don't, ask your local phone company.

Peterson's Business and Management Jobs: An annual listing of hundreds of employers plus essential background information on each.

Polk's Directories, R.L. Polk & Co.: Each major city has its own Polk Directory that is created by way of a door-to-door canvass of individuals and businesses in the area. Cross references by name, address, and type of business.

Professional and Trade Association Directories

These associations constitute another excellent avenue for getting information about where your kind of work might be found. Consider joining the associations that relate to the area that interests you, and then ask for their list of members – and contact them as sources of possible job leads. Association journals are also helpful in learning about what is going on in the field. Here are some sources of information.

Career Guide to Professional Associations: Garrett Park Press. Describes more than 2,500 professional associations. The information is more specifically oriented to the job seeker than is the Encyclopedia of Associations but has not been updated recently.

Encyclopedia of Associations, Gale Research Company: Gale Research. A listing of more than 22,000 professional, trade and other nonprofit organizations in the United States, representing more issues than you can imagine. It cross references them in various helpful ways.

Professional & Trade Association Job Finder: By career category, details over 1000 sources of information, referral, and more.

Bibliography

Reference Book of Corporate Management: Dun's Marketing Services. Provides information on the executives and officers of the 6,000 largest U.S. corporations.

Standard & Poor's Register of Corporations, Directors and Executives: Provides brief information on over 40,000 corporations and their key people cross referenced by names, types of businesses, and other methods. Also contains a listing of the parent companies of subsidiaries and the interlocking affiliations of directors.

The Career Guide – Dun's Employment Opportunities Directory: Aimed specifically at the professional job seeker. Lists more than 5,000 major U.S. companies that plan to recruit in the coming year. Unlike the other directories from Standard and Poor and Dun and Bradstreet, this guide lists personnel directors and gives information about firms' career opportunities and benefits packages. Also gives a state-by-state list of headhunters and tips on interviewing and resume writing.

The Job Bank Series: Bob Adams, Inc. A series of books aimed primarily at job-seeking professionals, each covers a different large city or metropolitan area. Each book also gives an introductory economic outlook for the covered area, followed by a listing of the area's major companies. Common positions within the company are listed.

The Job Hunter's Guide to 100 Great American Cities: Brattle Communications. Rather than concentrating on a particular locale, this guide gives the principal-area employers for 100 of America's largest cities.

Thomas Register of American Companies: Several related directories provide information on more than 100,000 companies and allows you to look them up by product, name, and by other means.

Where the Jobs Are: 1200 Journals with Job/Career Openings: Feingold & Winkler. A unique resource providing tips on responding to journal ads and a cross reference to specific journals by job type.

Where to Find Business Information: Brownstone and Curruth. This one lists and describes the many newsletters, journals, computer databases, books, and other sources of business information.

Resumes & Cover Letters

There are hundreds of resume books out there, but most offer bad advice. They assume that a resume will help get an interview while the research clearly indicates that this is not an effective way to do so. And many offer poor or unnecessarily rigid advice about the resume itself. Clearly, the importance of a resume is overrated, yet they are a standard and typically expected part of the job search process. I've selected a few that I particularly like and listed others that also have merits. There are many more...

Highly Recommended

Gallery of Best Resumes: *A Collection of Quality Resumes by Professional Resume Writers:* David Noble. The author is on JIST's staff and has done an excellent job of assembling over 200 sample resumes submitted by professional resume writers. Good advice and lots of excellent samples. A very good resource book that organizes resumes by occupational category.

High Impact Resumes & Letters: Krannich & Banis. In addition to the expected advice on constructing a resume, it provides worksheets on identifying skills and accomplishments, good job search advice, and plenty of sample resumes and letters.

The Quick Resume and Cover Letter Book – Write and Use an Effective Resume in Only One Day: J. Michael Farr. Starting with an "instant" resume worksheet and basic formats that you can complete in an hour or so, this book then takes you on a tour of everything you ever wanted to know about resumes and, more importantly, how to use them in your job search.

The Resume Solution – How to Write (and Use) a Resume That Gets Results: David Swanson. Lots of good advice and examples for creating superior resumes. Provides a step-by step approach to each section of a resume, providing lots of examples on how to handle problems, improve design, and to make your resume stand out.

Using WordPerfect in Your Job Search: David Noble. A unique and thorough book that reviews how to use WordPerfect to create effective resumes, correspondence, and other job search documents, including scannable and hypertext resumes. JIST.

Other Resume Books

College Student's Resume Guide: Marino.

Complete Resume Guide: Faux. Some good ideas and examples.

Damn Good Resume Guide: Yana Parker. An irreverent title, but it has many good examples and an easy-to-follow process for creating resumes.

Developing a Professional Vita or Resume: McDaniels. Special resume advice for professionals with advanced education or experience.

Don't Use a Resume: Richard Lathrop. A booklet providing good examples and advice on a special resume that emphasizes skills.

Dynamic Cover Letters: Hanson. A very focused book, just on cover letters.

Dynamite Cover Letters: Ron & Carol Krannich. Good content.

Dynamite Resumes: Ron & Carol Krannich. Lots of good examples and advice.

Encyclopedia of Job Winning Resumes: Fournier and Spin. Lots of examples in a wide variety of jobs.

How to Write a Winning Resume: Bloch. Good examples for college grads, more experienced job seekers, and professionals.

Job Search Letters That Get Results: Ron & Carol Krannich. Includes 201 sample letters.

Liberal Arts Power: How to Sell It on Your Resume: Nadler.

Ready, Aim, Hired: Developing Your Brand Name Resume: Karson.

Resume Kit: Beatty. Better than average advice on putting together effective resumes and cover letters.

Resume Pro: The Professional Guide: Yana Parker. A how-to guide for those who help others write resumes.

Resumes for Computer Professionals: Shanahan. Many examples.

Resumes for Executives and Professionals: Shy & Kind.

Resumes for High School Graduates: VGM editors. An unusual but useful focus.

Resumes for Mid-Career Job Changes: VGM editors.

Resumes for Technicians: Shanahan. Examples, tips for use, etc.

The Perfect Resume: Tom Jackson. A very helpful book on resumes that uses a workbook format. This approach makes it easy to identify skills, interests and achievements to support a clear job objective. Good examples.

The Resume Catalog: Yana Parker. 200 good resumes organized by job objective.

Writing a Job Winning Resume: John McLaughlin & Stephen Merman. A good book with examples that show how the resume covered a weakness.

The No Pain Resume Workbook: Hiyaguha Cohen.

School & Training Admissions, Financing, and Survival

More and more adults are going back to school to upgrade their career opportunities, and any young person should consider getting as much education and training as possible. There are many ways to finance post-secondary training or education, and that should not be a barrier. If you want to do it, seek and ye shall find a way. Here are some resources.

Highly Recommended

Career Connection for College Education – A Guide to College Education and Related Career Opportunities: Fred Rowe. Provides information on over 100 college majors and 1,000 occupations that are related to them. Includes information on salaries, course requirements, related high school courses, and other details useful in planning a college major. Published by JIST.

Career Connection for Technical Education – A Guide to Technical Training and Related Career Opportunities: Fred Rowe. Similar to the above, describes over 60 technical education majors and the careers they lead to. Published by JIST.

College Admissions Data Handbook: Published by Orchard House, this is the most thorough and up-to-date source of information on colleges available. There are four volumes covering different sections of the country.

Annotated Bibliography **491**

Tech Prep Guide: Technical, Trade, & Business School Data Handbook: Published by Orchard House, this is the most thorough reference of its kind, providing thorough information on over 1,600 schools plus summary information on another 3,000 schools. Four volumes cover different parts of the country.

More Good Books

Bear's Guide to Finding $ for College: John Bear. Well written, readable, helpful.

Brushing Up Your Clerical Skills: Steinberg. For new and returning office workers. Exercise on spelling, punctuation, typing, business letters, filing, etc.

College 101: Farrar. Primer for getting along in college.

College Degrees by Mail: John Bear. Brief descriptions for 100 nonresident schools.

College Majors and Careers: A Resource Guide for Effective Life Planning: Phifer. Good information on the college majors, skills, related leisure activities, personal attributes, and additional resource materials for major occupational interests.

College Survival Guide: Mayer. Well done. New student orientation to basics of making it.

Earn College Credit for What You Know: Simosko. On nontraditional college credit programs: types, application procedures, etc.

Electronic University: A Guide to Distance Learning Programs: Peterson's Guides.

Free Dollars from the Federal Government: Blum.

Free Money for College: A Guide to More Than 1,000 Grants and Scholarships: Blum.

Guide to Non-Traditional College Degrees: John Bear. Fun to read, well done, thorough.

Peterson's Independent Study Catalog: Guide to over 12,000 correspondence courses.

How to Apply to American Colleges and Universities: Brennan and Briggs.

Internships: 50,000 On-The-Job Training Opportunities for Students and Adults: Rushing.

Liberal Education and Careers Today: Howard Figler. I dropped out of premed in my junior year of college (a long story) and got a degree in liberal arts. And I turned out OK. Figler makes the same pitch for a liberal arts education and provides research and lots of advice on how liberal arts is a good way to go.

Major Decisions – A Guide to College Majors: Orchard House. Provides brief descriptions for all college majors.

Minority Student Enrollments in Higher Education: Provides information on 500 schools with the highest minority enrollments.

New Horizons – Education and Career Guide for Adults: Haponski. Methods of seeking and using education to get ahead.

Paying Less for College: Peterson's College Money Handbook: Provides costs, types of aid, and other details from over 1700 schools.

Peterson's Competitive Colleges: Data and tips on getting in to the top 300 schools.

Peterson's Guide to College Admissions: Student workbook on preparing and competing. Well done.

Peterson's Guide to Colleges and Programs for Students with Learning Disabilities: Mangrum and Strichart. Lists over 1,000 colleges with these programs.

Peterson's Guide to Four Year Colleges: 1900 schools & 400 majors. Organized to allow selection by many criteria plus tips on applying, etc.

Peterson's Guide to Two Year Colleges: Provides selection info on over 1400 schools with associate degrees.

Peterson's National College Databank: Data in over 350 categories, a major source of data for colleges of all descriptions.

Time for College – The Adult Student's Guide to Survival and Success: Siebert and Gilpin.

Who Offers Part-Time Degree Programs?: Peterson's Guides. Data on over 2500 institutions.

Winning Money for College: High school student's guide to scholarship contests.

You Can Make It Without a College Degree: Roesch.

Dress & Grooming

Initial impressions in the interview are very important. How you dress and groom is only one of the issues, of course, but it is one that most people can easily change and almost everyone can improve.

Dress for Success: John Molloy. Some of the advice is dated now, but this still gives good research-based advice on business attire.

Red Socks Don't Work: Karpinski. Dressing tips for men in corporations.

Women's Dress for Success: Molloy. Same thorough approach as for men.

Always in Style with Color Me Beautiful: Pooser. By a noted color consultant, clothing styles, colors, and make-up for women. Many photos.

Big and Beautiful: Olds. Larger women can be gorgeous, too.

Color Me Beautiful: Jackson. Discover your "seasonal" colors and coordinate your look. Color photos. Well done.

Professional Image: Bixler. One of few on dress, grooming, body language, and details for both men and women.

Self Employment, Consulting, Starting a Business

More and more people are working for themselves, starting small businesses, or working in small businesses. There are hundreds of books on these topics, and a good library will have more resources than I can list here, but here are a few suggestions.

The Small Business Administration: If you are considering self-employment or buying a franchise, the U.S. Small Business Administration (SBA) offers loans, training and planning, as well as many useful publications. There are SBA offices in every state. Their toll-free number is 1-800-U ASK SBA. In addition, their Service Corps of Retired Executives (SCORE) provides free training and counseling on how to set up and run a small business.

America's New Breed of Entrepreneurs: Presents collective experiences of 48 successful entrepreneurs and how they achieved their goals.

Beginning Entrepreneur: Matthews.

Best Home Businesses for the '90s: Edwards and Edwards.

Directory of Franchise Opportunities: U.S. Department of Commerce & LaVerne Ludden. Lists 1,500 franchise opportunities and information on selecting and financing a start up.

Directory of Microenterprise Programs: Lists loans and programs for low-income entrepreneurs.

Getting Business to Come to You: Edwards and Edwards. Low cost marketing tips.

Home Sweet Office: Meade. Telecommunicating from home to a regular job.

How to Build a Successful One Person Business: Bautista.

How to Run Your Own Home Business: Kern and Wolfgram.

How to Start, Run, and Stay in Business: Kishel. Good primer for the school of hard knocks.

Inc. Yourself: How to Profit from Setting Up Your Own Corporation: Shows financial and other advantages, plus how to set up.

Making It on Your Own – What to Know Before Starting Your Own Business: Feingold.

Mind Your Own Business – Getting Started as an Entrepreneur: LaVerne Ludden and Bonnie Maitlen. A good book for those considering their own business, with lots of good advice.

Opportunities in Your Own Service Business: McKay.

Running a One Person Business: Whitmeyer, Rasberry, Phillips. Practical.

Starting on a Shoe String: Building a Business Without a Bankroll: Goldstein.

Working from Home: Edwards and Edwards.

Future Trends/Labor Market Information

Projections 2000: U.S. Department of Labor. Provides detailed projections of the economy and labor force.

State and Metropolitan Area Data Book: U.S. Department of Commerce. Compiles statistical data from many public and private agencies. Includes unemployment rates, rate of employment growth, and population growth for every state. Also presents a vast amount of data on employment and income for metropolitan areas across the country.

Work in the 21st Century: Isaac Asimov and others: Anthology of well-done articles on work trends for the future. Stimulating.

Emerging Careers: New Occupations for the Year 2000 & Beyond: Based on years of research, details hundreds of new careers. Very good.

The Work Revolution: Schwartz & Neikirk. Thorough and well done. Predicts retraining, education, and other needs of rapid change.

Megatrends: Nesbitt. A best-seller that provides a review of where the economy is heading.

Trainer & Instructor Resources

While you should be able to find books on public speaking in most bookstores and libraries, more specific materials such as instructor's guides for a job search workshop are very hard to find. JIST does publish or carry a variety of these more specialized materials in their catalogs, should you be interested.

Career Exploration Groups: A Facilitator's Guide: Garfield & Nelson. Includes group activities and exercises to aid in self-knowledge, career information, and decision making.

Career Information Service: Norris. One of the few texts for university level career counseling & development courses. Thorough book for career counselors.

Career Planning Workshop Manual: Instructor's guide for life/work planning workshops. Includes group exercises, worksheets.

Developing Vocational Instruction: Mager & Beach. Easy-to-understand, step-by-step guidelines to developing good curriculum.

How to Organize and Manage a Seminar: What to Do and How to Do It: Murray. Budgets, plans, staffing, promotion, etc. Very Good.

Louder & Funnier: A Practical Guide for Overcoming Stage Fright: Nelson. Getting over fear of groups is a major obstacle to success as a trainer or presenter. Excellent.

Making Successful Presentations: Smith. Good for the new or moderately experienced trainer.

Making Vocational Choices: A Theory of Careers: John Holland: There are few career theory books, and this is one of the most influential. In plain and readable English, presents the research, rationale, and practical uses of his theory of six personality types.

The Business of Public Speaking: Good tips on business aspects of doing presentations.

Where to Start: An Annotated Career Planning Bibliography: Thorough, helpful. Organized by topic.

Interviewing

Dynamite Answers to Interview Questions: Ron & Carol Krannich.

Getting to Yes: Negotiating Agreements Without Giving In: Fisher & Ury. Good negotiating tips for anything.

How to Have A Winning Job Interview: Bloch. Good advice in a readable format, with lots of activities.

How to Make $1000 a Minute – Negotiation Your Salaries and Raises: Jack Chapman. Tips on getting more money and benefits during the critical part of a job offer.

Interviewing for Success: Ron & Carol Krannich.

Interviews That Get Results: Vik. Good tips for job seekers.

Knock'em Dead: With Great Answers to Tough Interview Questions: Martin John Yate

Make Your Job Interview a Success: Biegeleisen. Contains a variety of good checklists, interview answers, grooming tips, and other content.

Out Interviewing the Interviewer: Merman & McLaughlin. Good exercises, case studies, and tips for experienced and not-so-experienced job seekers.

Power Interviewing: Job Winning Tactics From Fortune 500 Recruiters: Yeager and Hough.

Ready, Aim, You're Hired!: How to Job-Interview Successfully Anytime, Anywhere with Anyone: Hellman.

Sweaty Palms Revised: The Neglected Art of Being Interviewed: H. Anthony Medley. Fun and factual tips for job seekers at all levels. Covers illegal questions, problem interviews, appropriate dress and behaviors.

The Evaluation Interview: Richard Fear. Considered a classic for anyone who is or wants to be a professional interviewer.

The Five Minute Interview: Beatty, Richard H.

The Ultimate Interview: How to Get It, Get Ready, and Get the Job You Want: Caple.

When Do I Start?: Clearly written, good content.

Winning the Salary Game: Salary Negotiations for Women: Chastain. Good strategies for men, too.

International Jobs

Researching the international job market can give you many clues about the careers, locations, and companies which look promising for overseas employment. Before you commit to an overseas job, however, carefully consider personal and family issues which might impede a full adjustment to your host country.

Publications

Directory of European Industrial and Trade Associations: CBD Research, Kent, England. Industrial and trade associations of Europe. Gives the principal trade and activities in which each engages.

Directory of European Professional and Learned Societies: CBD Research, Kent, England. Similar in format to Industrial and Trade Associations above, but deals strictly with learned and professional societies.

Encyclopedia of Associations – International Organizations: Gale Research. A listing of over 11,000 nonprofit organizations in 180 countries. Includes trade, business and commercial associations, and associations of labor unions.

How to Get a Job in Europe – The Insider's Guide: Surrey Books. Gives country-by-country listings of newspapers, business directories, regulations, organizations for further information, and other useful information.

How to Get a Job in the Pacific Rim: Surrey Books. Information similar to preceding book, but for countries bordering the Pacific Ocean.

International Careers: Bob Adams, Inc. Information on finding work overseas. Covers government, private corporations, and nonprofit groups.

International Employment Hotline: Names and addresses of governmental and nongovernmental organizations hiring for overseas work.

Key British Enterprises: Dun and Bradstreet. Detailed information on the 50,000 British companies which together employ more than a third of the British workforce.

International Jobs: Where They Are, How to Get Them: A Handbook for Over 500 Career Opportunities Around the World: Kocher.

Passport to Overseas Employment – 100,000 Job Opportunities Abroad: Information on overseas careers, study programs, and volunteer programs.

Principal International Businesses: Dun and Bradstreet. An international version of the *Dun & Bradstreet Million Dollar Directory*. While not aimed at the job seeker, it provides information on more than 55,000 companies in 143 different countries.

Teaching English Abroad: Griffith.

The Complete Guide to International Jobs and Careers: Your Passport to a World of Exciting and Exotic Employment: Ron & Carol Krannich.

International Agencies

These agencies maintain lists of consultants who are available to work overseas. Some agencies you might want to register with are: World Bank; U.S. Aid for International Development (USAID); United Nations Development Program; and United National Industrial Development Organization (UNIDO).

The U.S. Government: The federal government also has many jobs overseas. Don't overlook civil service announcements as a source of overseas employment. *Federal Career Opportunities* is available at most public libraries, and the publication *Federal News Digest* is available through subscription. State employment agencies offer computerized searches for federal job openings.

The Peace Corps: This is another source of jobs overseas. Wages are low, living conditions may be less than optimal, but if you are interested in helping people, the Peace Corps may be a possibility.

Job Loss, Survival & Success

Skills for Success: Scheele. Good advice on getting ahead in all sorts of careers.

Business Protocol: Yager. On-the-job manners.

Career Knockouts: How to Battle Back: Joyce Lain Kennedy. Avoiding, learning, and even benefiting from job failures.

Coping with Unemployment: Jud. Dealing with long-term unemployment.

Getting Things Done When You Are Not in Charge: Bellman.

How to Jump Start a Stalled Career: Prugh.

Moving Up – How to Get High Salaried Jobs: Djeddah. Techniques to get promoted or move out to a new job.

Not Just a Secretary: Morrow & Lebov. Techniques for doing well and getting ahead.

Sacked! Why Good People Get Fired and How to Avoid It: Gould.

Secretary Today, Manager Tomorrow: How to Turn a Secretarial Job into a Managerial Position: Marrs.

Termination Trap: Best Strategies for a Job Going Sour: Cohen. Excellent insights on avoiding or dealing with job loss.

Working Smart: Zehring. Advice on getting ahead, organizing time, dealing with people, and developing leadership skills.

Places to Live or Move To

Some people will be unhappy wherever they live, but living in a place you like does make life more enjoyable. Here are a few books that provide details.

Best Towns in America: Bayless. 50 of the U.S.'s most desirable places plus ways to evaluate all communities.

Country Careers – Successful Ways to Live and Work in the Country: Rojak.

Finding Your Best Place to Live in America: Bowman and Guiliani. Another good book providing information on good places to live.

Greener Pastures Relocation Guide: Finding the Best State in the U.S. for You!: Places Rated Almanac: Richard Boyer and David Savagean. Provides a thorough review of over 270 metropolitan areas, including information on housing, education, climate, health services, recreation, arts, transportation, crime, and income.

Special Populations

There are specialized materials written to help various segments of our population gain a competitive edge. Here are just a few.

Immigrants

Finding a Job in the United States: Friedenberg and Bradley.

Minorities

Best Companies for Minorities: Graham. Profiles of 85 companies.

Career Opportunities for Bilinguals and Mutliculturals – A Directory of Resources in Education, Employment and Business: Wertsman. Over 3,500 listings.

Directory of Special Programs for Minority Group Members: Willis L. Johnson. Over 2,800 sources of training, jobs, scholarships, and programs.

Minority Career Guide: Kastre, Kastre, and Edwards.

Minority Organizations – A National Directory: The largest source of information available covering over 7,700 professional organizations and resources.

Stepping Up: Placing Minority Women Into Managerial and Professional Jobs: Tips to replicate results of a program that increased the pay, advancement, and retention of minority women.

The Black Woman's Career Guide: Nivens. Good advice on over 50 good jobs, dress & grooming, skills ID, job search, and more.

Workers Over 40, Displaced Workers, Retirement Issues

Arthur Young's Pre-Retirement Planning Book: Very well-done book. Lots of worksheets.

Cracking the Over 50 Job Market: Conner. Good job search advice.

Getting a Job After 50: John S. Morgan, Petrocelli Books

Helping the Dislocated Worker: Ashley & Zahniser. Summary of suggested services, model programs, implementation strategies. Very helpful for program planners.

Job Hunting After 50: Strategies for Success: Samuel Ray.

Retirement Careers: Marsh.

Second Careers – New Ways to Work After 50: Bird. Analyzes career changes of over 6,000 people and how it worked out.

Mid Career Job Hunting: Official Handbook of the 40+ Club: E. Patricia Birsner. Facts on File. Solid advice on getting back on track and getting a job.

The Over 40 Job Guide: Petras.

People with Disabilities

A Helping Hand, A Guide to Customized Support Services for Special Populations: Thorough guide for program operators who emphasize employment: JTPA, older workers, offenders, others. Tips for improved services.

Americans with Disabilities Handbook: A JIST reprint of a USEEOC publication providing comprehensive information on the ADA legislation and how it is interpreted.

Americans with Disabilities Act: A Technical Assistance Manual: A JIST reprint of the USEEOC original.

Bouncing Back from Injury: How to Take Charge of Your Recuperation: Karen Klein and Carla Derrick Hope.

Complete Guide to Employing Persons with Disabilities: Henry McCarthy. National Rehabilitation Information Center, 8455 Colesville Road, Suite 935, Silver Spring, Maryland 20910-3319. (800) 346-2742; TDD 301-588-9284.

Job Hunting for the Disabled: Adele Lewis and Edith Marks. Interest surveys, programs, job descriptions, and job search tips.

Job Strategies for People with Disabilities: Witt. Good advice as well as lists of resource materials and programs.

Job-Hunting Tips for the So-Called Handicapped or People Who Have Disabilities: Richard N. Bolles.

Recovery

The Career Seekers: Tannenbaum. For anyone recovering from codependency or in a recovery program.

Clean, Sober and Unemployed: Elliot. Good advice for recovering substance abusers.

Spouses

Parents with Careers Workbook: Good worksheets and advice on getting organized, child care, home management, single parents, dual careers, time use, etc.

The Three Career Couple: Byalick and Saslow.

Surviving Your Partner's Job Loss: Jukes and Rosenberg.

Side by Side: Cuozzo and Graham.

Veterans/The Military

America's Top Military Careers: A JIST reprint of a DOD publication. Provides information on 200 enlisted and officer occupations, including civilian counterparts.

Complete Guide for Occupational Exploration : Among other things, this comprehensive career reference book cross references military occupations to the 12,000 civilian job titles. A JIST publication.

Resume and Job Hunting Guide for Present and Future Veterans: DePrez. Helpful book with some good techniques.

Veteran's Survival Guide to Good Jobs in Bad Times: Grant's Guides.

You and the Armed Forces: Marrs. Helps to better understand career options and what to expect from military life.

Young Person's Guide to Military Service: Bradley. Covers pros & cons of going into the services. Good sections for minorities and women.

Your Career in the Military: Gordan. Reviews advantages (education, money and others), plus enlistment options & procedures.

Women

More women are in the workforce today than ever before, and they tend to be better educated than average. But women without advanced education and who are single heads of households are not doing well, on average. Special advice and resources are clearly needed, and here are just a few.

Congratulations! You've Been Fired: Sound Advice for Women Who've Been Terminated, Pink Slipped, Downsized or Otherwise Unemployed: Emily Koltnow and Lynne S. Dumas.

Developing New Horizons for Women: Ruth Helm Osborn. Very good text to improve self-esteem, identify strengths, and develop long range life and career plans.

Directory of Special Opportunities for Women: Over 1000 resources for women entering and re-entering the workforce. Recommended.

Good Enough for Mothers: Marshall. Balancing work and family.

Homemaker's Complete Guide to Entering the Job Market: Lussier. Useful techniques to transfer homemaking skills to work-world and to find a job.

Resume Guide for Women of the '90s: Marino.

The Extra Edge: Mitchell. Success strategies for women, based on data from women grads of Harvard Business School.

The Woman's Job Search Handbook: Bloomburg and Holden. Well-done career planning and job search techniques.

Time for a Change: A Woman's Guide to Non-Traditional Occupations: For women considering nontraditional jobs: exercises & narrative plus a review of 10 growth oriented jobs.

Winning the Salary Game: Salary Negotiations for Women: Sherry Chastain.

Yes to Career Success!: Hennekins.

Salary & Benefits

Professional Associations

National and regional professional associations frequently conduct salary surveys. Contact your professional association and ask if they can provide you with salary information.

Your Network

Talk to colleagues in your professional network. Although people frequently don't want to tell you what they personally are making, usually they are willing to talk about salary ranges. Ask colleagues, based on their experience, what salary range you might expect for the position.

American Almanac of Jobs and Salaries: Wright. Covers hundreds of careers in the public and private sector.

American Salaries and Wages Survey: Gale Research. Detailed information on salaries and wages for thousands of jobs. Data is subdivided geographically. Also gives cost-of-living data for selected areas, which is very helpful in determining what the salary differences really mean.

AMS Office, Professional and Data Processing Salaries Report: Administrative Management Society. Salary distributions for 40 different occupations, many of which are professional. Subdivided by company size, type of business, region of the country, and by 41 different metropolitan areas.

Perks and Parachutes: Tarrant.

State and Metropolitan Area Data Book: Published by the U.S. Department of Commerce. Compiles statistical data from many public and private agencies. Includes unemployment rates, rate of employment growth, and population growth for every state. Also presents a vast amount of data on employment and income for metropolitan areas across the country.

White Collar Pay: Private Goods-Producing Industries: U.S. Department of Labor's Bureau of Labor Statistics. Good source of salary information for white collar jobs.

You Can Get Anything You Want: Dawson.

Tests & Test Taking

There are hundreds of career-oriented tests, and here are some resources to help evaluate or prepare for them.

American College Testing Program (ACT): Over 450 pages of skills, reviews, sample questions, study tips, and tips to raise ACT scores.

Book of U.S. Postal Exams: Bautista. Sample exams for 44 job categories.

Career Aptitude Tests: Klein & Outerman. Series of self-scored tests measuring aptitudes against over 250 jobs.

Civil Service Test Tutor: Practice drills & samples for government tests for beginning office jobs: accounting, file clerk, telephone operator, and similar jobs.

Counselor's Guide to Vocational Guidance Instruments: Kappes and Mastie. Reviews of many tests.

Career Finder: The Pathways to Over 1500 Entry-Level Jobs: Schwartz & Breckner. Checklists result in recommended jobs for more exploration. Lists salary, openings, etc.

Fairness in Employment Testing: National Academy of Sciences.

Guide to 75 Tests for Special Education: Up-to-date guide covering major tests, how to select, interpret, and use.

How to Get a Clerical Job in Government: Hundreds of sample questions & answers covering major topics on federal, state, and local exams.

How to Pass Employment Tests: Prepares job seekers to do well in tests they may encounter in their job search. Also has a section on tests often given to evaluate potential for advancement.

Making the Grade: Study habits and techniques for getting good grades by doing well on all sorts of tests.

Practice for the Armed Forces Tests: Drills, sample questions, test-taking tips, general review for all service tests.

Bibliography

Practice for Clerical, Typing, Steno Tests: Sample questions, drills, exercises to improve scores on most clerical tests.

Preparation for the GED: Thorough preparation to increase scores.

Preparation for the SAT: Thorough preparation to increase scores.

Assessment Tests and Instruments

Too many people think that there is a magical solution to their career planning problems that does not require effort. Tests are only tools to provide you with information and can't tell you what to do. I prefer assessment devices that encourage you to participate in the career decision making process. If you have access to a career center or counselor, ask about taking a career interest test. But remember that it can only provide you food for thought, not an answer to what you should do. Here are a few that I recommend.

Career Decision Making System (CDM): Thomas Harrington, Ph.D. & Arthur J. O'Shea, Ph.D. A popular interest test that is easy to use, self-scoring and interpreted. The Survey Booklet records stated occupational preferences, preferred school subjects, job values, abilities, plans for future education, and training.

Career Exploration Inventory (CEI): John Liptak, Ph.D. Published by JIST, this one provides a score that cross-references to major occupational interest areas and helps explore various alternative careers. Uses a unique past/present and future orientation and also helps create an action plan.

College Majors Finder: Cross-references Holland codes (which can be obtained from the **SDS** and **CDM** described in this section as well as from other devices) to over 900 college majors. Includes 2 year, 4 year, and advanced degree programs.

Leisure Search Inventory: John Liptak. An interesting approach to identify career interests based on what you enjoy doing rather than a more traditional approach. Cross-references to major career information systems. Published by JIST.

Self Directed Search (SDS): John L. Holland, Ph.D. This is the most widely used career assessment test available. Responses result in recommendations to consider occupations in one of six major clusters. Over 1,100 jobs are cross-referenced in a separate booklet in a logical manner.

World of Work: Published by JIST for use by young people, this is a 32-page booklet that provides activities and narrative to assist in self-understanding and in exploring career alternatives.

Computer Software and Information Services

Up until recently, there wasn't much software on career topics, other than some for use in schools. Resume software was among the first commercially available, but more and more career planning and job search material is now being released. Some of this stuff is junk, but there are also some useful materials available.

My selection here is limited, and I've only included software that is in a price range that might be attractive for an individual user. Some of the most useful programs are those like word processing and contact management ones that were not specifically done for job seekers. Having said that, here is a bit of information on what will become an increasingly important source of future career information.

Computer On-line Services

If you have a computer and know how to use a modem to get to various on-line computer services,

there is already a lot out there. Here are a few of the highlights.

Following are the major commercial sources of on-line services. You can get to them via the Internet or contact them directly. Each has a variety of services that can be helpful in your job search.

➤America Online (800) 827-6364

➤Bix (800) 695-4775

➤CompuServe (800) 848-8990

➤GEnie (800) 638-9636

➤PC-Link (800) 827-8532

➤Promenade (800) 827-5938

➤Prodigy (800) 776-0840

America Online has a career center with lots of career information on it as well as job listings. It is very good. GEnie has a service called *Dr. Job.* Dr. Job answers individual questions about career and employment issues through GEnie's electronic mail. Selected questions and answers also are published in a Dr. Job bulletin board.

If you are really interested in this subject, read *The Internet Job Search Companion.* It is the first book of its kind, and it's published by JIST.

Software Programs from JIST

At the time of this writing, these programs are available via JIST but in formats and prices intended for use in schools and programs rather than individuals. I mention them here to give you a glimpse of what is available and because versions for individual use may be released in the next year or so.

The Electronic OOH: Occupational Outlook Handbook: CD-ROM and disk versions. Fast lookup of the 250 occupational descriptions provided in the OOH, plus additional information on over 7,000 jobs that are related to the OOH jobs. A very helpful tool for use in the job search, since it allows you to identify job targets in industries and using skills that you may have previously overlooked.

The Electronic DOT/GOE: Dictionary of Occupational Titles/Guide for Occupational Exploration: This is a sophisticated CD-ROM program that includes the complete content of the *Dictionary of Occupational Titles, The Occupational Outlook Handbook, the Complete Guide for Occupational Exploration,* and over 60 additional details on over 12,000 jobs. While it is easy to use, it provides access to detailed technical information on over 12,000 jobs that has not been readily available in the past.

Other Software

Career Design: Career Design Software. A thorough program that provides content to help identify skills, select career options, prepare a resume, interview,

negotiate salary, and more. Based on the career planning principles of John Crystal.

Career Finder: Wintergreen/Orchard House. Very easy to use, just answer 18 questions, and it matches to 21 occupational clusters and lists the jobs that most closely match your preferences.

Free Phone CD ROM: Toll free numbers for over 1,000 business categories covering the entire country. Allows lookup by region and other criteria.

Information USA: Provides substantial information on federal jobs, government resources, agencies, grants, loans, scholarships, statistics, etc.

Letterwriter for Job Seekers: Wintergreen Software. Nifty program with section to write letters of applications, post-interview thank-you notes, and create your own letters.

Lovejoy's College Counselor CD ROM: Provides details on thousands of colleges and technical schools, 2,500 scholarships, and video clips of many schools. Excellent.

Perfect Resume Kit: Based on Tom Jackson's resume book, this program is flexible, powerful, and well done. A personal version is available.

PFS Resume Pro: A very popular and widely available program.

Quick and Easy for the SF-171: A program that helps you complete the complex federal employment application. About $50.

Select Phone CD ROM: Includes all listings in the White and *Yellow Pages* directories for the entire U.S. Search by name, region, business heading, etc.

Scholarships 101: Information on over 5,000 scholarship sources. Sorts by various criteria and helps write letters asking for additional information.

More Good Resources by J. Michael Farr

The Quick Resume & Cover Letter Book

Write and Use an Effective Resume in Only One Day!

ISBN 1-56370-141-3
$12.95
Order Code LP-RCLQG

The Quick Interview & Salary Negotiation Book

Dramatically Improve Your Interviewing Skills in Just a Few Hours!

ISBN 1-56370-162-6
$12.95
Order Code LP-J1626

Getting the Job You Really Want, 3rd Edition

A Step-by-Step Guide

Workbook
ISBN 1-56370-092-1
$9.95
Order Code LP-RWR

Instructor's Guide
ISBN 1-56370-196-0
$12.95
Order Code LP-RWRIG

The JIST Job Search Course

A Young Person's Guide to Getting & Keeping a Good Job *with Marie Pavlicko*

Workbook   **$8.95**
ISBN 0-042784-34-0
Order Code LP-YP

Instructor's Guide   **$12.95**
ISBN 0-042784-36-7
Order Code LP-YPTM

America's Fastest Growing Jobs, 5th Edition

Authoritative Information for Students, Career Changers, and Job Seekers on the Best Jobs in Our Economy.

ISBN 1-56370-289-4
$16.95
Order Code LP-J2894

America's Top Jobs™ for College Graduates, 3rd Edition

Detailed Information on Jobs and Trends for College Grads—and Those Considering a College Education

ISBN 1-56370-493-5
$16.95
Order Code LP-J4935

How to Get a Job Now!

Save Time, Find a Job, Earn More Money! Six Easy Steps to Getting a Better Job.

ISBN 1-56370-290-8
$6.95
Order Code LP-J2908

The Very Quick Job Search Video

An excellent Review of the Most Effective Techniques to Equip Job Seekers with the Very Best Job Search Tools.

ISBN 1-56370-283-5
$149.00
Order Code LP-JV2835

Look for these and other fine books from JIST at your full-service bookstore, or contact us for more information at 1-800-648-JIST.